# WOBBLY BITS

## AND

## OTHER EUPHEMISMS

John Ayto

A & C Black • London

First published 1993 as *Dictionary of Euphemisms*

This edition published 2007
Reprinted 2007
by A & C Black Publishers Ltd
38 Soho Square, London W1D 3HB

www.acblack.com

The moral right of the author has been asserted.

Copyright © John Ayto 1993, 2000, 2007

A copy of the CIP entry for this book
is available from the British Library.

ISBN 978 0 7136 7840 6

Typeset by A & C Black Publishers
Printed in Spain by GraphyCems

# CONTENTS

# INTRODUCTORY

Naming is magical. The delight, fear, reverence that we experience in the face of the phenomena of life, human behaviour and the world around us soak into the words we use to name them. When we utter the words, this power is released: the force of the original is reproduced, even magnified.

This is all very well when the import of a word is positive, or even – as is mostly the case – just neutral or mundane. But there are some experiences we would rather not conjure up quite so vividly. There are some things that are better left unnamed. Most people in most societies throughout history have found it difficult in many circumstances to refer directly to, for example, the excretion of waste matter from the body. Frank words for the sexual and excretory organs tend to be avoided unless particular social conditions permit them. Death and killing, disease, sexual activity, dishonesty, drunkenness, nakedness, fatness, ugliness, old age, madness – in short, anything that we are ashamed of: this is where the taboos of language operate.

But such topics must from time to time be addressed, however much we might prefer to avoid them. If we cannot bring ourselves to break the taboos, alternative methods must be found. This is the role of euphemism. As Robert Burchfield wrote in *Fair of Speech: The Uses of Euphemism* 1985, 'a language without euphemisms would be a defective instrument of communication'. Euphemism is the set of communicative strategies we have evolved to refer to a topic under a taboo, without actually contravening its terms.

This is a book about euphemistic words and expressions. Set out in thematic chapters, it looks at the various ingenious lexical formulae that speakers of English have come up with to tiptoe around conversational danger areas. It charts, for instance, the evolution of our terminology for a 'place for defecating and urinating'; it examines the rich

American vocabulary of funerals; it looks at the curious history of menstruation words; notes the effect of the invention of the zip on circumlocutory references to undone flies; takes in the chillingly bland official language of death and destruction in warfare; and includes the latest 'politically correct' vocabulary of the late 20th and early 21st centuries.

But there is more to euphemism than just words. Often we make body language or inarticulate sounds express what we are too embarrassed to talk about. 'Would you like to go to the . . . , before dinner?', the pause filled by perhaps a muffled cough or a furtive glance upstairs, can be readily interpreted as an invitation to visit the lavatory. And in the days when pregnancy was widely regarded as a taboo subject, the silence in 'I hear Mrs Jones is . . . again', with or without a meaningful look, could be made to speak volumes. (Suspension points ( . . . ), dashes (f–) and asterisks are printers' contributions to the armoury of euphemisms.)

Syntax and grammar can be euphemistic too. The use of the passive voice in place of the active is notoriously a way of blurring the directness of a message, often for self-exculpatory reasons (as in the case of the small boy who explains how the window has 'got broken').

The way we pronounce words can betray an impulse to euphemism. *Condom*, for example, has been around in the language since at least the early 18th century, leading a blameless and fairly low-profile existence, and not drawing attention to itself. But in the mid 1980s the AIDS epidemic forced it into the open, on radio and television. Hitherto it had been pronounced, in conventional fashion, 'kondəm, but now newsreaders and others began to articulate it with kid gloves, 'kondom, giving each vowel full value, as if it were a new and slightly distasteful term that could not be completely admitted to the language.

Euphemism can cover whole stretches of discourse too. It does not have to be lexicalized into individual words. 'It seems to me that what you are saying does not altogether accord with the truth' can be easily translated from euphemism to taboo as 'I think you're lying'. And consider these comments on David Owen, made by Shirley Williams in 1986 (quoted in *A Life at the Centre*, Roy Jenkins 1991): 'It does not follow that what the leader has said is the same and identical with the policy of the party . . . It would be excellent if he [were] prepared to listen to other points of view and possibly even consider whether there is room for some improvement on his part as well as on the part of the rest of us.' Decoded, this says 'The leader has been shooting off his mouth. He never pays any attention to others' opinions, and thinks he is always right.'

Utterances like these contain two key elements of euphemism: understatement and litotes. Litotes is a way of defusing a strong statement by expressing it as the negative of its opposite – so a 'problem of not inconsiderable proportions' could well be a major disaster, and 'not . . . the truth' equals 'lying'. A lot of euphemisms depend on this use of the negative. If you are 'not all there', you are mad. If people are 'not as young as they were', they are old. If you say that someone has 'never been a great reader', you may well be claiming that they are a philistine, illiterate, or of low intelligence. Someone described as 'no angel' could well be a vicious thug. A similar job can be done by negative prefixes. To say that someone is 'unwell' is a softer and more evasive statement than to say frankly that they are 'ill' or 'sick'. The chances are that work described as **uneven** is mostly bad. **Inappropriate** (as in 'inappropriate behaviour') can designate anything that falls foul of someone's (usually politically correct) prejudices. *Anti-* can imply the opposite of what it qualifies: *anti-Communist* is often a euphemism for 'Fascist'. The prefix *dis-* can be used in a similarly mealy-mouthed way – **disimprove**, for example, means 'worsen': 'a disimproved revenue position,' *Daily Telegraph* 1987, quoting the Irish businessman Tony O'Reilly. So can *sub-*: **sub-optimal** and **sub-prime** can both do duty for 'abysmal'. **Less than** (as in 'less than honest') is even less direct, and therefore more euphemistic. 'Oppositeness' can be suggested in more oblique ways: a **left-handed compliment** (first recorded in 1881) verges on an insult.

Understatement takes the heat out of a strong and perhaps upsetting statement – in what strikes many people as a pusillanimous way. A favourite modern understated euphemism is **robust**. Its up-front message is 'strong, sturdy', but behind this there often lurks 'rough, violent': someone who receives a 'robust reply' is likely to have had his ears scorched off, and a 'robust tackle' in soccer could easily result in a broken leg. In the same way **problem** frequently conceals something far more serious ('Houston, we have a problem' was the laconic message from the crew of Apollo 13 when their craft broke down on the way to the Moon; see also LITTLE LOCAL DIFFICULTY p 292); and in the late 20th century even admitting to a *problem* became too painful, and it transmuted into an **issue** (as in 'Other known issues with Windows Vista can be found in the Vista tracking bug', www.mozilla.com). Someone who is cantankerous, obstructive or otherwise objectionable can be euphemized as **difficult**. Something that is **awkward** can be downright dangerous: an 'awkward step' could deposit you on your back at the foot of the stairs, and an 'awkward customer' might black your eye. Arrangements that are **informal** probably go beyond the existing rules and may even be illegal. Arrangements that are **flexible** are not founded on any principled basis. Activities that are characterized as **fringe** (as in 'fringe banking') may well be fraudulent. Someone described, with apparent approval, as **hearty** may have an excess of back-slapping cheerfulness. A cricket pitch characterized blandly as **lively** could send good-length balls whizzing past the batsman's nose. Comments, looks, etc that are deemed **suggestive** could in reality be just plain lewd. And much of the euphemism of war entails understatement, as in *intervention* for 'invasion' (see p 300) and *stabilize* for 'conquer' (see p 300).

An even more popular euphemistic strategy is vagueness, the blanketing of a sensitive topic in the fog of a superordinate term of such high generality that you would be hard pressed to understand it out of context. There are few areas of taboo in which it is not deployed: *go* for 'urinate and defecate', for example (see p 163); *drink* for 'drink alcohol' (see p 45); *alter* for 'castrate' (see p 203); *language* for 'swearing' (see p 33); *thing* for 'genitals' (see p 124; *do* for 'arrest' (see p 24); *time* for 'term of imprisonment' (see p 28); *institution* for 'mental hospital' (see p 220); *appliance* for 'truss' (see p 154); *space* for 'grave' (see p 254); *asset* for 'weapon' (see p 304). Any change that is likely to prove embarrassing or unpopular can be hidden behind the broad screen of **adjustment**, a favourite word of euphemizers. **Certain** covers a multitude of sins: someone of a *certain age*, for instance (see p 230), is no longer young; a woman in a certain *condition* (see p 88) is pregnant; the term *a certain disease* (see p 205) was once upon a time all that some people could bring themselves to use for VD. Someone's disreputable sexual history can be disguised as a **past**, as in the confidentially muttered 'She has a past, you know' (a term mainly applied to women, since the mores of our society traditionally do not regard disreputable sexual histories in men in such a serious light – parallel euphemisms for men's behaviour, such as 'youthful **indiscretions**' and '*sow one's wild oats*', are markedly less disapproving; it is a product of the second half of the 19th century, and is now decidedly passé, but it still crops up if the context is right: 'Otto Habsburg . . . has approved his oldest son's decision to marry a woman with a past as rich as her fortune,' *Sunday Times* 1993). Films, scenes, photos, etc that are

**explicit** show sexual activity or sexual organs in graphic detail. Regular passengers on British railways are familiar with **operational difficulties** as the reason given for a delayed service, a term diffuse enough to cover virtually anything that could go wrong with a train. A patient exhibiting **challenging behaviour** may well be climbing the walls. **Care** is a term of high generality that has been shoehorned into a number of specific semantic slots in the field of sociology in order to make a more 'positive' impression: a child, for instance, that has been legally removed from its parents and is kept under the control of a local authority is described in Britain as *in care*; and the release of patients in mental hospitals to live at home goes under the name of *care in the community*. And one of the most recent examples of the phenomenon, emerging from America in the mid to late 1980s, is the use of **attitude** for 'hostility' or 'truculence', as in 'She's always giving me attitude'.

Then there is the 'blind-them-with-science' school of euphemism, which hides the unwelcome or the frightening behind a long word or a technical (-sounding) term (extra points can be scored if it is from a foreign language). So a tumour becomes a *neoplasm* (see p 200); the sexual organs are the *pudenda* (see p 134); and a dustman is metamorphosed into a *refuse operative* (see p 259). To air-traffic controllers, an incident in which two aircraft nearly collide involves merely a **loss of separation**, and those who have charge of the nuclear industry characterize a power-station meltdown as a **critical power excursion**. **Abuse**, one of the most pervasive euphemisms to emerge in the 20th century, perhaps comes into this category: it has an air of bureaucracy and officialdom about it. It has been used for 'wrong or improper use' since the 16th century, but in recent years it has come to euphemize sexual assault (as in *child abuse* and *satanic abuse*; see also ABUSE p 20) and illegal use of intoxicants (as in *alcohol abuse* and *drug abuse*; see also SUBSTANCE ABUSE p 62), and from there it has turned into a pompous synonym for *misuse* or *harm* (as in *racket abuse*).

The atavistic strand of placatory euphemism, which taps directly into the transformative magic of naming – as when the Ancient Greeks termed the ill-omened left side *euonumos*, literally 'of good name', and the modern Japanese call pornographic art *shunga*, literally 'spring picture' – is not much in evidence in modern English, although some American funeral terminology comes close – *beautiful memory picture* for a 'viewing of an embalmed corpse', for instance (see p 255), and some fossilized remnants survive from earlier times (e.g. **little people** and **wee folk** for (malevolent) fairies and **wise woman** for a witch).

But the subconscious notion that you can change the nature of something by changing its name persists – as witness British Nuclear Fuels' renaming of the nuclear reprocessing plant Windscale as Sellafield in 1981, in the apparent belief that the new designation would wipe out the negative connotations of the old one, and the altering of the Spastics Society's name to Scope in 1994 to avoid the dysphemistic *spastic*. Actors still seek to circumvent the taboo against referring to Shakespeare's *Macbeth* by calling it '**the Scottish play**'. And even 21st-century sophisticates can sometimes find themselves avoiding the name of God with some such humorous circumlocution as **the man upstairs**.

A more popular ploy is what might be termed 'making the best of a bad job', or 'damning with faint praise', according to your point of view. Into this category come such euphemisms as **interesting** for anything so bizarre or indeed boring that a more honest opinion would seem rude (as in 'The mixture of purple and green made an interesting effect'); **different** for anything so peculiar that you can't think of anything else to say about it; **invigorating** for 'unpleasantly cold' (as in 'an invigorating pre-breakfast dip in the sea'); **mixed** for 'bad' (as in 'mixed reviews' and 'a mixed reception'); and **uncertain** for 'bad and probably not going to improve' (as in 'Britain's economy faces an uncertain future'). **Courageous** can imply 'foolhardy', and in the case of politicians the subtext is often 'risking defeat in the next election': '"The President made the decision that we should stop at a given time . . . and I think it was a very humane and courageous decision," Gen Schwarzkopf said,' *Guardian* 1991. Evasions such as these perform a white-lying function, oiling the wheels with politeness, but if their code is subverted they can cut deeper than full-frontal dysphemisms. (Such is human nature that these 'favourable interpretation' euphemisms are likely to be bestowed on those at the top of the pile, with the most to lose from frankness: 'When a pro hits it to the right, it's called a fade. When an amateur hits it to the right, it's called a slice,' *Observer* 1992.)

The language of food offers a neat spectrum of the various modes of euphemism. Internal organs can bring out the squeamishness in us at the best of times, but the thought of eating them can certainly push us over the edge. Hence *offal* as a cover term for the insides destined to be eaten, unrecognizable as a euphemism now but originally (in the 15th century) simply and literally material that has 'fallen off' (American English uses the still manifestly euphemistic **variety meats**). The pancreas and thymus gland, especially of calves, used for food are disguised as **sweetbreads**, and the old word **lights** is still used for 'lungs' when they are for human or animal consumption. The early medieval distinction between the (Anglo-Saxon) terms used for live animals (*sheep, calf, deer* etc.) and the French-based ones for their flesh used for food (*mutton, veal, venison*) may well have had at least a partially euphemistic origin too. Animals turned to for food in times of need, or which perhaps bespeak a shortage of financial resources, may come in for facetious euphemistic camouflage: Australian, for instance, have christened the ubiquitous rabbit **underground mutton** when it goes into the pot, and in the USA during the Depression years of the 1930s the term **Hoover hog** (after the then president, Herbert Hoover) was applied to the same animal and also to the armadillo. Fishmongers have found that a palatable-sounding name can encourage customers to buy a fish which, if they knew what its real name was, they would leave on the slab: so in Britain, for example, first **flake** (first recorded in 1906) and later **rock salmon** have been used to disguise dogfish and wolffish; in Australia, *flake* does duty for shark, which in New Zealand is rechristened **lemonfish**. Inherently innocuous food may quickly attract taboos by association, notably in the arena of international rivalry or enmity: hence in the USA during World War I sauerkraut, associated with the German foe, was renamed **liberty cabbage**, and the reluctance of the French to cooperate with the USA during the 2003 invasion of Iraq led to the rechristening of french fries (i.e. chips) as **freedom fries**. The ultimate food taboo is eating the flesh of one's fellow human beings: hence the alleged euphemism among certain Polynesian peoples that translates into English as **long pig**.

The components of a language that its users can deploy euphemistically are by no means always straightforwardly benign in effect. For one thing, the euphemistic force of a word is often heavily dependent on its context. Most speakers of English would recognize *pass away* as an avoidance term, enabling one not to use the frank *die*. But what about *kick the bucket*? If someone were to say jokingly to a friend, 'Don't worry, I'm not about to kick the bucket yet', it would be quite reasonable to interpret their substitution of the trivializing idiom for the deadly-earnest *die* as euphemistic. But if a doctor were to say to someone waiting for news in a hospital, 'I'm so sorry to have to tell you, Mrs Bloggs, that your husband has just kicked the bucket,' the choice of words would be justly condemned as gratuitously insensitive.

(Keith Allan and Kate Burridge, in *Forbidden Words* (2006), characterize flippant or defusing usages of the *kick the bucket* sort as 'dysphemistic euphemisms' – in contrast with 'euphemistic dysphemisms', in which a milder term (e.g. *sugar!*) is substituted for a word that has offensive force (e.g. *shit!*).)

For another, the topics which we place under a taboo may change over the decades and the centuries, entailing a restructuring of our euphemistic resources. Many areas remain constant, of course – our Anglo-Saxon ancestors, for instance, seem to have been just as coy about defecation and urination as we are (see p 163) – but some are much more a prey to passing fashion. The sort of euphemisms for 'fat' that we use today, for example, were unheard of in the days when it was more socially acceptable or even desirable to be fat (see p 148). And the pathological reticence which so seized the Victorians when they referred to areas below the belt that they invented a range of repressed synonyms for 'trousers' – *unmentionables*, *ineffables*, etc (see p 153) – has long since passed (if indeed it ever existed among anything but a very narrow segment of society). It would be foolhardy to predict that any particular taboo is sacrosanct for all time. The sanctions against direct reference to sexual intercourse, which kept the word *fuck* out of the first edition of the *Oxford English Dictionary* in 1898, have given rise to a welter of circumlocutions (see p 37). But in 1972 *fuck* was admitted to the OED (along with *cunt*), and in 1992 it was announced that it was to be officially permitted in the text of an advertisement warning against AIDS: 'So if you are going to fuck, it makes sense to use one of the stronger variety [of condom].' A hundred years ago it would have been hard indeed to imagine the king of the four-letter words receiving the governmental imprimatur like this. As long as a taboo remains in force, it is not uncommon for a euphemism introduced to take the sting out of it to become contaminated by it. In such cases the old euphemism, no longer fit for purpose, needs to be replaced. **Genetically engineered**, for instance, as applied to crops, foodstuffs, etc. that have had their genetic make-up altered, was fairly circumlocutious, but soon the implication of scientists playing God began to cause concern, and it was replaced by **genetically modified** (often further disguised as **GM**). Even this was too strong meat for some (the idea of 'modifying' nature), and so the impeccably upbeat **genetically enhanced** was proposed. The lesson is that as long as such procedures and products are widely distrusted, any terminology associated with them will sooner or later lose the power to deflect such distrust (see also UNDERDEVELOPED and DEVELOPING, p 286).

By no means every usage that puts the best possible gloss on its referent is in strict terms euphemistic. The marketing industry, for example, subsists on words such as *bestseller, classic, masterpiece*, and *prime*, which in many cases seek to turn the ordinary into the special. Such hyperbole finds no place in this collection, which concentrates on efforts to rehabilitate the bad, the negative, the rude, the disturbing, the embarrassing. Nor does it include open-ended lists of metaphors and slang synonyms for taboo items. The judgment as to whether such words and expressions are truly euphemistic in force is necessarily somewhat subjective. It can be particularly tricky to make in cases (such as the sex organs) where no completely neutral, unmarked term exists, only formal or technical vocabulary at one extreme and highly colloquial words at the other. And as we have seen in the case of *kick the bucket*, what is euphemistic in one context may be taboo in another. But as a general rule, only those lexical items are included that genuinely represent an attempt to avoid a word that would give offence or seem too frank, and to replace it with something that either conforms with the politeness rules for its social context, or serves the user's purpose in concealing unpleasant truths.

At the back of the book there is a comprehensive alphabetical index that enables you to home in on any particular euphemism you may wish to refer to.

I am grateful to Jean Aitchison, Professor R L Brown, Irene Fairley, Eric Franklin, Bernard Johnson, Ann Kennedy and Don Peters for information and suggestions invaluable in the compilation of this book.

# CRIME

———

The **underworld** – itself an over-romantic collective synonym for 'criminals' – is unquenchably inventive in coining colourful terminology to denote its various activities. It is arguable that such words perform, or at least originally performed, a euphemistic function, in wrapping up the nefarious nature of their referents so that outsiders could not recognize it – that the British slang *blag*, for instance, is a way of avoiding officialdom's stark *theft* or *robbery*. There are certainly some individual instances where this is clearly so, but in general it seems closer to the truth to say that the slang of criminals (or thieves' cant, as it was known in previous centuries) is a private language meant primarily to reinforce group identity. Its role in protecting the delicate sensibility of group members from such frank vocabulary as *steal*, *policeman*, and *arrest* is certainly minimal.

The true euphemism of crime lies elsewhere, not amongst its professional exponents but amongst the mainly law-abiding, who seek to trivialize their own brushes with illegality, and to some extent amongst the law-makers and law-enforcers, whose interest occasionally lies in de-sensationalizing crime.

Even the most upright of us have probably at some point in our lives taken without permission something that does not belong to us, but we might be loath to own up to 'stealing'. Theft has probably inspired more double-speak than any other form of wrong-doing. A typical ploy is to disguise it by using a word that suggests that we gained possession of the stolen object by perfectly legitimate means. We might, for instance, say that we had **acquired** it, or **borrowed** it, or **found** it, or **obtained** it ('He left in a rush and flurry on a brand-new woman's bicycle that he had "found" in Besançon,' George Millar 1945 – in print it is common to signal the stretched meaning of these verbs with inverted commas), or even **attracted** it (a usage dating from the late

15

19th century which implies some strange magnetic force operating beyond the thief's will). **Gain** can be used in the same way (like *acquire*, it carries the useful implication that ownership was transferred without any positive action on the part of the beneficiary), as, at a more pompous level, can **alienate** (the underlying idea here is of separating the stolen object from its former owner, which can be expressed from the owner's point of view as '**deprive** someone of something' or '**relieve** someone of something' or '**part** someone from something'). Something that we suspect has been stolen can be said to have **gone walkabout** (as if it might make its way back of its own accord at some point), or simply to have **walked**.

Taking something by looting can be disguised (perhaps more ironically than euphemistically) as **liberating** or **salvaging** it: both usages originated in military contexts during World War II, but subsequently spread out to encompass more conventional theft. The intellectual dishonesty here lies in the hidden claim that one is performing a morally good act by taking something of someone else's – either by freeing it from tyrannous ownership or by rescuing it from damage or neglect. A similar nervously light-hearted attitude to theft inspired the use of **souvenir** for 'stolen object'. This too had a military origin, in World War I, when soldiers picking up unconsidered trifles among the ruins of battle would speak of 'hunting for souvenirs' or even, turning the word into a verb, of 'souveniring' something. Wartime looting has also been wryly disguised and excused as **redistribution of property**; and if a search has been conducted for something, from eggs to spare parts, which are successfully brought back without payment, you can say that they have been **foraged**.

If you do not feel brazen enough to claim that what you have done was not stealing at all, you can at least use a word that, while tacitly admitting the theft, seeks to mitigate it in some way. The approach may be pompous quasi-officialese: **appropriate** is the favourite here (as in 'Someone seems to have appropriated my pen'), with its hint of sanctioned confiscation; and **abstract** sounds too straight-laced to be really reprehensible. But the insouciant dismissal probably works better. **Pocket**, for instance (as in 'He sold it for more than he claimed and pocketed the difference'), openly admits theft, but says in effect 'Look here, it was only a tiny amount, hardly amounts to stealing, no one will miss it anyway.' Similarly trivializing in intention is **help oneself to** something, a development of the mid 19th century, which often implies bemused outrage at the effrontery of the theft but nevertheless plays down its seriousness. Into the same category come **bag**, the now rather dated **make away with** and **make off with**, and **lift**. This last, which reduces theft to the physical act of picking something up (not unlike American **move** for 'steal', and also **boost** for 'steal'), dates back to the 16th century. From the beginning it was commonly used in the context of stealing from shops (sometimes with *shop* as the grammatical object of the verb), and at the end of the 17th century we find the first instance on record of the term **shoplifting** (in an Act of Parliament): 'Preamble, the Crime of stealing Goods privately out of Shops and Warehouses, commonly called Shop-lifting.' It has now become so much the word for the thing that we scarcely notice its blandness compared with 'stealing from shops'. (The losses incurred through such thefts, by staff as well as customers, are delicately referred to by supermarkets and other shops as **in-store wastage**, **inventory leakage**, **seepage**, or **shrinkage**.) In US slang, shoplifting is further euphemized as a **five-finger discount**. A particular niche is occupied by British dialect **scrump** (first recorded in 1866), which contrives to turn the stealing of apples from other people's trees into a mischievous jape.

Theft by employees from their firms, by trustees from trusts, etc has a euphemistic vocabulary all of its own. To accuse someone of **siphoning off** company funds does not sound so drastic as a charge of 'embezzlement'. The message is less oblique in 'have one's **hand in the till**' or '**fingers in the till**' and in **line one's pockets**, but the metaphors soften it. Alternatively one can wrap the crime in the obscurity of a long word, **peculation** (which etymologically denotes 'stealing someone's cattle') or **misappropriation**. Or one can laugh it off by referring to it as **private enterprise** – a term (not necessarily restricted to nationalized industries) applied particularly to the illicit selling of a company's goods, the money paid being kept by the seller. Tampering with accounts is generally euphemized with **cook** – usually in the phrase *cook the books*, but also with other objects, such as *accounts* and *returns*. The usage, which dates back to the 17th century, comes from the notion of 'concocting' a dish. Alternatives include **doctor**, first recorded in the sense 'falsify' in the late 18th century, and also **salt**. This is used not only of accounts, possibly in imitation of French *saler*, but also with reference to the fraudulent introduction of precious metals, gems, etc into mines in order to make them seem more valuable than they really are.

The stealing of cars has for some reason attracted the circumlocutors. To start with, the crime has in Britain gone under the official designation **taking and driving away** – *take* being a remarkably restrained substitute for *steal*. A demotic alternative is the originally American **hot-wiring**, which refers specifically to the stealing of a car by by-passing its ignition system. The irony of the use of **joyriding** as a euphemism for 'stealing a car and driving it around recklessly for fun' (which seems to have evolved around 1970 from the earlier, broader sense 'taking a pleasure trip') has often been noted, in the light of the frequently non-joyful consequences of the undertaking. Also in the realm of car-crime euphemism is **put back the clock**, or **turn back the clock**, denoting falsification of the mileometer to deceive a potential purchaser.

Goods that have been stolen are **hot**, in the slang of the underworld (a usage first recorded in 1925), or, if someone is trying to sell them, **bent**. But the classic euphemism in this area is **fallen off the back of a lorry** (with vehicular variants such as *truck* and *wagon*). It is most characteristically used of goods offered for sale at surprisingly low prices, in markets, pubs, etc, which might reasonably arouse the suspicion that the seller did not come by them honestly, via the usual commercial channels, with all middlemen's needs satisfied. Its beginnings are not recorded, but it certainly seems to have been in use during World War II.

Someone with a tendency to steal may be at least partially excused with the light-hearted **light-fingered** (which dates back to the 16th century) and **sticky-fingered** (first recorded in 1890), which if not exactly hiding the truth, at least put it more kindly than *kleptomaniac*. Rhyming slang lowers the disapproval rating, too: **half-inch** for 'steal' (rhyming with *pinch* and first recorded in 1925) and **tea leaf** for 'thief' (first recorded in 1899). A person who gets or buys stolen goods knowingly from the original thief may be accused of **receiving** (mainly a British usage) or of **handling** – discreetly vague terms whose import is clear only in context.

Stealing shades into swindling in **clip**, now most familiar in **clip-joint** (first recorded in 1933), a term for a night club, bar, etc whose customers are charged extortionate prices; and in **ramp**, which denotes cheating someone out of their money, over charging them, etc. And it is not far from swindling to extortion. The king of the weasel words in this area is **protection**. As used in contexts such as 'protection racket', this ostensibly peaceable, comforting word denotes 'assurance against being beaten up, having one's premises destroyed, etc by a person who demands money for not doing so'. The usage seems to date back as far as the middle of the 19th century. Those who are initially disinclined to sign up for such 'protection', or indeed to fall in in any other way with demands made on them, may need to be **persuaded** or **convinced** – chilling euphemisms that may cover up a range of threats and **personal violence** (i.e. beating the victim up). Less mealy-mouthed but still euphemistic is **lean on**: '*Mirror* editors have always been leaned on, sometimes benevolently, sometimes not,' *Guardian* 1991. A peculiarly nauseating euphemism of the early 21st century is **happy slapping**, denoting the beating up of a child by a group of others who record the assault on a videophone and then send the images to friends.

The language of polite inquiry is easily perverted into the language of torture. Etymologically, an **inquisition** is merely an inquiry, but the torturous activities of the former Roman Catholic tribunal of that name that investigated and punished heresy have given it a permanent semantic slant. **Interrogation** when carried out by an oppressive security service, secret police, etc may be taken to depend more on the infliction of physical or mental pain than on tricky verbal questioning. An offer to **refresh the memory** of an uncooperative interviewee may in such a context turn out to be a threat of physical violence. In the midst of such doubletalk **third degree**, 'violent treatment to gain information or a confession', may seem shockingly frank, but its origins (in America in the late 19th century) were circumlocutious: it appears to have been based on the rigorous questioning to which a candidate for the rank of Master Mason, the highest order or 'third degree' of Freemasonry, was subjected.

The crime of rape is traumatic enough for the victim without rubbing it by using the stark word *rape*. An assortment of discreet alternatives is available. Suitably vague is **assault**, which in theory could denote anything from kicking someone in the shins to stabbing them (legally defined, it is an 'unlawful attempt or threat to injure someone physically') but which in the appropriate context clearly implies a sexual attack of some sort, possibly including forced sexual intercourse. In this sense it may well be an abbreviation of **indecent assault**, a term first officially introduced in Britain in an Act of Parliament of 1861. The Act gave no definition of the term, which is almost as vague (and therefore as euphemistic) as *assault*. It is taken strictly to apply to a sexually motivated attack that does not include intercourse or attempted intercourse, but in practice it is also used loosely for 'rape'. The term **criminal assault** behaves in a similar way.

If all this talk of *assault* seems too explicitly violent, the euphemism gauge can be turned up several notches by referring instead to **interfering with** someone. This excruciatingly discreet usage, first recorded in 1948, equates a potentially psychologically damaging sexual attack with a casual disturbance. To the same family belong **molest**, which again was originally a general word, denoting 'harmful attack', but has come euphemistically to include a sexual element; **harass**, simply meaning 'annoy persistently' for the first three hundred years and more of its existence, but at the end of the 20th century narrowing down to 'importune sexually'; **violate** which dates back to the 15th century; and **abuse**, used for *maltreat* in the sense 'give regular beatings to' since the 16th century but in the late 20th century applied to forced sexual intercourse with children ('He had files on all the boys and picked out those who had a sexual history or who had been abused before arriving at the school,' *Guardian* 1990; see also SELF-ABUSE p 83). The menace of the paedophile can be partially defused by the trivializing euphemism **kiddie-fiddler**.

If in general criminals feel little need to be euphemistic about crime, there is one sensitive area that provokes circumlocution: betraying other criminals to the police. The central term, **informer**, which dates back to the 16th century, bears the classic euphemistic hallmark of blameless generality covering up a specific taboo. Of the more colourful metaphors some, such as the British *nark*, are openly hostile, but others do offer a benigner alternative to *betray*. The oldest still in general use is **shop**, which dates from the 19th century. It evolved from an earlier slang use, 'imprison', which itself was derived from a now obsolete noun use of *shop*, for 'prison'; so etymologically it means 'cause someone to be imprisoned by betraying him or her to the police'. The British **grass** the noun, 'informer', and the verb, 'betray to the police', date from the 1930s; the noun came first, and may be short for *grasshopper* 'shopper'. The metaphor underlying **cough** (first recorded in 1901), **sing** (a 1920s American coinage), and **squeal** (which goes back to the 1840s) is fairly obvious, and the same notion of 'giving voice' inspired **canary** (the bird that 'sings'). There is an isolated instance on record of the use of **spill** for 'divulge' from the 1570s, but its modern use for 'divulge facts to the police' or 'confess', which probably derives from *spill the beans*, did not emerge until the early 20th century.

Moving from the specific to the general, English-speakers have evolved a number of highly discreet verbal strategies for suggesting illegality without openly referring to it. In legalese, a useful term is **unlawful**, which implies a technical breach of the law without the moral opprobrium that attaches to *illegal*: an 'unlawful killing' is a much less serious matter than murder. Activities which are clearly against the law, but which perhaps fear of libel might dissuade one from describing as such, can be discreetly characterized as **unconventional** or **questionable**: 'questionable dealings', for instance, almost certainly involve dishonesty. If arrangements are described as **informal** one might be justified in suspecting that they were not entirely within the law. And any proceedings or circumstances called, with great restraint, **irregularities** are liable to be decidedly illegal – fraudulently altered figures in an account, for instance. On a more colloquial level, a deliberate act in contravention of a law or rule may be disingenuously 'excused' as **bending the rules**, the suggestion being that the infraction is small and pardonable; and someone guilty of this can be said to have been **at it**.


## Some other assorted 'criminal' euphemisms:

**carrying** armed with a pistol or similar weapon – as in 'Are you carrying?' Euphemism by removal of the sensitive word from the phrase – here, 'carrying a gun'

**claim responsibility for** admit guilt for. Used particularly in relation to terrorist organizations owning up to their murders, bombings, etc, in such a way as to suggest that they were something to be proud of. The euphemism attracted much adverse comment when used in the British media in the 1970s with reference to the IRA, and the more acceptable 'admit responsibility for' came generally to be substituted

**family** in thieves' cant of the 18th and 19th centuries, 'the Family' was a collective term for robbers of all descriptions. It resurfaced in 20th-century America as a euphemism for the Mafia

**form** a criminal record (as in 'He's got form'), equated with the record of success or failure of a racehorse, athlete, etc. First recorded in 1958

**funny money** money acquired or produced in some unscrupulous or possibly illegal way – for example, illicitly inflated profits, or counterfeit money. A coinage of the 1930s

**gentleman of the road** in the 18th and 19th centuries, a conciliatory euphemism for 'highwayman.' When it was in common use, it was sometimes abbreviated to simply *gentleman*: 'Kate Hearn's husband collected his rents on the highway, like many another "gentleman" of the day,' Elizabeth Gaskell 1855

**launder** to pass illegally or unscrupulously acquired (e.g. stolen) money though some legitimate channel (e.g. a bank account) in order to disguise its provenance. A specific euphemism which emerged during the 1973–4 Watergate scandal in America out of an earlier more general sense 'change or tamper with in order to make legal or acceptable'

**operator** a person who skilfully uses devious, underhand or possibly illegal methods to achieve his or her ends: 'Peter Hedger has rightly earned a reputation as a shrewd operator,' *Guardian* 1991.

**under the counter** transacted in an underhand or unscrupulous way. From the notion of a sale not recorded in the conventional way (e.g. on a till), with the proceeds being improperly diverted, or of the clandestine selling of prohibited items. First recorded in 1926

# THE POLICE

The need to euphemize the police and their activities arises mainly out of either apprehension – the natural reaction of a normally law-abiding citizen suddenly brought into contact with the police – or secretiveness.

English has a rich variety of synonyms for *police* and *policeman*, but only relatively few can be said to be truly euphemistic. Many, indeed, are forthrightly dysphemistic: *the filth*, *pig*, *flatfoot*, *rozzer*, etc. Others have so melted into the background of the language (*bobby*, *copper*) that any euphemistic force they may originally have had has long since been dissipated. And others again (*the (Old) Bill*, *the fuzz*) draw too much attention to themselves to satisfy the self-effacing criteria of euphemism.

The true police euphemism is either placatory and flattering – elevating the status of policemen to ward off any unwelcome attentions – or disarming – seeking the same effect by taking away their aura of power. Such a subtle nuance as referring to a 'policeman' as a **police officer** (an early 19th-century coinage) has an elevating effect that draws attention to a need in certain circumstances to euphemize the bare *policeman* (although in the last third of the 20th century this role became mixed up with *police officer*'s non-sexist function). The same goes for the plain vocative **officer** (first recorded in 1899), the pompous and dated **officer of the law**, and the modern (mainly American) officialese **law-enforcement officer** (or **law-enforcement official**), and also, at the collective level, for **the force** for 'police force' and **the law** for the 'police' in general (first recorded in 1929). And **special** (short for *special constable*) is a much more flattering designation than 'part-time policeman'.

At the more light-hearted end of the spectrum is **boys in blue** or **men in blue**, a usage dating back to the 19th century: 'You must now begin to think seriously about handcuffs and prison, and men in blue,' Walter Besant 1882. The metaphor is based, of course, on the colour of police uniforms, and indeed in American slang policemen are known as **blues** *tout court*. The facetious and derisive **limb of the law** for 'policeman', a coinage of the 18th century, is now so dated that it can only be used ironically.

It is arguable that the American Citizens' Band users' **smokey bear** (or **bear** for short) for 'policeman' or 'state trooper' is euphemistic in origin, since like all such slang it began as an attempt to disguise the import of CB users' messages from the police and other outsiders. First recorded in 1974, it comes from the name of a bearlike character used in fire-prevention advertising in America. (Other CB police slang to have caught on more widely includes **bird in the air** and **eye in the sky** for 'police helicopter' and **feed the bears** for 'be fined for a traffic offence' – the implication being that the police will hang on to the money.)

The American **G-man** for 'FBI agent' (first recorded in 1930) was presumably prompted by the euphemistic urge – *G* is short for *government* – but it is now obsolescent at best. But the British **redcap** and American **snowdrop** for 'military policeman' – in both cases based on the colour of their headgear – are still very much in use.

All these circumlocutions are largely the work of the public euphemizing the police, but the police have their own circumlocutions to draw a veil of discretion over the more sensitive parts of their work. A favourite word is *special*, whose blandness can smother the most outrageous or shocking of activities – or conversely suggest exclusiveness where little exists. In particular, it is used to designate groups dealing with security, subversion, terrorism, and allied problems: the British term **Special Branch**, denoting the police department dealing with political security, is first recorded in 1894; **special patrol group**, another British term, names a police group equipped with firearms; and

**special police** is a broader term for 'anti-subversion police'. In Northern Ireland the *B Specials* were a pro-Protestant auxiliary police force (see also SPECIAL p 23). In America, **field associate** is the innocuous-sounding official title of a policeman appointed to spy on other policemen and report wrongdoings.

Arresting people is a point of maximum sensitivity in the relationship between the police and their clients, and the words *arrest* and *charge* themselves have acquired a number of more or less euphemistic synonyms. The one with maximum vagueness marks is **do** (as in 'I've been done for speeding again'), which appears to date from the late 18th century. Most are in a similar colloquial, whistling-in-the-dark vein: **haul in** and its partner **pull in** ('If you hadn't come voluntarily, I'd have pulled you in,' W M Duncan 1973), **pinch** (first recorded in 1837), etc. The notion of the policeman's heavy hand descending on the arrestee's collar is a rich source of metaphor: the use of **collar** for an 'arrest' (as in 'How many collars have you got this month?') goes back to late 19th-century America (in America an **accommodation collar** is an arrest made only in order to fulfil the required quota), and **feel someone's collar** for 'arrest someone' is first recorded in 1950. The handcuffs that may be a necessary part of the operation can be euphemized as **bracelets** (an early 19th-century coinage) or **cufflinks**. When the wrongdoer has been **apprehended** (a more discreet way of putting it), he or she may be described in the classic British police euphemism as **helping police with their enquiries** or *assisting police with their enquiries* (first recorded in 1957). The ostensible import of this formula is that the person concerned is merely being questioned in connection with a crime and has certainly not been charged with any offence, but the subtext is 'This person is definitely our main suspect, but we haven't enough evidence to charge them yet.' It also crops up in elliptical forms such as **helping the police** and **helping with enquiries**: 'A young man was helping police last night after the body of Susan Young, aged 12 . . . was found,' *Guardian* 1972. In the same vein, if the police announce that they would like to **question** someone in connection with a particular crime, it probably means that they would like to arrest them. If there emerges from the suspect's interrogation a self-incriminating statement that in fact has been cooked up by the police, it is termed in British slang a **verbal**; the euphemism can also be used as a verb: 'If one of us had signed anything, it would not have made any difference. They would have gone in and verballed us anyway,' *Guardian* 1991. On a rather less serious level, a legal summons issued for a minor offence, particularly a traffic-related one, may be trivialized as a **ticket**. The usage evolved in America around 1930, and indeed in American English *ticket* is also used as a verb, meaning 'issue with a summons'. In American Citizens' Band users' slang, a summons for speeding is a **piece of paper**. See also FEED THE BEARS (p 23). Paltry infractions such as these do not usually entail a trip to the **cop shop**, a rather cosy term (first recorded in 1941) that seeks to take the sting out of *police station*.

The long truncheon carried by the American police goes under the peculiarly bland name **nightstick** (first recorded in 1887) – it was originally used specifically for night-time protection. And an American policeman who is taking bribes is said discreetly to be **on contract**.

The central role of the police force is said to be the maintenance of **law and order**. This term dates back to the 16th century (it is first recorded in John Florio's *Worlde of Wordes* 1598, an Italian-English dictionary), but it was not until the 19th century that its use became widespread. In that period in America it began to be adopted as a political slogan, and more than one political grouping named itself the 'Law-and-Order Party'. The excessively and often violently repressive and anti-libertarian policies advocated by those who march behind the *law and order* banner (including those 19th-century US parties) reveal the descent of the term into doublespeak for (to paraphrase Hugh Rawson's *Dictionary of Euphemisms and Other Doubletalk* 1981) the 'imposition of order without too fine a regard for law'.

# PRISONS

The word *prison* can be an embarrassment, not just to those who bear the stigma of imprisonment, but also for those in charge of the prison system, who perhaps find it too insistent a witness of the criminality in their society.

The impulse to find an alternative, less stark term is nothing new. The now disused **house of correction** dates back to the 16th century (it was given official status in an Act of Parliament of Elizabeth I's time), and **place of correction** and **house of detention** have a long history too. The notion of **correction** is central to the euphemization of prisons, for it places the emphasis on rehabilitation, and plays down the sensitive issue of retribution. So in the late 20th century a prison may be referred to as a **correctional facility** or **correctional institution**. A prison guard can be a **correctional officer**. **Corrective training** is a form of prison regime that seeks the reform of the prisoner (although the term is also used of forced indoctrination of political prisoners). And the politically correct terminology for 'prisoner' is **client of the corrective system** or **guest in a correctional institution**. In a Russian **correctional labour camp** or **correctional labour colony** (a bleak political prison typically in the wastes of Siberia) the 'correction' on offer is of the ideological kind.

This by no means exhausts the official imagination. It has several other alternatives. *Adjustment* is a word beloved of circumlocutors, and in America a solitary-confinement cell can be euphemized as an **adjustment centre**, which makes it sound like a place where you drop in for a little mild therapy (other mealy-mouthed synonyms include **control unit** and **segregation unit**). The British **approved school**, introduced officially in 1932, denoted a penal institution for children, although it sounds more like a high-class academy with five stars from the educational equivalent of the *Guide Michelin*. It replaced **reformatory**, which continues in use in America as a term for a type of prison for first offenders and women (note again the stress on rehabilitation rather than punishment), and was itself replaced in 1969 by **community home**, which somehow calls up the inappropriate image of elderly inmates singing songs together (America has the similar-sounding **community treatment centre**, which denotes a type of local prison). Also for young British criminals is an **attendance centre** (coined 1948), a non-residential institution providing rehabilitatory training, but sounding every bit as much like a sort of youth club. The similarity is even more striking in the case of the American **youth centre** or **youth guidance centre**, denoting a sort of retraining centre cum prison for young criminals, which has replaced **state training school**, a former euphemism whose cover has been blown. American English also uses the curious euphemism *farm*: a **state farm** or **municipal farm** is a local prison. In Britain a cell in a police station or elsewhere may be called, with an exaggeration worthy of an estate agent, a **custody suite**, which makes it sound a good deal more comfortable than it no doubt is. (When in the 18th and 19th centuries British convicts were sent to prison in Australia rather than kept at home, the vague **transportation** was used to characterize their treatment.)

**Camp** is a key word in the euphemization of prisons for service personnel and civilians incarcerated in wartime: **concentration camp**, originally used during the Boer War for camps where all the civilians in a particular area were gathered together, but later applied to the exterminatory establishments set up by the Nazis before and during World War II; **internment camp**, first recorded in 1916; **labour camp**, a penal settlement where the prisoners do hard labour; **prison camp**, and **prisoner-of-war camp**. Places where Japanese residents were kept prisoner in America during World War II were known discreetly as **assembly centres** or **relocation centres**. The main metonym for such camps is **wire** (as in 'three years behind the wire' – the equivalent of **behind bars** for conventional prisons – and 'go over the wire' for 'escape' – corresponding to **go over the wall**); it is based of course on the barbed-wire perimeter fences. See also CORRECTIONAL LABOUR CAMP p 26. A more colloquial euphemism for a military prison is **glasshouse** (it was originally applied to the prison at North Camp, Aldershot, which had a glass roof).

Types of imprisonment are prone to official circumlocution too. **Detention** and **custody** sound more respectable than *imprisonmemt* (**custodial sentence** is a pompous way of saying 'being sent to prison', and the subtext of **preventive detention** is 'we are locking this person up because of the damage they would do if left at large'). Solitary confinement may become the rather attractive-sounding **seclusion**, and political imprisonmemt is mendaciously redefined as **political education** or **political re-education**. **Protective custody** may be genuinely for the protection of the person held, or it may not (the term came into English in the 1930s as a translation of German *Schutzhaft*, the name given to the Nazi programme of imprisonment of political opponents).

More colloquial terms for imprisonment are legion. Many rely on a sort of defensive humour. Prisoners may describe themselves facetiously as **enjoying Her Majesty's hospitality** or as being **guests of Her Majesty** (or in America **guests of Uncle Sam**). Vague adverbial allusion to imprisonment is by means of **away** or **down**, the latter probably from the notion of descending the court steps back to the cells after sentence (someone who is **put away** or **sent down** or who **goes down** goes to jail); by **in** (as in 'What are you in for?'); and of course by **inside**, first recorded in this sense in 1888. A term of imprisonment may be jocularly described as a **holiday** (American **vacation**), or as **periodic rest** (for recidivists). These are often used as excuses for absence to those encountered after release, as are implications of a journey elsewhere: the American **out of town**, **up the river** and **upstate** for 'in prison' were all inspired by the typical placement of US jails away from centres of population. The more colourful slang terms for '(term of) imprisonment' have largely moved beyond the realms of euphemism, but some retain memories of their origin, either in mysteriousness (**bird**, for instance, short for *bird lime*, long-lost rhyming slang for *time*, and **porridge**, which may have been inspired by stodgy prison food which has to be stirred – an allusion, perhaps, to slang *stir* 'prison') or in vagueness (**time** for 'period in prison' dates back at least to the 1830s).

Prisons themselves may be euphemized as the **big house** (an American term), the **brig** (originally a cell on board ship), and the **bucket** (short for *bucket and pail*, rhyming slang for *jail*). *Cell* has its rhyming slang too: *flowery dell*, usually abbreviated to **flowery**.

It is polite to refer to prisoners as **inmates** or **detainees** (a term generally reserved for political prisoners) and to criminals as **offenders** (**young offenders** if under age).

# ASSORTED SINS & NON-INDICTABLE OFFENCES

----

## LYING

There are two major ways of passing off a lie: to trivialize it, or to wrap it up in pomposity.

The trivializing school operates via comfortable colloquialisms, many of them handed down from the nursery, which seek to suggest that the statement in question was not untrue, or that if it was, it was only slightly untrue, or was not intended to be untrue, or was untrue only for the best of motives:

**fib** suggesting a small or trivial lie. It dates from the early 17th century, but its origins are obscure. It may be a reduced form of the obsolete *fible-fable*, which itself was a fanciful reduplication of *fable*

**story** as a euphemism for 'lie' it dates back to the 17th century. It is mainly used in the expressions *tell stories* or *tell a story*: 'You were always good Children, and never told stories,' John Wesley 1770. It has also been used in children's speech for 'liar', as in 'You story!'

**tale** used since the 13th century for a fictional rather than factual account, but only gradually shading into 'deliberate untruth intended to deceive'. Often in the expressions *tell the tale* or *give someone a tale*, *pitch someone a tale*, etc

**tall story** or **tall tale** ostensibly denoting nothing worse than an 'exaggerated account' (the usage originated in mid-19th century America, and arose out of an earlier notion of talking in a high-flown or grandiloquent way), but in practice often covering up a lie

**white lie** the intended message is 'a lie told for good motives' – for example, to avoid distressing someone by telling the truth. But often the motive behind the usage is merely self-exculpatory. The term dates from the 18th century

**whopper** originally, in the 18th century, it denoted literally a 'whopping' lie, a great falsehood, but since then it has also come to be used in a trivializing sense for any lie


It may not be accidental that the 20th century's two most notorious convoluted circumlocutions for 'lying' emerged from the world of politics and public affairs. In the House of Commons in February 1906, Winston Churchill, then a minister in the Colonial Office, pronounced that 'it [the Chinese labour contract] could not, in the opinion of His Majesty's government, be classified as slavery in the extreme acceptance of the word, without some risk of **terminological inexactitude**'. This pompous but fairly innocent euphemism for 'exaggeration' struck a chord, and has since been used to disguise downright lying.

Then in November 1986 Sir Robert Armstrong, former head of the British Civil Service, found himself in the witness box in an Australian court, giving evidence on behalf of the British Government in their case against Peter Wright, a former British agent who had published the revelatory book *Spycatcher*. He was challenged with making deliberately misleading statements; he admitted having been misleading, but denied telling lies, and went on to define misleading as being '**economical with the truth**'. This classic of bureaucratic weasel-speak enjoyed a considerable (ironic) vogue thereafter ('When Alan Clark, then a trade and industry minister, advised Matrix Churchill to be 'economical with the *actualité*' of how the machine tools it was exporting to Iraq could be used, he was repeating one of the canons of the arms trade,' *Independent on Sunday* 1992). But it was not in fact Sir Robert's coinage. The expression *economy of truth*, virtually denoting 'lying', dates back to the 18th century. According to the *Oxford English Dictionary* it had its origins in the theological use of *economy* for 'presentation of a concept in a way most acceptable to the recipient', but it presumably owes much too to the (euphemistic) use of *economy* for 'sparingness, stinginess'. By the 19th century the adjective *economic(al)* was being used in similar contexts: 'His economic management of Truth. I use this word though it may seem pedantic,' Frederick Robertson 1851. **Selective** is sometimes employed in the same way: a **selective fact** is a 'lie'.

America, too, has been a rich source of flim-flam. The 1950s saw the birth of the **credibility gap**, describing a disjunction between what

X says and Y is prepared to believe. The term really came into vogue in the 1960s, during the Vietnam war, in the context of the President and members of his administration making claims that are widely disbelieved. As R W Holder says in the *Faber Dictionary of Euphemisms*, a '"serious credibility gap" means everyone thinks you are a liar'.

The Watergate affair of the early 1970s encompassed one of the most concentrated extravaganzas of untruth on record, and much ingenuity was employed in covering it up. So swiftly did the officially sanctioned version of 'the truth' change that in 1973 Richard Nixon's press secretary Ron Ziegler applied the term **inoperative** to previously issued statements now acknowledged to be untrue (the current truth was *operative*). The same pair popularized the reflexive use of **misspeak** (originally 'fail to convey one's intended meaning') as a circumlocution for *lie* ('"The President," Ziegler said, "misspoke himself." He explained that the President had noted his error in reviewing the transcript of the press conference,' *Harper's Magazine* 1973).

The more the syllables, the greater the equivocation. *Telling untruths* or *falsehoods* somehow does not sound quite so reprehensible as *telling lies* (**untruth** as a posh alternative to *lie* dates from the 16th century, and **falsehood** in this sense is even older, although it originally had no euphemistic force). **Mendacity** (a 17th-century borrowing from Latin) seems more respectable than *lying*. The grandiloquent **prevaricate**, 'evade the truth', often shades imperceptibly into 'lie'. And **evasion** itself is sometimes used for 'lie'.

The notion of lying as the product of a fertile imagination, and hence as something positive rather than venal, inspires some common euphemisms. **Creative**, for instance, can imply an imaginative bending of the rules in order to mislead. It has been used with reference to accountancy since at least the early 1970s to denote the legal falsification of accounts, and more recently it has broadened out to suggest more generally 'misleading without necessarily lying': 'The ruler is also coming down on the knuckles of some of the more "creative" unit trust advertising and mail shots,' *Observer* 1988. **Imaginative** itself is used in the same way, commonly in the context of newspapers: 'imaginative reporting', 'imaginative journalism', etc, imply an overactive ingenuity that invents 'facts' when it cannot discover them. 'Creativity' reaches its apogee in **poetic licence**. This expression has been used since the 16th century to denote the supposed permission granted to creative writers to depart from grammatical rules, the factual representation of reality, etc, but in the 20th century it is also employed facetiously to sanitize deliberate distortion of the truth. It is not far from this to the use of **fiction** for 'lying' or 'a lie' (see also STORY, TALE).

The idea of 'decorating' the truth is a key source of euphemisms for lying by exaggeration. **Gild** is a classic instance: 'Cicero had prepared a speech in which he had gilded his own performances with all his eloquence,' J A Froude 1879. Its modern use (as in 'gild the truth,' etc) owes its existence mainly to *gild the lily*, 'exaggerate good qualities', a misquotation of 'to gild refined gold, to paint the lily . . . is wasteful and ridiculous excess,' Shakespeare *King John* 1595. In the same vein is **embroider**, which dates in this sense from the 17th century.

The notion of the truth as something elastic that can be **stretched** is an old-established one. In the 17th and 18th centuries, *stretch* was used intransitively to mean 'exaggerate'. More modern usage has turned to *stretch the truth* and simply *stretch it*. The notion of 'stretching' presumably also lies behind the now obsolescent expression **draw** or **pull the long bow** for 'exaggerate', which dates from the early 19th century.

One peculiarly bizarre euphemism for *lie* is **speak with forked tongue**, wished on North American Indians by writers of Wild West fiction (as in 'White man speak with forked tongue').

Lying sometimes hides behind rhyming slang. Two old stagers, covering up for *liar*, are **Dunlop tyre** and **holy friar**. *Tale* becomes **Daily Mail**. Of more recent coinage, and widespread in the 1980s, is **pork pie** for lie, often abbreviated to **porky** (as in 'Who's been telling porkies, then?').

The impressively technical-sounding **polygraph** is a useful verbal disguise for a lie-detector (based on a Greek model meaning literally 'much writing', it was applied in the 19th century to an instrument that recorded multiple physiological outputs; the use of some such outputs (e.g. pulse rate) in the 1920s to determine whether a person was telling the truth led eventually to the virtual synonymity of *lie-detector* and *polygraph*).

# SWEARING

The euphemism of swearing falls neatly into two categories: circumlocutions used for referring to or apologizing for swearing in general; and milder alternatives for individual specific swearwords.

**Swearing** itself is something of a euphemism, as is **oath**, at least in origin. Both historically convey the notion of making a solemn and binding declaration, reinforced by invoking the name of a god, a sacred object, etc. The invocatory part of the process would typically involve the use of a word or expression under some sort of taboo, and so eventually this 'use of taboo words' came to the semantic forefront. *Swear* in the sense 'use oaths profanely' dates from the 15th century, and over the years it broadened out to 'use expletives generally'. *Oath* made a similar transition even earlier, around the 12th century.

The blandest and in many ways the oddest piece of linguistic drapery for 'swearing' is **language**, as in 'pardon my language' and 'don't use language' ('Talking to the lamp-post . . . Using language . . . Singing in the W,' Dylan Thomas 1953). It is often used as an exclamation, admonishing someone for swearing – 'Now then, language!' It appears to date from the middle of the 19th century, and is now gradually dying out. It is curious indeed to use such a broad term as *language* for what in ordinary usage is only a fraction of its referent, but it could be that it is simply a curtailed version of **bad language**, first recorded around the same time. This itself has the vagueness of a typical euphemism: language can potentially be 'bad' in many other ways than profanity. **Strong language** denotes the use of frank, forceful, perhaps even taboo vocabulary, but probably not the most extreme obscenities. (The expression 'edited for language' which emerged in the 1990s with reference to the removal of rude words from films for television showing – 'When Harry Met Sally, which was shown at 10.05pm on Boxing Day, was "edited for language",' *Guardian* 1993 – carries perhaps unintended suggestions of the 'profanity' sense of *language*.) Other grammatically inspired euphemisms in this area are **adjective** and **adjectival**, standing in for an open-ended range of taboo adjectives: 'Beresford told him to take his adjectival charity elsewhere,' G Mitchell 1959. See also p 66.

A long-standing cover-term for profanities or obscenities in general is **four-letter word**, which dates from between the world wars. It refers to the coincidence that many of the main taboo words in English (*fuck*, *cunt*, *shit*, etc) have four letters. (Roughly contemporary is **four-letter man**, **type**, etc for an 'obnoxious fellow', the four letters here disguising *shit*.) The perception of such words as belonging to the plain, unvarnished Germanic element of the English lexicon, rather than polite Latin- and Greek-based vocabulary, has led to the use of **Anglo-Saxon** to characterize expletives, and strong language in general: 'I am not sure of the point of a dictionary of invective, unless you have tired of the usual Anglo-Saxon standbys,' *Guardian* 1991. But ironically, not many of the hard core of English expletives actually date back to the Old English or Anglo-Saxon period: *fuck* and *cunt*, for example, are not recorded before the 13th century, and the former may have been borrowed from Old Norse; even *shit* is recorded from the Old English period only in an isolated example of the past participle *beshitten*.

A common euphemistic strategy is to pretend that the unnameable thing is something quite different. This lies behind the use of **French** for 'bad language', which dates back to the late 19th century. It is usually used in a (not altogether sincere) apology for swearing, as in 'excuse my French!' and 'pardon my French!' ('Well I'll be buggered. Excuse my French,' Arthur La Bern 1966).

A more colloquial way of referring to swearing is **effing and blinding**, apparently a World War II coinage. *Effing* comes from a euphemism for *fuck* (see EFF), and *blind* is a relic of the archaic imprecation (*God*) *blind me*! (see BLIMEY).

The latest stratagem for referring indirectly to taboo words is the formula **the x-word**, where *x* equals the first letter of the word concerned. It originated in North America in the early 1970s. The leading exponent of the stratagem is *f-word* for *fuck* ('the appearance of the f-word in a City page A-3 news story in *The Gazette*,' *The Gazette* (Montreal) 1988), but it has also been widely applied facetiously to words tendentiously reckoned 'shocking', as in *l-word* for 'liberal'.

Such is the taboo against *bitch* as a term of opprobrium for a woman that when it comes to referring to a female dog (its original meaning), some over-delicate speakers have recourse, especially when addressing children, to **lady dog**.

**b** or **B** standing for *bastard* or perhaps more usually *bugger* – certainly *bugger* in the verbal use *b off*. In *silly b* it can also disguise *bitch*. As a typographical device for avoiding the full form in printed text, **b-** dates back at least to the mid 19th century, but as a fully fledged word in the spoken language it is not recorded before the 1920s.

**bally** a soft substitute for *bloody*, which dates from around the middle of the 19th century. It seems to have originated as a fanciful pronunciation of *bl . . . y*, a bowdlerized spelling of *bloody*

**bar steward** a wittily euphemistic transmogrification of *bastard*

**basket** bastard – but not *bastard* in its angry or insulting mode, more as a term of commiseration or even endearment, as in 'poor little basket', 'nice old basket'. It is first recorded in 1936

**beggar** a long-standing mild term of abuse, dating at least from the early 19th century. In part it may be a continuation of a much more ancient application of *beggar* 'mendicant' to a 'low fellow' (first recorded around 1300), but in its modern usage it is essentially a euphemism for *bugger*. It has never been used in the literal 'sodomite' sense, and it is increasingly rare to encounter it 'in anger'. Now, like *basket*, it is mainly indulgent: 'Poor old beggar!'

**bf** or **BF** bloody fool: 'Somebody you could really dismiss with easy conviction as an awful fool – a b.f.', Patrick Hamilton 1941. It is first recorded in the 1920s. Sometimes only the more offending part of the expression is abbreviated: **b fool**

**blank** used, as if in imitation of a blank space on a printed page, to avoid using a rude or taboo adjective or adverb (*bloody*, *fucking*, etc), and occasionally a noun or verb. It dates from the mid 19th century, and has been supplemented since then by **blankety**, **blankety blank**, and **blanky**

**blast** the mealy-mouthed imprecation and verb *blast*, and its adjectival derivative *blasted*, go back to the early 17th century. It originated as a truncated form of *God blast . . .*, meaning 'may God destroy . . .'

**blessed** a euphemistic substitution for *cursed*, which appears to date from around the end of the 18th century

**blighter** a softer British alternative to *bastard*, *bleeder*, *bugger*. It appeared towards the end of the 19th century, derived apparently from *blight* in the sense 'pernicious influence', and by the end of the 20th century had become decidedly obsolescent

**blimey** a mild exclamation, whose now virtually forgotten late-19th-century euphemistic origin is in *blind me*! (or possibly *blame me*!). An alternative spelling is *blime*. See also COR.

**blinking** a substitute for something stronger (*bloody*, etc) which dates from the early years of the 20th century

**blooming** like *blinking*, an alternative to stronger *b*-words, but somewhat earlier in origin – from the late 19th century. The underlying idea seems to have been of something full-blown, like a flower at its highest point of development – so a 'blooming idiot' is the most complete idiot imaginable

**blow** used in a range of fairly mild expletives, including *blow it*!, *blow me*!, *blow me down*!, . . . *be blowed*, and just plain *blow*!. It dates from the late 18th century, and early examples in the form *blow me up*! suggest that the original idea behind it may have been (like *blast*) 'destruction'. Another variant, now passé, is *blow me tight*!, expressing shocked surprise

**bluggy** a now disused euphemism for *bloody*, which enjoyed some favour in the late 19th century as a representation of a supposed 'child's pronunciation' of the word. It was used across the semantic spectrum, not just for the expletive

**bother** a mild substitute probably for *bugger*, first recorded in the 1840s

**buzzard** a fairly mild term of abuse (as in 'silly old buzzard'), which may be partly a euphemistic alteration of *bastard*. It is first recorded in 1939

**chuffing** a substitute for *fucking*, of Northern English origin

**confound** a euphemism with a very ancient lineage, dating back to the 14th century. Its original literal meaning was 'destroy, overthrow', but it was soon pressed into service as a roundabout way of saying 'consign to hell'. It was incorporated into curses and imprecations, which originally retained the full force of the sense 'send to hell' but have gradually, since about 1700, become milder and milder (as in 'that confounded cat')

**cor** a euphemism for 'God' in expletives, not recorded in print before 1931. Its usage does not actually mirror very closely that of *God*! Both can express exasperation, but there they part company: *God*! is used for angry outbursts, whereas the milder *cor*! is reserved for surprise. It commonly accompanies *blimey*: 'Oh cor blimey, I don't understand you people,' Alan Simpson & Ray Galton 1961. The alternative version **gorblimey** is first recorded at the end of the 19th century

**cripes** a euphemism for 'Christ' in exclamations, dating from the beginning of the 20th century. Alternative substitutions are the contemporary **Christmas**, and the much earlier **crikey**, first recorded in 1838

**d** or **D** a polite substitute for *damn*, *damned*, etc in the days when such a thing was deemed to be necessary. It presumably originated in the bowdlerized printed form of the word, *d-*. Rudyard Kipling is on record as using the extended spelling **dee**

**darn** a euphemistically tweaked pronunciation of *damn*, which originated in the US in the late 18th century: 'In New England prophane swearing . . . is so far from polite as to be criminal, and many . . . use . . . substitutions such as *darn* it, for d-m it,' *Pennysylvania Journal* 1781. Derived forms are **darnation** (for *damnation*) and the adjective **darned**. See also *goldarn* at GOLLY

**dash** a now distinctly dated substitute for *damn*, in expressions such as *dashed if I . . .*, *dash it all*, and the plain adjectival and adverbial *dashed*. It is first recorded in 1812, in the colourful *dash my wigs*!

**deuce** used formerly as a replacement for *devil* in various imprecations (*what the deuce*) and other expressions (*the deuce of a . . .*), but now distinctly passé. It goes back to the 17th century, and probably came from Low German *duus* 'the two at dice', used as a cry of exasperation at throwing the lowest possible score

**drat** a dated alternative to *damn*, which seems to have originated around the beginning of the 19th century. It is an eroded version of *'od rot*, which itself was a euphemistic alteration of *God rot*

**eff** a euphemism for *fuck*, based on the pronunciation of its first letter. Its range is restricted to figurative rather than literal uses of *fuck*, and in particular to *fuck off* and to **effing** as a replacement for the adjective and adverb *fucking*: 'He just told me I was past it and it was time I effing well retired,' *Guardian* 1991. It dates roughly from the World War II period. See also EFFING AND BLINDING (p 29)

**Fanny Adams** since World War I, *Fanny Adams* has been treated as a euphemism for *fuck-all* 'nothing' (often in the phrase *sweet Fanny Adams*, abbreviated to *sweet FA*). But it originated in the late 19th century as a piece of nautical slang, denoting 'tinned meat' – a black joke inspired by the name of a murder victim of the 1870s whose body was cut up

**flipping** a British substitute for stronger expletives – mainly *fucking* – which dates from around the beginning of the 20th century. **Flip** is not uncommon as a mild exclamation of annoyance

**frig** *frig* originally meant 'rub', but since at least the 17th century it has been used both in the sense 'masturbate' and as a direct euphemistic substitution for *fuck* ('Whenever Jeff Bridges said "fuck" it was changed to "frig", a standard euphemism used by Hollywood studios when they prepare a film for broadcast on television,' *Guardian* 1993). Unlike many such euphemisms, it replaces not just figurative usages (as in *frig around* 'fool about') but also literal ones: '"If you ask me, Sir," replied Taffy unabashed "like a pack of skeletons frigging on a tin roof",' T E Lawrence 1935. **Frigging** often takes over from *fucking* in adjectival and adverbial use. The overall status of *frig* in the language is dubious: there must be a suspicion that it is kept alive mainly in fictionalized representations of the language (books, films, etc), for it seems seldom to be resorted to in the speech of actual people

**Gawd** often regarded as simply a written representation of a 'vulgar' pronunciation of *God*, *Gawd* is in fact often used (in speech as well as writing, by people who would not normally pronounce it that way) as a euphemistic substitution for *God* in profanities

**G D** an American euphemism for *God damn*

**gee** a mild exclamation which originated in the US at the end of the 19th century. It probably represents a euphemistic shortening of *Jesus* (although *Jerusalem* has been suggested as an alternative source). Expanded forms include **geewhillikers**, **geewhillikins**, **geewhittakers**, and **gee whiz**. Cf. JEEZ

**Godfrey** the male forename *Godfrey* substituting for *God* in mild oaths. American English only, from around the turn of the 20th century

**golly** a euphemistic substitution for *God* as a mild exclamation of surprise. It dates from the late 18th century (although an earlier and now obsolete form *goles* goes back to the beginning of that century). In 1775 Gilbert White described it as 'a sort of jolly kind of oath, or asseveration much in use among our carters, & lowest people'. Extended versions include **golly gee** (mainly American), **golly gosh** (see GOSH), and **golly Moses**. And the element *gol-* is represented in the American **goldarn**

**Gordon Bennett** a British exclamation of surprise, annoyance, etc which appears to be a euphemism for a euphemism: it is a fanciful substitution for *gor blimey*, which itself is an eroded form of *God blind me* (cf. BLIMEY). It is not recorded in print until 1984, but it was certainly in circulation in the spoken language well before that. There were two famous Gordon Bennetts, one of whose names presumably inspired it: James Gordon Bennett (1795–1872), a Scottish-born US newspaper editor and publisher, and his son James Gordon Bennett (1841–1918), who gave his name to several motoring and aeronautical events

**gosh** an exclamation equivalent in mildness to GOLLY (indeed the two are sometimes combined to suggest a childlike purity even in extremis: 'Oh golly-gosh!'). Like *golly* it is an alteration of *God*, and it evolved around the middle of the 18th century

**great Scott** the most durable of a range of Victorian euphemisms for the exclamation *great God*! (others included **great Caesar**, **great grief**, and **great sun**). The identification of the *Scott* of *great Scott* with the intrepid polar explorer Captain R F Scott is chronologically impossible; his Antarctic exploits did not bring him fame until the first decade of the 20th century, but *great Scott* is first recorded in 1885

**gum** a substitution for *God* that exists only in the exclamations *by gum* and *my gum*. First recorded in the early 19th century, it is of dialectal origin, and *ee by gum* still has some currency as people's stereotypical idea of a Northern expression of surprise

**Halifax** since at least the mid 17th century, *go to Halifax* has been used as a euphemistic substitution for *go to hell*. It was probably at least partly inspired by the old beggars' and vagrants' prayer, 'From Hull, Hell and Halifax, Good Lord, deliver us', first recorded around 1660. The reference to Halifax is said to be due to the fact that anyone caught stealing cloth there was instantly beheaded

**Harvey Smith** the term *V-sign* is not as taboo as the gesture, but nevertheless this colloquial alternative probably serves some euphemistic purpose. It recalls an occasion in August 1971 when the showjumper Harvey Smith allegedly made a V-sign at one of the judges of a competition he was taking part in. Smith himself claimed it was a 'V for victory' sign, but the term stuck nevertheless

**heck** a euphemistic alteration of *hell* that first emerged in dialect speech in the second half of the 19th century

**holy moly!** an exclamation of surprise used mainly by American teenagers. It was popularized by the 1950s comic-book hero Captain Marvel. The model was probably *moly*, the name of a magical herb in Greek mythology, but the motivation was no doubt to de-fang the profane *Holy Moses!*

**Horlicks** the proprietary name of a beverage made by adding hot milk to a powder made from malt extract and milk. Its use in contexts such as 'make a right Horlicks of something', popular in British upper-crust slang from the 1970s onwards, strongly suggests a euphemistic substitution for *bollocks*

**jeez** or **jeeze** a euphemistic alteration of *Jesus*, first recorded in the 1920s. **Jeepers** is of similar antiquity

**Jesus H Christ** the addition of the *H* to the holy name apparently 'deconsecrates' it, making it more acceptable as an imprecation. It is first recorded in 1924. Some male homosexuals feminize the *Jesus* to **Jessica**

**Judas priest** a euphemistic substitution for the oath *Jesus Christ*, first recorded in 1914

**land** used as a substitute for *lord* in a variety of exclamations, particularly *land's sake*. First recorded in 1846, it is almost exclusively an American usage

**lor** an eroded form of *lord* (as in *God*), in use since at least the early 19th century in exclamations. The alternative spelling **law** may go back even further, but it could be that examples from the 16th and 17th century represent a variant of the interjection *la* or *lo*. The archaic **lawk** or **lawks** is also a euphemistic alteration of *lord*, probably influenced by *alack*

**mercy** as a mild exclamation, a euphemistic shortening of *Lord have mercy*!

**muck** a not very imaginative substitution for *fuck* in metaphorical contexts: 'You'll get nothing here, so just muck off, there's a good lad,' Richard Adams 1974. It dates from the 1920s, as does the adjectival and adverbial use of **mucking** for *fucking*

**mugger** a euphemistic alteration of *bugger* in various figurative senses – 'silly old mugger', 'mugger off', 'well, I'm muggered', etc. First recorded in 1945

**naff** used in British English in place of *fuck*, particularly in *naff off* ('Princess Anne . . . told [photographers] to "naff off",' *Sunday Times* 1982) and the adjective **naffing**. First recorded in 1959, but brought to wider public notice in the 1970s by the BBC television sitcom *Porridge*, it is not altogether clear where it came from: it may have developed from EFF, perhaps with an *n* grafted on from a preceding indefinite article, or it may be connected in some way with the obsolete backslang *naf* for *fan* 'female genitals' (cf. FANNY). It seems to have no connection with *naff* 'of poor quality, uncool'

**pheasant plucker** apparently some restricted currency as a euphemistic term of abuse, but the main role of this spooneristic euphemism is in a well-known tongue-twister whose quick-fire repetition leads back inevitably to 'pleasant fucker'

**Pygmalion** used in place of *bloody*, its inspiration being the phrase 'not bloody likely' spoken by Eliza Doolittle in Act III of Shaw's play *Pygmalion*, which scandalized audiences in 1913: 'My immediate reaction was to say, "Not Pygmalion likely",' *Times* 1976

**rats** a mild oath. In present-day usage it does not have any euphemistic flavour, but it may be connected with the now obsolete verb *rat*, itself a euphemistic substitution for *rot* (cf. DRAT)

**rollocks** a euphemizing alteration of the exclamation *bollocks*, probably influenced by *rowlocks* 'oar-holding devices', which rhymes with *bollocks*. It is first recorded from 1961. (**Rollicking** 'severe reprimand' would appear similarly to be a mealy-mouthed version of *bollocking* in the same sense, although in fact the first record of *rollocking* (1932) slightly predates that of *bollocking* (1938)

**round objects** = SPHERICAL OBJECTS

**ruddy** a euphemistic substitution for *bloody*, dating from the beginning of the 20th century. The impetus was partly rhyme, but partly also no doubt a common semantic element of 'redness'

**sanguinary** a pomposity dating from the late 19th century, used by those unwilling to soil their tongues or pens with *bloody*: 'The inhabitants raise up their voices and call one another sanguinary liars,' Bernard Shaw 1910. In its original literal sense 'characterized by bloodshed' it goes back to the 17th century

**shoot** an American exclamation of anger, frustration, etc, which probably arose at least partly as a way of avoiding *shit* in the same context. It dates from the 1930s

**shucks** a mild exclamation of annoyance, self-deprecation, etc which originated in mid 19th-century America, at around the same time as *shuck* 'pod' began to be applied to anything useless or valueless. Like *shoot*, probably a partial euphemistic substitution for *shit*

**so-and-so** originally a vague expression for something or someone not to be precisely identified, but pressed into service towards the end of the 19th century as a euphemistic alternative to taboo items such as *bastard*, *bugger*, etc. It is also used adjectivally: 'Some [clients] are a so-and-so nuisance,' *Listener* 1959

**s o b** an abbreviation of *son-of-a-bitch*: 'Why was he such a fickle little s-o-b? McBride offers the usual researched explanations about Frank's unaffectionate mamma,' *Sunday Times* 1992. (Incidentally, the literal *bitch* 'female dog' has now become so contaminated by *bitch* the term of abuse that it has given rise to the euphemism **lady dog**)

**socking** a euphemism for the intensive adjective *fucking* which enjoyed an apparently brief vogue around the middle of the 20th century (not to be confused with the rather older adverbial intensive use, as in *socking great*)

**something** used, mainly in reduplicated form, to avoid a string of expletive adjectives such as *bloody, damned, fucking* (as in 'you something-something idiot'). Users of the rarer **somethinged** presumably have more specifically *blasted, damned* or *confounded* in mind

**spherical objects** a euphemism for the exclamation *balls*!

**stuff happens** a euphemistic alteration of *shit happens*, a fatalistic admission that things will always go wrong and there is nothing much you can do about it. It came to prominence when US Defense Secretary Donald Rumsfeld used it in shrugging off the looting that followed the US capture of Baghdad in 2003

**suffering** used in a range of mild American oaths – mainly *suffering cats*, but there are other, even more bizarre options (e.g. *suffering succotash* – succotash is a dish of green maize and beans). It is not clear that it is a direct euphemistic substitution for anything, although it has been suggested that *suffering Christ* lies behind *suffering cats*

**sugar** a euphemistic alternative to the exclamation *shit*! *Be sugared* had some currency in the early 20th century as a way of avoiding *be damned* ('Real pilot be sugared. Real little show-off, more like!' *Tee Emm* 1942), but has now largely died out

**tarnation** a largely American alternative to *damnation*. It emerged in the late 18th century, via the intermediate form *darnation*

**thunder** used in assorted exclamations and imprecations, including *by thunder* and *in thunder* (as in 'What in thunder . . .?'), dating from the early 18th century. It is presumably a substitute for something stronger, probably *hell*. **Thundering** is used as a relatively mild intensifier: 'I was a thundering bad son,' Charles Dickens 1852

**tormented** a mild epithet suggestive of annoyance or frustration, used in American English in the days when *damned* was taboo. First recorded in 1825

**tunket** a euphemism of dubious origin, used in colloquial American English for *hell*. It goes back to the mid 19th century, and seems still to retain some residual usage, mainly in such phrases as *what in tunket . . .?*

## A Euphemistic Thesaurus of Expletives

**balls** round objects, spherical objects
**bastard** b, basket, blighter, buzzard
**bitch** b
**bloody** bally, blinking, blooming, bluggy, Pygmalion, ruddy, sanguinary
**bollocks** rollocks
**bugger** b, beggar, blighter, mugger
**Christ** Christmas, crikey, cripes
**damn(ed)** d, darn, dash, dee, drat, tormented
**devil** deuce
**fuck** eff, flip, frig, muck, naff
**God** cor, Gawd, Godfrey, golly, gosh, gum
**hell** heck, Halifax, tunket
**Jesus** gee, jeez, jeepers, Jessica, Jesus H Christ, Judas priest
**lord** land, law, lor
**shit** shoot, shucks, sugar

# GAMBLING

The risking of money on an uncertain result has always been regarded in some circles as a more or less reprehensible activity, and so it has naturally attracted a certain amount of circum locution. Gambling itself – the risking of money on games of chance such as cards, roulette, etc – is often dignified by the appellation **gaming**. This was originally, in the 16th century, a perfectly neutral term, but nowadays it is decidedly straight-laced. Apart from its use in certain fixed compounds, such as *gaming table* and *gaming board*, it is restricted to contexts in which *gambling* might seem too frivolous: the *Betting and Gaming Act*, for instance.

But on the whole it is betting rather than gaming that has accumulated euphemisms, and in particular betting on horse and greyhound racing. The business of taking such bets has long suffered a respectability gap. Since the early 19th century the book in which such bets are recorded has been known coyly as simply a **book**, and taking such bets has been termed **making a book**. From this period dates **bookmaker** for a professional bettor. (American English also uses **handbook** for such a book, and **handbook man** for 'bookmaker'.) But by the 20th century *bookmaker* had lost most of its euphemistic force, and new circumlocutions evolved: 1915 saw the first record of that classic genteelism **turf accountant**, which seeks to hitch betting to the staid, pin-striped world of accountancy (*the turf* as a metonym for 'horse racing' dates from the 18th century), and it was soon followed by **commission agent**, an obfuscatory use of a term which originally denoted simply 'one who transacts business for another in return for a percentage'.

Those who bet, too, are happy to be called something less blunt than *bettor*. **Punter** dates from the second half of the 19th century, but by now has become virtually standard English. Retaining their euphemistic flavour are **sportsman** (an American introduction dating from the mid 19th century) and **investor**. This is associated with **invest** 'bet' ('In bookie parlance, one does not bet on a horse; one invests, *Times* 1973), first recorded around 1950. *Punter* too has its related noun, **punt** 'bet', which comes ultimately from French *ponte* 'bet against the bank'. Like **flutter** (which evolved from a late 19th-century sense 'a try or attempt at something') it ostensibly denotes a 'small bet', but is often used to cover up a relatively large one. Another discreet way of referring to a bet is to say that you have a certain amount **on** a horse (as in 'I've got a couple of quid on Red Rum to win').

*Gee-gee* as a child's word for a 'horse' dates from the mid 19th century (it is a reduplicated form of the interjection *gee*, as used to urge a horse on). It has come to be used in the plural (**the gee-gees**) as a defensively playful way of referring to horse racing ('lost a packet on the gee-gees last week, old boy').

Debts incurred in betting and gambling are known with exquisite delicacy as **debts of honour**. This was originally because such debts are not legally enforceable, and therefore the creditor must rely upon the honour of the debtor.

# ALCOHOLIC DRINK

In the modern era, alcoholic drink has always had at best an equivocal status in Western society. For every one who uses and enjoys it, there has often been at least one who disapproves of it (or pretends to). So a subtle skein of circumlocution has evolved, with which one can allude to alcoholic drink without actually mentioning it by name.

The most powerful evidence of this is the extraordinary specialization of the term **drink**. Since Anglo-Saxon times this has meant simply 'imbibe a liquid'. But as long ago as the 15th century it has also been used specifically to denote 'take an alcoholic drink' – a sure sign of an underlying wish to muddy the waters, to equivocate about the true nature of the substance drunk. 'She drinks, you know' can scarcely be interpreted as other than 'She is a habitual drinker of alcoholic drink'. The noun works in the same way: 'Would you like a drink?' will in perhaps the majority of circumstances be taken as an offer of an alcoholic drink ('"Have you had a drink yet?" Peabody said, "I offered him one [it was malted milk] but he didn't want it." "I meant a real drink." Perron shook his head. "I don't want a real drink, either",' Paul Scott 1975). If even *drink* is too frank, **imbibe** is available as a more genteel alternative.

An allied strategy is to associate alcoholic drink with that most blameless of liquids, water. The language has not yet gone quite so far as to equate the two, but there are several expressions in which it stops not far short. The plural was often used in the past in a range of circumlocutions for 'distilled alcoholic drink', including **strong waters**, **distilled waters**, **hot waters** and the soothing **comfortable waters**: 'Some having good and comfortable waters, fetched them and drank one to another,' Captain John Smith 1624. **Water of life** in the same sense has never had much currency in English, but its Gaelic equivalent *uisge-beatha* lies behind English *whisky*, and French has the parallel *eau de vie* 'brandy'. In German, too, *Wasser* 'water' is used in compounds for 'distilled alcoholic drink', as in *Kirschwasser* 'distilled drink made from cherries'. The nearest modern English gets to it is the facetious **firewater**, a coinage of the early 19th century used originally in the context of strong drink consumed by North American Indians: 'I've brought you back a little souvenir – a bottle of the local fire-water made out of fermented bamboo shoots,' Richard Ingrams and John Wells, 1980. Then there is the **watering hole**, originally a pond in which animals drink, but used in the 20th century as a jocular circumlocution for 'pub' or 'bar': 'After two holes . . . the Duke turned to me and said: "Sod this for a lark, Thatcher. Where's the watering-hole?" (That's the way he talks.),' Richard Ingrams and John Wells, 1980. **Giggle water** is applied particularly to champagne, notorious for the rapidity with which it induces euphoria.

If *water* is too specific, try **liquid**. If you are offered **liquid refreshment**, it is likely that you will feel rather cheated if it turns out to be milk or orangeade. And a **liquid lunch** (first recorded in 1970) is decidedly a meal which consists mainly, if not entirely, of alcoholic drink. **Juice** is another alternative, mainly American. It presumably arose from a simple equation with the liquid obtained from fruit. Some connection has been mooted with *juice* 'electric current', but as this did not begin to appear until the end of the 19th century, nearly a hundred years later than 'alcoholic drink', any link can be nothing more than a posthumous reinforcement. Variations on the 'juice' theme include the American **joy juice**, **jungle juice** (originally Australian), and **stagger juice** (from its effect on the drinker). See also JUICED (p 52).

Perhaps the most well-worn excuse for drinking alcohol is that it is 'for medicinal purposes'. The bottle of sherry in the sideboard, the flask of brandy in the hip pocket have often relied on some phantom indisposition as a pretext for being brought out. And this is followed through in a range of medical euphemisms for 'alcoholic drink'. **Cough medicine** or **cough syrup** generally suggest spirits, and invoke the soothing effect of whisky, brandy, etc on the throat as they go down. The same notion of medicating the throat lies behind **gargle**, which dates back to the late 19th century: 'We're just going to have a gargle – will you join us?' *Sporting Times* 1889. And the idea of assuagement and comfort is followed through in **lotion**, another 19th-century coinage. **Tincture** comes from the medicine cabinet too: its use for a solution of some medicinal substance in alcohol paved the way for its facetious reapplication to alcoholic drink. The usage is first recorded in the early 20th century, and like many other saloon-bar circumlocutions it got a great boost in the 'Dear Bill' letters, written in the persona of Denis Thatcher, which appeared in the magazine *Private Eye* in the 1980s: 'No easy brief, Bill, as you will appreciate, especially after taking a few tinctures at lunchtime,' Richard Ingrams and John Wells 1980.

The 'medical' metaphor also manifests itself in a range of euphemisms suggesting that alcoholic drink has a beneficial or restorative effect on the drinker. **Restorative** itself comes into this category – someone offered a restorative after a hard day would expect to receive a drink of spirits, not a glass of medicinal tonic – as do **bracer** (an American coinage of the early 19th century), **reviver** (another 19th-century creation), and **stiffener** (which started life in Australia in the 1860s). In the same vein are **a fortifying drink**, **something to fortify you**, etc, and also **refresher**. If *refreshments* are available at a public function, you know you can expect tea, soft drinks, sandwiches, cakes, etc; but if you are offered **refreshment**, you may justifiably hope for something with alcohol in it. A **pick-me-up**, to revive flagging strength or vitality, is likely to contain strong spirits (yet another mid 19th-century American coinage); and an **eye-opener** (also American, from the early 19th century) has its (supposedly) invigorating effect on the sleep-clogged brain by virtue of its alcoholic content. Someone who has a liking for **stimulants** probably prefers whisky or gin to tea or coffee (or even amphetamines).

But one very high-profile substitute for 'alcoholic drink' takes quite the opposite tack – **poison**. To ask someone 'What's your poison?', or to invite them to 'name their poison', is to offer them an alcoholic drink and ask which sort they would like: '"What's your poison tonight, miss?" "Make it a gin and bitter lemon",' E Brown 1965. The usage apparently arose in early 19th-century America, and no doubt arose as a half-serious attempt to ward off alcohol's harmful effects by joking about them.

The drink often hides behind its container. 'He enjoys a **glass** occasionally' certainly does not imply water, and an offer of a 'glass of something' would be interpreted as containing alcohol. In Britain, **jar** stands unequivocally for 'beer' as do **tinnie** and **tube** in Australia.

The euphemism is all the more effective when the container is a small one: **noggin** (technically a quarter-pint measure) and **tot** both manage to suggest restraint in alcoholic intake: 'I'd intended to take a plate upstairs with a noggin or two out of my cache in the attic and watch the International Golf on the box,' Richard Ingrams and John Wells 1980. And this leads on naturally to another leading strategy for avoiding direct reference to alcohol: encouraging the inference that you are only drinking a very tiny amount. It is generally self-defeating, scuppered by the skill of the British at interpreting understatement. 'They say she enjoys a **drop** now and again' can be readily decoded as

'She drinks like a fish' (but 'I didn't touch a drop all evening' might be believed). Into the same category come **spot** ('May I offer you a spot? . . . I can recommend the Scotch,' P G Wodehouse 1936) and **little something** (often used for a slug of spirits added to a non-alcoholic drink, as in 'Would you like a little something in it?'). The Scots have contributed the **dram**, or more soberly still the **wee dram**, which somehow seldom stops at the official one-eighth-of-an-ounce limit. (*Wee* also goes with *drop*.) A **short** manages to highlight smallness of quantity, while brushing alcoholic content under the carpet (first recorded in print in 1953, it is an abbreviation of the much earlier **short drink**, denoting a single measure of spirits; but the 'shortness' has become so much more shadow than substance that *short* is now applied to any drink of spirits, of whatever size). Etymologically, a **chota peg** is a 'small drink': Hindi *chota* means 'small,' and *peg* is a now super-annuated British term for a drink of spirits, especially brandy and soda. *Chota peg* was the preferred alcoholic diminutive for the British Raj in India.

A round-the-houses way of implying the smallness of your alcoholic drink, and hence the extent of your own sobriety, is to emphasize how short a period of time it will take to consume. This stratagem lies behind the **quick one** or **quickie** (first recorded in 1941), and is also responsible for the **swift half**, a quickly consumed half-pint of beer. **One for the road**, ostensibly a drink before departure, draws a discreet veil over the possibly considerable number of drinks that preceded it (the expression is first recorded in the title of the Johnny Mercer song 'One for my baby (and one more for the road)' 1943). **Nightcap** strays into similar territory, suggesting rest and sleep as the motive for drinking it rather than alcohol-induced revelry (the word originally denoted a 'cap worn in bed', and was not used for an 'alcoholic drink before bedtime' until the early 19th century).

## A range of other 'alcohol' euphemisms:

**amber fluid** also **amber beverage**, **amber liquid**, **amber nectar** an Australian circumlocution for 'beer' (after the colour, naturally), first recorded in 1909. **Amber** is occasionally used on its own in the same sense: 'It's too cold for beer anyway . . . Never too cold for the old amber, love,' A Seymour 1962. In the 1980s it became familiar in Britain as the result of advertisements for Australian lager: 'sustained in their gruelling flight in an army ambulance across the Sahara by the thought of that glass of sparkling amber nectar awaiting them,' *Sunday Times* 1992

**antifreeze** alcohol freezes at a lower temperature than water, but mainly from its warming effect on the drinker

**beverage** in Britain usually in the expression *alcoholic beverage*, which somehow succeeds in giving off an aura of wholesomeness, or at least of non-dangerousness (it feeds, of course, off the standard application of *beverage* to non-alcoholic drinks). In North America *beverage* on its own is used for 'alcoholic drink' (in Canada, a *beverage room* is a bar where beer is served). The colloquial British abbreviation **bevvy** (first recorded in 1889) means decidedly 'alcoholic drink', usually 'beer'

**dry** applied to countries, states, etc in which the sale of alcoholic drink is prohibited. (In Wales the term refers to towns and villages where alcoholic drink cannot be bought on a Sunday.) With its opposite, **wet**, the usage originated in the US in the late 19th century

**electric soup** any strongly intoxicating beverage: 'I furnished our mortician friend with a dollop of electric soup', *Private Eye* 1992

**freshen** an offer to 'freshen your drink' is to be interpreted as a proposal to add more alcoholic drink to an emptied or partially emptied glass. 'Can I **top** you **up**?' means the same

**grape** *the grape* is a long-standing euphemism for 'wine'. *Grape or grain* is sometimes used to contrast wine and whisky

**hospitality** often a lexical disguise for the proffering of alcoholic drink. It is used particularly in the context of providing drinks for guests at a television studio, clients at a trade exhibition, etc. Favoured guests will be ushered into the *hospitality room* or *hospitality suite* and given drinks from the *hospitality cabinet* (which is normally kept locked to prevent staff members from getting to the contents). The usage evolved in the 1950s

**libation** in modern usage, a saloon-bar euphemism for an 'alcoholic drink', which began to evolve in the 18th century from the earlier specific sense 'drink poured out in honour of a god'

**moonshine** a discreet American verbal disguise for illegally distilled spirits, usually whiskey. It evolved in the second half of the 19th century from an earlier sense, 'smuggled spirits' – the underlying idea presumably being nocturnal importation by the light of the moon. Alternative circumlocutions are **mountain dew** and **prairie dew**

**mother's ruin** a euphemism for 'gin', based on the idea of it as typically a women's drink. Its dated air suggests the gin-soaked 18th-century harridans of Hogarth's *Gin Lane*, but in fact the earliest record of it in print is not until the 1930s. The earlier term for 'gin', dating from the beginning of the 19th century, was *blue ruin*

**nineteenth hole** when golfers have finished their eighteen holes, they traditionally repair to the club house for some alcoholic refreshment – hence the facetious name *nineteenth hole* for the club-house bar, which emerged in America around the turn of the 20th century

**nip** originally, in the late 18th century, a half-pint of beer, but in more recent usage an (abstemiously) small drink of spirits. It is short for the obsolete *nipperkin* 'half-pint or less of liquor', which was probably adapted from Dutch *nippertje*, a derivative of *nippen* 'sip'

**sauce** a euphemism for 'alcoholic drink', originally American, and first recorded in 1940. It is usually *the sauce*, and appears in expressions like *be on the sauce* and *hit the sauce*

**sherbet** recorded in Albert Barrere and Charles Leland's *Dictionary of Slang, Jargon and Cant* 1889–90 as 'popular' term for 'a glass of any warm alcoholic liquor, as grog', *sherbet*'s euphemistic career really got under way in Australia in the early 20th century. There, it operates as a facetious alternative to *beer*, or occasionally to *alcoholic drink* in general. It is a re-application of the original sense 'cooling drink'

**snifter** the denotation is a 'small drink, typically of spirits', suggesting temperance, but in practice the intake is not necessarily limited to one: 'I couldn't help thinking pretty enviously of you, Monty and the Major enjoying a few pre-match snifters at the 19th,' Richard Ingrams and John Wells, 1980. The usage originated in America in the first half of the 19th century. It was presumably an extension of an earlier meaning 'sniff, snuffle', although the sense development is not altogether clear (cf. SNORT); perhaps there was originally some suggestion of sniffing a drink in order to evaluate its quality, but there is no documentary evidence for this

**snort** virtually identical in meaning and connotation to SNIFTER, and like it an American coinage (though from the end of the 19th century): 'Emboldened by the odd snort of Old Stag's Breath, and possibly just a touch blotto, I embarked on a harangue,' Richard Ingrams and John Wells, 1980. There is perhaps some allusion to the clearing of the nasal passages by a particularly strong drink

**tipple** an alcoholic drink, particularly a person's habitual drink: 'What's your tipple?' means 'What do you usually drink?' The word gives off an aura of innocence, as if half expecting the answer to such questions to be 'ginger beer', but in practice there are no holds barred in its range of application. The noun, which dates back to the 16th century, is a derivative of the verb *tipple* 'drink alcohol', which itself was a back-formation from *tippler* 'bartender', a word of unknown origin

**top up** See FRESHEN

**wet** See DRY

# DRUNKENNESS

*Drunk* and *drunken* themselves were originally just as euphemistic in intent as *drink* is today (the usage dates back to the early Middle English period), but in modern English they are the standard neutral terms for 'intoxicated by alcoholic drink'.

Many of the contemporary synonyms for *drunk* are decidedly too graphic or forceful to qualify as euphemisms: *pissed*, *smashed* and *stinking*, for instance, scarcely soften the impact of their message. Most strategies for circumventing the subject involve either a very formal or technical term, or a word which in one way or another makes light of drunkenness.

Into the former (rather limited) category come **intoxicated** itself, **inebriated** (dating back to the 17th century, and based ultimately on Latin *ebrius* 'drunk'), and **under the influence** (a late 19th-century development, with *of alcoholic drink* understood). **Intemperance** delicately suggests a considerable fondness for alcoholic drink, and **incapable** has become detached from the legalese *drunk and incapable* to suggest drunkenness. A literary flavour is given to alcoholic intoxication by **Bacchanalian** (from the name of *Bacchus*, the Roman god of grape-growing and wine): we assume that a *Bacchanalian orgy* involves drunkenness as well as fornication. **Bibulous** (related to Latin *bibere* 'to drink') politely implies a tendency to excessive alcohol intake. The originally American **pixilated** tries to be a solemn word, but really isn't. It was based on *pixie*, perhaps with the addition of *elated*, and to begin with meant 'whimsical'; 'somewhat drunk' is a later semantic development. **In one's cups** is a high-falutin way of saying 'drunk', which originated, probably in the 16th century, in the more neutral sense 'while drinking'. But the most rarefied synonyms for *drunk*, so sesquipedalian that no one uses them any more, are **temulent** (ultimately from Latin *temetum* 'intoxicating drink') and **titubant**, whose original literal meaning was 'staggering, reeling'.

A classic recipe for making drunkenness acceptable is to focus on its positive side: that it (supposedly) makes you feel good. That is the motivation behind **happy** (dating from the late 18th century), **merry** (which goes back even further, to the 16th century), and **euphoric**. Into the same category come **mellow** (17th century) and the now rather dated **elevated**, whose implication of drunkenness evolved from an earlier sense 'elated, exhilarated'. (The same semantic development is responsible for **high** 'drunk', which emerged in the 17th century from a probable earlier *high* 'elated', now found only in *high spirits*. **High as a kite** 'very drunk' is first recorded in 1939.) Happiness, or the search for it, is also implied in **drown one's sorrows** – although alcohol as an antidote to unhappiness is more likely to achieve its effect through oblivion than through joy. A similar up-beat message is delivered by the mainly American **comfortable** (one can picture the alcohol-induced stupor of well-being) and **celebrate** (when uninhibited or rowdy behaviour is explained with 'Oh, they've been celebrating', we guess that alcohol has been high on the list of entertainments), and also perhaps by **ebullient**, which suggests positive high spirits ('when he [Harold Wilson] was weak, and when he was strong, . . . when he was distinctly ebullient, and when he was bleakly sober,' Roy Jenkins 1991). An occasion described as convivial may well end up with everyone **under the table**. The subtext of all these 'happy drunkenness' terms is that the intoxication is mild in degree and socially acceptable in form, not aggressive and unpleasant: but it is intoxication none the less.

There inevitably comes a point, however, when gloom succeeds happiness, and many are the euphemisms that exploit the downside of intoxication. **Maudlin** originally meant 'weepy, crying' (it was an adjectival use of a now obsolete form of the name of (Mary) Magdalene, who was depicted in Christian iconography as a weeping penitent). In the 16th century the term *maudlin drunk* evolved, denoting someone who has reached that stage of drunkenness that ends in tears; and by the end of the next century we find *maudlin* itself being used in this sense. **Tearful** makes the same point more directly, and the American **discouraged** exploits the same onset of alcoholic gloom. Another way of putting it, euphemistically, is **emotional**. This seems to have had its genesis in the 1960s. Its usual habitat is the expression

**tired and emotional**; this was particularly linked in its early days with the Labour politician George Brown, whose liking for strong drink was occasionally obvious, and it is still common in the world of politics: 'A tired and emotional Connor Pickering, the chairman of the Conservative students' organisation . . . saw Norman Lamont being interviewed by hacks. . . . Pickering approached the group and loudly exclaimed: "You're full of shit! When are you going to resign?",' *Private Eye* 1992. An early alternative was **tired and overwrought**.

Which brings us conveniently to another aspect of the effect of alcohol that lends itself to circumlocution: its tiringness. Drink does take it out of you, leaves you absolutely exhausted. Besides **tired** itself, we have the genteel **fatigued**, and, really turning the ironic screw, **over-tired**.

From tiredness it is a short step to more serious symptoms: blurring of the mental capacity, and downright illness. Into the first category come **confused**, **fuzzy**, **hazy**, and **muzzy**, all suggesting the mental fog of forgetfulness in which the drunkard wanders. But the main exponent of this notion is **fuddled**. In fact, 'alcoholically intoxicated' appears to be the original meaning of this (it is first recorded in the late 16th century), with the more general 'confused' being a later development, but there is no doubt that in modern usage *fuddled* relies on its connotations of 'confusion' for its euphemistic force.

As well as furring up your brain, alcohol can make your eyes go all funny. Many euphemisms exploit this curious effect. **Cock-eyed**, for instance, which originated in America, possibly as long ago as the early 18th century. **Glassy-eyed** and **glazed** continue the same theme, as does the originally American **pie-eyed**. This emerged around the turn of the 20th century, but its etymology is far from clear. There is no plausible connection with the *pie* made from pastry, but perhaps the expression is a remembrance of the rare adjective *pied* 'jumbled, confused', which itself came from the *printers' pie*, a term for a confused mass of type. But alcohol's effect on the vision is most powerfully evoked by **blind**, short for *blind drunk*, which dates back at least to the early 17th century: 'On the night he arrived in London he would get blind, he hadn't been drunk for twenty years,' Somerset Maugham 1930. In the 20th century the nouns **blind** and **blinder** have been derived from the adjective, denoting a drunken binge.

The next stage after visual impairment may be some loss of sensation or of motor function. The use of **paralytic** for 'in the advanced stages of drunkenness' dates back to the early 20th century (the *Oxford*

*Dictionary of Slang* quotes a choice example from the *Daily Express* 1927: 'Woman at the Thames Court: I was not drunk. I was suffering from paralysis. Mr. Cairns: I have heard being drunk called being paralytic') (see also PLASTERED p 51). A similar point is more colloquially made by **legless** (first recorded in the 1970s), which implies that you are too drunk to stand up. The anaesthetizing effect of alcohol is more pleasingly evoked in **feeling no pain**, which dates from around the World War II period. But an altogether more grisly image is conjured up by **embalmed**, suggesting that the alcoholic torpor has reached a deathlike state (see also PICKLED p 51). In more florid vein, **look on the wine when it is red** echoes Proverbs 23: 31-32: Look not thou upon the wine when it is red, when it giveth his colour in the cup, when it moveth itself aright. At the last it biteth like a serpent, and stingeth like an adder.

More generalized intimations of illness brought on by alcoholic intake are expressed by **damaged** (mainly American), **fragile**, **under the weather**, **the worse for wear**, and that all-purpose euphemism **indisposed** (Hugh Rawson in his *Dictionary of Euphemisms and Other Doubletalk* quotes from Elizabeth Longford 1969: 'There had been an officer "staggering on parade" through "indisposition"'). The circumlocutory potential of **unwell** was im mortalized in *Jeffrey Bernard is Unwell*, the title of Keith Waterhouse's play about Jeffrey Bernard, the *Spectator* writer whose occasional absences from the magazine when too drunk to write his column were thus accounted for to readers. **The worse for drink** has all the mealy-mouthedness of euphemisms at their most sanctimonious.

A traditionally delicate way of referring to drunkenness is by winding the clock back a little to the consumption of the alcohol that led to it. The verb **drink** can do this quite succinctly: 'He drinks, you know' is readily interpreted as 'He drinks far more alcohol than is good for him and is regularly drunk'. To **enjoy a drink** or **like a drink** put it even more genteelly, **hit the bottle**, **be on the bottle**, **put it away** and **knock it back** more bluntly. **Bend the elbow** and **lift the elbow** are quaintly circumlocutious, relating excessive alcoholic intake to the arm action used in raising the glass to the lips. And **indulge** and **partake** make use of two key weapons in the armoury of euphemism, vagueness and pomposity ('Would you care for a small sherry?' 'I don't indulge, thank you' (i.e. I never get drunk)). Similarly tiptoeing round the subject is **to have drink taken**, whose evasiveness is nicely brought out in Rudyard Kipling's 'not drunk, but all – *all* havin' drink taken' (1926).

Extent of alcoholic intake can be put to euphemistic use, too, although it runs the risk of excessive frankness: **loaded** (which comes from late 19th-century America, and is also used of intoxication with drugs) is scarcely a prudent choice if one is aiming for verbal damage-limitation. Nor does **to have had a skinful**, which implies a stomach awash with beer, do much to mitigate the large consumption (it dates back to the late 18th century). More discreet, in suggesting only a minimal amount more than is prudent, are **one too many** and **one over the eight**, first recorded in 1925, which appears to rest on the assumption that the average adult male can consume eight pints of beer without becoming incapacitated (this from before the days of medically recommended safety limits – four pints a day, according to the Royal College of Psychiatrists in 1979). Both expressions are open to variation – 'a glass too many', for instance: '"Did I have one over the regulation number last night?" "Not at all . . . you were perfectly all right",' R J B Sellar 1925. The introduction of legal penalties for having more than a specified amount of alcohol in the blood while driving led in the 1960s to the use of **over the limit** as virtually a euphemism for 'drunk'; and in the late 1980s the acronym **dumbo**, variously interpreted as 'drunken upper-class middle-aged businessman over the limit' or 'dangerous upper-middle-class businessman over the limit', enjoyed a brief vogue. But simplest (and vaguest) of all is just **full**. In the generalized sense 'having eaten or drunk as much as one can' this dates back to the Anglo-Saxon period, but it has two specific developments relating to alcoholic intake: the Scottish form **fou**, used for 'drunk', and a range of colloquial Australian similes, notably **as full as a tick** and **as full as a bull**, also meaning drunk.

The action of alcohol in loosening the drinker's inhibitions is often compared to the effect of lubrication on machinery. The American **greased** comes into this category, as does **lubricated** itself (first recorded in 1927) and **oiled**, which dates back to the early 18th century (it usually comes in the form **well-oiled**). These very fluid metaphors contrast strangely with **plastered**, which emerged around the beginning of the 20th century. Its origins are not entirely clear, but probably it was intended to compare the stiffening effect of alcohol with that of a plaster cast (here we are back in the territory of PARALYTIC – see p 53). This is supported by the now dated American **shellacked** 'drunk', which literally means 'covered with stiff shiny shellac varnish'.

The long-term effects of excessive alcoholic consumption are fore-shadowed in various 'drunkenness' metaphors based on the notion of 'preserving food in liquid'. **Pickled** dates from the first half of the 19th century, **soused** (literally 'preserved in vinegar or brine') from the second. **Sozzled**, also late 19th-century, is probably related to *soused*. And from that point it is not far to the more macabre EMBALMED (see p 54).

A range of cookery terms has been used to disguise drunkenness, notably **boiled**, **cooked**, **steamed** (although the variant **steamed-up** suggests that its origins may be more general), and (probably the most widely used) **stewed**, which originated in America in the early 18th century and often occurs in expressions such as *stewed to the eyebrows* and *stewed to the gills*.

## Some miscellaneous 'drunkenness' euphemisms:

**blitzed** devastated as if by a lightning assault; mainly an American usage

**blotto** a coinage of the early 20th century, with a P G Wodehousian flavour to it. It is presumably derived from *blot*, but how and why has never been satisfactorily explained

**Dutch courage** alcoholic drink taken to stiffen one's resolve in a tricky situation. Originally probably a reference to the supposed heavy drinking habits of the Dutch (in the 18th century a *Dutch feast* was much the same as what we would now call a *liquid lunch*), with the additional implication that these 17th-century enemies of Britain were only brave when they were drunk; but there may also be some allusion to gin as the Dutch drink

**far gone** a classically vague euphemism for 'drunk' which probably dates at least from the 18th century: 'Charles Lamb . . . [drank] too much wine. He was not so far gone as to be outrageous . . . but he was flurried in his manner,' Crabb Robinson 1815

**half cut** meaning 'drunk', and dating from the late 19th century. The source of the metaphor is far from clear, but presumably there is some connection with the equally mysterious and now obsolete American **half shaved** 'drunk'

**half seas over** originally *half sea's over*, that is, 'halfway across the sea'. It was applied metaphorically to any halfway condition, and by the end of the 17th century it was being used specifically for a condition halfway between sobriety and drunkenness. Like almost all expressions that start out meaning 'half-drunk', it eventually turned into simply 'drunk'

**hollow legs** if you are said to *have hollow legs*, the implication is that you can drink large quantities of alcohol without getting drunk (or alternatively that you have a prodigious capacity for food)

**juiced** mainly an Americanism for 'drunk', dating from the mid 20th century. It is often followed by *up*. See also JUICE (p 41)

**lit** probably from the equation of being elated (as when drunk) with being illuminated like a lamp. It dates from the early 20th century, and like *juice* is often followed by up

**soaked** dating back to the early 18th century, and fairly obvious in its metaphorical descent. In modern usage it has all but lost its euphemistic force, particularly when preceded by the names of drinks (*gin-soaked*, *rum-soaked*, etc)

**splice the mainbrace** originally a piece of naval slang, meaning 'hand out the ration of grog (rum and water)'. Literally to splice the mainbrace is to rejoin the rope controlling a ship's mainsail when it has broken. This is quite a hazardous procedure, particularly in heavy seas, and a tot of grog was deemed an appropriate reward for those who undertook it. It has subsequently become a hearty euphemism for 'have an alcoholic drink'

**squiffy** a British colloquialism that makes drunkenness seem cosy, amusing even: 'She would boldly admit that she had had . . . one "over the eight", and had been a little "squiffy" (the feminine Plumleigh-Bruce word for inebriation, and, pronounced as "Squiffeh", suiting this particular feminine Plumleigh-Bruce's voice and accent to perfection),' Patrick Hamilton 1953. It dates from the mid 19th century, but its origins are obscure. A variant sometimes encountered is **squiffed**

**stoned** a term that emerged in America around 1950 with reference to both alcoholic and narcotic intoxication. The source of the metaphor is not clear, but there may be some connection with *ossified* and *petrified*, also used in American English for 'drunk'

**three sheets in the wind** a nautical euphemism for 'drunk'. A *sheet* on a ship is a rope controlling a sail. If three of them are 'in the wind', or flapping about loosely, things are pretty unsteady. The usage dates at least from the early 19th century

**tiddly** drunk in a frivolous or childlike way, or so the implication goes. The adjective emerged around the turn of the 20th century from an earlier and now obsolete noun *tiddly* 'drink'. Its ultimate origins are not clear, but one possibility is that it was short for the obsolete rhyming slang *tiddlywink* 'drink'

**tie one on** an American expression meaning 'get drunk'. It has a curious history. It appears to be short for *tie a bun on*, which together with *get a bun on* and *have a bun on* was used in the US in the first two thirds of the 20th century for 'get drunk'. It has been suggested that this use of *bun* for 'drunken state' (which also spawned *bunned* 'drunk') may go back to the 18th-century *bungey* 'drunk', itself perhaps a derivative of *bung* 'stopper for a cask'

**tight** at the end of the 20th century scarcely euphemistic any longer. Presumably the original impetus behind the usage, which appeared in the first half of the 19th century, was to soften the impact of *drunk*, but the source of the metaphor is not clear. The likeliest explanation is some sort of allusion to a stomach full or 'tight' with alcoholic drink. This may be supported by the parallelism between the similes *as tight as a tick* and AS FULL AS A TICK (see p 51)

**tipsy** a light-hearted word suggesting a mild light-headedness, but in practice someone described as 'tipsy' can be fairly thoroughly drunk. The word evolved in the 16th century, and explains itself: someone who is tipsy is liable to 'tip over' due to excessive alcohol consumption

**well away** a typically vague euphemism which can mean 'thoroughly embarked on any reprehensible or disapproved-of activity' – asleep and snoring, for instance. But the target is usually someone who is far down the road to alcoholic insensibility

**wet the baby's head** celebrating the birth of a child offers a welcome excuse for drinking alcohol, and *wet the baby's head* provides the necessary verbal camouflage. The usage dates from the late 19th century

**wet one's whistle** a very ancient synonym for 'take a drink' ('of alcohol' nowadays usually understood), which dates back to the 14th century. It depends on an otherwise obsolete use of *whistle* for 'mouth or throat, as used in speaking or singing'. Variants recorded from former centuries include *wet one's mouth*, *wet one's throat*, and *wet one's weasand* ('throat'), and from more recently *wet one's beak* and *wet one's beard*

**zonked** usually *zonked out*. It comes from the verb *zonk* 'hit', which imitates the sound of a heavy blow. An American coinage of the late 1950s, it is also applied to the effects of narcotics

And finally, some British rhyming slang. **Elephants** (short for *elephant's trunk* 'drunk') goes back as far as the 1850s. Much more recent are **Brahms and Liszt** and **Mozart and Liszt**, both covering for 'pissed', both apparently arbitrary uses of the composers' names, dating from the 1970s.

# DRUGS AND DRUG-TAKING

Few areas of activity produce such a kaleidoscopic, and such a rapidly changing range of terminology as the world of drug-taking and the making and selling of narcotics. But much of it that finds its way into treatments of euphemism amounts to little more than colourful synonyms. It acts, in the common way of slang, as a form of private code amongst members of the culture, excluding outsiders. As such, it is the very antithesis of euphemism, whose role is to mollify and soothe, to present a benign face, not to exclude.

But there are some categories of drug-speak that meet the euphemistic qualifying standard. A common form of verbal camouflage in this area is the use of an extremely general term with a highly specific meaning. This is often done by deleting *drugs* as the object of a transitive verb and using the verb intransitively. For example, to *use drugs* becomes to **use**: 'Why don't you bust a cap with me? It's choice. I used this morning and I'm still nice,' C Cooper 1960. To **deal** is to sell drugs (from the transitive usage *deal drugs*), to **carry** is to *carry drugs*, to have illegal narcotics about one's person, and to **hold** is similarly to have drugs in one's possession. To **smoke** non-euphemistically is to inhale tobacco smoke, but in drug-users' terminology it covers up the smoking of cannabis, opium etc.

Innocent-looking nouns can conceal a drug-connection too. A **pill** is a pill containing an addictive drug, particularly a barbiturate or amphetamine: 'The police were not too hip on drugs, and pills used to be passed out at clubs like ordinary cigarettes,' *New Statesman* 1970. A **piece** is about an ounce of an illegal drug, especially morphine or heroin (an American usage first recorded in 1935). **The business** is either an injection of a drug, or the equipment for heating and preparing it. And a **habit** is to be understood as an unbreakable habit – an addiction to drugs. The usage began in America, and seems to go back as far as the 1840s. Aficionados recognize various subcategories:

a **belly habit** involves swallowing the drug; if you have a **lamp habit**, you smoke opium; someone with a **mouth habit** smokes the drug; intravenous injectors have a **needle habit**; and those who take drugs by sniffing have a **nose habit**. Someone with an **ice-cream habit** is a recreational drug user, not a hardened addict – the idea being that you take the drug as an occasional treat, like ice cream.

But the ultimate in cryptic abbreviation must be **on**. If someone is said to 'be on', it means they are taking drugs, or are addicted to drugs: 'She's high right now, can't you see it? She's been on for three days,' William Gaddis 1955. A shortening of *on drugs*, the usage emerged in America in the 1930s.

In the quest to disguise the dark side of addictive drugs by verbal sleight of hand, three other main strategies can be discerned. The most popular is to associate the drug with innocent pleasure by lending it the name of something harmless or desirable. Alternatively, you can hide behind technical terminology, and adopt an air of clinical detachment; or you can play it (fairly) straight by using the name of the plant from which the drug was obtained.

What could sound more innocent than **angel dust**? It blends the notions of heavenly purity and divine approval with a suggestion of golden motes shimmering in a sunbeam. Surely nothing with a name like that could do you any harm? But behind the euphemism is just the hallucinogenic drug phencyclidine. Your trip on angel dust may take you to heaven, but if you are unlucky you could stay there – the blackly humorous side of the metaphor is that angel dust can kill. Also exploiting the angelic theme is **yellow angel**, a name for a pentobarbitone tablet (from its colour, of course).

*Dust* features in several drug euphemisms: besides *angel dust* there is **dream dust**, a drug in powdered form (**dreamstick** was once used for both an 'opium pipe' and a 'marijuana cigarette', the allusion in all cases being to the pleasant reverie produced by the drug); **gold dust** is cocaine, white and powdery, as are **happy dust** and **heaven dust** (back amongst the angels again). The powdery image is followed through in **joy powder** 'morphine' or 'cocaine' and **joy flakes** 'cocaine', and also in **Bolivian marching powder** 'cocaine' (Bolivia is a major producer). Most of these names operate by suggesting the euphoria produced by the drug (as do **giggle stick** and **joy stick** for 'marijuana cigarette'); **gold dust**, by contrast, sets out to create an aura of opulence, although the cynic might also discern in it an allusion to the profits made by its sellers.

This ambiguity is certainly present in **Acapulco gold** and **Colombian gold**, two names for high-grade marijuana, produced respectively near Acapulco, Mexico, and in Colombia. The product is typically brownish- or greenish-gold in colour, and is highly desirable because of its quality, but also it does wonders for the bank balances of those who trade in it.

A similar golden glow suffuses **California sunshine**, or **Hawaiian sunshine**, or **yellow sunshine**, all American names for LSD (from the colour of the tablets).

Back among the angels, **blue heaven** is amytal, a type of barbiturate, which comes in blue capsules; and other 'colour' euphemisms that trade on positive associations are **blue velvet**, a mixture of turpine hydrate and codeine that was introduced to a wider audience via the 1986 film *Blue Velvet*, and **black beauty**, a tablet usually of biphetamine. (*Purple heart* 'tablet of Drinamyl', not strictly a euphemism, borrows the name of a US medal awarded to those wounded in action.)

Another favourite verbal disguise is to rename a drug after a foodstuff, particularly something sweet and toothsome favoured by children – what could be more benign? Into this category come the American **candy**, which originally denoted cocaine, then LSD on a cube of sugar, and finally broadened out to any narcotic (**nose candy** is an inhaled drug, typically cocaine); **fruit salad**, an assortment of different drugs, typically one assembled by experimenting teenagers rifling their parents' medicine cabinets; **jellybean**, an amphetamine tablet; **ice cream**, a drug in crystalline form, from the white colour and perhaps also the resemblance to ice crystals on ice cream; and **sugar**, any white narcotic in powdered form, from its resemblance to white sugar (a similar resemblance underlies the use of **snow** for cocaine). In the same spirit an addiction to drugs can be coyly termed a **sweet tooth**.

Marijuana is sometimes known as **baby** – ostensibly because it is the drug for newcomers, who when they 'grow up' move on to something harder, but usefully also suggesting innocence and harmlessness. Picking up on similar resonances is **doll**, a term for a tablet of methadone which was brought to a wider audience by Jacqueline Susann's 1968 novel *Valley of the Dolls*. **Girl** for 'cocaine' also projects an image of wholesomeness, but apparently has its origins in the notion that cocaine has an aphrodisiac effect on women.

Giving a drug a human name is a surefire way of defusing its threat. That was no doubt the impetus behind **Mary Ann**, **Mary Jane**, **Mary**

**and Johnny**, and **Mary Warner**, fanciful alterations of *marijuana* which emerged between the two world wars.

There is a fine line between medicinal drugs and illegal recreational drugs, which can be usefully exploited by pretending that the latter are the former. Morphine when taken addictively has been euphemized by the term **medicine** (sometimes inflated hyperbolically to **God's own medicine**, or **gom** for short). Illegal drugs can take refuge behind the respectable-sounding **pharmaceuticals**, and **pharmacy** can disguise a person's stock of drugs.

The circumlocutionary function of this high-sounding terminology brings us close to the world of double-speak in which drug addiction masquerades pusillanimously as **dependency** (as in 'She has a dependency problem'), and legal mumbo-jumbo covers up illegal drugs as **controlled substances** (**substance abuse** is an all-embracing euphemism for the taking of any drug or intoxicant, from injecting heroin to sniffing glue: 'A look at the lethal craze of volatile substance abuse – the practice of sniffing common domestic products,' *Radio Times* 1993). An antique delicacy rather than legal fictionalizing lies behind **Eastern substances**, which alludes coyly to the Orient as the traditional source of opium and other drugs.

Marijuana sounds much less threatening if it can be made to share the name of the plant it is made from: **hemp**, or **Indian hemp** ('Its votaries have taken to opium and hemp, the latter of which Sir Lepel Griffin says is far more injurious than tobacco,' *The Nation* 1893). Failing that, any of a number of botanical subterfuges can be resorted to: you can call marijuana **grass** (a usage which dates back to the 1940s), **hay** (rather earlier, and now superseded), **the weed** (a euphemism also applied to tobacco), or **the herb**. Similarly cocaine is termed **the leaf**, because it is obtained from the leaf of the coca plant; and **hop** has been used in American English since the late 19th century for a narcotic drug, particularly opium. **Tea** as a euphemism for 'marijuana' (first recorded in 1935) depends partly on a resemblance to dried tea leaves (although it is also used for a drink made by brewing marijuana in hot water).

# AVARICE

An accusation of miserliness is a pretty serious matter. It cuts to the quick. Many of the words we use to make it have a very high acid content: *avarice*, *cupidity*, *meanness*, *stinginess*, and so on. The flip side of this is that we often find it politic to tone down the accusation, to soften its impact without leaving it unsaid.

The classic strategy is to look for positive behaviour traits that are closely related to avarice and parsimony, and to use the words for these positive traits to describe the negative ones. For example, most of us would regard economy as more or less of a virtue, the opposite of wastefulness. So how better to euphemize people with padlocked wallets than as **economical**. Equally useful weasel words are **careful**, implying a worthy caution over the expenditure of even the smallest amount of money, and **thrift**: 'Manning's personal life seems to offer little cause for reproach, beyond . . . a reputation in some quarters for extreme thrift,' *Observer* 1992. Hugh Rawson in his *Dictionary of Euphemisms and Other Doubletalk* quotes from Anatol Rapoport's *Semantics* 1975: 'A game said to have been invented by Bertrand Russell is called "Conjugating Adjectives." It is played by mentioning three adjectives having the same denotation but different connotations. Example: I am thrifty, you are tight, he is stingy.'

As Rapoport's conjugation implies, **tight** can be middlingly euphemistic – more outspoken than *thrifty*, but milder than *stingy*. It probably combines the image of the tightly clenched hand unwilling to let go of money with more abstract notions of constriction and retention. But that is mainly in American English. For British speakers, *tight* is fairly strongly condemnatory, in much the same league as the insulting *tight-fisted*. In Britain, the parallel euphemisms are **close** and the now seriously dated **near**. Both go back to the 17th century, and like *tight* depend on the idea of keeping the hand firmly closed (at that period *close* was used where we would now use *closed* and *near* had a more general sense 'narrow, constricted' which it has since lost).

Negative understatement is always a useful way of meaning what you don't say, so a verdict of **ungenerous** can be readily interpreted as 'mean bastard'. And apparently 'He's **no tipper**' enjoyed a vogue as an expression characterizing someone reluctant to part with money.

Direct references to money include **counting** or **watching the pennies** (implying an obsessive retention of the pounds – the related *penny-pinching* is no longer euphemistic) and **money-conscious** (we assume that the consciousness embraces getting and saving rather than spending).

The stereotypical English view of the Scots as stingy has made **Scottish** available as a sly insinuation of meanness.

# COWARDICE

The language of cowardice received its major euphemistic boosts of the 20th century in two world wars and subsequent military encounters. Soldiers have always run away from the enemy, been overwhelmed psychologically by the experience of battle, etc. But as the speed and thoroughness of the reporting of war increased, so those in authority sought to disguise these failings linguistically, so as not to shatter illusions on the home front.

The classic World War I term was **shell shock**, first recorded in 1915. Ostensibly based on the ennervating effect of continuous exposure to artillery bombardment, it officially covered a form of neurosis brought about by the prolonged horror, noise, violence, fear, etc that was the general experience of men in the front line. One of the effects of this horror, noise, etc was to make you want to run away from it, and so *shell shock* soon side-slipped partially into the role of a euphemism for 'cowardice in the face of the enemy', or for a less specific disinclination to fight. Shortly after the war it was abandoned as an official term in favour of *psychoneurosis*.

In World War II the vogue term was **battle fatigue** or **combat fatigue** – the latter officially adopted in 1943. By now, the linguistic manipulation of reality had become more sophisticated. *Fatigue* has a fairly comfortable sound, suggesting that those affected are merely a little tired – nothing a good night's sleep or at most a week's break will not put right. But in fact it names a serious psychological disorder, and again has frequently been used informally as a euphemism for 'cowardice'.

Another World War II coinage was **lack of moral fibre**, often abbreviated to **LMF**. RAF aircrew grounded for displaying conspicuous lack of courage would have *LMF* noted against their names in their records.

This is a far more direct euphemism than *battle fatigue*: it was deliberately devised to denote 'cowardice', while wrapping it up in gobbledegook.

In the Vietnam war, the Americans took the art of circumlocution to new heights with **acute environmental reaction**.

During World Wars I and II, people who were in reserved occupations, such as coal-mining, were exempted from conscription into the armed forces. To counter any suggestion that this was a soft option, it was dubbed **work of national importance**. But the expression was quickly subverted in the services, where it came to be regarded as a euphemistic cover-up for those who were afraid to fight.

Away from the battle-field, cowardice is not a quality much euphemized. Colloquialisms such as *yellow* and *lily-liverered* scarcely have any euphemistic force in present-day English, even if they did originally, and *funk* has a certain cruel directness about it. *Shit oneself* suggests the effects of fear too graphically to qualify as a circumlocution. But **have** or **get cold feet** has more of the authentic coyness. It emerged in America towards the end of the 19th century, and supposedly describes one of the symptoms of fear. So too does **butterflies (in the stomach)**, which originally (around the turn of the 20th century) denoted the tremors in the stomach caused by fear, and by extension has come to signify 'fear'.

Cowardice's opposite, courage, is not the sort of concept that one would think of as requiring a euphemistic cover-up. But one of its more colloquial synonyms, *guts*, is too much for some sensitive stomachs. Hence the ponderous **intestinal fortitude**, coined around 1915 by Dr John W Wilce, professor of clinical medicine at Ohio State University, and used sporadically since – as often facetiously as in earnest.

# SEX

———

The Anglo-Saxon peoples, and particularly the British, are famous for being embarrassed by sex, so it is hardly surprising that the English language contains more euphemisms for sexual activity than for any other topic.

Even when we talk about talking about sex, we cannot bring ourselves to do so directly. Hence all those adjectives that tiptoe around the edge, not conceding pleasurableness, not daring to condemn outright as obscene, but just hinting at a vague naughtiness: the likes of **Rabelaisian** (an insipid fate for the wholeheartedly vulgar French satirist François Rabelais), **suggestive**, **near the knuckle** (with its synonyms **near the bone** and **near the mark**), **off-colour** (referring especially to jokes), **fruity** ('The Queen was said to be entranced by [the Duchess of York] and the Duke of Edinburgh was said to like her fruity jokes,' *Guardian* 1990), **risqué** (borrowed from French in the 1860s), **piquant** (another French loanword – English likes to take refuge in French when alluding to sexual matters), **earthy**, **spicy**, **racy**, **broad** (now rather dated, but once popular for its extreme allusiveness: 'a collection of comic but extremely broad ballads,' Henry Traill 1882), **loose**, and (quintessentially euphemistic) **equivocal**.

We are even squeamish about using the word *sex* when it refers inoffensively to males or females collectively, rather than to their reproductive association. Tongue-tied allusions to 'the opposite . . . er . . . you know' have become a cliché, and **gender** is often resorted to as a lexical escape route: 'Age really matters with goat. Too old and it will surely be tough . . . So does gender: it's always best to use castrated males,' *Guardian* 1990.

# FOREPLAY AND AFTER

Vagueness is the soul of euphemism, so it is not surprising that circumlocutions for sexual activity often fail to distinguish between copulation and the stimulatory activities that precede it, nor that many euphemisms whose overt message is the latter conceal a subtext of the former. The classic case is **make love**. When this came into English towards the end of the 16th century (as a translation of French *faire l'amour* or Italian *far l'amore*), it denoted the attempt to initiate a sexual relationship – a more refined version of what in modern parlance might be termed *chatting up*. But by the middle of the 20th century it had, while retaining its butter-wouldn't-melt external appearance, moved decisively in meaning via petting to downright copulation: 'One of the Carvers made love to her and she had a baby,' Mervyn Peake 1950. Similarly shifty in the past, although now pretty dated, was **embrace**, which was used to denote not an innocently friendly clasping with the arms but (typically in the plural) sexual intercourse.

There remains a residue of euphemisms for sexual activity that are interpretable, at least by the less cynically minded, as not necessarily connoting vaginal or other penetration.

Many of them equate sex with play or boisterousness. Into this category come **fun and games** ('Beneath the orderly conduct of her bar there was always present the possibility of "fun and games",' Edward Grierson 1952) or simply **fun**, a usage which appears to date back to the late 19th century; **romp**, as both a verb and a noun (the latter is also used for a play, film, etc featuring light-hearted titillation); **slap and tickle** (first recorded in 1928); and **tumble** (as in 'a tumble in the hay' – the presumption of copulation is quite strong in this case). The notion of 'play' also features heavily in **indoor sport(s)**, which originally denoted such pastimes as cards, chess, Monopoly and blow football but has increasingly come to be interpreted, and used, as a facetious euphemism for 'sexual activity': 'We once again indulged in the oldest of indoor sports,' R Perry 1972.

Another key euphemistic strategy is to admit playfully that sex is slightly wicked. This lies behind **hanky panky**, originally used in the 1840s for 'mischievous activity' in general, but later narrowed down to 'improper sexual conduct' (the word was an arbitrary coinage, probably inspired by *hocus pocus*); **monkey business**, another innocent 19th-century coinage that has got into more knowing hands; and **naughty**, implying unspecified sexual escapades (in Australia and New Zealand it has been used straightforwardly since the 1950s as a noun meaning 'sexual intercourse' and as a verb meaning 'have sex with').

The notion of 'doing more than has been permitted' lies behind **take liberties**, which dates back to the mid 18th century, while **familiar** in the sense 'presuming on acquaintance to go beyond what is sexually proper' is as old as the 15th century.

**Amorous** could connote anything from unrequited serenading outside a lady's window to sexual intercourse, and **favours** (as conferred by a woman on a man) could be anything from a kiss to copulation. The latter usage dates from at least the early 19th century, and the 17th century had the much more specific but still deeply euphemistic **last favour** for 'intercourse' (inspired by French *les dernières faveurs*).

A particular subset of precopulatory activity that has attracted its own euphemisms is fondling of the genitals and other erogenous areas, particularly by a male of an unwilling female. *Grope* is fairly vague, but too coarse to qualify as a euphemism; **feel** and **touch**, however, fit the bill admirably. Both disperse the force of the message by their high generality. *Feel* in this context is mainly a noun ('give someone a feel', 'cop a feel') while *touch* is a verb (as when the embarrassed inquisitor of the victim of a sexual attack might ask 'Where did he . . . "touch" you?'); the addition of *up* reduces the euphemistic force of both. **Fumble** suggests inexperienced and fairly unsuccessful attempts to penetrate a woman's outer garments ('Boys could not be bothered to fumble with all those buttons,' *Guardian* 1990), but it has also been applied to copulation.

**Nonsense** (as in 'Now then, let's not have any of that nonsense') can disguise anything from exploratory caresses to full intercourse.

When it comes to the actual insertion of the penis into the vagina, there are no euphemisms like the old euphemisms. *Fuck* may be marginally less taboo now than it has been in the past (see p 12), but for most people in most situations the embarrassment of referring directly to this action is so great that, if it cannot be avoided, they are glad to take refuge in the flowery vagueness of antique diction. Into this category come **act of love** ('Less overt is the man who asks his wife to "play dead" and keep quiet while he performs the act of love without her assistance,' Brian Masters 1993; **love** is a key euphemism for 'sexual intercourse' – a **night of love** is unlikely to be spent gazing into each other's eyes, and an enquiry about someone's **love life** will be interpreted as a question about the frequency and quality of their sexual intercourse; see also MAKE LOVE p 67); **commerce** ('Sophia's virtue . . . made his commerce with Lady Bellaston appear still more odious,' Henry Fielding 1749; there is no imputation of payment – it is simply a narrowing down of the more general sense 'dealings'); **congress** (etymologically a 'coming together': 'The contrasting heights of two animal species "would be a bar to any congress of an amorous kind",' *Sunday Times* 1993, quoting Gilbert White); **connection** (a classic euphemistic exploitation of vagueness, dating back to the late 18th century); **coupling** (which has been around since the 14th century); the verbs **enjoy** and **possess** 'have sex with', usually used of a man, and **give oneself** and **surrender**, similar in connotation but applied typically to women; to **oblige**, again used of a woman allowing a man to have sex with her, with occasionally the implication of payment, and to **pleasure**, a unisex verb redolent of former centuries ('"His Grace" wrote Sarah, Duchess of Marlborough "returned from the wars this morning and pleasured me twice in his top boots",' *Guardian* 1990) that has enjoyed something of a revival in the second half of the 20th; and **union**, like *connection* and *coupling* a rather coy exploitation of the 'joining' notion (see also COITION p 70).

The two crucial adjectives in this area are **carnal** and **connubial**. *Carnal*, which crops up in expressions like 'carnal thoughts' and of course 'carnal knowledge' (a resounding circumlocution for 'sexual intercourse'; see KNOW p 69), makes the straightforward puritan equation of the body with (sinful) reproductive activity – a notion also embodied in the archaic use of **the flesh** for sensual appetites and their assuagement ('the sins of the flesh' were basically copulation), and in the late 20th-century use of **physical** to connote penetrative sex (as in 'Let's get physical', or 'I no longer have a normal physical relationship with my husband and he cannot come to terms with this,' *Guardian* 1990). *Connubial* means literally 'of marriage', but in its commonest environment, the expressions 'connubial bliss' and 'connubial pleasure', it is the connotation of sexual intercourse that is uppermost, not marriage.

A small but important subset of ornate sexual euphemisms consists of two verbs closely linked in people's minds with the Bible. Indeed, when **know** is used for 'have sexual intercourse with' in modern contexts, it is almost invariably qualified by 'in the biblical sense' ('in the **biblical** sense' has virtually become a euphemism for 'in a sexual sense'). It is a literal translation of a Hebrew euphemism. The other verb is **lie with** (intransitively **lie together**), which is also used for 'copulate (with)' in the King James Version: 'Lift up thine eyes unto the high places, and see where thou hast not been lien [i.e. lain] with. Thou hast polluted the land with thy whoredoms and with thy wickedness,' Jeremiah 3:2. It ties in with the modern use of such euphemisms as SLEEP WITH and BED for sexual activity (see p 73), and has a direct descendant in LAY for 'have sex with' (see p 72).

The law casts a certain respectability over an officially sanctioned set of copulatory vocabulary. The notion of having to **consummate** a marriage – i.e. to make it somehow mystically 'complete' by having sexual intercourse – is essentially a legal one (the term is first recorded in an Act of Parliament of – appropriately enough – Henry VIII's time). The vague **relations** for 'sexual intercourse' (in fact short for **sexual relations**) smacks of mealy-mouthed divorce evidence in the days when it had to be spied out by private detectives ('She had relations with the respondent on numerous occasions'). (US President Clinton relied on the supposed ambiguity of the full form when he denied having 'sexual relations' with Monica Lewinsky.) But the classic divorce-court evasion was **intimacy**. Indeed, whenever the account of extra-marital goings-on reached an interesting stage, it seemed that the verbal curtains were pulled with some such formula as 'Intimacy then took place'. The saccharine circumlocution has survived the liberalization of the divorce laws, evidently fulfilling a need for a warm, cosy, non-salacious-sounding term for 'sexual intercourse': 'Roy Castle and Maggie Philbin return with a report from John Pitman on intimacy in later life,' *Radio Times* 1993. (The corresponding adjective **intimate** is used in the same way – 'Were you ever intimate with her?') Also from the legal textbook is, or was, **crim con**, an abbreviation of *criminal conversation*, a superannuated euphemism for 'adultery'.

Technical terms are always serviceable for covering up embarrassment, and copulation is no exception. Indeed, the word *copulate* itself spread into the general language in the 20th century from the specialized terminology of zoology. It is now perhaps too much of a core term to be still regarded as a euphemism, but the much more formal **coition** (etymologically a 'coming together'; compare UNION p 69) is certainly language with its starchiest clothes on. It dates from the early 17th century.

At the colloquial end of the spectrum, there is a constant danger of copulation euphemisms toppling over the edge into taboo. Some verbs and verb phrases that most of the time maintain their equilibrium:

**at it** see p 74

**attend to** perpetuating the male fantasy that females' needs are met by being copulated with. A coarser but still euphemistic synonym is **see to** (as in 'I wouldn't mind giving her a seeing-to')

**been with** at the extreme of allusiveness (it is, after all, possible to 'be with' someone without having sex with them) and now, like the similarly inspired *go with* (see below), rather passé – but still to be heard (as in 'She's been with half the boys in the classs')

**dip one's wick** from the image of the male inserting his penis (see WICK p 130). First recorded in 1958

**do it** to copulate. Allusion could scarcely get more oblique. First recorded in 1922, but the most famous example is perhaps in the title of the Beatles song 'Why don't we do it in the road?' **Do** is also used independently for 'copulate with'. On the use of IT for 'sexual intercourse' see p 74

**do what comes naturally** representing (and exculpating) sexual intercourse as an instinctive activity imposed by nature. An expression given a boost by the Irving Berlin song *Doin' what comes naturally* (1947)

**drop your pants/knickers/drawers**, etc a necessary preparation for sexual intercourse, and used as a metaphor for it. Applied to women

**frig** barely exempt from taboo, but qualifying as a euphemism on the grounds that it substitutes for *fuck*. It dates back to the late 16th century, and may ultimately be a variant of the obsolete *frike* 'dance, move briskly'

**get into** to succeed in having sex with (a woman) – a coinage of the late 19th century. To **get into someone's knickers** could in theory be no more than a successful attempt at a grope, but in practice it generally refers to copulation

**get your end away** to succeed in having sexual intercourse. An almost exclusively male usage – from the notion of the genitals as the terminal point of the trunk

**go** to copulate enthusiastically – but mainly manifested as the agent noun **goer** (as in 'Is she a goer?', asked by the pub bore about his companion's wife in the celebrated *Monty Python* 'nudge-nudge wink-wink' sketch). The rather dated **go with** is used for 'have sex with': 'I heard one Soviet girl . . . describe her country as being like a prostitute . . . who will go with anyone,' *Guardian* 1990

**go upstairs** one could in theory have a number of destinations in going upstairs (and indeed *go upstairs* is used as a euphemism for visiting the lavatory), but in the context of sex, the metaphor is based on the location of the bedroom: 'Not a word was said about getting undressed, or doing a striptease, and definitely nothing was said about going upstairs . . . There's no mention in the contract about going upstairs or about prostitution at all,' *The Women Trade*, BBC1 1992

**have** highly allusive, but in practice (as in 'He boasts about how many women he's had') the meaning is usually fairly obvious. The usage dates back at least to the late 16th century. **Have your way with** is a much more 'literary' alternative, tied in even more strongly than *have* to men ('He had his wicked way with her')

**have it off (with)** to have sex (with). A Briticism dating from the pre-World War II period. A variation is **have it away (with)**

**lay** as both a verb, meaning 'have sex with', and a noun, meaning a 'person (typically a woman) considered for their part in or proficiency at copulation' (as in 'She's a great lay'), it originated in 1930s America. The underlying metaphor ties in strongly with the sexual use of BED and SLEEP WITH, and reinvents the 'biblical' figure of speech LIE WITH

**let in** a rather graphic euphemism for a woman permitting penetration by the penis (as in 'Oh why did I let him in?'). Now fairly dated

**make** in American slang, if a man makes a girl, he successfully chats her up – the usual implication being that he has achieved his copulatory goal. First recorded in 1918. The synonymous **make it with** is more restrained in expression but amounts to the same thing. It is more recent, dating from the 1950s

**make babies** an excruciatingly coy circumlocution, even when it does truthfully reflect the purpose of the exercise. Often followed by *together*. Compare PLAY MOTHERS AND FATHERS

**make out** another Americanism for 'succeed in having sex with someone'. First recorded in 1939

**party** a verb that in America has careered from 'attend a party' via 'enjoy oneself as at a party (or perhaps an orgy)' to 'have sex'

**perform** a classically vague way of saying 'copulate to the satisfaction of your partner'. Often used in the context 'perform in bed'. The majority of the usage is probably applied to men, and there is sometimes a connotation of 'ability to have an erection'

**play around** another application of the 'children's games' metaphor to sexual intercourse, defusing its seriousness (compare FUN AND GAMES p 67). The element *around* often connotes promiscuousness. **Play games**, too, suggests a compromising of monogamy

**play mothers and fathers** again, a 'children's game' – the innocent pastime of changing the doll, putting it to bed, etc uprated to X. Compare MAKE BABIES

**put out** a woman who 'puts out' is willing to have sex. An Americanism dating from the 1940s

**roger** to copulate (with). A piece of archaic slang (first recorded in 1711) sometimes revived for comic effect. It is probably a verbal use of the now obsolete *roger* 'penis', one of a range of male forenames applied to that organ

**score** (of a man) to succeed in having sexual intercourse (with the most conveniently available partner). Probably not so much a sporting metaphor as an extension of earlier uses of *score* for 'succeed in obtaining something', applied for example to drugs. Originally American, first recorded in 1960

**sleep with** together with its intransitive partner, **sleep together**, one of the key verbal 'sexual intercourse' euphemisms. It dates right back to the Anglo-Saxon period, but it seems to have died out towards the end of the Middle Ages, and there is no evidence of the modern usage before the early 19th century. It is part of the whole '*bed* = sex' euphemistic nexus (see p 77), but in this instance the metaphor is carried beyond *absurdum* – presumably at least one of the partners must be awake for sexual intercourse to take place. The offshoot **sleep around** (first recorded in 1928) implies promiscuous sexual intercourse. And a **sleeping dictionary** is a foreign woman from whom in the course of a brief affair or one-night stand a man learns the rudiments of her language in the intercopulatory intervals

**spend the night with** an even more coy circumlocution than *sleep with*: we are invited to consider the possibility of the two people sitting up until dawn discussing ancient Chinese philosophy or the current economic crisis. The form of the idiom is quite fixed: *stay the night with* is perfectly innocent, with no sexual subtext

**swing** to have promiscuous sex at every opportunity, and in particular to engage in wife-swapping. First recorded in 1964. Compare SWING BOTH WAYS (p 111)

**take** as in '"Take me!" she cried' or 'He took her on the kitchen table'. A bodice-ripping metaphor bulging with imagery of male sexual rapaciousness and female passivity: 'Less overt is the man who asks his wife to "play dead" and keep quiet while he performs the act of love without her assistance; I know some happily married women who are pleased to gratify their spouses in this way and simply be "taken",' Brian Masters 1993. It is first recorded in the works of D H Lawrence

**take advantage of** to have sex with a woman who, the implication goes, was too guileless to know what was going on and object

The human brain responds with extraordinary fertility to the challenge of finding acceptable ways of referring to 'sexual intercourse' itself. The classic euphemistic strategy of vagueness provides several important ones. If a man says he is looking for some **action**, the context may allow the inference that he wants a woman to copulate with. A person's **adventures** may well be his or her past acts of sexual intercourse. And **fate worse than death**, applied to premarital loss of female virginity, often specifically by means of rape, is nothing if not cryptically allusive – although nowadays it is much more often used facetiously than with a straight face (the idea, if not the precise verbal expression, goes back to the 17th century).

Then there's the 'I've-forgotten-what-it's-really-called' school, always a useful approach when trying to avoid embarrassment. In the area of sexual intercourse its main contributions are **how's your father**, British and now rather dated, and **you know what**. And perhaps **the other** belongs to this category too. Short for the obsolete *the other thing*, this is first recorded in 1922. It encapsulates a curious existential split, with sexual activity on one (tabooed) side and the whole of the rest of human life and existence on the other. Its commonest context is the expression 'a bit of the other'.

But for vagueness none of these can compete with **any**, **bit** and pre-eminently **it**. They depend for their particular interpretation upon context – either of situation or of collocation. The expression *getting any*, for instance – as in 'Been getting any recently?' – instantly suggests male success in persuading a woman to copulate. Similarly someone who had *had a bit* might well have been having sexual intercourse (see also BIT ON THE SIDE p 113). But the king of the sex euphemisms is certainly *it*. Running for the cover of the neuter pronoun when we want to mention sexual intercourse dates back at least to the 17th century, and still we refer to people being *at it*, or *getting it*, or *having it*, or *wanting it*, the *it* sometimes in inverted commas or otherwise typographically marked if the point needs to be hammered home: 'I was lugged off to their secret meeting-place . . . to be asked what IT was like,' Nancy Mitford 1949. See also DO IT (p 71).

Then there are all the playful colloquialisms, first cousins to the 'children's games' metaphors (see FUN AND GAMES p 67), which defuse the seriousness of sexual intercourse. Into this category come **jollies** (typically in *get one's jollies*, which can refer to gratification or excitement in general, but usually has copulatory connotations); **nookie**, first recorded in 1928, which may have referred originally to furtive sexual activity in secluded corners or 'nooks'; **roll in the hay**, an apparently bucolic image that may in fact have originated in the metaphorical use of *hay* for 'bed,' as in *hit the hay* 'go to bed' (**roll** has been used on its own for 'act of copulation,' generally in the phrase 'have a roll': 'Your Rosemary has been having a roll with a Cabinet Minister,' Paul Ferris 1976); the British **rumpy-pumpy**, which exploits the graphic imagery of 'rumps' and 'pumping' for playful purposes ('There is a bit of rumpy-pumpy, first on the stairs and then in a bed,' *Observer* 1993; it is first recorded in 1986, and has alternative formulations such as **rumpty-tumpty** and **rumpo**); **jig-a-jig**, which dates from the 1930s, and mimics the jerking movements of intercourse; and **yum-yum**, which as a general term for any sort of pleasurable activity, based on the exclamation *yum!*, dates from the late 19th century – the specific application to sexual intercourse has also produced **yum-yum girl** as a euphemism for 'prostitute'.

A curious subset of colloquialisms for 'sexual intercourse' is represented by **corn** and **oats**, which are usually used (of men) in expressions such as 'get one's corn' and 'want one's oats'. They seem to be based on the notion of sexual intercourse as something that men require regularly, as horses require to be fed (on corn or oats), although in the case of *oats* (first recorded in this sense in 1923) there may also be some allusion to the expression *sow one's wild oats* 'behave promiscuously in youth'.

So allusive as to be impenetrable to the uninitiated is **Ugandan**. This euphemism (as in **Ugandan activities** or **Ugandan discussions** 'sexual intercourse') emerged from the pages of the British satirical magazine *Private Eye* in the 1970s. It has gained some minimal wider currency, but the *Eye* remains its major habitat: '[The] university vice chancellor

. . . was caught by Inspector Knacker discussing Ugandan further education policy in [a] red-light [district],' *Private Eye* 1993. Its inspiration is said to have been the discovery of a female Ugandan government minister having sex in an airport lavatory – or 'discussing Ugandan affairs', as she claimed.

Not surprisingly, the word **sex** plays a major role in the euphemization of copulation. Not that there aren't taboos against its use too, but in the second half of the 20th century they became much weaker, and anyway it causes far fewer shivers than *fuck*. Its central role is to stand in for *copulation* itself, particularly in the expression 'have sex (with)', but also in a wide range of other contexts, such as 'good sex' and 'safe sex': 'Only 10 per cent of women [were] aware it could be taken up to 72 hours after unprotected sex,' *Guardian* 1990. 'Have sex' itself dates back to the 1920s (it is first recorded in the works of D H Lawrence), but it does not seem to have become widespread until the 1950s. Some purists still affect to find the usage solecistic, as if *sex* could only mean 'gender'. But more important from the point of view of sheer frequency is **sexual intercourse**, which has become so much our everyday term for 'copulation' that we forget its circumlocutious origins, and scarcely regard it as a euphemism. First recorded in 1799, it depends on a general use of *intercourse* for 'communication, dealings' (compare COMMERCE p 69) which is now very rare – not least because of contamination by sexual connotations. From the beginning we find *intercourse* used in other combinations with the sense 'copulation' – as in 'illicit intercourse', 'fleshly intercourse', 'promiscuous intercourse', etc – but it does not seem to have been until the 1960s that **intercourse** came into its own as a free-standing euphemism for 'copulation' – as in 'have intercourse with someone'. See also SEXUAL RELATIONS (p 70).

Position and location have an important role to play in our verbal disguising of copulation. Most positional euphemisms take their cue from the standard lying-down attitude adopted for sexual intercourse. **Horizontal**, for instance, is used in a variety of nudge-nudge contexts to suggest intercourse (compare GRANDE HORIZONTALE p 97), and **on your back** goes one step further to exploit the stereotypical copulatory position of the female (see also LIE WITH p 70). Other positionally based euphemisms are **knee-trembler** 'act of copulation performed standing up', from its weakening effect upon the knees (first recorded in 1896) and **leg over**, generally applied to males, from the traditional man-on-top position, and possibly a lineal descendant of an 18th-century euphemism *lift a leg over* 'have sex with'. The colloquial name of the commonest Western copulatory position, which might possibly be regarded as euphemistic, is **missionary position** (first recorded in 1969), so called apparently because Christian missionaries told benighted heathens that it was sinful to copulate in any other way than with the female beneath and facing the male.

Location euphemisms centre predictably on the bed. **Go to bed with** for 'have sex with' is first recorded in 1945, and the use of **in bed** with sexual overtones (as in 'good in bed' or 'discovered them in bed together') is presumably of similar if not earlier vintage. The mainly American synonym **sack** is used with the same connotations (as in 'She's great in the sack'). And **between the sheets** is a more allusive way of putting it. The focus can be lengthened by moving from the bed itself to the room in which it is situated: **bedroom** is widely used with connotations of 'sexual activity' ('the bedroom secrets of Farrah and Ryan,' *Guardian* 1990), and **bedroom eyes** (first recorded in 1947) denotes a 'look that invites sexual intercourse'. Promiscuity can be trivialized as **bed-hopping**. A very specialized location euphemism is **casting couch**, with its connotation of sexual intercourse with a film's producer or director as the way for an actress to secure a part in it.

The notion of copulation as the ultimate goal and extreme point of sexual activity is embodied in a small group of euphemisms, all usually preceded by *go*: **all the way, the whole way**, and, more colloquially, **the whole hog**. A common context for them is young girls contemplating the loss of virginity: 'I'm still a virgin. How will my boyfriend take it? Is there a right age to "go all the way"?' *Guardian* 1990.

Knowledge about human sexual intercourse is traditionally euphemized as the **facts of life**, an expression which dates from the late 19th century. A favourite metaphor used when explaining them is the **birds and the bees**, which shunts the embarrassing connotations on to non-human species.

Virginity in danger and chastity are not the burning issues they once were, and the euphemisms used to talk about them have a dated air. **Honour** and **virtue** are, or were, key terms, and a woman attempting to avoid unwanted sexual intercourse might be said to be '**defending** her honour'. A woman penetrated for the first time could formerly have been described as **deflowered**. A more modern euphemism for 'virginity' is **cherry**, coined in America in the 1920s. It comes from an earlier use of *cherry* for 'hymen', and its most common context is probably 'lose your cherry'.

Unwelcome or illicit sexual attentions that go beyond mere touching (see FEEL p 68) have a euphemistic vocabulary all of their own, but as is characteristic of many euphemisms, their vagueness can make it difficult to tell whether copulation or some other form of sexual activity is being referred to, or indeed in some cases whether some form of non-sexual assault is meant. Leading exponents include ABUSE, HARASS, INTERFERE WITH, MOLEST and VIOLATE (see p 20).

A miscellaneous selection of other 'copulation' euphemisms and general sexual circumlocutions:

**beastliness** somewhat harsh for a euphemism, but it qualifies on the grounds of its vagueness. It seems to have been applied to any sort of sexual activity of which the speaker disapproves, from masturbation to copulation

**bundle** a verb used for the traditional practice, in Wales, Scotland, New England, and elsewhere, of engaged couples sleeping in the same bed (supposedly) without copulating. The tacit knowledge that in many cases proximity overcame chastity will have turned *bundle* into a euphemism

**console** euphemistically, the 'consolation' may consist of sexual inter-course, particularly as offered to a person deprived of their usual sexual partner

**fraternize** a euphemism which emerged from the immediate post-World War II period in Germany. The word had been used for 'asso-ciate in a friendly way with the enemy' since the late 19th century, but it was the particular conditions of occupied Germany that led to its being applied specifically to voluntary sexual intercourse between soldiers and women of a conquered country. The colloquial abbrevia-tion **fratting** is first recorded in 1945

**free love** sexual intercourse outside marriage. First recorded in 1822, but since the concept is no longer taboo, it now sounds very dated. Its connotations are of early 20th-century sandal-wearers who found that conventional sexual restrictions chafed their libidos, and used *free love* as a slogan to persuade female partners into bed

**night starvation** originally, in the 1930s, a promotional phrase denoting the supposed nocturnal malnutrition that could be warded off by a bedtime drink of Horlicks; subsequently, though, it came to be used with a knowing wink to imply famine on the sexual-intercourse front

**one-night stand** a sexual liaison that lasts for only one night, or for a very brief period. A development of the earlier sense, 'theatrical engagement for a single night', first recorded in 1963

**on the job** a colloquial euphemism for 'engaged in sexual intercourse' that dates from the early 1960s

**penetration** used since at least the early 17th century as a technical and particularly a legal term denoting the insertion of the penis into the vagina, as defining sexual intercourse for the purposes of the law. It does not, however, seem to have come much into the public domain until the second half of the 20th century. From then dates the use of the verb **penetrate** for 'insert the penis into the vagina of (a woman)'. But it may be the AIDS epidemic of the 1980s and 1990s that propelled the word and its derivatives into wide and euphemistic use, as in '**penetrative** sex', denoting sex involving the insertion of the penis into the vagina or anus

**up** a graphic enough metaphor, but euphemistic in its exploitation of a very general word. A man who is 'up' a woman is having sexual intercourse with her. The usage dates from at least the 1930s

**use** as an elegant but now decidedly archaic euphemism for 'have sex with (a woman)' this dates back to the 14th century

# AROUSAL AND CLIMAX

In the late 20th century, *erection* is the common coin of newspaper advice columns, women's magazines, etc. But previous decades found it rather strong meat, and tended to leave it in the decent obscurity of medical textbooks. Alternatives included the pompous quasi-scientific **tumescent**; the coy **uncomfortable** (a reference to the constrictive effect of garments on the growing penis); the descriptive but vague **rise** and **stand** (both nouns, the latter with the decidedly non-euphemistic variant *cockstand*); the military **present arms** (a reference to the drill manoeuvre in which a rifle is held up vertically in front of the body) and **stand to attention**; and the high-flown literary **pride**. More down-to-earth discussions of erection tend to use the vague circumloction **get it up**. Failure to do so owing to excessive consumption of beer or other alcohol can be euphemized as **brewer's droop**.

Parallel physiological signs of preparedness for intercourse in females have inspired no such cornucopia of metaphors, although **damp** may be used to suggest the flow of lubricative vaginal secretions, and **cream** has stood for the secretions themselves (a woman who **creams for** a man wants sex with him).

**Arousal** is a suitably discreet word for suggesting the relevant physiological changes in the genitalia of both sexes.

In the euphemization of orgasm, **come** has a long and honourable history, stretching back to the mid 17th century. Its underlying metaphor of reaching a goal has kept it in constant use since then, and in more recent years has contributed to **completion**, **finish**, and the important **climax** (first recorded in 1918). The extended form **come off** is equally old.

But it has not had it all its own way in the interim. The notion of orgasm as a sort of death is of even longer standing, and in the 17th and 18th centuries poets were fond of using **die** and **expire** to describe the orgasmic moment. Vestiges of the metaphor live on in the romantic imagination, although in modern usage they would more likely suggest a swoon than an orgasm.

In the 19th century *come* was strongly challenged and almost eclipsed by **spend** (first recorded in this sense in 1662). Amateur psychologists have seen in it a reflection of the commercial spirit of the age, the ejaculation of semen being equated with the paying out of money. Certainly it must have begun as an exclusively male term, but erotic writers of the 19th century liked to identify a parallel female effusion of vaginal secretions accompanying orgasm, and used *spend* of women too.

Orgasm verbs that specifically rely on the notion of ejaculating semen include **cream**, **discharge**, and **spill**, and the noun **effusion** is similarly inspired. **Release** implies the breaking of tension that accompanies orgasm.

Unconscious ejaculation of semen while asleep seems to cause embarrassment. Amongst the verbal cover-ups for it are **nocturnal emission**, first recorded in 1928, and the very dated **night loss**. The sort of erotic dream that gives rise to such 'emissions' is euphemized as a **wet dream**, a term dating back to the mid 19th century.

A man who **fires blanks** ejaculates semen that is not capable of impregnating a woman. But one who has **lead in his pencil** (a metaphor first recorded in 1941) is both potent and virile, or more generally vigorous.

# VARIATIONS

Beyond straight vaginal penetration, the language comes under still more strain. The range of other sexual gratification techniques require careful verbalization.

A popular cosy cover term in British English since the late 1950s has been **kinky**. To define it as 'sexually deviant' begs the question of what constitutes deviance. In practice, it seems to have been applied to any sexual practice beyond conventional heterosexual intercourse (including homosexuality), but it can also have specific connotations of clothing fetishism. More condemnatory, but still euphemistic in its extreme vagueness, is **unnatural**. It is so broad as to be virtually open-ended, but in practice it tends to be applied to homosexuality in general, and anal intercourse in particular ('However the issue was dressed up, "we are still talking about the unnatural, offensive, and abominable act of buggery",' *Guardian* 1991), and also to intercourse with animals.

If there is one activity that stands out from others for its ability to inspire circumlocutions, it is anal intercourse. This presumably reflects a high embarrassment factor. Several euphemisms in this area make coy use of the notion of 'behind'. Indeed, to 'have/take someone from behind' can refer to buggery (it may also denote vaginal penetration from the rear). **Backward** means 'anally' in the context of penetration, and the **back door** contrasts explicitly with vaginal intercourse via the 'front door'. Earthier, but still euphemistic in its allusiveness, is **brown**, used in a variety of contexts to denote anal intercourse: to 'do a brown', for instance, is to sodomize someone. The reference is, of course, to the colour of shit.

Anal sex is illegal in Britain and America, but the framers of laws have experienced some difficulty in calling a spade a spade in this area. In Britain in the 19th and 20th centuries, good old-fashioned buggery often went under the legal disguise of **gross indecency** (the term is also applied to sex with animals). In America, sodomy is a **statutory**

**offense** – a term used by journalists to spare the sensibilities of their readers (and presumably often also to mystify them).

Oral sex provokes its fair share of mealy-mouthedness too. Presumably the Latinate *cunnilingus* and *fellatio* performed a euphemistic function to begin with (both first appeared in print in the 1880s), but after a hundred years they have achieved the status of standard terms. The vaguest synonym available is **go down on**, first recorded in 1916; the metaphor combines the notions of the forward and downward inclination of the performer's head and the necessary movement down the body to the genitals. It refers to both cunnilingus and fellatio, but a **blow job** is almost always fellatio, and the verb **blow** (first recorded in this sense in 1933) denotes exclusively 'stimulate the penis with the mouth'. To **give head** is to perform either cunnilingus or fellatio. The two carried out mutually and simultaneously are termed **sixty-nine**, or in the decent obscurity of French **soixante-neuf**, a euphemistic notion which crossed the English Channel in the 1880s. The configuration of the two heads and bodies supposedly resembles the figure 69.

Sexual activity that involves the exertion of control and often the inflicting of humiliation or physical pain can be euphemized as **discipline** or **dominance** (the female provider is termed a **dominatrix**). The bare initials **S and M**, or **S-M**, first recorded in 1965, disguise sadism and masochism.

Sexual gratification achieved by being urinated on, or by using urine as general sexual prop, goes under the very jolly names of **golden showers** and **water sports**: 'I have mentioned . . . water sports to otherwise sophisticated . . . girls, only to have them blanch with horror and gasp "I couldn't do that!",' *Cosmopolitan* 1988. **Urolagnia** achieves the same euphemistic effect by the 'blind-them-with-science' technique (it is based on Greek *lagneia* 'copulation, lust', and dates from the beginning of the 20th century). Similar gratification obtained from faeces is termed **coprolagnia**.

The use of **bestiality** to denote sexual intercourse with animals dates back to the 17th century. In the Bible, Leviticus 20:15 ordains that 'if a man lie with a beast, he shall surely be put to death,' and in the preamble to the 1611 translation the sin is referred to as *bestiality*.

A tradition has grown up of referring to a range of 'non-core' sexual activities by the name of the nationality that supposedly favours them. Thus, for example, **Greek** denotes anal intercourse (a reference to the male predilections of Classical times rather than a slur on modern Greek manhood). **French** alludes to oral sex (the use of **French kiss** for an 'open-mouthed kiss with extensive tongue-contact', which dates from the 1920s, is a product of the more general reputation of the French for sexual naughtiness). The **English** supposedly prefer whipping, bondage, etc.


# MASTURBATION


The official attitude to masturbation over much of the past three or four hundred years is encapsulated in two of the main words sanctioned to name it during that period: **self-abuse** (first recorded in 1728) and **self-pollution** (first recorded in 1626). Both signal clearly that in the 18th, 19th and early 20th centuries, all right-thinking people publicly avowed it to be disgusting and degrading (whatever they did in private). 'Pollution' is pretty strong, and 'abuse' is now reserved for sexual attacks on children and women. That it was an offence not just against oneself but also against God was made clear by another condemnatory circumlocution, **solitary sin**. And the notion of guilty masturbatory seclusion is neatly encapsulated by **secret vice**.

Clearly, the age that was so hung up about masturbation that it invented quasi-medical appliances to prevent children from doing it, and concocted myths that it made you go mad, was unlikely to be able to talk about it openly. Indeed, the editors of the first edition of the *Oxford English Dictionary* were so coy about it that the definitions of *masturbation*, *self-abuse*, and *self-pollution* simply refer back to each other in a neat circle ('*masturbation* the action or practice of self-abuse'; '*self-abuse* self-pollution'; '*self-pollution* masturbation, self-abuse') without ever saying what they refer to (the deficiency was remedied in the second edition).

Another favourite of the 19th century was **onanism** (the OED copped out again with 'self-abuse, masturbation'). This puts all the blame on a suitably obscure character in Genesis, Onan, a son of Judah. He was forced to marry his brother's widow, but he was unwilling to impregnate her, so he 'spilled [his seed] on the ground' (38:9). This 'displeased the Lord: wherefore he slew him' (38:10). It seems to have been more a case of birth control by the withdrawal method than masturbation, but it is as a **wanker** that the unfortunate Onan has been commemorated in the English lexicon.

The word *masturbate* itself came into English in the early 17th century in the form *mastuprate*. This may reflect a remodelling based on the (still unsubstantiated) supposition that its Latin original, *masturbari*, was a blend of *manus* 'hand' and *stuprare* 'defile'. The orthography we are familiar with today is not recorded before 1855. Its original habitat seems mainly to have been medical and psycho-sexual texts, and it was not until after World War II that it began to creep out more confidently into the public domain. A society that was beginning to come to terms with the fact that manual stimulation of the genitals is not unnatural was looking for a straightforward, non-judgmental term to denote it, and *masturbate* seemed by far the best candidate.

This by no means spelled the end for euphemisms, however. The starkness of *masturbation* will not do for all contexts. But the new generation of circumlocutions, while discreetly avoiding any directness of reference, tend to be positive, or at least neutral in tone, rather than condemnatory.

Many, not surprisingly, incorporate the notion of 'self' or 'oneself'. **Relieve oneself** (with its unfortunate suggestion of urination), **satisfy oneself** and **work oneself off** all imply the achievement of orgasm, as does **finish oneself**, with the additional connotation of masturbatory orgasm following joint foreplay or inconclusive intercourse. On the other hand **play with oneself**, **rub oneself** and the colloquial **diddle oneself** (used mainly of children) simply suggest manual stimulation. Many of the more delicate exponents of this formula refer mainly to female masturbation: **caress oneself**, **do oneself**, **do it with oneself**, **make love to oneself**, **touch oneself** ('Little girls are told not to touch or play with themselves,' *Family Circle* 1973). The verb **finger**, too, generally refers to manual stimulation of the female genitals. The 'self' theme is carried through in **self-gratification** and the rather flowery **self-pleasuring** (another mainly female usage), and also in the technicalism **auto-erotic**, a late 19th-century coinage of the English sexologist Havelock Ellis, based on Greek *autos* 'self'.

Present-day sex therapists may refer to masturbation as **genital sensate focussing**, reflecting the positive modern view of the practice as a normal part of sexual life and as a necessary forerunner to intercourse. A rather sadder circumlocution is **solitary sex**.

At the more colloquial end of the spectrum, **hand job** (first recorded in 1969) and the rarer **wrist job** often connote masturbation of a male by another person. And a prostitute may disguise masturbatory services as **massage**, **hand relief**, or a **body rub**.

The American *beat one's meat* (cf. MEAT 'penis,' p 128) is probably too graphic to qualify as a euphemism, but **beat off** (used of males) is rather more discreet. The graphic **come to a sticky end**, again of males, is based on the notion of ejaculated semen, and also includes a pun on *come*.

In military slang, **blanket drill** has been used to cover up masturbatory activity (from bed being its standard venue).

Surreptitious manipulation of the genitals with the pocketed hand is jokingly referred to as **pocket billiards**. First recorded in 1940s, it probably originated as a piece of schoolboy slang. The underlying pun, based on the notion of billiard balls and possibly also the cue, is not overly subtle.

The use of **beastliness** for 'masturbation' conjures up the scenario of outraged schoolmasters excoriating their young male charges for goings-on in the dorm.

Finally, some British rhyming slang: **J Arthur Rank** (or **J Arthur** for short) for the far-from-euphemistic *wank* commemorates the English film magnate J Arthur Rank (1888–1972) in a way he can scarcely have expected; and **Barclays Bank** (or just **Barclays**) commandeers an even more august British institution ('Quite the barclays before bed. Masturbatory success is the result of imaginative conceit', Kenneth Williams, diary, 12 August 1976).

Mechanical or electrical adjuncts to masturbation can be an embarrassing topic to drop into general conversation, so verbal camouflage is often called for. **Marital aid** is a weaselly cover word for a range of items sold in sex shops, many of them masturbatory in application. A battery-powered dildo is usually discreetly disguised as a **vibrator** or a **cordless massager**.

# CONTRACEPTION

The era of AIDS has put us all on speaking terms with condoms (albeit not without a certain amount of discreet phonological hedging – see p 6). But for previous generations they, and anything else to do with artificial prevention of impregnation, were firmly unmentionable.

Earlier centuries disguised the condom as **armour** (a favoured term of James Boswell's when describing his trips to the park) or as a **purse**, but its modern euphemization really begins with **French letter**, first recorded around 1856. The English habitually turn to *French* as a shorthand for sexual naughtiness (see also p 83), but in this case it is not clear what the original connotation of *letter* was: possibly it was derived from *let* 'prevent' (as in 'without let or hindrance'), and only later came to be associated with the sort of letters you post. The French got their own back by calling condoms *capotes anglaises* 'English cloaks'.

Other circumlocutions at the colloquial end of the scale include the American **cardigan** (a charmingly domesticated image), **doodah** (a specialized use of the all-purpose euphemism), the British **johnny** (first recorded in 1965), **plonker** ('"Oh, French letters." "That's it, plonkers. We've got no plonkers"',' *Personal Services* 1987; also used for 'penis'), the mainly American **rubber** (from the material of which condoms are commonly made (see also RUBBER GOODS); first recorded in 1947), **rubber johnny**, **safety**, and the originally American **skin** (probably from the notion of putting a metaphorical second skin on the penis, but animal skin has been used in the manufacture of condoms; first recorded in 1960).

A greater air of medical seriousness is engendered by the weasely and mainly American **prophylactic**, a euphemism of the 'blind-them-with-science' school, first recorded in 1943. Etymologically something which 'guards against' (its ultimate origin is Greek *phulax* 'guard'), it encapsulates the dual role of the condom: guarding against not only unwanted pregnancy but also disease – in the days of its coinage vene-real disease, now, AIDS. (The same duality underlies **protector**.) Although it is mainly applied to condoms, it is also used for other barrier devices, as are the nouns **preventive** (first recorded in 1822) and **preventative**.

The most neutral of the euphemisms for 'condom' is probably **sheath**, first recorded in this sense in 1861, although despite its apparent blandness, which commended it to polite usage in the days before it became OK to say 'condom', it does subconsciously call upon images of the penis as a 'sword' or 'weapon'.

Manufacturers of condoms have an image problem to cope with. In the AIDS-released 1980s and 1990s they have been very up-front about it, but in former decades they were glad to hide behind the discreet **rubber goods**, a euphemism which dates from the early 20th century. And the company that makes Durex condoms hides the nature of its product under the name 'London Rubber Company'. See also RUBBER above.

In East Africa, where Roman Catholic teaching has made the condom taboo but the AIDS epidemic necessitates the promotion of its use, the picturesque circumlocutions **American sock** and **gumboot** are used.

The American police sometimes refer to condoms as **collapsible containers**, presumably from their post-use detumescence.

But the prize for oblique reference must certainly go to the question traditionally posed by barbers to their customers as they brushed the hair-clippings from their shoulders: 'And **something for the weekend**, sir?' Barbers' shops, with their exclusively male clientele and remotely paramedical associations, were in former years perhaps the main retailers of condoms, and the import of the question would have been understood by all but the most naive of clients. (It also gives a view of sexual intercourse as an activity strictly demarcated to the work-free weekend, not as one to be indulged in whenever the fancy takes you.) A scenario even more redolent of embarrassment – certainly in the not very distant past and perhaps still to some extent today – is the chemist's shop where the male would-be condom-buyer is confronted by a female assistant and asks 'Could I see a male assistant, please?' – a question amounting virtually to a euphemistic request for condoms.

Other methods of contraception have not attracted nearly so much euphemism, although **the pill** as a vague reference to contraceptive pills has enjoyed a vigorous existence since it first came on the scene in 1957 (**birth pill** was an early alternative that did not wear so well), and **cap** (first recorded in 1916) may serve a euphemistic function in sounding more commonplace, less clinical than *diaphragm* (although that is apparently a later term). **Vatican roulette** (first recorded in 1962) as a facetious epithet for the rhythm method of birth control puns on *Russian roulette*, the risk of death from a single bullet being replaced by the risk of pregnancy from ill-timed copulation, and *Vatican* referring to its being the only form of contraception sanctioned by the Roman Catholic church. (**Rhythm method** itself, which dates from around 1940, is somewhat mealy-mouthed, skirting round what it really denotes, and the less common synonym **safe method** – based on the notion of the **safe period**, when conception supposedly cannot occur – might well be open to prosecution under the Trades Description Act.) The withdrawal method – withdrawing the penis from the vagina just before ejaculation – has been camouflaged with a range of euphemisms of the pattern **get off at X**, where X is the name of a railway station immediately before a main terminus of a line: hence, among others, *get off at Gateshead* (before Newcastle), *get off at Paisley* (before Glasgow), *get off at Clapham Junction* (before London Victoria and Waterloo) and, in Australia, *get off at Redfern* (before Sydney).

More general euphemisms include **birth control**, a coinage of the second decade of the 20th century (the true object of control is presumably conception rather than birth); **family planning**, a post-World War I introduction which in practice more often than not denotes the prevention of 'families'; and **safe sex**, which in the late 20th century has moved from referring to contraception to denoting the avoidance of sexually transmitted diseases.

More colloquial, and now rather dated, are the vague **take precautions** ('Neither had taken any precautions . . . Miss Morrison was pregnant,' Tim Heald 1975) and **take care**. In the early part of the 20th century **precautions** was used in a concrete sense for 'contraceptive device' (as in 'use precautions'); and *take care* is first cousin to the cautionary cliché 'If you can't be good, be **careful**!'

Euphemisms for sexual intercourse without contraception include **unprotected** (as in 'unprotected sex') and the more colloquial **bareback**.

# PREGNANCY

The taboo in Western society against referring openly to a condition which in its later stages is fairly obvious to all is on the wane, but it has left a rich legacy of doubletalk in the language.

Our lexicon of pregnancy can be roughly divided into two categories: the delicate circumlocution and the colourful metaphor. The first treads gingerly round the subject without ever getting to the point, and its classic weapon is the impenetrably vague **condition** (as in 'A woman in your condition ought not to . . .'). Elaborated versions include **in a delicate condition** and the notorious **in an interesting condition** which, with variants such as *in an interesting situation* and *in an interesting state*, goes back at least to the mid 18th century. It has also had the offshoot 'be **interesting**' for 'be pregnant'. See also INTERESTING EVENT (p 88). Similarly vague is **that way** for 'pregnant'.

The notion of looking forward to the time of birth provides a key pregnancy euphemism: 'be **expecting**'. This dates from the beginning of the 19th century – the earliest record of it in the OED is from a letter of Jane Austen's, written in 1817. The related and rather curious **expectant mother** for 'pregnant woman' appeared around the middle of the 19th century. A more genteel alternative to *expecting* is **anticipating**. And rather in the same vein of twee evasiveness is **eating for two**, referring to the extra nourishment needed for the developing foetus.

The biblical **with child** for 'pregnant' dates back to the Old English period, but no longer has any genuine currency.

The guilt-ridden **fall** for 'become pregnant', which makes pregnancy sound like moral turpitude, has all but died out, but it leaves a legacy in the dated-sounding **fall pregnant** for 'become pregnant', which contains a suggestion of unplannedness or unwelcomeness.

In the colloquial department, the three leading metaphors are **in the club**, **up the spout** and the now rather dated **in the family way**. The last, which emerged at the end of the 18th century, is probably just a semantic specialization of an earlier *in the family way* meaning 'in a domestic manner'. The more aggressive *in the club* and *up the spout* (and the similar **up the pole**) appear to be post-World War I creations. *In the club* is a shortening of **in the pudding club**, which bears a strong family resemblance to 'have a **bun in the oven**', seemingly a post-World War II coinage. Both exploit the notion of the developing foetus in the womb being like a dish cooking in the oven. The mainly American **knock up** 'impregnate' can phase British speakers, for whom it also (and chiefly) means 'to wake someone up in the morning'.

*In the club* and *up the spout* often have strong connotations that the pregnancy is unwanted; and when in addition the woman is unmarried, the time-honoured euphemism is the vague **in trouble** (first recorded in 1891). When a man impregnates an unmarried girl, he 'gets her into trouble' – or did until the latter part of the 20th century, when more readily available abortions reduced the troublesomeness, and the taboo against unmarried motherhood weakened. Another distinctly passé euphemism for 'unwillingly pregnant' is **caught** or **caught out** ('Very often it happens that you get "caught", and you know that the baby that you feared might come has really begun,' Marie Stopes 1919). **Sprain one's ankle** as a euphemism for 'become pregnant outside marriage' dates back to the 18th century but is now little more than a memory.

Men expected to marry the woman they had impregnated were said to **do the right thing**, or to **make an honest woman of** her (first recorded in 1818).

Coyer, but still fairly colloquial, are **carry** for 'be pregnant with' (as in 'When I was carrying Giles . . .'), first recorded in 1776, and **bump** or **lump** for a 'pregnant woman's expanded abdomen'.

The use of **gone** to denote the period of time elapsed during a pregnancy (as in 'four months gone') dates from the mid 18th century.

# ABORTION

The modern euphemism of abortion is distinctly high-tech. **Termination** is the all-purpose term (in essence a shortening of 'artificial termination of pregnancy'), which since it first came on the scene in the late 1960s has emerged from medical jargon into the general language. It has been joined by the clinically precise but nevertheless evasive **voluntary interrupted pregnancy** (further disguised by the abbreviation **VIP**) and **therapeutic interruption of pregnancy**.

These are the linguistic products of an age when legal abortion has become much more widely available, but the subject is still controversial, and the word *abortion* still carries too many negative associations to be freely usable in all contexts.

In the days when aborting any foetus was a crime, the vague and circumlocutory **illegal operation** and **criminal operation** were widely used to euphemize the procedure. And more recently **dilatation and curettage** (**D&C** for short), strictly speaking a term for an operation to remove the lining of the uterus for therapeutic reasons, has been used as a piece of convenient humbuggery to disguise an abortion operation. (The informal synonym is a **scrape**.)

At the more colloquial end of the spectrum is **bring off**, meaning 'to abort (a foetus)'.

The liberalizing of the abortion laws in many Western countries in the last third of the 20th century left a sizable minority of the population still opposed to abortion. As they began to organize and lobby, they needed an epithet without the negative vibrations of *anti-abortionist*. The alternatives they came up with were the disingenuous and somewhat euphemistic **right-to-life** (a product of the early 1970s) and **pro-life** (which emerged in the mid to late 1970s). While the pro-abortionists were still in the ascendancy they had no need to euphemize themselves, but in the 1980s, when the antis gained ground and the pros began to feel embattled, it was felt that something a little less strident than *pro-abortionist* would be helpful: the coyly vague **pro-choice** was the result.

# CHILDBIRTH

The taboos of childbirth have fallen away rapidly in Western society over the past half century (one of its few residues in Britain is the ban on male midwives). The sight of a woman giving birth on television is relatively commonplace, and the husband or male partner who does not wish to be present and assist at the birth of his child may be considered distinctly perverse.

With the taboos has gone the language used to circumvent them. Most English euphemisms for 'childbirth' now have a very dated air. The days when one spoke mysteriously of **accouchement** for 'giving birth' are long gone (it came into English in the early 19th century from French, where it meant literally 'putting to bed', and it is in effect a double euphemism: semantically 'put to bed' covers up 'give birth' – an evasion lexicalized in English as 'be **brought to bed** of a child', first recorded in the early 16th century – and an extra layer of disguise is afforded by the obscurity of the foreign language). Even **confinement**, described by the OED in 1891 as 'the ordinary term for [childbirth] in colloquial use', now sounds hopelessly coy (the underlying metaphor is apparently not the notion of being simply 'confined to bed', as when one is ill, but something rather more violent: the expression *Our Lady's bands* or *bonds*, used in the Middle Ages for 'childbirth', suggests a continuing tradition of birth as something that as it were physically tied a woman to her bed).

Also well past their prime are **time** – as in 'She's near her time', meaning 'She's soon going to give birth' – and **lie in** for '(be in bed in readiness to) give birth', which goes back to the 15th century and is preserved in aspic in the term *lying-in hospital*, still to be seen carved above the door of old maternity hospitals.

**Interesting event** for a 'birth' has gone the same way (compare INTERESTING CONDITION p 88), but the continuing currency of its synonym **happy event**, which probably emerged in the late 19th century, reminds us that we are still not always inclined to be terribly up-front and frank when talking about childbirth. Indeed, much contemporary childbirth terminology that we use without thinking had euphemistic origins. **Delivery** for 'childbirth', first recorded in 1577, has the diagnostic attribute of vagueness; **labour** for '(effort involved in) giving birth' is a similarly specific application of a general term; and **maternity** in contexts such as *maternity hospital* and *maternity leave* is a rather coy way of referring to childbirth and the succeeding period. And it may well be that some people still speak tweely of the **patter of tiny** (or **little**) **feet** (a cliché dating back to middle of the 19th century) when anticipating the birth of children. To prospective siblings, the impending new arrival may be euphemized as the **little stranger**.

A child born as the result of an unplanned pregnancy may be euphemized as an **accident**, while one who arrives unlooked-for in the wake of one or more siblings may be termed (with rather cruel dismissiveness) an **afterthought**.

The disguising of childbirth and its attendant circumstances with the concept of the **gooseberry bush** in the face of children's awkward questions (as in 'You were found under a gooseberry bush') has not been traced further back than the 1940s. But the legend of the **stork** that delivers babies, which is of German origin, is far older. It has even spawned an American verb *stork*, meaning 'make pregnant'.

# BASTARDS

In an age when the parents of an increasingly large proportion of the population are unmarried (28 per cent of babies born in Britain in 1990 were 'illegitimate'), bastardy no longer bears the stigma it once had. We still have some difficulty finding the right words for addressing the topic, but this may be because it is no longer a subject for comment, and the old words and phrases sound awkward and out of place.

The standard legal term, **illegitimate**, dates back to the early 16th century (indeed, 'born to an unmarried woman' is the earliest recorded sense of the word in English). It has certainly played a euphemistic role over the years, in avoiding the taboo *bastard*, but it now tends to be widely avoided, as perpetuating an outdated censorious attitude. (The term **illegit** used as a noun could be heard in colloquial speech in the 1990s.)

The euphemisms of the past have come into a number of categories. There has been the romantic: **love child**, first recorded in the early 19th century in the works of the somehow appropriately named Eugenia de Acton (the obsolete *love brat*, dating from the 17th century, does not paint such a rosy picture). The vague: **misfortune** was a popular way of avoiding the word *bastard* in the 19th century; it came from the equally circumlocutious *have* or *meet with a misfortune*, meaning 'give birth to such a child' ('"If you please, ma'am, I had a misfortune, ma'am", replied the girl, casting down her eyes,' Frederick Marryat 1836). **Mishap** was used in a similar way. The flowerily metaphorical: **born on the wrong side of the blanket**, dating from the late 18th century, implies that impregnation took place elsewhere than its sanctioned location – between the sheets of the marital bed. The colloquially dismissive: the now superannuated **by-blow** 'illegitimate child' dates from the late 16th century, its underlying metaphor partially illuminated by the OED's 1888 definition 'one who comes into the world by a side stroke'. The heraldic: **bend sinister** as a metaphor for illegitimacy exploits the convention that a band from the upper right-hand corner of a shield to the lower left-hand corner denotes a bastard.

**Natural** is a word much used over the centuries in tiptoeing around the subject of legitimacy. From the 15th century it was actually used for 'legitimate', but from the late 16th century the completely antonymous 'illegitimate' began to gain ground. The two obviously could not co-exist. It was the latter that survived, and expressions such as *natural child* and *natural son* for one born outside marriage (particularly in relation to a father) can still be heard today. A child's *natural father* is the man who impregnated but (by implication) is not married to its mother. (A child's *natural parents*, on the other hand, are the original parents of a child that has been fostered or adopted.)

The parents' plight is euphemized by **single parent** (first recorded in 1969), which serves the double purpose of avoiding the condemnatory *unmarried mother* and allowing that the partnerless one may be male. A further layer of padding is added by **lone parent**, which gets away from *single*'s implication of unmarriedness and embraces divorced or widowed parents. In present-day America, the parents of an illegitimate child are known as its **birthparents**. She or he presides over a **one-parent family**. A parent who has absconded or bolted is an **absent parent**.

# PROSTITUTES

The word *whore* has been with us since Anglo-Saxon times. Its origins are fairly positive: it is distantly related to Latin *carus* 'dear', and its Germanic ancestor may at first have meant 'dear one' – evidence, perhaps, that even in its infancy the **oldest profession** (a term first recorded in 1922) was in need of euphemizing. But many of the oldest examples of the word that survive in English have heavily negative connotations, and throughout its subsequent history it has been a word to avoid in polite conversation. In modern usage (when not used as a deliberate archaism) it is decidedly abusive.

One interesting attempt to soften its impact has involved a sort of phonetic plastic surgery. From the 17th to the 19th century there is evidence that the word was often pronounced to rhyme with *viewer*, retaining its 16th-century long *u* sound, although regular phonological development had taken its standard pronunciation to a rhyme with *shore*. John Walker, the 18th-century phonetician and lexicographer, conjectured that this reflected an unconscious desire to 'soften the coarse effect of a coarse word'. And Hugh Rawson in his *Dictionary of Euphemisms and Other Doubletalk* 1981 records the spellings **hoor** and **hooer** as representing the same phonetic euphemization in 20th-century American English. (Compare the late 20th-century phonological alteration of *condom* p 6.)

But this phonetic tinkering was not enough to save the reputation of *whore*. An early substitute was *harlot*, widely used by 16th-century translators of the Bible in place of *whore*, the usual term in Wycliffe's 14th-century version, presumably because it was less offensive. But it too has long since gone to the bad.

Early in the 17th century English acquired the noun *prostitute*, which had been used in Latin for a 'woman who offers sex for money' (etymologically it denotes 'someone who sets themself in a public place'). Since then it has become the closest thing to a neutral term in this sensitive area, sanctioned by formal and legal usage.

But it has retained enough of a shudder factor not to cut off the flow of euphemistic alternatives. Closest to home, late 20th-century feminist consciousness has altered it to **prostitute woman**, seeking to defuse its negative connotations by turning it from a stark noun into an adjective.

But the noun **pro** (first recorded in 1937) seems more likely to be an abbreviation of *professional prostitute* than of *prostitute* itself.

One of the most obvious avoidance strategies is to hide behind some other occupation. The reputation of the theatre as an environment of sexual laxity has led in the past to the use of **singer** and particularly **actress** as euphemisms for 'prostitute'. A subspecies is the **sing-song girl**, a Chinese female entertainer who may be expected to offer sexual intercourse after finishing her singing. But by far the commonest late 20th-century disguise is **model**. This usage, which seems to have established itself in the late 1950s and early 1960s, presumably arose out of the use of *model* for 'woman who poses for photographs' – 'camera clubs' at that time being a popular camouflage for men wishing to view naked women. Since then its regular appearance on advertising cards in thousands of newsagents' and corner shop windows up and down the country has confirmed its status. Along rather similar lines is **masseuse**, whose massaging activities may be limited to particularly sensitive portions of her clients' anatomies (see also MASSAGE PARLOUR p 102).

Getting slightly nearer to the truth, but still euphemistic, are **escort**, mainly used in the context of the ESCORT AGENCY (see p 102), and **hostess**, which typically denotes a woman paid to entertain male customers in a nightclub, ply them with drink (at their expense and at inflated prices), and then have sex with them – the usage established itself in the 1930s.

As an alternative to these very specific bogus job titles, prostitutes may be designated by a broad euphemism that suggests paid employment – for example, the originally American **working girl**, first recorded in 1968 (note the crucial distinction from *working woman*). Of similar inspiration is **business woman**, which ties in with prostitutes' use of **business** both to designate their occupation and as a shorthand euphemism for their services – as in 'You want business, love?' 'The **profession**' is a grandiloquent name for prostitution (compare OLDEST PROFESSION p 94), and its members may call themselves **professionals** (a usage going back at least to the mid 19th century). Those less ambitious for status may be content with 'the **trade**' (a term first recorded as long ago as 1680) and the quaintly genteel designation **ladies of trade**. (*Trade* is also a collective euphemism for prostitutes used by male homosexuals, a usage first recorded in the 1930s. **Rough trade** is uncouth or aggressive males sought out as (paid) homosexual partners. Individual young male homosexual prostitutes are **rent boys**

– a usage first recorded in 1969 – or **chickens**: 'The chickens . . . these days are much wiser. They don't hang around Euston Station, they come straight to the places they have read about where they know they could do business,' *Guardian* 1988.)

A more colloquial designation of prostitution is 'the game', which typically occurs in the expression **on the game** 'working as a prostitute', first recorded in 1898. An alternative, reflecting a standard place of assignation, is **on the street** or **on the streets**. The notion of the public streets as the place where prostitutes pick up their clients dates back to the 16th century, and the euphemism **street-walker** for 'prostitute' is first recorded in 1592 (the synonymous **street girl** is 20th-century). Vaguer still is **woman of the town**, still sufficiently current in the late 19th century for the OED to use it as a synonym definition of *courtesan* but now decidedly passé.

The classic euphemistic ploy of vagueness inspired **personal services** as a circumlocution for the services sold by prostitutes (it can also be applied to non-professionals: 'One of them . . . endeavoured to provide personal services by removing her clothes in broad daylight,' *Observer* 1993).

As an alternative strategy to pretending that prostitutes are not prostitutes, one can give them a fancy-sounding foreign name to push them up the status ladder. Not surprisingly, these tend to be French, and to refer to high-class (i.e. expensive) prostitutes. Probably the earliest in this category was **courtesan**, borrowed from French in the mid 16th century. From the beginning it seems that it had a euphemistic function (Ephraim Pagitt in his *Christianographie* 1635 wrote that 'the name Courtezan (being the most honest [i.e. respectable] synonymy that is given to a Whore) had his originall from the Court of Rome'), and in modern usage it connotes a prostitute used by men of great wealth or high rank, especially in former times. Its Edwardian successor was **demi-mondaine**, a borrowing of the 1890s. It denotes a woman of the **demi-monde**, literally the 'half-world' – a term coined by the novelist Alexandre Dumas the younger to suggest the fringes of polite society, inhabited by women with slightly tarnished sexual reputations, but increasingly coming to imply high-class prostitution. Closely synonymous is the now archaic **demi-rep**, first recorded in the middle of the 18th century, and suggesting a woman whose 'reputation' (i.e. for chastity) is at least fifty percent compromised. And from the same stable comes **demi-vierge**, literally 'half-virgin', a borrowing from

French of the early 20th century which denotes a woman who is physically a virgin but engages freely in sexual activity.

*Demi-mondaine* and *demi-rep* contrive to give the impression of amateur status, or at least of indirect payment. A **poule de luxe**, literally 'luxury hen', is still expensive, but available for more general hire: 'The girls, they come around the whole time: they practically picket the place. When I tell these pictures and visions, little duchesses, dazzlers and *poules de luxe* that Mark Asprey isn't around – they're devastated,' Martin Amis 1989. The term first appeared in English in the 1930s. Much older is **fille de joie**, literally 'girl of pleasure', which goes back to the early 18th century (**fille de nuit** 'night girl' is on record too). **Grande horizontale** 'great horizontal' has been applied to celebrated prostitutes – 'l'horizontal' because of their typical working posture. Rather more discreet is **grande amoureuse**, first recorded in English in 1925 and guardedly defined by the *Oxford English Dictionary* as 'a woman skilled in the arts of love'.

A glossary of miscellaneous terms for those who give sex in return for money or other reward:

**bad girl** apparently derogatory, but its actual mode is understatement, and viewed in that light it is euphemistic. An American usage

**B girl** another Americanism, dating from the 1930s. It is generally said to be short for **bar girl**, another euphemism, which overtly denotes a girl paid to encourage customers at a bar to drink; but it could also be an abbreviation of BAD GIRL

**brass** a piece of British slang, first recorded in 1934. It is short for *brass nail*, rhyming slang for 'tail'

**call girl** a prostitute whose services you hire by 'calling' her on the phone. The usage originated in the US after World War I. An establishment from which such prostitutes operate is known as a **call house**

**camp follower** a prostitute who follows an army around from place to place on campaign. Now largely a historical term

**of a certain description** a euphemism of extreme delicacy, used in the 19th century in expressions such as 'a woman of a certain description' and 'a lady of a certain description' to denote a prostitute

**fallen woman** originally, in the 18th century, a woman who had blotted her moral copybook by having sex outside marriage, but increasingly in the 19th century just a euphemism for 'prostitute'. Now obsolete, the most powerful image it conjures up is probably that of William Gladstone prowling the streets of London at night looking for 'fallen women' to save

**gay** now firmly attached semantically to the concept of homosexuality, but in the 19th century used as a euphemistic adjective denoting 'prostitution': a *gay woman*, for instance, was a prostitute, and the *gay life* work as a prostitute

**girlie** a noun used attributively to denote women as sexually stimulating objects. Often it refers to pornographic material featuring naked women (as in 'girlie magazines'), but it also serves as a cover for prostitution: a **girlie bar** or **girlie house** is likely to be a brothel

**good-time girl** a young woman who lives only for pleasure (first recorded in 1928), but frequently a euphemism for 'prostitute'

**hustler** a usage dating from the early 1920s, and probably based on the notion of importuning potential clients like a salesman who 'hustles' customers. Nowadays its euphemistic force has all but disappeared. The verb **hustle** is used for 'work as a prostitute'

**lady of the night** from prostitutes doing their work mainly at night. Now decidedly superannuated

**painted woman** from the days when facial make-up was considered a sure sign of the harlot. Now therefore obsolete

**pleasure** euphemistic when the pleasure in question is commercial sex. Used in former times in the expressions *lady of pleasure* and *woman of pleasure* for 'prostitute'

**scarlet woman** originally the great whore of Babylon, as described in Revelation 17:4, 'arrayed in purple and scarlet colour', but subsequently any prostitute, or more loosely any sexually promiscuous woman. Now largely a literary relic

**sleepy-time girl** mainly American. 'Bed' links the euphemism with its subtext, 'sexual intercourse'

**tom** British slang for 'prostitute', first recorded in 1941. It may have evolved from the earlier Australian slang *tom* 'girlfriend', itself short for *Tom-tart*, rhyming slang for *sweetheart*

**totty** more of a sexually promiscuous woman than a professional prostitute, although the distinction is not always easy to draw. (It can also be used to refer to a woman in general and, increasingly, as a collective term for fanciable women.) British slang dating from the late 19th century. Probably a pet-form of *tot* 'little child'

**unfortunate** used as a noun in the 19th century meaning 'prostitute'

**white slave** a relic of the first half of the 20th century, when British middle-class mothers kept their daughters on the straight and narrow with cautionary tales (largely apocryphal) of young white girls kidnapped and sent abroad to be the sexual slaves of rich and swarthy foreigners. The term actually originated in America in the late 18th century, with reference to white Europeans imported as slaves along-side black Africans

There is a linguistically grey area between women who offer sex for money or other direct reward and those who arouse similar disapproval by having many (non-paying) sexual partners. The terminology, both dysphemistic and euphemistic, for each tends to overlap. The key words in the latter category are **easy** and **loose**, both of which are derogatory euphemisms for women who distribute their sexual favours too liberally, whether on an amateur or a professional basis. The use of *loose* for 'free from any moral restraint, licentious' dates back at least to the late 15th century, and the expression 'loose woman' has come to denote a sexually promiscuous one, not necessarily a prostitute (although from the mid 19th century for about a hundred years **on the loose** meant specifically 'working as a prostitute'). *Easy* has a similar history, its underlying connotation being 'compliant, easy to persuade to have sex'. 'Easy woman' has now passed out of use, but 'woman' or 'lady of **easy virtue**' is still current, albeit decidedly dated in feel. This is the vocabulary of an age when a multiplicity of sexual partners was much more of a taboo than it is now, especially for women, and to it also belong 'woman of **doubtful reputation**' (compare DEMI-REP p 96), **adventuress** (the implication is often of sexual favours offered in return for material ones), **abandoned**, and **fast** (a 'fast' woman outraged the sexual mores of her day). The same note of disapproval was sounded more colloquially by the enigmatic **no better than she should be**. But the early 21st century does have its own euphemism for promiscuous sexual activity, and quite a witty one at that – the American **distributive sex**, first recorded in 1986.

The vocabulary of male heterosexual prostitution is far more limited than that of female prostitution, no doubt because the phenomenon is far less widespread and the transaction implied is hedged about with more deep-rooted taboos. To a much greater extent than with female prostitution, the terminology trades on the ambiguous middle ground between payment for sexual intercourse and payment for the company of someone of the opposite sex. The general assumption is, though, that the now rather dated **gigolo** includes sexual intercourse among his services. First recorded in 1922, it is a borrowing from French, where it is a masculine formation based on *gigolette* 'female dancing partner', a derivative of *giguer* 'dance'. The etymology lays bare the underlying euphemistic metaphor, which followed the word into English: the paid sexual partner masquerades as a professional dancing partner.

The period of time that a prostitute spends with a client is known euphemistically as a **trick**, a usage which originated in the USA in the 1920s. A *trick* is also a prostitute's client, as is a **john**, a term first recorded, in America, in 1928. In British English, the readiest euphemism is **punter**: 'For the working girl and her punter, this may be so (though a recent survey of prostitutes put straight sex a long way down the list of requirements),' *Sunday Times* 1993. The services offered may be coyly disguised as a **nice time** (as in 'Can I give you a nice time, love?') more commercially as BUSINESS (see p 95) or (getting closer to the nub of the matter, but still conveniently vague) **relief**. The use of the term **soliciting** as a rather po-faced officialism for 'offer sex to a potential client for payment' has its origins in the early 18th century, although it does not seem to have become institutionalized until the late 19th century. An even more solemn alternative is **importuning**, first recorded in this sense in an 1847 British Act of Parliament. Both *solicit* and *importune* are also used of male homosexuals seeking partners. Driving slowly along the edge of a road trying to pick up a prostitute has been euphemized since the 1940s as **kerb crawling** (the contemporary and synonymous **gutter crawling** never caught on to such an extent).

In the early 21st century, when the work of prostitutes is no longer as universally stigmatized as it was, and moves are afoot to legalize it, the tawdry connotations of much of the vocabulary of prostitution stand in the way of its rehabilitation. The politically correct lobby's contribution to a new non-judgmental terminology includes **sex worker** or **commercial sex worker** (**CSW** for short), and also **sex care provider**, which makes the job sound like a social service. A more upmarket-sounding alternative is **executive-stress consultant** ('knickerless Ukrainian executive-stress consultants', A A Gill, 2007).

# BROTHELS

Historically, the most popular verbal disguise for *brothel* has been **house**. From the 18th up to in some cases the 21st century, variations on the *house of . . .* theme have furnished polite ways of referring to establishments where prostitutes work. The best known allude to such places' reputation: **house of ill fame** (first recorded in the 1750s) and **house of ill repute**. Another set focusses on the meeting between prostitute and client: **house of accommodation** (first recorded in 1749) probably refers discreetly to the 'accommodating' of the client rather than the lodging of the prostitute, given that the 'lodging' sense of *accommodate* did not begin to emerge until the early 18th century (although the later **accommodation house** for 'brothel' may owe more to the notion of a lodging house); **house of assignation** dates from the early 19th century, and like **house of resort** (i.e. a place to which men go to . . .) is now distinctly passé. **House of pleasure** and **house of sin** represent the opposite ends of the approval spectrum. And *house* has in the past been used on its own to signify, albeit cryptically, a 'brothel'.

The main modern survivor of the 'house' tendency is the legal term **disorderly house**, which can technically refer to any establishment whose habitués regularly disrupt public order, but which in practice usually denotes a 'brothel'.

As with prostitutes themselves (see p 94), so with their places of work, a popular way of disguising commerciality with a veneer of sophistication has been to borrow foreign terminology – in the case of brothels, generally from Italian rather than French. The oldest is the now barely euphemistic **bordello**, acquired in the late 16th century and replacing the now obsolete *bordel*, which had come via French. In the 17th century came Italian **bagnio**, literally 'bathhouse', suggestive of naughty goings on in public baths and prefiguring in its way the modern use of MASSAGE PARLOUR and SAUNA PARLOUR (another part of the same semantic jigsaw is the now obsolete *stew* 'brothel', which also originally meant 'steam bath'). And **seraglio** (etymologically a 'locked-up place'), which standardly denotes a 'harem', has been used allusively for a 'brothel'.

The majority of modern euphemisms for 'brothel' depend on pretending that it is something else, more respectable. The vaguest is

**night club**, which can sometimes conceal something less innocent than its name suggests. Establishments where men take their clothes off and are physically manipulated by female attendants are begging for their name to be used as a euphemism, and that is indeed what has happened to **massage parlour** (the circumlocution is first recorded in 1913; compare MASSEUSE p 95). Saunas standardly lack the female attendants, so there is less room for euphemization, but nevertheless **sauna parlour** has occasionally stood in for *brothel*. (Note how the straight-laced *parlour* is hauled in to lend an air of respectability, as it is also in **encounter parlour**, denoting an establishment where men can meet prostitutes.) Another sort of pretence is represented by **escort agency**, which would have us believe that the only function of the women hired there is to accompany their clients to dinner, the theatre, etc.

The cryptic American **chicken ranch** supposedly commemorates a real brothel in Gilbert, Texas whose poorer clients, being mainly agricultural workers, paid for the prostitutes' services in kind – in the form of chickens (although it is hard to believe that it was not at least powerfully reinforced by the traditional metaphor of *chicken* applied to prostitutes – cf. POULE DE LUXE p 97).

**Hourly hotel** comes clean about the virtually euphemistic use of *hotel* (and *motel*) for an establishment with rooms that can be hired for sexual intercourse (professional or amateur) as opposed to overnight accommodation.

**Meatrack** for an area where prostitutes assemble in search of clients (and also for a place where male homosexuals meet for pickups) is probably too savage in its imagery to count as a true euphemism (it taps into the metaphor of prostitutes as commercially available flesh, which dates back at least to the 16th century, and also crops up in present-day English in such expressions as **white meat** for 'white-skinned prostitutes'). The slang **knocking shop** for 'brothel', too, is a bit near the knuckle, with its reminder of the vulgar *knock* or *knock off* for 'copulate with', but its element of earthy humour may just qualify it for euphemistic use in appropriate circumstances. It dates from the mid 19th century.

But perhaps the most pervasive of circumlocutions used to suggest the presence of prostitutes and brothels is **red light**, first recorded as an adjective (in America) in 1900. Its most typical habitat is the expression 'red-light district'. It comes from the use of a red light in the window as the sign of a brothel. **Red lamp** is an occasionally encountered alternative. A **red-lighter** is a 'prostitute'.

The designation of places where women may go to meet men for sexual intercourse is in its infancy, but an early euphemism, from America, is **microwave club** – the implication being that the microwave oven enables her still to prepare her husband a meal after spending the afternoon in extra-marital intercourse.

# THE EMPLOYERS

*Pimp* and *ponce* are terms with a high contempt factor, and the impulse to avoid them when talking about men who make a living from the control of prostitutes is easy to resist. The main softer alternative available is **procurer**, which dates back to the early 17th century. It has a distinctly legal flavour, as do the verb **procure** 'obtain as a prostitute', and even more the noun **procuration**. The basic rule of euphemism – it's more discreet in a foreign language – has encouraged the use of the French version **procureur** in English, and French **procureuse** has sometimes stood in for the English feminine form **procuress**: 'What a coarse face . . . she looks like a *procureuse*,' Evelyn Waugh 1930.

More colloquial is the prostitutes' **husband** for the man who controls their activities.

The use of **madam** for a 'female brothel-keeper' dates back, perhaps rather surprisingly, no further than the early 20th century, although its French form (and presumable model) **madame** is first recorded in English in 1871. The much older euphemism **mother** is now obsolete.

The group of prostitutes controlled by a pimp can be euphemized, using horse-racing metaphors, as a **stable** (first recorded in 1937) or, in American English, as a **string**.

The classic legal circumlocution for the activities of a pimp is 'living off **immoral earnings**'.

# PORNOGRAPHY

In the past, book-collectors with a penchant for pornography covered their tracks with the vague **curious**: 'That redoubtable suppressed *Life and Loves* of his ... which is sought after by collectors of "curious" books', H.G. Wells 1934. The collective term for such books, **curiosa**, exploits the classic euphemistic smokescreen of Latin. Even more obscure is **amusing**, which in an art dealer's catalogue can signal 'pornography' to those in the know. The more utilitarian modern euphemism for such material is **adult**. Magazines featuring mainly photographs of naked women are **men's magazines**, on which a more modern variation, taking advantage of their usual location in a newsagents (out of the reach of children) to make allowance for a less exclusive audience (e.g. gay magazines with photographs of naked men), is **top-shelf**. See also SKIN FLICK, p 157.

# HOMOSEXUALITY

The word *homosexual* entered the English language in 1892, in C G Chaddock's translation of *Krafft-Ebing's Psychopathia Sexualis*. From that moment on, as it began to establish itself, the euphemizers have had something to get their teeth into.

The taboos against homosexuality militated against direct reference to it throughout at least the first two thirds of the 20th century. But hostility towards it has ensured that many of the synonyms for *homosexual* are decidedly derogatory.

This taints a major strain of homosexuality euphemisms, based on the notion of being 'unusual' or 'strange'. Its most familiar exemplar is *queer*, which dates from the early 1920s as an adjective (as a noun it is first recorded in 1935). The usage originated in America, and to begin with its function was at least partly as a verbal camouflage. Over the decades it has sunk to the status of a term of abuse, although gays are now reclaiming it.

Other euphemisms in the same vein have held up better, perhaps in consequence of being less commonly used. They are far from complimentary, but they go no further than drawing attention to the (statistical) non-normality of homosexuals. They include **abnormal**, **curious**, **funny**, **odd**, and **peculiar** (major players these last two). In the same semantic realm but much more condemnatory is **unnatural**, which has been used in legal contexts (as in 'unnatural acts' and 'unnatural practices'; US legal terminology has in the past plumped for the impeccably vague **crime against nature** to denote buggery). (The use of **straight** for 'heterosexual', first recorded in 1941, contrasts implicitly with these 'unusual' euphemisms, although in present-day English *straight* is typically paired with *gay*.)

Towards the most cryptically discreet end of the euphemistic spectrum are vague references to 'that which one prefers'. They may or may not be partially disambiguated by an explicit mention of *sex*, but the fact that 'that which one prefers' is members of one's own sex has to be inferred from the fact that a comment on what one prefers has been made in the first place – heterosexuality usually elicits no such observation. Into this category come **orientation**, **predilection**, **preference**, and **proclivity**, all of which may be preceded by *sexual* and all of which carry the strong suggestion of 'homosexuality'. Closely related is **tendencies**, an extremely roundabout way of saying 'homosexuality' that apparently came on the scene between the two world wars: 'Now the Egyptians, they don't give a damn about a man if he has Tendencies,' Lawrence Durrell 1958.

But even these wispy allusions do not plumb the depths of lexical evasiveness. The prize must go to a set of euphemisms that rely on little more than a demonstrative pronoun or adjective (perhaps supported by a raised eyebrow or knowing look) to get across their message. The vaguest of all, **so** (as in 'Did you realize he was "so"?'), emerged in the interwar years and is now decidedly superannuated. The almost equally cryptic **that way** is first recorded around 1960, but probably goes back further than that (the expanded form **that way inclined** is scarcely more explicit). (The related 'the **other way**' is slightly more upfront, not that that is saying much; it dates back at least to the 1930s.) **Like that** is another way of (not) saying the same thing. So ostensibly are **one of them** and **one of those**, but in practice they are more condemnatory; they are still firmly euphemistic, in that they avoid the use of the frank *homosexual*, but their use is basically homophobic. Among gay men, the term **one of us** is frequently used with obviously positive connotations.

An obvious euphemistic ploy, in the case of male homosexuality, is to allude to femaleness. This is the rationale of **effeminate**, whose avowed message is 'unmanly' but which frequently disguises 'homosexual'. Women's names have in the past been a popular cover-up. Names based on flowers have struck a particular chord, as if to emphasize the femininity: **daisy**, **lily**, and the particularly successful **pansy** (first recorded in 1929). Others include **Mary** or **Mary Ann** (first recorded in 1880 and mainly applied to homosexuals taking the female role), **Maud** (often a paid homosexual prostitute), and pre-eminently **nancy**, a coinage of around the turn of the 20th century. This was short for the former, now obsolete, *Miss Nancy* 'effeminate or homosexual man', and it has since spawned the derivative **nancy boy**. Of all these, the two which have survived longest, *pansy* and *nancy*, have, whether by coincidence or not, become strongly derogatory – enough to fall under a modern taboo on negative words relating to homosexuality. Both now have a very dated air. (**Lizzie** for 'lesbian', first recorded in 1905, is an alteration of *lesbian*, although no doubt it was partly inspired by the female name *Lizzie*. The derivative **lizzie boy** was presumably modelled on *nancy boy*.)

Other words with 'female' connotations that have attached themselves euphemistically to male homosexuals in the past include **auntie**, applied to men of late middle age or beyond; **cissy**, an adjective suggestive primarily of girlishness in young boys, but also used with more serious imputations of adult males (the word comes ultimately from *sister*); **fairy** (fairies being stereotypically female and delicate), a usage which dates from the late 19th century and is now both derogatory and taboo; and, returning to the theme of flowers, **lavender**, used in American English as an adjective denoting homosexuality: a *lavender boy* is a male homosexual, and a *lavender convention* is attended by them (the metaphor is apparently based on the stereotypical use of perfume by male homosexuals, of which lavender in the past was a widely used ingredient). The use of *queen* for 'male homosexual', particularly one of mature years, scarcely qualifies as a euphemism any longer; it dates back to the 1920s.

The negative understatement, a potent tool of euphemizers, has been put to work on homosexuality. To say that a person is **not interested in the opposite sex** is a well-worn formula, and variations on the theme of **never married** have long been a code in newspaper obituaries and elsewhere (the simple **unmarried** sometimes carries the same connotation, and the positive **confirmed bachelor** usually does). **Unhealthy** betrays a more censorious attitude, but is still firmly euphemistic. The *locus classicus*, though, of negative designations is Lord Alfred Douglas's **the Love that dare not speak its name**. It comes from a line in his 1894 poem 'Two Loves', and achieved notoriety when it was referred to during the trial of his 'friend' (see p 108) Oscar Wilde for homosexuality in 1895. The notion of unspeakability is expressed more succinctly, and opprobriously, in **the nameless crime**, a term for those to whom *buggery* would give the vapours.

The long-winded, the high-falutin and the legalistic have all proved useful in throwing a smokescreen around homosexuality. **Invert** 'homosexual person' and **inversion** 'homosexuality' were adopted into English from the work of continental psychologists in the 1890s. Their introduction as technical terms can be dated from 1897, when the British sexologist Havelock Ellis used them in his *Studies in the Psychology of Sex*, although *inversion* is recorded in 1895 in a letter of Aubrey Beardsley. They were in common use as delicate but technical-sounding alternatives to *homosexual(ity)* throughout the first half of the 20th century, but since then the vogue for them has waned. The usage is based on the notion of the interchange of sexual preference. Branching off from the 'normal' preference lies behind **divergence**, used occasionally for 'homosexuality'.

**Homo-erotic** (etymologically 'same-loving') was an early alternative to *homosexual*. It was introduced into English in 1916 in Ernest Jones's translation of *Ferenczi's Contributions to Psycho-analysis*. It never caught on in the language at large to the same extent as *homosexual*, but for that very reason it has remained available as a technical-sounding and therefore euphemistic synonym. A rather similar role is performed by **homophile**, coined around 1960 as a sociological rather than a psycho-sexual term.

Legal jargon has presented the language with **consenting adult**. In Britain, the Wolfenden Report on homosexuality, published in 1957, introduced the notion of homosexual acts performed 'by consenting adults in private', which were no longer to be illegal, and it did not take long for *consenting adult* to become shorthand for *homosexual* (in practice it is also applied to heterosexuals, especially when they are engaged in some out-of-the-ordinary sexual activity). An earlier legal circumlocution is **indecent**, which is the only way the law in the 19th and early 20th century could bring itself to refer to homosexuality: an *indecent offence*, for instance, probably involves two people of the same sex (see also GROSS INDECENCY p 81).

Interest in the arts could be taken as a sign of homosexuality, and indeed in the obfuscatory language of the early and mid-20th century, both **artistic** and **musical** could stand as code-words for 'homosexual'. The world of the arts has also contributed **aesthete**, a throw-back to the aesthetic movement of the late 19th century and its stereotype of the effeminate artist. And classical mythology makes its contribution with the curious **Uranian**, standing in for *homosexual* as both adjective and noun. It is derived from the name of Urania, the Roman muse of astronomy. This in turn came from Greek *Ourania*, literally the 'heavenly one', which was used as an epithet of Aphrodite, the goddess of love. And it is supposedly a reference by Plato to Aphrodite in his *Symposium* that inspired the modern application to homosexuality. The word was coined in English in the 1890s (and has maintained a tenuous toehold ever since), but its ancestry is German. **Uranism**, a contemporary synonym of *homosexuality* that has not survived so well, is a direct adaptation of German *Uranismus*. And even more bizarre is **urning**, a noun meaning 'homosexual' which was acquired from German in the 1880s. This was coined in 1864 by K H Ulrichs, again based on the name *Urania*. Not surprisingly, it did not have a very lengthy career in English.

The use of **male** to denote 'male homosexual' one might have thought carries allusiveness *ad absurdum* – but 'male magazines', 'male movies', etc are produced for the delectation of gay men (compare the very different connotations of 'for men').

The relationship of a homosexual to his or her partner has always presented lexical problems. The standard solution has been to use **friend**, but heavily hedged about with written or spoken inverted commas, so that (nudge-nudge, wink-wink) we all know what is being referred to. **Companion** and **long-term companion** are used in the same cryptic way.

The notion of unavowed homosexuals being 'in the **closet**' dates from the early 1960s. Amongst its spin-offs are **closet queen** 'secret male homosexual' and **come out of the closet** 'declare one's homosexuality', abbreviated for extra euphemistic effect to **come out**. This in turn produced the verb **out** 'reveal someone's homosexuality', first recorded in 1990.

On the use of **cottage** as a term for a 'public lavatory' when used as a place for male homosexual pickups, see p 186. Another euphemism that has arisen out of a place where homosexuals meet for assignations is **in the park**: 'If the Prime Minister were arrested in the park . . . it would come to me to deal with, you know,' Roy Jenkins 1991.

Some other 'homosexuality' euphemisms at the colloquial end of the spectrum:

**camp** a word of uncertain etymology, suggestive of highly histrionic male homosexuality. It appeared on the scene in the first decade of the 20th century

**cruise** to go around the town in search of homosexual pickups. Originally an American usage, first recorded in 1903

**friend of Dorothy** an allusion to Dorothy Gale, the young heroine of Frank L. Baum's *The Wizard of Oz* (1900), who in the 1939 film version was played by Judy Garland, later a gay icon

**fruit** a male homosexual – a usage that originated in America in the 1930s. Euphemistic to begin with, but the effect has worn thin

**iron** short for *iron hoof*, British rhyming slang for the decidedly non-euphemistic *poof* 'male homosexual'. First recorded in 1936

**left-handed** an American usage, comparing 'wrong' handedness with 'wrong' sexual orientation. Compare AMBIDEXTROUS (p 111)

**limp-wristed** from the stereotypical image of the effeminate male homosexual making misguidedly stereotypical female gestures, such as allowing the hand to flop forward limply from the wrist. It appears to have originated as the attributive *limp-wrist* around 1960, but the *-ed* form is now commoner

**swish** an ostentatiously effeminate homosexual male; an American usage, first recorded in 1941. The adjective **swishy** derives from it

No account of colloquialisms for 'homosexual' would be complete without a mention of **gay**, which towards the end of the 20th century had become virtually the neutral term, particularly for male homosexuals. Its origins are unclear. As long ago as the 17th century it was being used euphemistically for 'sexually dissolute' (a usage which survives, just, in the cliché *bachelor gay*), and by the early 19th century it was being applied specifically to female prostitutes. It is possible that the coexistence of the 19th-century heterosexual underworld with the world of male prostitution and secret homosexual activity originated a crossover of *gay* to homosexuality: Hugh Rawson in his *Dictionary of Euphemisms and Other Doubletalk* 1981 quotes one John Saul, a male prostitute of 1880s London, using the word both of female prostitutes and of his male friends. An earlier clue still is a reported 1868 song called 'The Gay Young Clerk in the Dry Goods Store' by the US female impersonator Will S Hays, but the precise semantic status of *gay* here remains speculative. It seems likely that *gay* was used as a private word in the homosexual community throughout the first half of the 20th century, but it did not begin to emerge into the general language until the 1950s. By the 1970s it was ousting the more traditional uses of *gay*, and now, as we have seen, it is a widely used standard term.

*Lesbianism* as a term for female homosexuality dates from the 1870s. Its origins are presumably euphemistic (an obscure classical allusion to Lesbos, the island where the homosexual Greek poet Sappho lived), but at the end of the 20th century it was a standard term, preferred by many female homosexuals to *gay*. Sappho retains her euphemistic role, however, in **sapphic**, **sapphist**, and **sapphism**, coinages of the late 19th century which have always remained in the realm of the high-flown and literary. Similarly obscurantist is **tribadism**, both a general term for lesbianism and a more specific reference to lesbian intercourse in which one woman lies on top of the other for the purpose of clitoral stimulation. A derivative ultimately of Greek *tribein* 'rub', it came into English in the early 19th century.

The new euphemisms of the last third of the 20th century, touched with the spirit of political correctness, are **male oriented** or **male identified** for male homosexuals, and for lesbians **female oriented** or **female identified**. The unisex catchall is **same gender oriented**, or **SGO** for short: 'Today's SGO girl takes her style cues not from k d lang or Jeanette Winterson, but from the pages of Elle or Vogue,' *Sunday Times* 1993.

# BISEXUALITY

**AC/DC** from the abbreviations for 'alternating (electric) current' and 'direct current', suggesting alternative preferences. First recorded in the US in 1960

**ambidextrous** from the shared notion of 'bothness'. The facetious alteration **ambisextrous** dates back to the 1920s

**bi** not exactly original, but less frank than the full form *bisexual*. It functions as both an adjective and a noun. First recorded in 1966. The derivative **bi-guy** denotes a bisexual man

**ladyboy** a young male transvestite, especially an oriental one, and particularly one who is a prostitute

**swing both ways** based on the use of *swing* for 'have sex promiscuously' (see p 73). First recorded in 1972

**switch hitter** a metaphor from baseball, where a *switch hitter* is someone who can bat both right-handed and left-handed

**versatile** a classically vague euphemism – the versatility in this context consists of having intercourse with both sexes. First recorded in 1959

# WOOING, WINNING AND WANDERING

The euphemistic notion of the male as a suppliant at the court of which his prospective sexual partner is the queen appears to date from the late 16th century – that, certainly, is the period when the verb *court* 'try to win the sexual favour of' and its noun *courtship* entered the language.

In the succeeding centuries *court* gradually made itself more at home in the language, alongside the much older *woo*. Its connotations of courtliness seeped away, and by the 1890s the *Oxford English Dictionary* was describing its usage as 'homely'. For those with long enough memories, the last vestige of its serious use in Britain is probably the question 'Are you courting?', regularly asked by Wilfred Pickles of embarrassed young single contestants in his radio programme *Have A Go* in the 1950s and 1960s.

In the wake of the liberated 60s, the notion of trying to get accepted as a sexual partner is no longer one that needs to be hedged about with heavily circumlocutious or flowery language. Nor do we care any longer to maintain the pretence that all such efforts are directed towards the ultimate goal of marriage.

Some linguistic reminders of a less upfront past remain, however. **Proposition** used as a verb, meaning 'make an offer of sexual intercourse to', originated in America in the 1930s (compare the similarly allusive but much more respectable *propose*, meaning 'make an offer of marriage', which dates from the mid 18th century).

More importunate demands, typically by a male of a female, have been euphemized with the verb **bother** (as in 'Has he been bothering you, dear?'). It usually refers to verbal suggestions rather than a physical assault (although it is also applied to unwelcome attempts at sexual intercourse within marriage). A still more genteel way of putting it is **attentions** (as in 'She repulsed his unwelcome attentions'). An **improper suggestion** could in theory be encouraging fraud or theft, but in practice the term is interpreted as referring to an (unwelcome) request for sexual intercourse. More colloquially, an overenthusiastic suitor might be said to be getting **fresh**.

In the past, having convinced the parents of his prospective sexual partner that his **intentions** were **honourable** (i.e. that he was not going to try to have intercourse with her before marriage), a man might aspire to **win** her, which in polite usage connoted the extraction of a promise of marriage. In modern parlance **get off with**, vague enough to qualify as a euphemism, implies a successful opening of sexual negotiations but not necessarily the achievement of full intercourse. It is first recorded in 1915.

A woman who readily or even eagerly accedes to the sexual requests of a male may be euphemized as **available**. Someone of either sex who has had many sexual partners can be described as **experienced** – a euphemism that can be positively approving in the case of men, but as applied to women is decidedly a cover-up. For actual, if coy, disapproval of a woman as a prospective wife there is, or was, **damaged goods**, which equates loss of virginity with damage to merchandise in a shop: 'Donald Farfrae is not aware when he marries her that Lucetta is damaged goods,' *Essays in Criticism* 1952. A more discreet and slighly less judgmental way of putting it is to say that a woman has a *past* (see p 8); while a man who has many unacknowledged sexual liaisons could be said to have a **secret life**, a euphemism first recorded as, and perhaps inspired by, the title of a volume of soft-porn memoirs published in 1880 by the pseudonymous 'Walter'. The adjective **fast**, as applied to a sexually immoral life or to the people who lead it, dates from the 18th century. A woman, by contrast, who is unwilling to engage in pre-marital sexual intercourse may be critically euphemized by men as **saving it** (preserving her virginity until after marriage). Dismissing promiscuity as **playing the field** draws on the terminology of the racecourse: betting on several runners in the same race.

A collective euphemism in the days of the British Empire for girls sent abroad (especially to India) to find a husband who had proved elusive in Britain was the **fishing fleet**.

Someone who marries, or has as their sexual partner, a person younger than themselves (much younger in the case of men) may be disapprovingly termed a **cradle-snatcher** (originally an Americanism, first recorded in 1925) or a **baby-snatcher** (which apparently dates back still further, to the pre-World War I period).

If a marriage takes place to avoid the social taboo of bastardy, the man is euphemistically said to **make an honest woman of** his wife (an expression often also used jocularly for 'marry' with no imputation of pre-marital pregnancy) or to **do the right thing** by her.

A marriage in which by agreement each partner raises no objections to the other having extra-marital sexual relationships is euphemistically termed an **open marriage**. By contrast, a marriage in which sexual intercourse has never taken place may be discreetly described as a marriage **in name only** or, hiding behind the even thicker disguise of French, as a **mariage blanc**, a term first recorded in English in the 1920s (in French it means literally 'white marriage', probably a delicate reference to the lack of hymenal blood on white sheets).

A wife or especially a husband who is always on the look-out for opportunities of extra-marital flirtation or intercourse is said to have a **roving eye**, a term first recorded as long ago as 1596. If the propensity is frequently translated into action, the guilty party may be said to **wander** or **stray** or **roam**, or to have **itchy feet** (a reminder of the **seven-year itch**, a camouflage term for a supposed tendency to seek another sexual partner after seven years' marriage). Such affairs are often jokily euphemized as '**extracurricular** activities', and the objects of the **errant** spouses' passion as a **bit on the side**. Sporting imagery is invoked in **playing away**.

Much more condemnatory, but still euphemistic, terms for the taking of an extra-marital lover are **cheat** and **deceive**, which stress the duplicity towards the spouse (the more colloquial **two-time** perhaps more commonly refers to non-married partners). They lead on to the key nexus of euphemisms in the area of staying with one sexual partner or abandoning them for another: **faithful/fidelity** and **unfaithful/infidelity**. The specific sexual connotations of these words do not seem to have emerged out of the general notion of 'loyalty' before the end of the 17th century, but they are now so firmly established that we scarcely think of them as circumlocutions any more. A more 'literary' alternative to *infidelity* is **inconstancy**.

A person discovered by their usual partner copulating with someone else is said to have been caught **in flagrante**. This is short for *in flagrante delicto*, a piece of legal Latin that means 'with the crime blazing' – 'red-handed', in other words. The (semi-)humorous sexual application evolved in the 20th century. Another contribution by the law to the euphemism of sexual infidelity is **co-respondent** 'person cited in a divorce case as having had sex with the spouse of the person seeking the divorce' (etymologically the person being cited 'with' the 'respondent' – who is typically the petitioner's wife). In the days when the divorce laws gave prominence to such people, the term became almost a euphemism for a 'promiscuous male who has sexual liaisons with married women': *co-respondent shoes* were two-tone leather shoes supposedly worn by such lotharios.

A person who is not married or otherwise encumbered by a sexual partner may be euphemized as **free**.

The offering of excuses by a partner unwilling to engage in sexual intercourse probably comes into the category more of euphemistic behaviour than of euphemistic language, but two particularly high-profile words stereotypically used in such contexts by women deserve a mention: **headache** and **tired**.

# SEXUAL PARTNERS

A glaring vacancy has existed in the English language until very recently for a word for a 'permanent cohabiting sexual partner'. Social introductions would trail off along the lines of 'This is X, my, er . . . '. Various more or less euphemistic stabs were made at filling it in the last third of the 20th century, from the rather coy **live-in lover** to the bizarre American acronym **posslq** (standing for 'person of opposite sex sharing living quarters'). Towards the end of the 20th century there were signs that the simple (but still euphemistic) **partner** was gaining general acceptance.

The lexical uncertainty has been caused at least partly because in the past the category of unmarried cohabitee was so socially taboo that no mere euphemism could make it mentionable in polite society. When reference to it was unavoidable, probably the pretence would be made that the couple were legally married, so there was no call for a separate generally usable word to denote the concept. The only specific terminology available was the legalistic **common-law wife/husband** (a coinage of apparently the turn of the 20th century), which officially denotes a marriage sanctioned in law even though not formalized by a legal or religious ceremony (its precise status varies in different legal jurisdictions), but which in practice usually alludes to any unmarried couple living together.

But partly too it reflects a general squeamishness about referring directly to a sexual partner of any sort. Whatever the precise refinements of their status, a delicate way of referring to them has been evolved. It could even be argued that metaphors for 'husband' and 'wife' such as *old man*, *her indoors* (popularized by the Thames TV series *Minder* 1979–93), *good lady*, and particularly **lady wife** serve some euphemistic purpose.

Unmarried sexual partners using the same accommodation have inspired two verbal usages that are among the classics in the canon of English euphemism: **live together** and **cohabit**. *Live together*, and its transitive partner *live with*, score heavily on the vagueness scale: their surface meaning is all innocence, applicable to anyone sharing a residence with another, and it is only context that allows one to draw out the concealed implication of regular sexual intercourse. *Live with* seems to have been in use by the middle of the 18th century, and Jane Austen employs both *live together* and *live with* in this sense. (The related **live in sin**, more condemnatory but still euphemistic, dates from the early 19th century.) Their legalistic cousin *cohabit* deploys formality as a cover for embarrassment. Its specific connotations of living together as husband and wife date back to the early 16th century, although in early usage there was not necessarily any implication of being unmarried (an Act of Parliament of 1548 refers to a 'Sentence for matrymonye, commanding solempnizacion, cohabitacion, consumacion and tractacion [conduct] as becometh Man and Wyef to have'). This euphemistic connotation developed later, and has now taken the word over completely.

Sexual partners who do not live together may still be bashful about specifying their relationship too baldly. This in the past has been the world of pink frilly language, the perfumed vocabulary of the boudoir, much of it borrowed from or inspired by French or Italian, the languages of the hot-blooded. So in former times a lady might have had her **gallant**, her **beau** (an introduction of the early 18th century), or, especially if married, her **cavalier-servant** (brought into the language by Lord Byron) or her **cicisbeo** (an early 18th-century borrowing from Italian, which may etymologically mean 'beautiful chickpea'). **Paramour**, acquired from French in the 14th century and now only used ironically, is a unisex term. French has been amply resorted to in euphemizing the sexual relationships themselves as well: the use of **affair** for such a relationship dates from the start of the 18th century (the non-euphemistic *love affair* is not recorded before 1862; the ultra-euphemistic **affaire**, a return to the original French, was introduced into English in the 19th century; both the anglicized and the French form have embroidered versions as **affair of the heart** and **affaire de coeur**); English borrowed French **amour** for 'love affair' in the 16th century; and the use of French **liaison** for 'love affair' dates from the early 19th century (Lord Byron again being apparently instrumental in its introduction). **Dalliance** for 'flirtation' is also of French origin.

The euphemistic use of **mistress** for 'woman who has an ongoing sexual relationship with a man to whom she is not married' dates back to the 15th century, although the full modern panoply of connotations – the woman financially supported by the man, the man married to another woman – do not seem to have developed until the 17th century. In present-day usage, the term has a decidedly dated air. Its nearest male equivalent, also now somewhat overtaken by the relaxation of social taboos, is **lover** 'male sexual partner of a married woman'. *Lovers* in the plural has an important euphemistic function as a fig leaf for 'partners in sexual intercourse' (as in 'They were lovers' or 'Have you and she ever been lovers?'; compare MAKE LOVE); and, in keeping with late 20th-century aspirations towards sexual equality, *lover* is increasingly used for a man's (female) sexual partner.

The now very dated-seeming (but not entirely defunct) scenario of a female unmarried sexual partner financially supported by a (married) man has left a tidemark of euphemisms in the language. **Keep** is a key term, and a fairly derogatory one too; the notion of the **kept** woman, 'maintained or supported by a paramour,' as the *Oxford English Dictionary* resoundingly defines her, dates from the late 17th century (there is some modern homosexual usage of the term applied to men). The 1920s euphemized a 'mistress' as an **affinity**. Redolent of the same bygone era is **protector** 'man keeping a mistress', a quintessentially 19th-century usage. But **sugar daddy** 'old man who lavishes money on a young woman in return for or in hopes of sex', an American coinage of the 1920s, is still very much with us. The closest approach to a balancing expression in terms of male female relations is probably **toy boy** 'young male lover of an older woman', first recorded in 1981.

In the wider sphere of sexual relationships as a whole, probably the most overused camouflage word is **friend**. On the surface it has no sexual connotations at all, but this makes it perfect for the euphemistic innuendo: a newspaper reporting on a person's *friend* could make it clear by context that the two were heterosexual or homosexual partners – if there were any room for doubt, a pair of quotation marks or the adjective *close* would remove it. Then there are all the *-friend* compounds. **Boyfriend** and **girlfriend** purport to denote young sweethearts – those much beyond their teens need not apply. But minimalization of age, a central euphemistic strategy, makes them ideal coy terms for adult sexual partners. Less age-shy but still euphemistic are **man friend** and **woman friend**, while a more genteel note can be struck by **gentleman friend** and **lady friend**. People who are **just good friends**, on the other hand, (supposedly) have only a platonic relationship. Another link in the 'friendship' chain is **constant companion**, used with heavy allusiveness by the press when identifying an unmarried sexual partner. Similarly **close** can imply much more than it states (as in 'The two have been close for several years').

US sociological jargon of the 1970s came up with the non-sex-specific **significant other**.

A less prolific tactic, but one popular for disguising a woman's male sexual partner, is to invoke a role or duty of accompanying. A woman's **escort**, who goes around socially with her in public, will not, if she is married, be her husband (a female *escort* is likely to be a prostitute; see p 95). The more up-to-date terminology for such a man is a **walker**.

In keeping with the vagueness principle, the crucial term in the euphemization of sexual relationships, particularly among adolescents, is *out*: if two people **go out** together, or someone **takes** another person **out**, we assume that it is ultimately for some sexual purpose, not merely to get into the open air. The largely American **go with** similarly implies a sexual relationship. **See** can have distinctly sexual connotations (as in 'Are you still seeing that boy?'). In former decades the equally vague **take up with** denoted the formation of such a relationship. Almost as dogeared are **carry on with** and **run around with**, which carry a strong note of disapproval.

The discreet language of yesteryear disguised a male suitor as an **admirer** or, in the case of the lower orders, a **follower**, a term coined in the 19th century to denote a man courting a female servant ('No followers', the conditions of employment would sternly state). A rendezvous for sexual purposes was in those days an **assignation** or, if a touch of Wardour Street poetry-ese were desired, a **tryst**. Also from the 19th century come **lady's man** 'man who is sexually stimulated by the company of women (and has the same effect on them)' and **lady killer** 'man sexually irresistible to women'. To the same era belongs the concept of the **other woman**, a married man's alternative sexual partner (the term is first recorded in 1855, in Robert Browning's *Men and Women*). But lest we should pride ourselves on having done away with such nebulous allusions, we should remind ourselves that 'the other woman' is not far from such modern circumlocutions as 'Is there someone else?' (meaning 'Do you have another sexual partner?').

Another 19th-century introduction is **ménage à trois**, in French literally 'household of three'. Its euphemistic cover (for 'sexual relationship involving three people living together') is maintained by its foreign disguise. It is not to be confused with **troilism**, which refers to sexual activity involving three people. In this case the foreign disguise (it is probably based on French *trois* 'three') is reinforced by the *-ism* suffix, which gives an air of technical detachment. It is first recorded in its current sense in 1951.

The latter part of the 20th century was on the whole much less coy about naming sexual associations, but one notable euphemism emerged in the 1940s and has been making headway ever since: **relationship** for 'sexual relationship' or 'love affair' (as in 'I'm not in a relationship at the moment'). Roughly the same period saw the emergence of **sexual athlete** as a metaphor for a person of great sexual appetite and prowess.

Even in the 21st century there may remain vestiges of that most homely of sexual euphemisms, the courtesy title **uncle** bestowed on a mother's male lover as a reassurance for her children: 'The play is a simple tale of a boy who, lacking a resident father, grows up under the influence of various temporary "uncles",' *Listener* 1968.

# THE BODY & ITS PARTS

---

So great is our fear in Western society of revealing intimate parts of our body to strangers that many people's literal nightmares contain scenes in which they find themselves naked in a public place. And if a part is intimate enough to keep covered up, it is likely enough that we will experience some sort of difficulty or embarrassment in talking about it.

The genital organs are at the greatest extreme of the taboo spectrum, a position reflected on one hand by the unprintability of some of our words for them and on the other by the fact that some people have *no* words with which to refer to them (a survey reported in 1992, for instance, found that many mothers do not use a name for their daughters' genitals). Less taboo but still embarrassing enough to evoke many euphemisms are the buttocks and the female breasts.

Any part of the body, in other words, that is connected with reproduction or sexual activity, is an erogenous zone, or is associated with excretion or odours is liable to circumlocution. From the late 18th century through the high summer of Victorian prudery, legs were considered so sexually improper that even the garments that concealed them could not be directly named (see p 153). It was this period, particularly in America, that gave birth to the euphemism **limb** for 'leg': 'I am not so particular as some people are, for I know some who always say limb of a table, or limb of a piano-forte,' Frederick Marryat 1839 (this has now died out, but Robert Burchfield, in *Fair of Speech: The Uses of Euphemism* 1985, sees a relic of it in *artificial limb*, which avoids a direct reference to 'leg' – or 'arm'). The word *thigh* might be too suggestive for some excitable folk, who would prefer a less sensational alternative such as 'upper leg'.

The abdomen, immediately above the genitals and generally kept covered up in public, presents some linguistic problems. The word *belly*, in particular, is under a cloud. Until the 18th century it was simply the standard term for the 'abdomen'. But the Victorians took against it (it was expunged from many versions of the Bible published in the 19th century). They preferred *stomach*, which had been used in this wider sense since the 14th century. This is now such a central usage that it cannot be regarded as a euphemism, but **tummy** for 'stomach' certainly is, particularly when used amongst adults (by a doctor to a patient, for instance). It originated as a nursery word in the middle of the 19th century. An even coyer alternative is **tum-tum**: 'Make some toast and coffee. My tum-tum's empty,' P. Mallory 1981. Similarly **tummy-button** (first recorded in 1945) replaces 'belly-button' or 'navel'. And the same prudery lies behind the use of **Middle Eastern dancing** for 'belly dancing.' A curious early 20th-century contribution to the repertoire of 'abdomen' euphemisms was **Little Mary**, from the title of a play (1903) by J.M. Barrie.

Because of its strong (repellent/attractant) smell, the hollow beneath the arms needs to be referred to with care. The word *armpit* (which dates from before 1400) is a bit strong, especially for advertisers. They will not use it, preferring the much more sanitary-sounding **underarm**. This began to be used as an adjective with reference to armpit smells and their alleviation in the mid 20th century (see p 192), and it has since become a direct nominal synonym for *armpit*.

Physical shortcomings also produce circumlocution. Baldness and fatness are less uncomfortable to talk about if we can wrap them up in euphemisms. A pimple becomes, amongst cosmeticians, a **beauty spot** or a **blemish**. An unshaven face is euphemized with **five-o'clock shadow** (first recorded in 1937) or **designer stubble**.

At the most general level of all, *body* itself can be an uncomfortable word. It is very direct, almost unclothing its referent in a way that may seem appropriate only in moments of sexual intimacy. There are connotations of 'dead body' to it too. To get around this, we may make use of **anatomy** (as in 'She poked him in a tender portion of his anatomy'). At a more colloquial level, **chassis** for 'body' is a product of the motor-car age (it is first recorded in 1930); it is mainly used in contexts of male admiration for the female body.

# GENITALIA

Of the linguistic taboos that have us in their grip, the ban on naming the external genitals is amongst the strongest (rivalled as a ring-fenced area only by sexual intercourse and prostitution). The more anxious we are about referring to something openly, the more likely we are to invent circumlocutions for it: and surveys have revealed over a thousand synonyms for 'male genitals', and in excess of twelve hundred for the apparently even more taboo 'female genitals' (see Keith Allan and Kate Burridge *Euphemism and Dysphemism* 1991, p 96). Not all of them are euphemisms, of course. A good many (*pisser, cock, cunt*, etc.) are decidedly not for sensitive company. But a lot of creative thought has gone into ways of making these ostracized organs more respectable.

It is in line with the vagueness principle of euphemism that some 'genitalia' terms make no distinction between male and female. Sexual ambiguity in this area is apparently reassuring, and tones down the embarrassment factor. A prime example is **genitalia** itself, and its anglicized cognates **genitals** and **genital organs**. The latter two have been in English since the Middle Ages, but particularly since the 18th century they have come to have the status of 'technical terms', used by scientists and doctors. They were joined in the late 19th century by *genitalia*, which has the additional obfuscatory advantage of being Latin. As in the case of PENIS and VAGINA, the late 20th century saw an enthusiastic adaptation of this 'medical' vocabulary into a euphemizing role.

Alternatively, one can soften the focus on the genitals themselves by referring in more general terms to the part of the body in which they are situated. The biblical **loins** exploits this strategem. It originally denoted the part of the body below the ribs and above the hips (it is etymologically related to *lumbar*), but its use in Bible translations from the 16th century onwards for the 'part about which one puts clothes to cover one's nakedness' (as in *gird up one's loins*) led to its being interpreted as 'part of the body containing the genitals'. This is reinforced by its further biblical use for 'source of offspring or of future generations' (although in this context it is mainly a male, not a unisex term).

Similarly non-committal are **groin** and **crutch**. *Groin* originally denoted the crease or depression where each of the thighs meets the body, but its proximity to the genitals makes the word irresistible as a euphemism (mention of a 'groin strain' in a sportsman can be relied on to produce schoolboy sniggers in some quarters). The use of *crutch* (or **crotch**) for the 'part of the body where the legs meet at the top' derives from an earlier sense 'fork, bifurcation'; again, the organs very prominently situated there make the euphemistic transfer an obvious one. Both terms can be used for either sex, but in practice are more male-oriented.

Vaguer still is **abdomen**, which technically covers the entire trunk from the chest to the pelvis. Greater precision can be suggested by the still inexact **lower abdomen**. These are commonly resorted to by sports commentators reluctant to refer directly on radio or television to the genitals – when a boxer has been struck there, for instance (**below the belt** is another way of saying this), or when the ball finds its way to a batsman's testicles (see also ABDOMINAL PROTECTOR). A less genteel, but still euphemistic, alternative is **belly**.

The location of the offending organs can be used as a verbal figleaf – 'down' in the body's basement, away from the higher and nobler functions of heart and brain. So **down below**, **downstairs**, **down there**, and the **nether parts** or **nether regions** are all mealy-mouthed alternatives for 'genitals' – the first three, in particular, favoured in embarrassed conversations between patient and doctor or nurse ('A programme devoted to problems "down there" was too shy for anything but innuendo', *Radio Times* 1998). A jokey variant on the theme, now obsolescent, is **Low Countries**, from the name formerly applied to the area of Belgium, the Netherlands, and Luxembourg. It was mainly applied to the female genitals – not surprisingly in view of the pun in the second element.

The 'secrecy' of the genitals is another theme that can be exploited. They may not be seen by other people outside a strictly limited set of circumstances. Here, the classic euphemism is **private parts**. The notion goes back at least to the 13th century, when it was expressed by the word *privy*: *privy parts*, *privy members*, *privy limbs*, and (in the case of the vagina) *privy chose* (= 'private thing') were all used for 'genitals'. The present-day usage *private parts* seems to have emerged in the second half of the 18th century. Records of the colloquial abbreviation **privates** date only from the 20th century, but a pun in *Hamlet* (to Hamlet's question 'Then you live about her [Fortune's] waist, or in the middle of her favours?' Guildenstern replies 'Faith, her privates we') suggests that it is of far greater antiquity. Certainly antique, and now quaintly so, is just plain **parts** for 'genitals': 'Wash the parts with Juice of Calamint,' John Wesley 1747. Part of the same family is **personal parts**.

Coyer than most is the use of **person** for 'genitalia', a piece of legalese which goes back to the early 19th century (it is first recorded in an Act of Parliament of 1824), and is as extreme an example of the whole standing for the part as can be imagined. It is most commonly associated with the male genitals, and as a piece of legal circumlocution it most often crops up in the expression *expose one's person* (cf. EXPOSE ONESELF p 158), but it is applied to the female genitals too: 'He held me round the waist with his right arm and used his left hand. He put his hand on my person,' *Straits Times* (Singapore) 1911. And without actually lexicalizing the concept as *person*, it is quite common to generalize from the unmentionable genitals to the safer territory of the entire body, provided that the context makes the reference clear: a woman discussing many women's ignorance of the appearance of their genitals, for instance, wrote coyly 'We don't really know what we look like' (*Observer* 1992).

At the cosy-colloquial end of the spectrum come a range of nonsense words for 'thing whose name is unknown or not remembered, or which you do not want to say,' applied specifically to the 'penis' and the 'vagina': **thingummy, thingy, whatsit, whatchamacallit**, and the like. And of course **thing** itself performs the same role: 'One had opened his pants and was shaking what my circle called "his thing",' Lilian Hellman 1969; as does, on a more high-falutin level, **affair**. Other 'genital' euphemisms include the flamboyant **sex**, whose natural habitat is purple-patch sex scenes in novels ('the narrow white briefs that barely captured her sex,' Ted Allbeury 1977); the practical **equipment**, which is mainly but not exclusively applied to the penis; the similarly inspired **gear**; and the jokey **naughty bits**, which picks up on the wider use of *naughty* to connote 'sexual activity' (see p 68). The last can be shortened to simply **bits** ('Gay characters have to . . . be more honest and decent to sugar-coat . . . the unpalatable truth of what they do with their bits,' A A Gill 2000).

The unisex euphemism for 'pubic hair' is **short hair** or **short hairs** (even though, as R W Holder points out in the *Faber Dictionary of Euphemisms* 1989, the pubic hair is considerably longer than other body hair). The more common colloquial version of it is **short and**

**curlies**. Both are found much more often in such expressions as *have someone by the short and curlies* 'have someone at a disadvantage' than in literal use. An alternative is **pubes**, the medical term for 'pubic hair' when pronounced /pyoobeez/, but commandeered into colloquial language as /pyoobz/.

More outlandish metaphors for 'pubic hair' tend to be applied to the female variety, although not exclusively so. Vegetative imagery includes **bush** (first recorded in 1922), the American **cotton** (an allusion to the fluffy balls, not to the thread), and GRASS (see p 138). **Beard** is based on a fairly obvious analogy, and **busby** recalls the fur hats worn by certain British soldiers. Cosmetic depilation of that area can be thinly disguised as a **Brazilian wax** (microscopic Brazilian bathing costumes leave little option). See also ACE OF SPADES (p 137), BEAVER (p 134), MUFFIN (p 137), PUFF (p 137), PUSSY (p 134).

# Male Genitals

No confidence trickster in history can have had as many aliases as the penis. The taboos surrounding it are so strong that English speakers over the centuries have been unable to settle on a single neutral term for it that is usable in all circumstances. Instead, it goes under a range of names, from which a selection is made, appropriate to the circumstances in which the speaker finds him- or herself. The character of many of them is so up-front and frank that strong taboos apply to *them*. *Cock*, for instance, *prick*, and *pisser* are strong and above all serious words for the penis. They do not seek to defuse its threat by obfuscation or jokiness. Therefore in many social contexts, alternatives for such words have to be sought. (The taboo against *cock* in American English is so strong, incidentally, that it is not even used for 'male chicken'; the term **rooster** was coined in the second half of the 18th century to replace it.)

**Penis** itself is something of a euphemism. It began to be used in English in the late 17th century (it is a direct adoption of Latin *penis*, which originally meant 'tail'), and for much of its career has been used mainly in medical and similar technical contexts. Its Latin obscurity and medical respectability have made it a useful word for referring to the embarrassing organ in polite circles. Towards the end of the 20th century there were signs that it might be moving beyond this role into the language at large, and providing for the first time in the modern era a genuinely neutral term for the male sex organ.

The more dainty, formal end of the euphemistic spectrum makes, as might be expected, much use of obscurity and vagueness when dealing with the male sex organ. Leading circumlocutions in this category include **appendage** (recalling the far more down-to-earth *tail*), **implement**, and **instrument** (both high-falutin alternatives to TOOL (see p 130)). **Organ** has a noble ring to it: in theory it could refer to any of scores of structures within the human body, but unmodified, and in the appropriate context, it is readily decoded as 'penis' (and it is also useful material for double entendres, as regular readers of that respected organ of satire, *Private Eye*, know: 'It is good to know that this organ is fingered in the furthest corners of the Roman Empire. My article on Vanduara. . . ,' *Private Eye* 1992). In the same vein is **member**. This is descended from Latin *membrum*, which originally meant 'limb' but came by extension to be used for 'sex organ'. When English acquired it in the 13th century it brought this extended meaning with it. At first it was a unisex term, but over the centuries it came to be restricted to 'penis'. Its status in modern English is dubious. It is certainly still used, but it is so antiquated that its effect, whether solo or in the expression **male member**, is often risible. The Latin **membrum virile** (literally 'male member') cloaks it in more respectable obscurity. See also PECULIAR MEMBERS (p 131). The euphemistic use of **manhood** for 'penis' dates back at least to the erotica of the 18th century (John Cleland uses it in his *Memoirs of a Woman of Pleasure* 1749, better known as *Fanny Hill*). *Root* for 'penis' is rather more recent – apparently it dates from the early 19th century. Its imagery is too earthy to qualify it as a euphemism, but the quaint **man-root** coined from it, with its simple imagery suggestive of early medieval poetic diction, certainly serves a circumlocutory purpose.

But such elevated penile vocabulary is far outnumbered by colloquialisms, intended for the most part to put us at our ease when referring to this sensitive part of the male body. Familiarity and humour dispel taboo. And one of the surest ways to familiarity is to give the little fellow a name. A range of male forenames have been applied to the penis, notably *Cecil, Charlie, Dick, John Thomas, John Willie, Percy, Peter, Roger,* and *Willy*. Of them, **Cecil** is perhaps the least often encountered. **Charlie** is an all-purpose euphemism of wide application, but in this instance there may be some link with *Charlie* 'fool' (first recorded in 1946), since 'penis'-words are often used as terms of abuse for foolish people. *Dick* dates from the late 19th century (an earlier sense 'riding whip' may have suggested a phallic image), but for some reason – perhaps its phonetic similarity to *prick* – it does not function euphemistically in the way these other personal names do. **John Thomas** has a long history, going back to the mid 19th century, but perhaps received its biggest boost from Lady Chatterley's enthusiastic endorsement: '"John Thomas! John Thomas!" and she quickly kissed the soft penis,' D H Lawrence 1928; a variant is **John Willie**, and it is also shortened to **John**. **Percy** is encountered mainly in the expression *point Percy at the porcelain* 'urinate' (see p 176); it may be a punning reference to PERSON (see p 124). **Peter** is mainly American, dating probably from the late 19th century, and perhaps partially suggested by a phonetic similarity to *penis*. *Roger* was widely used colloquially for the 'penis' in the 17th and 18th centuries, but now (barely) survives only in the verb *roger* 'copulate (with)' (see p 73) and in the folk-mythical *Roger the Lodger*, the sexually voracious paying guest. But undoubtedly the best-established of all in British English – so much so that it is scarcely perceived any more as a personal name, and is not spelled with a capital letter – is **willy**, which dates from around the turn of the 20th century. It received a scarcely needed but no doubt welcome boost in the 1980s with the publication of a series of cartoon books by Peter Mayle and Gray Jolliffe featuring a penis-like character called 'Wicked Willie'.

Many of these 'name'-euphemisms, and particularly *John Thomas* and *willy*, have a distinct air of the nursery about them. They come into their own when adults are trying to avoid alarming their children – or more likely themselves – with grown-up words for the penis. The care of children is for many people the only context in which they cannot avoid referring to the penis, so it is not surprising that a number of 'penis' euphemisms have the winsomeness apparently considered appropriate in such circumstances. Into this category comes also **ding-a-ling**, dating from the early 1970s, and sometimes shortened to **ding** or altered to **ding-dong**. Its immediate source may have been the notion of the penis swinging like a clapper in a bell, but no doubt it was also influenced by German and Dutch *ding* 'thing', which crossed the Atlantic with immigrants and gave English *dingus* 'gadget, thingummy' (and also occasionally 'penis') (cf. THING p 124). It sounds innocent enough, but when it reared its head in 1972 in the song 'My Ding-a-ling' recorded by Chuck Berry, the BBC banned the record from its programmes. (Apparently in a similar vein is the mainly American **dong**, which emerged in the 1930s and may contain some subliminal memory of Edward Lear's 'Dong with the Luminous Nose' 1877, but in practice it is more of an adult's than a child's word.) Other nursery words for 'penis' are **sausage**, **whistle**, from the general shape of a metal whistle, and **winkle**, which graphically compares the young boy's minimal member with the small spiral shell.

*Sausage* is no doubt mainly a matter of shape (cf. PUD p 129), but its suggestion of meat content ties in with other 'meat' euphemisms used for 'penis'. **Meat** itself in this sense dates back to the 16th century, and seems to have been in continuous use since then, mainly in the context of sexual intercourse. The carnivorous imagery is suggestive of red-blooded virility. (See also MEAT 'vagina' (p 137), BEAT ONE'S MEAT (p 85), and MEAT AND TWO VEG (p 132).) Of similar inspiration are **beef**, **mutton** (also used for the 'female genitals', as indeed is *meat*), and **pork**. **Joint** for 'penis' is probably another metaphor from the butcher's shop, but its etymology is uncertain.

## Some other miscellaneous colloquial 'penis' circumlocutions:

**dork** an American coinage of the 1960s. Its origins are not clear; it might be an alteration of *dirk* 'dagger' (the phallic imagery is obvious), and no doubt *dick* 'penis' is in the background. The majority of its current usage is in the extended sense 'fool' (a common semantic development of 'penis' words)

**gadget** see TOOL (p 130)

**hampton** short for *hampton wick*, rhyming slang for *prick*; see WICK (p 130)

**joy stick** a reapplication, for fairly obvious reasons, of *joy stick* 'aircraft control column', with a reinforcing rhyme on *prick*

**key** from the notion of inserting the penis into the vagina, like a key into a keyhole (see KEYHOLE p 136)

**knob** or **nob** apparently in circulation since at least the 19th century, and its euphemistic status is at best dubious; it has a vividness and a forthright monosyllabicness that do not suit it to circumlocution. The source of the metaphor is presumably the glans penis, not the entire organ

**length** an erect penis, thought of in terms of its extended size. Most often encountered in the expression *slip someone a length*, i.e. (of a man) to have sex with someone

**middle leg** the euphemizing of the penis as a 'limb' of the body has a long history (see MEMBER p 126), but *middle leg* seems to date from no earlier than the World War I period. An alternative form is *third leg*. Cf. SHORT ARM (p 129)

**old man** dating from the turn of the 20th century. Not, as might be supposed, a female usage, from *old man* 'husband', but a male one, generally referring to the unerect penis

**pecker** a mainly American usage, dating from around the turn of the 20th century. It may have arisen out of some mental link between *cock* 'male chicken' (that 'pecks' for food) and the taboo *cock* 'penis'. It appears to be quite distinct in origin from the British *keep one's pecker up* 'maintain one's courage', where *pecker* probably equals 'beak', with the notion of 'keeping one's nose in the air, holding one's head up high'

**pencil** a fairly obvious visual metaphor ('long thin object'), first recorded in 1937, oblivious to the etymological connection between *penis* and *pencil* (*pencil* comes ultimately from Latin *penicillus*, a diminutive form of *penis*)

**plonker** a word of uncertain history. It originally turned up as a dialect term for anything spectacularly large, and was commandeered by Australian services' slang in the first half of the 20th century for an 'explosive shell'. Its use for 'fool' dates from the mid 1960s, but was popularized by the character Del Boy in the 1980s BBC sitcom *Only Fools and Horses*. It appears to predate its use for 'penis', but as the more normal semantic progression is from 'penis' to 'fool', this may be a misleading impression created by lack of early written evidence

**pud** like the now largely obsolete *pudding*, of which it is an abbreviation, used mainly in the expression *pull one's pud/pudding* 'masturbate'. The basis of the metaphor is the 'sausage' type of pudding (as in *black pudding*), not the 'dessert' (see also SAUSAGE p 128)

**rod** largely an American term for the 'penis,' dating from around the turn of the 20th century. As the imagery suggests, it is generally applied to the erect penis

**schlong** a Yiddish term for 'penis,' introduced into American English in the mid 20th century. It is descended from a Middle High German word for 'serpent', exploiting the same Freudian imagery as SNAKE

**short arm** as with MIDDLE LEG, an image based on the notion of an additional limb. Its use in the military euphemism *short-arm inspection* 'inspection for venereal disease' (see p 208) was partially inspired by *small-arms inspection* (small arms are pistols, rifles, etc)

**snake** Freud's analogy between the penis and a snake is lexicalized as *snake* in American Black English. But among British and Australian speakers its best-known context is **one-eyed trouser snake**, a coinage of the Australian comedian Barry Humphries. See also SYPHON THE PYTHON (p 175)

**third leg** see MIDDLE LEG

**tool** an ancient usage, dating from at least the mid 16th century. The notion of the penis as something with which a man goes to work is also exploited in *gadget*, IMPLEMENT, and INSTRUMENT

**weapon** the oldest of all 'penis' euphemisms still in general use, dating from the Anglo-Saxon period. The persistence of the metaphor would no doubt be regarded as highly significant by psychologists

**wick** generally taken to be short for *Hampton Wick*, rhyming slang for *prick*, which is also abbreviated to *hampton*. Hampton Wick is a locality in SW London, opposite Kingston-upon-Thames on the west bank of the Thames. **Wick** does not have much currency as an independent synonym for *penis*; it mainly occurs in the expressions DIP ONE'S WICK 'copulate' (see p 71) and *get on someone's wick* 'annoy someone'

**yard** a euphemism in very common usage between the 14th and the 18th century, but now obsolete. It made no extravagant claims: the metaphor is based on another now disused sense of *yard*, 'rod, stick, staff', so there is no implication of 'three feet long'. The comparison between an '(erect) penis' and a stick goes back at least to classical times (Latin *virga*, literally 'rod', was also used for 'penis'). See also ROD (p 129)

# Testicles

Compared with the penis, the testicles are relatively little euphemized. Among the items available for avoiding the technical *testicles* and *testes* and the still taboo *balls* and *bollocks* are:

**acorns** see NUTS

**cojones** an importation from Spanish, where *cojon* means 'testicle' (it is related to the long obsolete English *cullion* 'testicle'). It was originally taken over, in the 1930s, in the metaphorical sense 'courage'; there are no records of its literal use before the 1960s

**fry** a euphemism for the testicle of an animal, particularly a lamb, cooked as food. The metaphor is from the literal 'frying' of the dish, not from any tenuous connection with *fry* as 'offspring'. Cf. PRAIRIE OYSTER

**glands** a classically vague euphemism – there are after all lots of other glands in the male body, never mind the female body. It seems to have been particularly popular in newspaper English in the 1920s and 1930s, when editors dared not even print the medically respectable *testicles*. A slightly more explicit alternative was **sex glands**

**gonad** a much more technical word than *testicle*, but nevertheless some colloquial euphemistic use in the late 20th century. It received a considerable boost from Buster Gonad, a character with extraordinarily large testicles in the comic magazine *Viz*

**nuts** a usage apparently dating from the early years of the 20th century, and fairly obvious in its visual imagery. It is more commonly used to replace *balls*! as an exclamation than in strictly anatomical contexts, but cf. *get one's nuts off* 'copulate to the point of ejaculation'. *Acorns* was no doubt similarly inspired; it is probably just a coincidence that Latin *glans*, from which we get *gland*, meant 'acorn'

**orchestras** short for *orchestra stalls*, British rhyming slang for 'balls'

**peculiar members** a bizarre testicular euphemism coined by the American lexicographer Noah Webster for his bowdlerized version of the Bible, published in 1833. For example, he rendered Leviticus 21:20, 'hath his stones broken' in the Authorized Version, as 'have his peculiar members broken' (quoted in Hugh Rawson, *A Dictionary of Euphemisms and Other Doubletalk* 1981). *Peculiar* in this instance actually means 'own personal', not 'odd', so the general drift is intended to be much the same as PRIVATE PARTS. Cf. MEMBER (p 126)

**pills** from a more general substitution of *pill* for *ball* that emerged around the turn of the 20th century, probably by reference back to the ultimate source of *pill*, Latin *pila* 'ball'

**plums** from their shape and perhaps also their pinkness

**prairie oysters** an American and Canadian term for the testicles of a calf served as food. *Oyster* is presumably a reference to the testicles' status as a delicacy, and also to their roughly oval shape, similar to that of oysters. (The French, incidentally, call animal testicles used as food *rognons blancs*, literally 'white kidneys')

**rocks** an Americanism, first recorded in 1948, and used almost exclusively in the expression *get one's rocks off* 'copulate to the point of ejaculation'

**stones** an obviously similar inspiration to *rocks*, but the two could scarcely be more different in history and usage. It dates from the Anglo-Saxon period, but by the 20th century it had virtually died out (the *Oxford English Dictionary* described it in 1917 as 'obsolete except in vulgar use')

On the euphemisms for testicular protection worn by sportsmen, see p 154. A player struck a paralysing blow in that area is often delicately said to have been **winded**.

A residue of genital euphemisms refer to the penis and the testicles considered together, as a unit. Some stress the extreme value of these particular organs, to both the man and his partner: into this category come the American **jewels**, and the extended forms **family jewels**, also American in origin (it is first recorded in 1946) but now well known in Britain, and **crown jewels**. (Yiddish *schmuck* 'penis' is descended from German *Schmuck* 'ornament, jewellery', but when it passed into American slang use in the late 19th century it was only in the further extended sense 'idiot'.) Others use food as a metaphor for the penis and testicles: the underlying meaning of **meat and two veg** becomes clear once you know that MEAT is a euphemism for 'penis' (see p 128); and the relative newcomer **lunchbox** supposedly contains a sausage and two Scotch eggs: 'This didn't deter *News of the Screws* editor Patsy Chapman from creeping in and grabbing Kelvin by his lunchbox while he was listening to Mr Major's blandishments,' *Private Eye* 1992.

The relative size of the genitals is euphemized by two adjectives: the genteel **endowed**, which views them as a gift of nature (bountiful or otherwise), and the rather franker **hung**, which is based on their pendulousness. Both are most commonly encountered qualified by *well*, indicating admirably large size. *Well-endowed* is first recorded in 1951. *Well-hung* is much longer established, dating back to the mid 19th century. Also occasionally used in the same sense is **equipped**: 'He says he has been well endowed and you must know this means "heavily equipped sexually",' *Maledicta* 1983 (cf. EQUIPMENT p 124).

**basket** male homosexuals' argot for the penis and testicles as displayed by revealingly tight trousers

**cluster** similarly used for the genitals as outlined by the trousers, but not a homosexual usage

**jock** an ancient term, now best known in the compound *jockstrap* 'garment for holding the male genitals in place during strenuous activity'. Originally, in the 18th century, it was applied to both the male and the female genitalia, but in the course of the 19th century it became exclusively a male-oriented word. Its origins are unknown, but there is presumably some connection with the obsolete slang *jockum* 'penis'

**load** an American male homosexuals' term for the male genitals

**vitals** a very vague term, whose use dates back to the early 17th century. Etymologically it denotes 'the organs essential to supporting life', but it has been applied to a range of internal structures, including the viscera and the brains. Amongst its referents are the male genitals, and sometimes more specifically the testicles

**wedding tackle** male equipment essential to the consummation of a marriage; commonly used in contexts of protecting the genitals from untoward damage

**wobbly bits** a unisex euphemism for those parts of the body that may continue to move when the remainder has come to rest: in the case of males, the genitals. Cf. NAUGHTY BITS (p 124)

The question of which trouser leg accommodates the genitals is one which requires very delicate verbal handling by gentlemen's tailors. The traditional way of getting round this conversational obstacle at fittings is to ask 'Does sir **dress** to the right or to the left?'

On *expose oneself* and other euphemisms for the public display of male genitalia, see p 158.

# Female Genitals

The female genitals are the most difficult part of the body to name. Many people, of both sexes, go through life without doing so: it is not beyond human ingenuity to invent linguistic strategies for skirting round the subject if it should come into view. Even in circumstances which make it very difficult to avoid, such as parents talking to very young children about their bodies, about urination, etc, a way out can be found (the results of a survey released in 1992 suggested that many mothers do not use a name for their daughters' genitals).

*Cunt* and *twat* are impossibly taboo, especially in their literal sense. At the other end of the spectrum, **vagina** would until comparatively recently have been viewed as too much of a doctor's or anatomist's word for general use, but there are now signs that, like its male counterpart *penis*, it may be escaping from this specialized enclave, and becoming available as lay euphemism (in the process its meaning has broadened out, from 'passage from the cervix to the vulva' to 'external female genitals in general').

The number of synonyms for the 'female genitals' outnumbers those for 'male genitals' (by a ratio of 6:5, according to figures given by Keith Allan and Kate Burridge, *Euphemism and Dysphemism* 1991, p 96), and many of them serve a euphemistic function.

Of them, the majority that rely on the classic euphemistic defence, vagueness, are so vague that they can be used indiscriminately for both the female and the male genitals (*affair*, *equipment*, *instrument*, *thing*, etc; see p 124). But the French **belle chose** (literally 'beautiful thing') for specifically 'female genitals' enjoyed some currency in English in former centuries (note the additional disguise of the foreign language).

The most widely used of the formal, respectable class of verbal subterfuge has always been **pudendum**, a Latinism of admirable obscurity introduced into English probably as early as the 14th century. It is a derivative of the Latin verb *pudere* 'be ashamed', so etymologically it denotes 'that of which one should be ashamed' – a suitably defensive and apologetic term for organs which we are indoctrinated to associate with wrong-doing (German genital vocabulary – *Schambein* 'pubis', literally 'shamebone'; *Schamglied* 'penis', literally 'shame-limb'; *Schamlippen* 'vulva', literally 'shamelips'; *Schamteile* 'genitals', literally 'shameparts' – is even more guilt-ridden). Technically it is a unisex term, but in practice it is virtually always used with reference to the female genitals. Reflecting a general tendency to regard the genitals as a multiple concept, it is mainly used in the plural form, *pudenda*.

Terms at the more colloquial end of the spectrum fall into a number of distinct categories. Amongst the most notable is the comparison with small furry animals. The general inspiration for this is of course the female pubic hair, which forms the most obviously visible adjunct to the genitals on a woman's body, and is therefore fair linguistic game for a metaphorical transfer to the genitals themselves. Both **cat** and **kitty** are in current use in this sense, but the commonest present-day (apparent) animal 'vagina' euphemism is the catlike **pussy** (first recorded in 1880). 'Apparent' because its origins may in fact have been far from feline. It has been suggested that the short form **puss** may be of independent Germanic origin, quite distinct from that of *puss(y)* 'cat'. Low German had the word *pūse* for 'vulva', and Old Norse had *púss* 'pocket, pouch', so it is quite possible that *pussy* 'female genitals' is in origin not an 'animal' metaphor but a 'store-place' metaphor. It is not inconceivable that it could even represent an alteration of **purse**, itself used as a euphemism for *cunt*, and, like the American **pocket-book**, inspired both by the appearance of the female genitals and by the notion of them as a 'store of wealth'. But either way, there is no doubt that its use must have been strongly reinforced by the image of a furry cat, and the word is intimately associated in the public subconscious with cats (helped along by almost weekly *pussy* double entendres perpetrated by the character Mrs Slocombe in the BBC television sitcom *Are You Being Served*? 1972–1985). The theory that *pussy* is short for *pussycat*, rhyming slang for *twat*, is based on this association.

Another seeming zoological metaphor is **beaver** (a 'hot beaver shot' in a pornographic magazine is an explicit photograph of the female genitals). First recorded in 1922, this again is a transference of a term for the 'pubic hair' or 'pubic area', but in this case the immediate source of that figure of speech is a still earlier *beaver* 'beard'. On the face of it, it would seem likely that 'beard' was inspired by the hairy wood-gnawing animal, but in fact no direct connection has ever been established between the two, so the ultimate origins of *beaver* 'female genitals' remain uncertain.

The euphemistic use of **bun** and **bunny** seems still to have some currency (it goes back at least to the late 18th century), although they are under challenge from the semantic proximity of BUNS 'buttocks' (see p 141). They are a reminder of the embarrassment caused in former centuries by the now archaic *coney* 'rabbit', which was generally pronounced to rhyme with the possibly related (and now obsolete) *cunny* 'female genitals'. The modern rhyming of *coney* with *phoney* appears to be the result of a conscious early 19th-century phonological clean-up.

Another fairly obvious source of metaphor is the configuration of the vulva, as an indentation or cut. This has produced a whole range of euphemisms, from **slit** (first recorded as long ago as 1648) through **cleft**, **gap**, **gash** (first recorded in 1893) and **nook** (probable source of NOOKIE 'sexual intercourse'; see p 75) to the more refined, but rare, **alcove**. Also exploiting the 'split' metaphor are the nursery coinages **front bottom** and **bottom in front**, which draw an analogy between the gap between the buttocks and the gap between the lips of the vulva. A related notion is of the genitals as a 'hole'. The use of **hole** itself in this sense dates back at least to the 16th century. A punning alternative, with an allusion to the 'sacredness' of the genitalia, is **holy of holies**, while **keyhole** recalls the use of KEY for 'penis' (see p 128). The idea of a hole also underlies **buttonhole** (**button** in this context is a euphemism for *clitoris*) and the Australian **golden doughnut**, first recorded in 1972 – the doughnut is evidently of the American ring-shaped variety, not the traditional British bun.

The notion of the vagina as a receptacle is realized in the mainly American **box**, a mid 20th-century coinage (Tok Pisin, a Melanesian pidgin of Papua New Guinea, has *bokis*, an alteration of *box*, for 'female genitals'); **boat** (in this image, the clitoris is euphemized as **the man in the rowboat**); **cockpit**, not exactly the subtlest play on words in the history of the English language; **nest**, or in full **bird's nest**, in which the image of the receptacle is combined with that of the shagginess of the pubic hair; and **oven**, which has additional connotations of the heat of passion. See also PURSE and POCKETBOOK (p 134).

Physiological position determines two or three important euphemisms. The fact that the external female genitals are on the anterior part of the body, as opposed to the posterior (with connotations also of vaginal rather than anal sexual intercourse), underlies **front door**, **front garden**, and **front parlour** (the more direct **front passage** contrasts explicitly with BACK PASSAGE 'rectum' – see p 141). See also BOTTOM IN FRONT (above). Their location in the lower part of the body inspires vague circumlocutions such as **down below, downstairs**, and **down there**: 'I discovered that lots of women view themselves as abnormal "down there". We don't really know what we look like and are very frightened of being exposed in that way,' *Observer* 1992. See also LOW COUNTRIES (p 123).

Location is also highly relevant to the use of **tail** in this context. It began, not surprisingly, as a euphemism for 'buttocks' (see p 142), but in the latter part of the 20th century it has undergone a specialization of application to the female anal-genital area considered as an object of male lust – originally, presumably, from the point of view of rear penetration.

Foodstuffs are an important source of female-genital euphemism – it does not take a Sigmund Freud to work out the implications of that. The vagina is a **cabbage** in modern American Black English slang (an image supposedly based on appearance), or a **cake**; it used also to be a **jelly roll** (originally and literally a cylindrical cake containing jam); the hymen is a **cherry** (a usage mainly associated with expressions denoting loss of virginity, such as *lose one's cherry*, which emerged in America in the 1920s); the external genitals in general are a **honey pot** (a usage dating back to the early 18th century); in modern American slang the labia majora are one's **muffin** (a usage possibly in conscious response to BUNS for 'buttocks' – see p 141); and more carnivorously, the female genitals are also euphemized as **meat**, a usage of 17th-century vintage, and as **mutton** (to 'hawk one's mutton' is to work as a prostitute) – both also applied to the penis (see p 128).

The pubic hair, which indirectly inspires many 'animal' euphemisms for the female genitals (see p 134), provides a synonym for 'female genitals' itself in **muff** (a 17th-century coinage), whose starting point as a metaphor is a resemblance between the female pubic hair and a fur muff (a *muff-diver* is someone who practises cunnilingus). The rhyming **puff** seems to rely on a resemblance between the pubic hair and a powder puff; it is mainly used in the expression *powder one's puff*, a more risqué substitute for the euphemism *powder one's nose* 'urinate'. The modern American **ace of spades** 'female genitals' may likewise be at least partly inspired by the roughly heart-shaped outline of the female pubic hair. The genitals as consumed by a cunnilinguist are sometimes euphemized as **hair pie** (with a pun on *hare*).

A very genteel verbal disguise is provided by the now rather dated **feminine gender** (the underlying notion of identifying the genitalia with abstract sexuality also inspired SEX for 'genitals' – see p 124). More highly embroidered variations on the femininity theme are **Lady Jane**, which achieved a certain notoriety from its use in D H Lawrence's *Lady Chatterley's Lover* 1928 ('In her maiden-hair were forget-me-nots and woodruff. "That's you in all your glory!" he said. "Lady Jane, at her wedding with John Thomas",' and so in the same vein), and the less common **lady flower**, **lady star**, and just plain **lady**.

The use of **fanny** for the 'female genitals' dates roughly from the middle of the 19th century. Its origins are not clear. The banal truth is perhaps that it is simply an application of the female name (a phenomenon common in the case of the penis and male forenames – see p 127), but if it is older than the written record shows, it could have been inspired by Fanny Hill, the sexually adventurous heroine of John Cleland's *Memoirs of a Woman of Pleasure* 1749. It is exclusively British usage, and in America, where *fanny* means 'buttocks' (see p 141), it can cause consternation. On the use of the same term for 'female genitals' and 'buttocks' see TAIL (p 142).

More recent than *fanny* is **snatch**, which emerged around the turn of the 20th century. Perhaps it arose from the notion of a quickly 'snatched' sexual encounter – a swift grope, as it were – but in truth its origins are lost in history.

The use of **treasure** for 'female genitals' recalls the use of JEWELS for 'male genitals' (see p 132) – the owner's most valuable and precious possession.

**Garden** for 'female genitals' exploits the twin images of a 'place for relaxation and pleasure' (made more explicit in **garden of Eden**) and 'cultivation' metaphorically associated with sexual intercourse. There may also be some subliminal reference to **grass**, an American euphemism for 'female pubic hair'.

Rhyming slang in this area is based, unsurprisingly, on *cunt*. Best established is **grumble and grunt**, often shortened to **grumble**, followed by **sharp and blunt**.

Of a somewhat different order of euphemism is **the monosyllable**, which was in widespread use in the 18th and 19th centuries as a polite substitute for the word *cunt*. Not so much euphemistic as eulogistic was the elaborated version, **the divine monosyllable**.

Vaginal secretions produced before and during copulation are euphemized by the more luridly buttock-heaving school of soft-core pornographers as **love juice**.

# BUTTOCKS

In the Old English period, *arse* was a perfectly respectable word. But over the centuries it has gradually gone to the bad. The late 17th century saw the start of its decline, and it is now firmly taboo. It was probably around 1700 that *ass* began to be used as a euphemistic substitution for *arse*. This still survives as the American form, but it has long since lost its euphemistic force. (It probably also, incidentally, played a part in the introduction of the word *donkey* in the 18th century, to replace the by then rather rude *ass*.)

The majority of modern polite alternatives exploit the idea of the buttocks' position relative to the rest of the body, as being below or behind. The best-established of the 'below' words is of course **bottom**. The first record of this anatomical use is from no earlier than 1794, but as Joseph Shipley said in *In Praise of English* 1977 (quoted by Hugh Rawson in his *Dictionary of Euphemism and Other Doublestalk* 1981), the fact that Shakespeare transformed a character called Bottom into an ass (in *A Midsummer Night's Dream* 1594) may suggest that it is considerably older than that (although of course this interpretation depends on *ass* for *arse* being older than we know too). As is inevitable with euphemisms, *bottom* has lost some of its protective power over the centuries, and it is now euphemized itself in the abbreviation **b t m**, first recorded in 1919. Personal names of the type *Ramsbottom* and *Shufflebottom* (which are based on an earlier use of *bottom* for 'valley') can cause embarrassment, and the *-bottom* element is often disguised as *-botham*; and in the case of *Sidebottom* further camouflage is provided by the mincing pronunciation /sidibə'tam/. The nursery form **botty** is first recorded in print in 1874.

Even older than *bottom* is **backside**, which dates from around 1500. It is firmly in the colloquial levels of the language, but it is available as a euphemism. Much further up the scale of mealy-mouthedness is **behind**, which probably originated in the latter part of the 18th century. In a classic euphemistic move this was soon cloaked in the decent obscurity of a foreign language: **derriere** (from French *derrière*, literally 'behind,' first recorded in 1774). Both were probably inspired by *posteriors* 'buttocks', an early 17th-century coinage which itself was based on late Latin *posteriora* 'buttocks', literally 'behind parts'. The English usage evolved in the 19th century from the plural to the present-day singular **posterior**. Other exploitations of the 'behind' and 'below' themes include the rare **after part**, the vague **end**, the slightly more explicit **latter end** or **latter part**, the related **rear end**, often shortened to simply **rear** (first recorded in 1796), and the nautical **stern** (a metaphor dating back to the 17th century). **Hindquarters** is generally applied to the rear part of animals, but there is some euphemistic use with reference to the human buttocks too (cf. RUMP p 142).

Another popular ploy is to concentrate on the buttocks' role in sitting. **Seat** in this sense goes back to the early 17th century (the 18th and 19th centuries used the coy elaboration **seat of honour**). The rather juvenile **sit-upon** and **sit-me-down** are much more recent coinages, first recorded in 1920 and 1933 respectively: 'The "little man" was enormous, bulging over a small stool at his doorway, smoking a hubble-bubble. He rose affably and Mrs Stitch immediately sat in the place he vacated. "Hot sit-upon," she remarked,' Evelyn Waugh 1955.

**Buttocks** itself dates from around 1300. It is probably a descendant of Old English *buttuc* 'round slope' – a metaphor derived therefore from shape rather than position. This in turn would have been a diminutive form of an unrecorded *butt*, which apparently originally meant 'strip of land'. The relationship of this with present-day *butt* 'buttocks' is far from clear. That usage emerged around the middle of the 15th century, roughly contemporaneously with *butt* 'thicker end, stump', but a direct connection with *butt* 'strip of land' cannot be demonstrated. Perhaps they are the same word, perhaps they are unrelated, or maybe *butt* is an abbreviation of *buttock*. Whichever, in modern usage *butt* (which is confined to American English) is decidedly non-euphemistic. The rather straight-laced *buttocks*, on the other hand, clearly operates as a socially acceptable alternative to *arse* and its ilk, but in ordinary colloquial speech it would usually be replaced by something less formal, such as *bottom*.

The best-established contributions of rhyming slang to 'buttock'-vocabulary are **Khyber**, short for *Khyber pass*, and **bottle**, short for *bottle and glass*, both rhyming with *arse*; and **kingdom**, short for *kingdom come*, rhyming with *bum*.

The anus and rectum have their own small clutch of particular euphemisms. The latter, both on street corners and in doctors' consulting rooms, regularly goes under the discreet name **back passage** (a less common alternative is **back way**). The circularity of the anus is the basis of the metaphor in **ring** (first recorded in 1949), and also in euphemistic application of *eye* in **second eye** (an American homosexuals' usage). Australians use the rather charming **freckle**. And from the world of (approximately) rhyming slang comes **elephant and castle** for *arsehole* (from the name of an area of London to the southeast of Waterloo).

## Some other buttocky circumlocutions:

**bum** in British English probably still too 'rude', even if only jokingly so, to count as a euphemism, but milder in effect in America. It is an ancient word, dating from the 14th century, but its ultimate origins are obscure

**buns** an Americanism, which emerged around 1960. Presumably from the hemispherical shape, but there may also be some connection with the use of *bun* as a euphemism for the female genitals (see p 135)

**cheeks** the basis of the metaphor is obvious – two round paired symmetrical parts. It dates back at least to the late 16th century: 'spied both his great cheekes full of small blisters,' Thomas Deloney *c*.1600. The use of the singular *cheek* for each half of the buttocks is perhaps more mainstream, less euphemistic than the plural usage

**duff** an American usage, probably of military origin. Hugh Rawson, in his *Dictionary of Euphemisms and Other Doubletalk* 1981, conjectures that it may be short for the *duffel bag* on which soldiers often sit

**fanny** in British English used chiefly for 'female genitals' (see p 138), but to Americans exclusively the 'buttocks'. In early usage (it seems to have emerged in the early 20th century) it was distinctly a vulgarism, but over the decades it has slipped from under its taboo, and it is now available as a euphemism. The 'buttocks' use presumably arose out of the 'female genitals' use – the tendency to linguistic confusion between the two is not uncommon (see TAIL p 142)

**fleshy part of the thigh** a circumlocution most famously applied to the shooting of Lord Methuen in the buttocks during the Boer War. As R W Holder points out in the *Oxford Dictionary of Euphemisms* 2003, the main reason for the delicacy was to avoid any suggestion that his lordship was not facing the enemy at the time

**fundament** an ancient term for the buttocks, or more specifically the anus, dating back to the 13th century, and now firmly in the category of pompous euphemism. Etymologically it denotes the 'lower part', the 'bottom part'

**heinie** an American usage of fairly recent coinage, also spelled **hiney**. It is probably an alteration of *behind*, perhaps influenced by the already long-established *Heinie*, an American slang term for a 'German'

**honkies** another Americanism, not quite so polite as *heinie*, but available as a euphemism. An alternative spelling is **hunkies**, revealing its probable origins in *hunkers* 'haunches'

**keister** originally an American slang term for a 'satchel', 'bag', or 'burglar's tool-case', and also a 'safe, strong box'. It may well be that its use for 'buttocks' (first recorded in 1931) comes from the use of the rectum as a hiding place (e.g. for illegal drugs)

**rump** a usage dating back to the mid 15th century. Its core application is to the rear part of the body of animals and birds, near the tail, but it can also be used by extension of human buttocks (cf. HINDQUARTERS p 140)

**Sunday face** an ironic comment of some sort, perhaps inspired by the earlier Scottish use of *Sunday face* for a 'sanctimonious expression'

**tail** first used (for fairly obvious reasons) for 'buttocks' as long ago as the early 14th century, but no longer generally available as a euphemism, at least in British English – it is commoner in America. In modern usage it is for the most part either restricted to metaphorical expressions (such as *work one's tail off*), or it has side-slipped into connotations of the female anal-genital area as an erogenous zone (on the interchangeability of terms for the buttocks and female genitals see also FANNY pp 138 and 141, and BOTTOM IN FRONT p 136)

**tochus** an Americanism, first recorded in 1914. It is an adaptation of Yiddish *tokhes*, and is spelled in a variety of other ways, including **tuchus** and **tokus**

**tush** also mainly American, but apparently some Australian usage too. First recorded in 1962, it may be an alteration of TOCHUS. It also comes in the diminutive forms **tushie** and **tushy**

# BREASTS

English-speakers of the modern era have problems with breasts. Even in purely functional contexts we may seek to avoid the word (references to breast-feeding, for instance, may be got around by talking about '**nursing** mothers'). And any whiff of their other role as erogenous zones has us reaching fast for terms less direct than *breasts*. The taboo is in some ways a curious one: it is not as if *breasts* were in any sense vulgar, as other tabooed terms for body parts are, but rather perhaps that it has power as a word to be used privately and intimately, and therefore is embarrassing if generally bandied about. Many of its synonyms are too earthy to be available as euphemisms (*tits*, for example, *titties*, *knockers*), but there are many halfway-houses to choose from.

The main representative of the discreet end of the spectrum is **bust**. This originally meant (and still does mean) in English a 'sculpture of the head and shoulders', but Italian *busto*, from which it ultimately derives, denotes 'upper body', and this sense began to come into use in English in the 18th century. Until well into the 19th century it could be used of male chests as well as female ones, but gradually the modern specialization of meaning hardened. Its commonest context is perhaps dressmaking and fashion, in which women (and men) who would not otherwise refer to breasts are forced to find an inoffensive term for discussing measurements. (It is interesting that the derivative *busty* 'having large breasts', first recorded in 1944, is decidedly non-euphemistic.)

Equally respectable is **bosom**. This is an ancient word, originally meaning 'front part of the body, chest, regardless of sex' (etymologically it may denote the 'space encompassed by the two arms'). Its euphemistic use for 'breasts' seems to have sidled surreptitiously into the language in the past 150 years. Arising from this, and somewhat less mealy-mouthed, is the use of the plural **bosoms** for 'breasts'. In case any embarrassment should still be caused, this can be further disguised phonetically as /bə'zoomz/, realized in print as **bazooms**. An even more impenetrable camouflage is provided by the back-slang version, **mosob**.

Other polite ways of referring to the breasts include **chest** (as in 'a woman with a big chest'; safely androgynous, but the bizarre **chests** rather gives the game away); **front** (exploiting the classic euphemistic strategy of vagueness, and mainly used in ambiguous contexts where it could plausibly also be interpreted as 'front part of a garment, covering the chest or breasts'); the peculiar **lungs** (from their physical contiguity and a passing resemblance in outline); the biological-obfuscatory **mammary glands** (*gland* is a word beloved of circumlocutors); and the graphic **shelf** (connoting breasts prominent and substantial enough to rest a plate on). In a more poetic vein is **globes**, which assumes relative largeness.

At the more colloquial end of the spectrum come the originally American **boobs** (first recorded in 1949; originally apparently a male usage with strong overtones of sexual appreciation, but more recently, increasingly used by women as a neutral (but perhaps excessively winsome) euphemism); **boobies** (also originally American, and the probable source of *boobs*; *boobies* itself is very likely an alteration of the dialectal *bubbies* 'breasts'); the almost exclusively male **bristols** (first recorded in 1961; short for *Bristol Cities*, British rhyming slang for 'titties', after the name of Bristol City Football Club); **charlies** (a use of the male forename, which dates back to the mid 19th century); the Australian **norks** (an early 1960s coinage, allegedly inspired by the picture of well-endowed cows on the packaging of the products of Norco Co-operative Ltd, a New South Wales butter manufacturer); and the simple **pair** (impeccably vague, but instantly interpretable in – usually admiring – context).

Other circumlocutions include **big brown eyes** (possibly an allusion to the darker-coloured nipples); the American **headlights** (likewise exploiting the ideas of duality and prominence, and based on the large prominent headlights on cars of the 1940s); and **wobbly bits** (a term also used to euphemize the male genitalia). A range of fruit names have been used as stand-ins for *breasts*, of which the most firmly established are **grapefruit**, **melons**, and **water melons**.

English is well equipped with adjectives describing women with large breasts, many of them decidedly flowery. In some cases a general fatness is implied, but with an underlying emphasis on the breasts. **Buxom** is the key word here. It originally meant 'obedient', but it evolved semantically via 'biddable, obliging', 'lively, jolly' and 'healthily plump and vigorous' to (of a woman) 'large-breasted'. **Rubenesque** (inspired by the plump, large-breasted women painted by

Rubens) comes into the same category; it dates from the early 20th century. **Junoesque** on the other hand (after the stately Roman goddess Juno) can be a discreet way of saying simply 'large-breasted'. At the other end of the formality spectrum, expressions used of men to denote large genitals are applied to women with reference to their breasts: **well-endowed** is a particular case in point, but **well-hung** is also used in the same way. Another *well*-term applied to large-breastedness is **well-built**.

Given the general preference in modern Western society (with occasional departures) for the hourglass female shape, with large breasts, narrow waist and prominent hips and buttocks, it is not surprising that a range of terms has evolved to refer discreetly to this set of characteristics. Some of them seem to stress particularly the breasts: **voluptuous**, for instance, and **pneumatic**, apparently introduced by T S Eliot in 1919 in the phrase 'promise of pneumatic bliss', and suggestive of artificial inflation. Cryptic references to a woman's **physique**, too, can be taken as meaning her breasts. Most, though, are all-embracing. Both the delightfully vague **shapely** (flat-chested women have a shape too) and the pseudo-technical **curvaceous** (first recorded in 1936, in reference to the famously shapely Mae West) come into this category. The use of **curves** to euphemize the prominence of breasts and hips dates back to the mid 19th century, and it has also produced the adjective **curvesome**: 'Mazeppa, traditionally played by a curvesome female,' *Time* 1940. The word **figure** in female contexts must be interpreted not as the entire form of the body, but as a reference to the breasts, waist, and hips and their relative size. To 'have a good figure' is to have fairly large breasts and hips, defined by a thin waist; **a fine figure of a woman** expresses the same idea in a more pompous way. If a woman 'loses her figure', the desirable harmony between the three elements has gone – perhaps the breasts have sagged, or the thinness of the waist has been obliterated by an expanding abdomen. **Full** in the context of the body as a whole tends to be merely a euphemism for 'fat' (see FULLER FIGURE p 149), but when applied to breasts it is a decidedly positive term, implying a sensuous largeness. The use of **vital statistics** for 'measurements round the breasts, waist and hips' dates from around 1950 (its original sense was 'data relating to significant events in human beings' lives').

The use of **cleavage** for the gap between a woman's breasts, especially as revealed by a low-cut dress, dates from the mid 1940s. That too was the era of the **sweater girl**, a term for a young woman with large breasts, which were made more apparent by the wearing of a tight sweater (it was popularized by its application to the US film star Lana Turner).

So shy were 19th-century gentlefolk of referring directly to the breasts that rather than ask for the 'breast' of a chicken or turkey at table, they would request **white meat** – a usage which survives to today. (A similar sensitivity about *leg* and *thigh* resulted in **dark meat**.)

# BALDNESS

The loss of head hair is a decidedly sensitive subject for men. Discussion of it in the presence of one afflicted is likely to avoid the frank *bald* (which may be descended from an unrecorded Old English *ball* 'white patch') in favour of more discreet verbal hairpieces.

A slight reduction in candour can be achieved by calling a man **balding** (first recorded in 1938) rather than *bald*, implying that the process of going bald is far from complete. In practice there is no hard-and-fast criterion, in terms of percentage of hairless scalp, for pronouncing a man 'bald'. Someone with anything less than a completely bare crown could equally well be termed 'balding' or 'bald', opening the way to the euphemistic use of *balding*.

More circumlocutious still is **thinning**, as in 'thinning hair' and 'He's thinning a bit', and the related **thin**, as in 'thin hair' and 'He's getting a bit thin on top': 'When he [Michael Heseltine] tosses it back these days, you can see he is beginning to go rather thin on top,' *Guardian* 1991. The usage, which dates from the mid 19th century, exploits the literal meaning 'not dense' to suggest a scarcely noticeable diminution in the amount of hair, while in practice being used in cases where bare patches of scalp are distinctly visible.

When matters have gone beyond mere reduction of hairs per square inch to decided areas of hairlessness, one can turn to **receding**. This can be used with reference to the man himself (as in 'I must admit I'm receding a bit'), but its starting point was the expression *receding hair-line*. This implies baldness working its way backwards from the forehead, a condition also euphemized by **high forehead**. When it advances via a side route it can be disguised as a **wide parting**.

Firms which market techniques or preparations for remedying baldness are understandably coy about using the actual word *bald*. The preferred terminology in advertising material is **hair loss**. This is scarcely less frank than *bald* in its denotation, but it functions euphemistically by avoiding the sheer starkness of the word *bald*, and by suggesting a certain scientific detachment.

American politically correct language of the 1980s, 1990s, and 2000s even has a term for 'baldness' – three of them, in fact: **differently hirsute**, **follicularly challenged**, and **hair disadvantaged**.

For euphemisms for *wig*, see p 161.

# UGLINESS

Ugliness is a matter of opinion, not of fact, so the number of euphemisms associated with it is low. If mentioning it would cause offence, the opinion can be left unspoken. But if it must be voiced, and you fight shy of the frank *ugly*, the classic alternative is **homely**. This usage evolved in the late 16th century, apparently from earlier connotations of 'commonplaceness', 'humbleness', and 'lack of sophistication and distinction' associated with 'home'.

**Plain** is perhaps a little too direct to function as a full-fledged euphemism, but it is less brutal than *ugly*. Originally, in the mid 18th century, it was intended to soften the blow of *ugly*, but over the decades its association with 'ugliness' has gradually robbed it of its circumlocutory power. To describe a woman as a *plain Jane* (first recorded in 1912) could not be interpreted as anything other than frankly derogatory.

If *plain* and even *homely* do not wrap the message up sufficiently, an alternative strategy is to use some sort of negative understatement, such as **less attractive**, **not much to look at**, or **unprepossessing**. The politically correct way of expressing 'ugly' is **cosmetically different**.

# FAT

Attitudes to adipose tissue have fluctuated over the centuries – particularly in its role as a yardstick of female sexual attractiveness. One age likes its women more or less fat, the next demands thinness, then fat is back, and so on. At the present time in Western society, under additional pressure from the health lobby, fat is in the doldrums, for men as much as for women, and the past hundred years have seen a proliferation of ingenious and ingratiating ways of avoiding calling a fat person 'fat'. (The adjective *fat* itself, incidentally, has always had a derogatory aspect, going right back to Old English times: an Anglo-Saxon riddle has *Mara ic eom and fættra ðonne amæsted swin, bearg bellende on boc-wuda* 'I am larger and fatter than a pig, a barrow [castrated boar] grunting in the beech-woods,' where the implication of *fat* is clearly 'obese'. But it has also until comparatively recently been available as a neutral or even appreciative term with reference to human beings; it is doubtful if today anyone would exclaim so gleefully 'My fat baby is a great darling!' as Princess Alice did in her *Memoirs* 1864.)

Adjectives denoting 'fatness' can exploit the distancing effect of formal, rhetorical, or even pompous language: **corpulent**, **rotund**, **ample** (as in 'a woman of ample proportions'). Or they can attack the problem from the other end, trivializing fatness with jokey colloquialisms: **chubby**, **roly-poly**, **tubby**. It is a short step from this to insinuating that fatness is a virtue: **comfortable**, **well-built**, **well-covered**, **well-rounded**, **well-upholstered**. **Plump** itself has positive connotations. Other supposed attributes of fat people that have contributed to the 'fat' lexicon are their cheerfulness (if someone is described as 'a **jolly** old man' the automatic assumption is that he is fat) and their sensuality (**cuddly** has become synonymous with *fat*). The comparative mode performs its usual softening role in **larger** ('for the larger figure'), which sounds a lot less bad than *large.*

Many 'fat' euphemisms are more or less sex-linked. In the case of women, these often shade into the more specific 'large-breasted' (e.g. *buxom*, *a fine figure of a woman*, *Rubenesque*; see p 144). Men's blushes are spared with adjectives that could be indulgently interpreted as referring to excess of muscle rather than unsightly fat: **burly**,

**chunky**, **stocky**, **strapping**. Both sexes share **stout** (which barely disguises spreading girth, but is less direct than *fat*) and the curious **big-boned**, which attempts to put the blame for excess size on the skeleton rather than its padding. Similarly unisex is **generously proportioned**; and the politically correct **circumferentially challenged** ('An ad in *The Stage* asking for 17-stone extroverts brought 200 replies from the severely circumferentially challenged,' *Observer Magazine* 1993), **differently sized**, **horizontally challenged**, and **person of size** of course avoid any sexist differentiation. Clothes advertised as 'for the **fuller figure**' will fit fat people – particularly large-breasted women.

## The Topography of Fat

The urge to euphemize fat often homes in on particular parts of the body – especially, of course, the abdomen, but also, in the case of women, the hips and breasts (see p 143):

**bagels** in American English, fatty bulges around the hips and thighs, especially in women. Literal bagels are ring-shaped buns, so the metaphor presumably arose from the resemblance to a ring of fat around the waist, but in specializing its application to women, the centre of reference has shifted sideways to the hips

**bay window** a fat abdomen. A figure of speech comparing the convexity of the window to the bulge of the stomach. It seems to have originated in American English

**brewer's goitre** a man's obese abdomen, as caused by excessive consumption of beer (the image is somewhat lurid, but it probably still counts – just – as a euphemism)

**corporation** a British term for a fat abdomen. The usage dates back to the mid 18th century, and it is generally assumed that it was inspired by the fat bellies that mayors and their corporations acquired through attending too many municipal banquets

**embonpoint** a fat abdomen. French *embonpoint* 'fatness' is a nominalization of the phrase *en bon point* 'in good condition'. English borrowed it in the mid 18th century, delighted to be able to clothe the potbelly in the discreet disguise of a foreign language

**hipsters** an American term equivalent to BAGELS. The usage originated on the West Coast of America. *Hipster* was coined, around 1960, as a term for trousers, skirts, etc that hang from the hips rather than from the waist, but the metaphorical shift to 'bulges of fat around the hips' was an obvious move

**love handles** fatty bulges around the hips. Mainly an American usage, dating from the 1970s. What better way of defusing disapproval for what might otherwise be viewed as a sexual turn-off, than by suggesting that they are useful adjuncts to sexual intercourse? The notion is that oversize hips provide something to hang on to in a clinch

**rubber tire** the American equivalent of SPARE TYRE

**spare tyre** a roll of fat around the waist; a fat abdomen. The inspiration in the shape of the tyre is obvious, but the metaphor also usefully suggests 'something additional', an excrescence that is not part of a person's standard equipment in the fat line. It appears to date back to around 1960 (the first recorded example of it is in an advertisement in *Harper's Bazaar* December 1961: 'The deep diaphragm section slims you . . . That "spare-tyre" has vanished!'). American English also uses *rubber tire*

# The Ages of Fat

The brutal truth is that obesity is caused, in the vast majority of cases, by simply eating too much. One of the ways in which people seek to cover up this unpalatable fact is by ascribing a person's fatness to the age he or she has reached.

**the mature figure** the physique of a fat person, typically female, of middle age or over. A euphemism of the clothing retail industry, which dare not call its customers 'fat'. See also OLDER WOMAN

**middle-age spread** or **middle-aged spread** increase in waist measurement that coincides with the onset of middle age. The term carries derogatory undertones of slothful inactivity that besets those of advancing years. It appears to have originated in the 1930s (*John O'London's* 29 January 1937 carried an advertisement inviting readers to 'join the happy throng who have learnt to control the "middle-age spread" by wearing the . . . supporting belt'). The alternative **middle-age bulge** is sometimes encountered

**the older woman** if a garment is advertised as 'for the older woman', the chances are that its seller is drawing attention not to its restrained, classic style but to its size. The unspoken assumption is that women of middle age and above will be looking for 'large' and 'extra large', and the equation of age with fatness is widely enough accepted to make the euphemism clear. See also MATURE FIGURE

**puppy fat** fatness in children or adolescents. Implicit in the term is the comforting assumption that the fatness will disappear with maturity, when the stage of being a 'puppy' or youngster has passed. It dates back at least to the 1930s

# Weight

It is comforting to substitute the notion of 'weight' for that of 'fat'. To say 'I'm trying to lose weight' is less stark than to say 'I'm trying to lose fat', or even 'I'm trying to become thinner'. If someone becomes fatter, it is polite to say that they have 'put on weight'; and people who are on a diet often call themselves **weight-watchers**, a term which originated as a trademark in the USA in 1960. H G Wells satirized the circumlocution in his story 'The Truth about Pyecraft' 1903. A fat man called Pyecraft, anxious to thin down, took an ancient potion which he was assured would make him lose weight. And that is exactly what happened. He ended up floating around the ceiling (his waistband still the same circumference), and had to put on lead-weighted underwear when he wanted to come down to ground level. As his friend said to him, 'You committed the sin of euphemism. You called it, not Fat, which is just and inglorious, but Weight.'

**overweight** too fat; obese. The adjective *overweight*, in the general sense 'too heavy', dates back to the early 17th century, but its specialized application to excessive fatness did not emerge until the end of the 19th century. Not long afterwards it began to be used as a noun, signifying 'obesity': in August 1917 the *Medical Times* of New York reported 'reduction cures for overweight' (to **reduce** in the sense 'become thinner', which dates from the early 20th century, is the classic dieting euphemism)

**weight-conscious** anxious about obesity; conscious of a need to remain or become thin

**weight gain** becoming fatter (also used non-euphemistically as a technical term in medicine and veterinary science)

**weight problem** someone who *has a weight problem* is too fat

The use of **heavily-built** for 'fat' plugs into similar semantic territory.

## Fat and Science

A standard way of disguising the unacceptable is to hide it behind scientific (or pseudo-scientific) terminology, and fat is no exception:

**adipose tissue** technically, *adipose tissue* is connective tissue in which fat is stored. Each cell contains a large globule of fat. The clinicalness of the term has a euphemistic appeal, and has inspired the use of **adipose** for simply 'fat': an 'adipose wife looms threateningly on the doorstep of her husband's mistress,' *Sunday Times* 1990. Similarly **adiposity** is used for 'obesity'. The word *adipose* goes back ultimately to Latin *adeps* 'fat'

**cellulite** a term for a particular sort of body fat that came into English via the health-clinics of Switzerland and France. It denotes a water-retentive tissue that gathers around the hips, thighs, buttocks, and upper arms, particularly of women, and gives a pitted appearance to the skin covering it (the effect has been compared to orange peel). It is supposedly difficult to remove by dieting. The term was borrowed from French in the 1960s, and was enthusiastically taken up by promoters of weight-reducing schemes as a way of avoiding the dreaded *f*-word

Thinness has no need of euphemization in modern Western society – *slender*, *svelte*, and *sylph-like* come closest in their determinedly positive connotations, but they are not true euphemisms. Shortness, or smallness, on the other hand, can be a problem. Tiny women might prefer to be called **petite** (first recorded in the late 18th century, and now widely used as a euphemistic dress size) or, if their facial features are sufficiently refined to carry it off, **elfin**. See also VERTICALLY CHALLENGED (see p 213).

# CLOTHING

---

## CLOTHING

The urge to euphemize articles of clothing relates directly to the part of the body they cover. Garments below the waist, and underclothing in general, get the treatment. Any indecent limb lurking underneath provokes a circumlocution.

Proverbially, Victorians had an attack of the vapours at the very thought of a leg. Hence their habit of covering up table legs, piano legs, etc. Hence too their reputation for a reluctance to use the word *trousers*. But in fact the range of quaint euphemisms associated with trousers had its beginnings rather earlier, towards the end of the 18th century. Virtually all of them are variations on the theme 'too rude to be spoken about in polite company', and are cast in the form of a plural noun based on an adjective ending in *-able* or *-ible*.

The earliest on record, from 1790, is **inexpressibles**, which had a long and vigorous career ('The episcopal inexpressibles . . . for obvious reasons will be unsuited to lay legs,' *Spectator* (Melbourne) 1875), followed in 1794 by **indescribables** ('Mr Trotter . . . gave four distinct slaps on the pocket of his mulberry indescribables,' Dickens, *Pickwick Papers* 1837). But undoubtedly the best known today is **unmentionables**, first recorded in 1823. Others include **ineffables**, **inexplicables**, **unexpressibles**, **unspeakables**, **untalkaboutables**, **unutterables**, and **unwhisperables**. Another coy alternative to *trousers*, *breeches*, and the like was **continuations**. This was originally applied to clerical gaiters, but in the course of time came to be transferred to trousers (from the notion that trousers are an extension of the waistcoat above them).

As people's delicacy in referring to trousers waned, these usages mostly died out. But in some cases they were applied to other below-the-waist garments (the earliest known use of *inexpressibles* refers to petticoats and smocks as well as breeches), and this strand has survived, or been revived, in *unmentionables*, now widely used for 'underpants' ('Fear of being ambulanced away to a place where nurses will . . . snigger at your frayed unmentionables,' *Times* 1974). The semantic duality persists in **nether garments**, used by the mealy-mouthed for both 'trousers' and 'underpants'. The most widespread 20th-century British euphemism for underclothes in general has undoubtedly been **smalls**. Now rather passé, it is used mainly in the context of laundry: 'washing one's smalls'. It is first recorded around the middle of the century, and appears to be a development of an earlier, also euphemistic and now obsolete, use of **smalls** for 'breeches'. This in turn was short for *small-clothes*, first recorded in the late 18th century.

Garments which mould or control various parts of the body are naturals for a euphemistic cover-up. The term **foundation garment** (or in American English plain **foundation**) for 'corset' dates back at least to the 1920s. It is a product of the fashion industry rather than the everyday language, and contrives to suggest that the role of the corset is to form the underlying structure on which the outer garments are built, rather than to control unruly fat.

Sportsmen who wear very tight or specially adapted underpants in order to restrict the free play of their genitals while running may choose to dignify them with the name **athletic supporter**, rather than use the more direct *jockstrap*. And in the same general area, the triangular plastic or metal cup worn by batsmen to guard their testicles against a direct hit is often genteelly termed an **abdominal protector** (reflecting the euphemistic *lower abdomen* for 'genitalia': see p 123), even though most of the abdomen is left undefended. The alternative **box** (first recorded in 1950) is no less euphemistic in its origins, but has now virtually become the accepted term.

**Appliance** is a classic euphemism, covering up embarrassment with vagueness. Short for *surgical appliance*, it can in theory stand for any garment, prosthesis or other contrivance worn on the body for therapeutic purposes, such as a surgical collar or an artificial leg; but in practice, if someone says they wear an appliance, you can be almost certain that they are referring to a truss, a sort of belt worn to keep a hernia from protruding.

Clothing, and particularly shoes, that are sturdy, hardwearing or just plain dull, as opposed to fashionable or elegant, may be charitably (or damningly) described as **sensible** (a usage dating back to the 1880s).

The word typically conjures up an image of a tweedy woman with brown lace-up brogue-style shoes, suitable for cross-country walking ('Forty, if she's a day, wears pince-nez and sensible boots and an air of brisk efficiency that will be the death of me,' Agatha Christie 1924).

# NAKEDNESS

If certain items of clothing may not be mentioned by name, how much greater is the taboo on complete nakedness, and on the revelation of certain parts of the body. *Naked* has been the standard adjective describing unclothedness since Anglo-Saxon times, but around the second half of the 18th century, people seem to have started to take against the word's directness, and to explore softer alternatives. **In a state of nature** dates from this period ('My first impression was amazement, at beholding the women from 15 to 70 almost in a state of nature,' C Wilmot 1802), starting off a long line of metaphors in which lack of clothing is linked with 'nature'. The association is partly with the nakedness of the newborn child (cf. BIRTHDAY SUIT below), but mainly with the notion that clothing is a product of civilization, a veneer not shared by the rest of creation (primitivism and the cult of the 'noble savage' provided fertile ground for such figures of speech in the late 1700s); cf. IN THE RAW below. Variants on the same theme include **in nature's garb** and the French borrowing **au naturel**, literally 'in the natural (state)'.

*Nature* also provides a linguistic fig leaf for those who like to congregate in unclothed groups. The cult of nudism emerged in Germany after World War I, and by the end of the 1920s had made itself known in the English-speaking world. Its earliest terminology was *nudism* and *nudist* (both first recorded in 1929), but before long these words came to seem too sniggeringly explicit, and so the more innocent- and respectable-sounding **naturism** and **naturist** were coined as alternatives (on 30 October 1961, the *Daily Telegraph* reported that 'Delegates . . . at the annual conference of the British Sun Bathing Association . . . agreed . . . to substitute "naturism" for "nudism"'). As the name of the organization reveals, nudists have often disguised their activities under a further layer of euphemism as **sun bathing**, and the places where they gather are coyly **sun clubs**

('Although Lancashire has four Sun Clubs (naturist terminology for nudist camps), none is on the coast,' *Lancashire Life* 1978).

It is ironic that *nudism* and *nudist* should need to be toned down, since **nude** itself has served as one of the main genteel alternatives to *naked*. Etymologically meaning simply 'bare', *nude* was introduced into English from Latin in the 16th century, as a legal term, but for a long time made little headway (Dr Johnson does not mention it in his *Dictionary* 1755, although he does include *nudity*). However, in the 18th century it did begin to be used in art criticism, on the model of French, as a term for the unclothed human figure, and in the 19th century it spread into the general language, both as an adjective and as a noun (as in *in the nude*). In its avoidance of the frank *naked*, *nude* almost invariably succeeds in suggesting that nakedness is improper, compromising its euphemistic force. A further softening is effected by **nuddy**, which apparently originated in Australia some time after World War II.

Most other verbal strategies for tiptoeing around nakedness can be divided between the pompously mealy-mouthed and the nudge-and-wink jocular. Into the former category come **disrobe** for 'undress', which dates back to the 16th century; **undraped** for 'wearing no clothes', which occurs mainly in the expression *the undraped (female) form* or *figure* and probably came (like *nude*) from the language of art criticism; and the noun **undress**, as in *a state of undress*.

A similarly prim impulse lies behind the use of **decent** for 'clothed', usually in the context of an embarrassed enquiry through a closed door about whether the person behind it has any clothes on: 'Are you decent?' The usage appears to have originated outside the dressing rooms of theatres, and does not necessarily imply that the person is fully clothed, merely that they have enough on to satisfy the demands of propriety.

The more jovial approach is represented by such expressions as **wearing (only) a smile** (mainly American), **not have a stitch on** (*stitch* here standing for the garment it holds together), and **birthday suit** ('I will strip this holy father to his birthday suit,' Benjamin Malkin 1809). This last, which dates from the early 18th century, originally referred to an especially splendid suit of clothes which was ordered for a king, emperor, etc on the occasion of his birthday, but it was not long before the usage was subverted by associations with the nakedness of the newborn child. Earlier variants, long defunct, include **birthday attire**, **birthday clothes**, and **birthday gear**. British upper-class slang of the post-World War I period produced the jokey **starkers** from *stark naked* ('It shows his 22-year-old girlfriend completely starkers and vulnerable,' *Guardian* 1991) and the synonymous but rarer **starko**. And a range of circumlocutions for 'naked' come in the form *in the* . . . :

**in the altogether** dating from the late 19th century, an expression probably based on the notion of being 'altogether' or completely naked, although it has also been suggested that there is some connection with John 9:34, 'Thou wast altogether born in sins'

**in the buff** from *buff* meaning 'leather', originally as made from buffalo hide, from a comparison between the animal's skin and the bare human skin. In early use, from the 17th to 19th centuries, the phrase was generally *in buff*, and the modern form probably dates from the late 19th century

**in the raw** meaning literally 'in its natural, unrefined form', it is often used to denote the most unsophisticated or even savage aspect of something, without the veneer of civilization, but it also denotes 'naked': 'Auberon surprised her in her bath and is thus one of the very few men who can claim to have seen his great-great-grandmother in the raw,' Evelyn Waugh 1944

**in the skin** from the notion of the unclothed skin (as in IN THE BUFF). Other euphemistic equations of skin with nakedness crop up in SKINNY-DIPPING and in **skin flick**, a film featuring extensive erotic exposure of naked (female) flesh

The deliberate revealing of parts of the body, and particularly of the sex organs and other erogenous zones, whether by amateurs or professionals, is something that people shy away from referring to directly. A range of colloquialisms exists for various aspects of the activity, among them:

**flash** to reveal one's sex organs in public. The word is applied typically to men (though not exclusively: 'His latest film . . . features Sharon Stone who last year attained notoriety and stardom by flashing in *Basic Instinct*,' *Radio Times* 1993). The standard scenario is of a dirty old man in a dirty old raincoat, lurking in some secluded spot and whipping the coat open to startle passing females with his unencumbered genitalia. The word is actually recorded in slang dictionaries and the like from the 19th century (the *Swell's Night Guide* of 1846, for instance, has '*Flash*, to sport, to expose, he flashed his root [penis])'. But its modern proliferation in usage appears to date back no further than the 1960s

**moon** to show one's buttocks. The vogue for mooning, either as a form of protest or as a sign of contempt, appears to have begun in the USA in the late 1950s. The word supposedly reflects a resemblance between the pale naked buttocks and the full moon

**streak** to run naked through a public place as an act of bravado. Streaking apparently originated on the West Coast of the USA in the early 1970s. As a widespread fad amongst American college students it did not last very long, but the occasional streaker still braves the wrath of the ground authorities at sporting events, such as test matches and rugby internationals. The term probably comes from the notion of running very fast, or 'streaking' along

But the classic euphemism in this area is **expose oneself**, which could logically refer to any part of the body normally clothed, but which by common consent is taken as referring specifically to the genitals. Its nominalization is **exposure**, or in full **indecent exposure**, which dates back as a legal term in Britain to an Act of Parliament of 1851. Someone who goes in for such exposés can be verbally disguised as an **exhibitionist**. This was originally a technical term in sexual psychology, introduced in the 1890s, but has since become available in the general language.

The weakening of the taboo in Western society on revealing the female breasts in public in the final third of the 20th century created a gap in the lexicon, which was filled with a word that showed that the taboo was still very much alive and kicking: the circumlocutious **topless**. First recorded with reference to women in 1964, it designates a garment (originally a swimsuit) that extends no further up than the waist, and hence by extension a woman wearing such a garment, a place where such garments are permitted, etc: 'Anguished Fergie and her pal Johnny Bryan are suing . . . over the topless holiday snaps that led to her being exiled from the Royal Family,' *Guardian* 1991. We have now got used to the metaphor, so that the notion of a 'topless woman' no longer strikes us as odd. But the more recent **bottomless**, a euphemism for 'completely naked', can still produce surreal effects: one might well think that 'bottomless dancers' are the last thing male punters in a nightclub would want to see.

To **go commando** is to go about with a full complement of outer garments but no underpants (the implication is perhaps that 'real men' scorn such cissy accessories).

The viewing of naked or semi-naked women for payment has naturally produced its own euphemisms. The high-falutin **ecdysiast** for 'striptease-dancer' was coined in 1940 by the American journalist H L Mencken, apparently in response to a request from stripper Georgia Sothern for a classier job-title. It is based on Greek *ekdysis* 'moulting'. Its force today, though, is more pompously humorous than truly euphemistic, and those who require a modest cover-up will more likely plump for **exotic dancer**, which emerged in the USA in the early 1950s: '"Exotic dancer" – "A euphemism for stripper",' R Hardwick 1965. Photographs of naked women may be linguistically camouflaged as **artistic**.

Swimming naked is often coyly referred to as **skinny-dipping**. The usage originated in the USA in the 1960s, and makes an anomalous use of *skinny* (which usually means 'thin') as the equivalent of *in the skin*.

Modern adherents of witchcraft like to go naked in the open air when enacting their rituals, and the word they prefer for covering their nakedness is the romantic-sounding **sky-clad**, first recorded in 1909: 'Pagans in Britain are hard pushed to go sky-clad at midsummer, let alone the other yearly festivals,' *Radio Times* 1992.

# ADJUSTMENT OF DRESS

There is one aspect of male clothing that presents a particular danger to the absent-minded: the flies (the term *fly* was originally applied, incidentally, to the flap covering the trouser buttons, from the notion of its being fixed along one edge and free to fly, like a flag, from its attachment). Inadvertent failure to do up buttons or zip can, if self-discovered, lead to panic-stricken attempts to remedy the omission unobtrusively, while the mind races over such questions as how long have they been undone, who will have noticed and how much, etc. But if the unintentional revelation remains undiscovered, the ball is in others' court. Most people probably say nothing and try to look anywhere else. A few bold spirits come straight out with 'Your flies are undone', but for many a circumlocution is indispensable.

In the days before zips (invented in 1891), the oversight was made more obvious by a row of buttons. In the British Army, the resemblance between a button and a medal led to a succession of euphemistic metaphors varying on the theme **have a medal showing**. Late 19th- and early 20th-century campaigns in foreign parts gave rise to more specific expressions, such as **Abyssinian medal**, **Egyptian medal**, and (during World War I) **Turkish medal**. And more generally, there was the **canteen medal**, which started life as a dismissive term for a campaign medal (awarded to everyone regardless of merit).

Euphemisms in this area tend to be winsomely allusive, whether they refer to the open fly itself (**the shop door is open**), to its admitting external influences (**you're catching a cold**), or to what may be revealed as a result (**Johnnie's out of jail** and **flying a flag**). But they can be so oblique that it is hard to see how the recipient gets the message (as in **your nose is bleeding**, or the cryptic American **one o'clock at the waterworks**).

But the most widespread present-day circumlocution is certainly the injunction to patrons of gentlemen's public lavatories, 'before leaving, please **adjust your dress**'.

The only female sartorial solecism to be euphemized in this way is the slip protruding below the hemline. In former times, when direct reference to underwear was taboo in polite circles, 'your slip's showing' would be replaced by coy expressions such as **it's snowing down south** (a reference to the usual white colour of slips) and the enigmatic **Charlie's dead**.

# EMBELLISHMENT

The beautification of the body, or at least the masking of its blemishes, is a rich area for linguistic mystification, but often it is more a case of hyping the commonplace than disguising the unpalatable. Those who call a *hair dresser* a *hair stylist* are no doubt prompted more by a desire to sound sophisticated than by any sort of taboo attached to *hair dresser*.

But there is one aspect of hair care that certainly does attract euphemisms: the wig – and in particular the male wig. The word *wig* seems to have a peculiar horror for men, with its implication of covering the entire head, and hence of complete baldness, and the words used instead of it seek to suggest that only the tiniest patch is lacking in hair, scarcely worth bothering about. The classic circumlocution is **toupée**, which was introduced from French in the early 18th century as a term for a topknot on a periwig, but in the 20th century came to be used for a small wig covering the top of the head. But somehow the flight from reality is even greater in **hairpiece**, which strains to suggest smallness, triviality, even superfluity, but succeeds only in sounding pompous. It appears to have come into use in American English sometime between the two world wars, and this was also the period which saw the introduction of such jokey, but equally euphemistic alternatives as **rug**, **divot**, and **doily**. Rhyming slang contributions include **Irish jig** and **syrup of figs**. See also BALDNESS, p 146.

The other hair dresser's activity that calls for some verbal wrapping is the dyeing of grey and white hair to disguise the effects of aging. The two main alternatives to the *d*-word, **rinse** and **tint**, began to be deployed in the early years of the 20th century (*blue rinse* has come to be symbolic of well-groomed elderly women). They have been joined by **touch up**, which contains the comforting implication that only a few stray hairs need to be dyed to restore a youthful appearance.

The treatment of body hair is even more embarrassing. Its removal can be concealed in the Latin obscurity of *depilation*, but the popular euphemism is **waxing**, from the application of hot wax to the skin, which is pulled off when cool, taking the unwanted hair with it. Excess female pubic hair is removed with **bikini wax**, if it is liable to protrude beyond the **bikini line** – the line formed by the top edge of bikini briefs.

But when beauty treatment reaches the operating theatre, things are clearly getting serious; the surgeon's scalpel is a great encourager of euphemism. The term *plastic surgery* dates back to the 1830s (it was probably adapted from German *plastische Chirurgie*, and *plastic* has the sense 'formative'), but its association with major reconstructions of disfigured features no doubt led those merely in search of beautification to prefer the softer-sounding **cosmetic surgery** (first recorded in 1926). The process is disguised even more coyly by such expressions as **aesthetic procedure** and **surgical improvement** (or, in the case of increasing breast size, **surgical enhancement**), and also **streamlining**, which denotes the surgical removal of unwanted fat. More colloquial is the notion of *lifting* the face, of picking up its sagging parts and replacing them higher up. The terms **face-lift** and **face-lifting** emerged in the 1920s ('A youthful appearance is considered an advantage, and face-lifting is a common thing among men,' *Sunday Dispatch* 1928), and for a time faced competition from **face-raising**. A more recent introduction along the same lines is **tuck**, which borrows the terminology of dressmaking to describe an operation in which subcutaneous fat is removed and the overlying skin replaced more tightly. The entire procedure, including the initial incision, is a **nip and tuck**.

Overall, any surgical intervention designed to improve the appearance, from hair to teeth to facial wrinkles, is often euphemized as **enlisting the help** or **aid of science**.

# BODILY FUNCTIONS & SECRETIONS

## DEFECATION AND URINATION

So keenly do we desire to conceal the process of elimination of the waste products of eating and drinking that many of our commonest euphemisms even hide which of the two functions we are referring to. The vaguest of all originally shifted the attention from the action itself to the journey necessary to reach the place where the action may be performed: **go**, and its past form, **been** ('But I been three times . . . I can't pee any more!' William Golding 1959). The usage is not recorded before 1926, but it echoes uncannily euphemisms used by our Anglo-Saxon ancestors for 'place for defecation and urination': *gang*, literally a 'going' or 'journeying', which is related to modern English *go*; and compounds such as *gang-ærn* 'going-place', *gang-tun* 'going-building', and *utgang* 'outgoing'. It is now so firmly established that the notion of movement to a place has virtually disappeared (as in 'I had to go in my pants'). It remains, of course, in expressions such as **go to the lavatory, go to the loo, go to the bathroom**, etc, where the journey anticipates and symbolizes its purpose. **Go upstairs** reflects the usual location of a lavatory. An even vaguer formula is sometimes adopted – **go somewhere**: '"Dadda! I wanna come in!" "Well, you can't. Clear out!" "But dadda! I wanna go somewhere!" "Go somewhere else, then. Hop it. I'm having my bath." "Dad-*da*! I wanna *go some-where*!" No use! I knew the danger signal. The WC is in the bathroom – it would be, of course, in a house like ours,' George Orwell 1939.

Another popular strategy is to acknowledge that the process is 'natural', and therefore unavoidable, and common to all people – as if this will camouflage it in the general hurly-burly of life. **Call of nature** is the locus classicus, dating back at least to the mid 18th century. The mysterious urgings of one's body summon one imperiously from one's civilized concerns to perform some action linked with one's animal past; this could in theory be anything from sneezing to giving birth, but everyone understands that the call (which must be **answered**) is to urinate and/or defecate. The formula can be switched round to **nature's call**, or even pared down allusively to just **call** ('*Warder . . . Where's your mate? Fellow Convict.* 'Ad a call, sir . . . Went over to that wall,' John Galsworthy 1926). Other elaborations on the same theme include **demands of nature**, **nature's needs**, **natural functions**, and **natural purposes**. Then there is the now rather dated **pay a call**, which bears a superficial resemblance to *call of nature* but is in fact a variant of **pay a visit** – i.e. to the lavatory.

Another strand that keeps surfacing is the notion of necessity, of something no one can avoid doing. **Feel the need** can stand elliptically for 'need to urinate or defecate', and various coy formulae with **necessary** or **necessity** serve the same purpose.

The desire to be more down-to-earth, while at the same time preserving a decent vagueness, is met by **bodily functions** (which again could theoretically apply to any of scores actions and processes) and **bodily waste**, or alternatively **waste matter**.

But perhaps the commonest strategy is to account for one's departure to urinate or defecate by pretending either to be going to the lavatory for some other purpose, or to be going somewhere else altogether. Into the first category come **to freshen up** (the overt suggestion being of washing one's face and hands, tidying one's hair, etc; often used on arrival at a place, or before a meal); **to wash one's hands** ('I wonder if Rosie could, perhaps, take Miss Malloney to, er, to wash her hands,' John Gardner 1974); and, of women, **to powder one's nose** (first recorded in 1921, and providing an ideally genteel excuse for a woman to retreat to the lavatory (see also POWDER ROOM, p 182): 'I'll use your bathroom. To powder my nose, as nice girls say,' L P Davies 1972).

If one wants to conceal one's destination completely, a number of even more outlandish fibs are available. Many of them seem to involve going into the garden – presumably a hang-over from the days of outside lavatories. One can claim to be going to **look at** or **see the garden**, or various parts of it, such as **the lawn**, **the flower beds**, **the compost heap**, etc. Some mileage can be got, too, out of picking or plucking various sorts of flower, although for the most part this metaphor seems to apply specifically to urination. At the end of the 20th century these all have a decidedly dated air, but the more general

**stretch one's legs** is still very much in use (usually in the context of a need to urinate or defecate after long confinement in a vehicle), as is the still vaguer **adjourn** and **disappear** (if someone says 'I must just disappear for a moment,' their companion does not expect them to vanish in a puff of smoke). Other bizarre alibis include **going to feed a dog**, **going to feed the goldfish**, **going to post a letter**, and the versatile **going to see a man about a dog** (first recorded in the 1860s).

The discomfort of an urgent need to urinate and/or defecate provides a hook for a further range of circumlocutions. **Relieve oneself**, which has been dated back to the 1930s and is probably a good deal older than that, encapsulates the bliss of an overloaded bladder at last emptied ('Motorists in continental Europe are familiar with the sight of drivers relieving themselves on the side of any road,' *Guardian* 1991). It echoes the earlier and now obsolete **ease oneself**. The same impulse lies behind the use of **comfortable** in expressions such as 'make oneself comfortable' (a suspension of proceedings to allow participants to urinate or defecate can be euphemized as a **comfort break**; see also COMFORT STATION p 182).

The school-room has produced its own particular euphemisms. To **be excused** is to be given permission to go to the lavatory, and by extension simply to urinate and/or defecate (not necessarily restricted to schoolchildren: 'He arranged for a friend with a padlock to hang around, asked to be excused, bundled his two escorts into the lavatory . . . and he was off,' *Guardian* 1991) and a child's request to **leave the room** or **class** is likely to be interpreted the same way. In a younger age-group still, **potty-trained** or **toilet-trained** implies the attainment of a more or less adult level of control over the bladder and bowels (the related **house-trained**, which dates from the 1920s, is applied mainly to household pets). A parent inculcating these skills may encourage its offspring to **perform**. Any lapse in this area is apt to be coyly described as an **accident** ('Then a new child had, as Mabel calls it, an "accident". She may have been afraid of asking to go out,' *The Nation* 1926); the term is also applied to an adult's involuntary urination or defecation. A baby whose soiled nappy is replaced by a clean one is said to have been **changed** – although of course the baby remains the same.

**Incontinent** now comes across as a fairly neutral term, but originally it was much wider in application, referring to any sort of self-restraint (notably sexual). The sense 'unable to control urination or defecation', which appears to date from the late 18th or early 19th century, is no doubt euphemistic in inspiration. There is some ambiguity as to which of the excretory functions it refers to; with no further qualification, urination is generally assumed, and when both are meant, **double incontinence** (which somehow turns up the euphemism rating again) may be used.

One rather curious circumlocution is **be caught** or **taken short**, meaning 'be seized with a sudden need to urinate or defecate, particularly in circumstances which make it difficult to fulfil'. First recorded in the 1890 edition of *Funk and Wagnells' Standard Dictionary*, it appears to be a specialization of an earlier sense 'be caught suddenly at a disadvantage'. This in turn depended on a now obsolete sense of *short*, 'abruptly, suddenly'.

# Defecation

Indoctrination in the ways of negotiating the lexical minefield of faeces begins at the earliest possible age. The infant performer is bombarded with winsome circumlocutions; the habit, once learnt, persists into later life, often bringing parts of the nursery vocabulary with it. A leading feature of this vocabulary is the use of simple single-syllable words, often reduplicated, and often imitative in origin – like much of the other language used by adults to babies and very young children. **Pooh**, for instance, is a nominalization of the exclamation of disgust at a bad smell (it appears to be a product of the 1950s). **Poop** suggests a similar origin, perhaps via a reduplicated form *poo-poo*, but in fact it seems to have begun as an imitation of the sound of farting or defecating ('Little Robin red breast, Sitting on a pole, Niddle, Noddle, Went his head, And Poop went his Hole,' goes an early 18th century nursery rhyme). There are no consistent records of it until the 1930s, but since then it has been moving steadily away from 'farting' towards 'defecating' ('Five-year-old eyes grow wide with wonder at the memory of the elephant "pooping" on the carpet,' *Cape Times* 1974). It has been slow to catch on in British English, but its cause has been helped by the *poop scoop*, or *pooper scooper*, an implement used for removing dog faeces from public places (first recorded in 1978). In the same category comes the American **do** (as in *doggy do*), probably partly nonsense-syllable but partly also chosen for the extreme vagueness of the verb *do*, which makes it a perfect vehicle for euphemism (defecating is diluted to 'doing something'). The metaphorical possibilities of its reduplicated form were publicized by George Bush's 'in deep **do-do**' (i.e. in serious trouble: 'That sums up the Bush approach in this campaign: whatever kind of deep doo-doo our health system is in now, is nothing compared with what Clinton would get us into,' *Observer* 1992). American English also has **boom-boom**, which is generally explained as being onomatopoeic, and **ca-ca**. The immediate source of this was probably French slang *caca*, but it goes back ultimately to the ancient Indo-European stem *kakka-*, which produced words for 'faeces' or 'defecate' in a range of descendant languages (e.g. Latin *cacare*, Spanish *cagar*, Russian *kakat*). English too used to have *cack*, which now survives only in *cack-handed* 'awkward' (originally 'left-handed', perhaps from the 'mess' made by a left-handed person). Another vividly onomatopoeic nursery word is **plops**, from the sound of the shit hitting the water. And babies are very much the focus of **top and tail**, a metaphor taken from the trimming of fruits such as gooseberries and applied to the cleaning up of babies that have vomited and defecated. But the most high-profile of the baby words are probably **jobs**, which reflects the notion of defecation as a task to be performed, also present in the adult *do one's business*; and **number two**, which is probably an allusion to the greater psychological significance of defecation compared with urination (compare NUMBER ONE p 173) and the greater physical and psychological volume of faeces compared with urine. The form of the first combines with the motivation of the second in **big jobs**, sometimes familiarly shortened to **biggies**: 'He's a bit erratic where he does his biggies, now he's a grown up parrot,' Angus Wilson 1967.

Another product of nursery mentality is **whoopsie**. It is a derivative of *whoops*, an exclamation of dismay and apology for some inadvertent mistake, and as its origins suggest, it refers mainly to embarrassingly accidental or untoward defecation: 'The owner had a dog who did a "whoopsie" in the middle of the restaurant floor,' *Observer* 1993. Its use was popularized in Britain by Michael Crawford in the BBC sitcom *Some Mothers Do 'Ave 'Em* 1974–9.

The word *shit* goes back to Anglo-Saxon times, and to begin with was quite a respectable word. It is not until the 17th century that we begin to find instances of its being printed *s . . t*, signalling its exit from polite conversation. At the end of the 20th century there are some slight stirrings of partial rehabilitation, but on the whole it is a word still avoided. Alternative strategies have to steer a course between the technical/medical/high-falutin (**faeces**, **defecate**, **excrement**, **ordure**, **solid waste**, **evacuate**, etc), which themselves can play a euphemistic role, and colloquialisms (such as *crap* and *crud*) which quickly fall under the same taboo as *shit*.

One or two general themes can be picked out amongst the skein of circumlocution. Movement figures strongly, presumably in allusion to the involuntary muscular contractions of the intestine that propel the faeces. Since the 17th century, **move the** or **one's bowels** has been a polite way of saying 'defecate'. The corresponding nouns are **movement**, applied both to defecation and to the faeces, most commonly encountered as **bowel movement** (abbreviated to **BM**); and **motion**, which dates back to Shakespeare's time ('Shall I lose my doctor?' asks the host of the Garter Inn in *The Merry Wives of Windsor*; 'no; he gives me the potions and the motions'). Mention of the double entendre *passing a motion* is always good for a cheap laugh.

As already noted in the case of *job*, the idea of defecation being a piece of work one has to perform has taken quite a strong hold. The euphemism **do one's business** dates back at least to the early 17th century, and remains in circulation now, albeit with a slightly dated air. There is some evidence for the use of **duty** or **duties** in the same sense.

The attitude taken up by the defecator accounts obviously for the verb **squat**, but also by a more indirect route for the now mainly medical euphemism **stool** for 'piece of excrement' – what in more down-to-earth language would be a *turd*. It is the same word as *stool* 'seat'. From the 15th to the 19th centuries, people sitting on the privy or commode would be decorously described as *on the stool*. By the 16th century *stool* had come to be used for 'the action of defecating', and its current surviving sense was not long in following.

In this as in other areas, rhyming slang plays its obfuscatory role. **Tom-tit** (or **tom** for short) stands for *shit*; **Richard** leads by way of *Richard the Third* to *turd* – the choice of the vilified Richard among other potential 'Thirds' being presumably far from accidental; **my word** (from the exclamation) is applied particularly to canine excrement on pavements.

Two other mainstays of euphemism, propitiation and irony, are represented in the use of **honey** for 'faeces'. Initiated perhaps by some resemblance in colour, the metaphor really depends on the ironic contrast between the sweetness and desirability of honey and the opposite characteristics of faeces. It is of North American origin, and occurs almost exclusively in compounds. A **honey bucket** (first recorded in

1931 but apparently dating back at least to the World War I period) is a depository for faeces; a **honey wagon** is a truck or other vehicle that comes round an army's lines or trenches collecting the contents of the honey buckets (the term is also used for a portable outdoor toilet); and a **honey cart** is the vehicle used at airports for emptying and removing the contents of the aeroplanes' lavatories. During the Vietnam War, latrine cleaners were known as **honey dippers**.

Another theme, not surprisingly, is 'dirt' (indeed, English **dirt** is related to Dutch *dreet* and Norwegian *drite* 'excrement', and is often itself used euphemistically in that sense, as in *dog dirt*). **Make a mess** often implies 'defecate' – usually, though not exclusively, of an animal ('It's the dog. It made a mess on the carpet,' *Woman's Own* 1960); **mess** itself is often applied to animals' faeces, as in *dog mess*. **Muck** has almost lost its euphemistic force in agricultural contexts, where it has become a virtually neutral term for cattle excrement used as fertilizer, but elsewhere (especially in *dogs' muck*) it retains its evasiveness. **Dirty** when used as a verb in relation to underwear is taken to refer not to any old dirt, but specifically to faeces (or urine); an even more mealy-mouthed alternative is **soil**, used particularly by medical and social workers of involuntary defecation by children, patients, etc. When it is animals rather than people that are responsible, the euphemism is **foul** (as in 'Penalty for fouling the footway £50').

Animals' excrement has its own particular coy terminology. **Droppings** is the all-purpose euphemism for anything from mice to elephants, based on the notion of that which falls from the body (not so far, in fact, from the notion of 'separation' or 'splitting off' which appears etymologically to underlie *shit*). The singular usage *dropping*, which has now died out, dates back to the 16th century; there is no evidence for the plural *droppings* before the 19th century. **Cow-pat** for 'flat mass of cattle faeces' is not on record before World War II, but it is predated by various dialectisms such as *cow-clap*, *cow-clot*, *cow-dab*, *cow-flop*, and *cow-pad*. **Pancake** is an alternative. In the days when piles of horse faeces adorned the roads of towns and cities, they were often euphemized in America as **horse apples** or **road apples**.

Two animal-excrement words in particular have gone through curious cycles of euphemism: **dung** and **manure**. *Dung* originally denoted specifically 'excrement used as fertilizer' (much as *manure* now does); it derives ultimately from an Indo-European root meaning 'cover'. It then broadened out to 'animal excrement in general', and in present-day English it has a special role as a permitted alternative to 'animal *shit*', sanctioned because of its down-to-earth, agricultural connotations. The etymological meaning of *manure* is 'hand-work'. It comes from Old French *manoevrer*, which contained elements descended from Latin *manus* 'hand' and *operari* 'to work'. The original sense 'work by hand' passed via 'till, cultivate' to 'fertilize', and the noun derived from the verb has come to mean 'animal excrement used as fertilizer'. Its status hovers uncertainly between neutral term for the substance and euphemism for something more outspoken. A similar niche of sanctioned technical term (although without the farming connection) is **sewage**, a derivative of *sewer*, which comes ultimately from a Vulgar Latin compound meaning literally 'water drain'.

Some other defecatory euphemisms:

**body wax** a bizarre and now defunct term for 'faeces', sometimes shortened to simply **wax**. Perhaps there is an underlying notion of wax as something excreted, as in *beeswax* or *earwax*

**clear-out** applied usually to fulsome defecation initiated by a laxative

**grunt** a verb used for 'defecate' in American English; apparently imitative of the effortful noises that may accompany the process

**hock(e)y** or **hook(e)y** a term for excrement, particularly dogs'. Of uncertain origin, but current in American English since at least the 1960s

**night soil** a polite way of referring in the 18th and 19th centuries to human faeces collected for use as fertilizer. Its removal from cesspits and the like would take place discreetly at night – hence the name. The link with fertilizer might seem to suggest that the *soil* element denotes 'earth', but in fact it is the *soil* that also means 'dirt, discoloration' – a different word. This used to be commonly used for 'faeces', but now survives only in the technical term *soil pipe* 'pipe for carrying off lavatory waste'. The corresponding verb is still alive and well in excrementitious contexts (see p 169)

**open the** or **one's bowels** to restore the passage of faeces, generally by means of some sort of laxative ('The bowels should be well opened at the onset by a brisk purgative,' *Allbutt's System of Medicine* 1897). Once this has been achieved, the aim is to **keep the bowels open**

**pure** a 19th-century term for dogs' excrement, as gathered from the streets for use in the processing of leather (an alkaline solution was made from it, which removed grease). The underlying allusion was to 'purifying' the hides, not to any quality of 'purity' in the excrement, but to modern noses at least the smell of euphemism is unmistakable

**regular** defecating at healthily regular intervals – i.e. not constipated. A euphemism favoured by the manufacturers of proprietary laxatives, bran breakfast cereals, etc

**skidmarks** excrement stains on underpants

**solids** an abbreviation of *solid waste* (see p 168), a euphemistic substitution particularly in *when the solids hit the fan*

**use paper** to defecate – a euphemism used mainly in hospitals, and contrasting with (in the case of males) 'needing the bottle' (see BOTTLE p 175), in which case no wiping is deemed to be necessary. The range of euphemisms applied, incidentally, to the paper used for cleaning up after defecation and urination is largely restricted to a 'lavatory' word plus *paper*: **toilet paper**, **loo paper**, **bog paper**, etc. This may be further distanced by substituting the form in which the paper is usually sold – *roll*: **toilet roll**, **loo roll**, etc. A more delicate note is struck by *tissue*: **toilet tissue**, first recorded in 1968 ('Lavatory paper, or, in the genteel euphemism of Adspeak, toilet tissue,' *Verbatim* 1982), and the even more tangential **bathroom tissue**; both tend to be applied by manufacturers to the softer, more up-market brands. *Bumf* started life, in the late 19th century, meaning 'lavatory paper' (it is short for *bum fodder*), but that application has now virtually disappeared in the face of the contemptuous 'unwanted or tiresome documents'.

The genteel vocabulary of defecation includes circumlocutory references to constipation. **Bind** is a favourite word in this area, used particularly with reference to foods that as it were 'tie knots in' the intestine and prevent the free passage of faeces: eggs, for example, might be described as 'very binding'. **Cement** is used as a verb in the same sense, and often also with the connotation of arresting diarrhoea (as in 'These tablets'll cement you up').

# Urination

Many of the standard colloquialisms for 'urination' are based ultimately on 'sound' imagery: the sound of the stream of urine being discharged from the body, or falling into a receptacle. *Piss* itself is descended from an onomatopoeic Vulgar Latin verb *pisare*. And several of the best-known nursery substitutions are similarly inspired. **Wee** and its duplicated form **wee-wee** (both noun and verb) were supposedly suggested by the sound (they are first recorded from the 1930s); and if the resemblance seems slightly implausible, it is corroborated by the American **whizz**, of similar antiquity. **Pee** is often explained as a euphemistic replacement of *piss* (and when it is written **P** the avoidance of taboo is obvious), but it too must surely be in part an echo of the sound. Dating back at least to the 1780s, it has transcended the nursery, and is used as a rather winsome 'urination' word by adults. The double **pee-pee** has a more infantile ring to it, but in fact much of its usage seems to be in facetious imitation of foreigners speaking English, in expressions such as *do pee-pee* and *make pee-pee* (French for example has *pipi*). **Piddle**, which dates back to the 18th century, suggests a similar sound-symbolism. In fact there existed an earlier *piddle*, which meant and still means 'spend time aimlessly', but it seems likely that *piddle* 'urinate' may be a different word, blended from *piss* and perhaps *puddle* ('making a **puddle** on the floor, carpet, etc' remains a coy way of referring to involuntary urination by pets or children). The story that the name of the Dorset village of Tolpuddle (as in 'the Tolpuddle Martyrs') was euphemistically changed from Tolpiddle in the 17th century to save puritan sensibilities seems to be apocryphal (spellings with *-puddle* date back at least to the 13th century), but certainly when Dorset County Council proposed in 1956 to change the name of the nearby Puddletown to Piddletown, to harmonize with other local names, the outraged populace rose up against it (the names in their various forms come from the River Piddle, and have nothing to do with urination). It is pure coincidence, but a neat one, that another nearby village is called Tincleton; for another acoustically inspired expression for 'urination' is the British 'have a **tinkle**', first recorded in 1965. This rather charmingly finds a resemblance between drops of urine hitting water or porcelain and the sound of tiny bells.

The corresponding American term is the verb **to tinkle**, which emerged slightly earlier.

Still in the nursery, one of the most high-profile childhood terms for 'urination' or 'urine' is **number one**. This forms a pair with *number two* for 'defecation' or 'faeces', the logic of the numbering presumably being that urination has some precedence because of its relative frequency, while defecation is a more serious affair meriting a higher number. The usage is first recorded in John Farmer and William Henley's *Slang* 1902.

An obvious euphemistic strategy is to associate urine with a less sensitive liquid – water. Indeed, **water** has been used for 'urine' since at least the 14th century. It was formerly very common (the 1885 Revised Version of the Bible, for instance, translated 2 Kings 18:27 as 'To drink their own water with you,' which in the Authorized Version had been 'drink their own piss with you'), and it was used particularly in the context of medical diagnosis by means of a patient's urine. Nowadays it is largely limited to the expressions **make water** and **pass water**, meaning 'urinate', and the rather odd *feel something in one's water*, denoting intuition – all of which have a decidedly dated air.

Other metaphors continue the watery theme. **Wet** has been used since the 18th century to mean 'urinate into or on', as in *wet the bed* and *wet one's pants*; but *wet oneself* meaning 'urinate involuntarily' (often substituted euphemistically for *piss oneself* in the metaphorical sense 'laugh uncontrollably') and the plain intransitive *wet*, meaning 'urinate', seem to be 20th-century developments. *Wet* is occasionally used as a noun, too, in the senses 'act of urinating' (as in *to have a wet*) and 'urine'. But *wet the bed* remains the commonest of these expressions, giving rise in the late 19th century to the familiar compound **bed-wetting** (which no one interprets as involving any other liquid than urine).

Water also figures prominently in many of the more far-fetched excuses coyly offered for leaving in order to urinate. As noted above, these often involved 'going into the garden' in the days of outdoor lavatories, and this presented a splendid opportunity for heavy-handed humour along the lines of **watering the garden**, **watering the flowers**, **watering the roses**, etc. Another former variant on the horticultural theme was **pluck** or **pick a rose**, applied to and used almost exclusively by women. It was subtler than the punning **pick** or **plant a pea** and the more delicate but scarcely less obvious **pick** etc **a sweetpea**. The image behind the florid **shake the dew off the lily** (which apparently dates from the 1930s) is presumably shaking the remaining drops of liquid from the penis after urinating.

The classic circumlocution used by patients tongue-tied about discussing urinary problems (and by patronizing doctors) is **waterworks**: 'Trainee medicos soon conquer anxieties such as waterworks phobia, caused by working on a ward full of ailing kidneys, bladders and prostates,' *Guardian* 1991. *Waterworks* in its literal sense 'installation for providing a public water supply' dates back to the 16th century, but this euphemistic application was not coined until the turn of the 20th century.

## Other metaphors with 'liquid' connections include:

**one's back teeth are afloat** or **floating**, suggesting such a great need to urinate that the body's liquid level has risen to the top of the throat

**leak** mainly a noun, as in *have* or *take a leak*, but this is actually quite recent (from about the 1930s), and the verbal use goes back much further, to Shakespeare's time

**to pump ship** a nautical euphemism dating from the late 18th century, based on the notion of pumping out water from the bilges, with the penis being likened to the hose used: 'A couple of men had come in to pump ship at the stand-up urinals,' Douglas Rutherford 1977

**run-off** an act of urination – first recorded in the 1961 supplement to Eric Partridge's *Dictionary of Slang*. The underlying idea is of running off liquid from a cask

**to shed a tear** to urinate – a circumlocution of ridiculous delicacy, based on an analogy between two different sorts of bodily secretion

**to splash** or **spatter one's boots** to urinate – used of males, with reference to the scattering of splashed urine, particularly when standing at a urinal. It is a lineal descendant of **to cover one's feet**, a direct translation from Hebrew used in the Bible ('And he came to the sheepcotes by the way, where was a cave; and Saul went in to cover his feet,' 1 Samuel 24:3). A similar inspiration (if such it can be called) lies behind **to wring out one's socks**

**to strain the potatoes** of a male, to urinate – an Australian euphemism, one of the multitude of colourful metaphors introduced to the language in the 1960s by Barry Humphries in his ocker persona Barry McKenzie

**to syphon the python** of a male, to urinate – the 'python' of course being the penis, commonly the subject of snake imagery

There is also a liquid connection with the British **slash**, as in *have a slash* 'urinate'. This has nothing to do with *slash* 'cut', but comes from Scots *slash* 'large splash of liquid', which in turn was probably descended from Old French *esclach*. It is first recorded in 1950. Its Cockney rhyming-slang transformation is reputedly **J Carroll Naish** (from the name of the actor who played the Chinese detective Charlie Chan).

Pressure within the bladder provides another hook to hang a euphemism on. If anyone says they are **bursting**, the interpretation is either (depending on context) that they are too full to eat any more or that they have an urgent need to urinate. In such circumstances they will be desperate to **empty** or **ease their bladder**. The verbal usage **to slack** or **slack off** is also suggested by a releasing of bladder pressure.

Medical circumlocutions include **bottle** (if a male patient in hospital is asked if he 'wants the bottle', it can be assumed that the bottle-shaped urine receptacle is meant, not a bottle of alcohol) and **sample** or **specimen**, which, without further qualification, is taken to refer to a few centilitres of urine provided by a patient for diagnostic examination.

The best-known piece of urinary rhyming slang is **Jimmy Riddle** ('piddle'), first recorded in 1937. It is often abbreviated to **Jimmy**. Another – reputedly – is **Mike** or **Mickey Bliss**, which has been claimed as the origin of *take the mickey out of* (modelled on *take the piss out of*), but there is little satisfactory evidence for this. **That and this** ('piss') is used as a noun, in the sense 'urination'.

A miscellany of other alternatives to *urinate*:

**to cock** or **lift a leg** scarcely a necessary posture for human urination, but occasionally used with reference to men. The usual beneficiary of the euphemism is a male dog

**to commit a nuisance** a piece of legal periphrasis which has now largely died out. It is gloriously vague in its surface meaning, but the underlying message is generally accepted as being 'urinate in a public place so as to give offence to those in the vicinity'. Its commonest context was on notices bearing the injunction 'Commit no nuisance'

**to make** an American usage which is apparently a shortening of *make water*. It may well have originated in the language of parent to young child (as many euphemisms for urination and defecation do, for that is a context in which people who would otherwise not refer to such topics have to find a vocabulary for them)

**to point Percy at the porcelain** an alliterative encapsulation of male urination: *Percy*, of course, is the penis, *porcelain* the lavatory bowl, urinal, etc. The anonymous coiner of the phrase was presumably unaware that the word *porcelain*'s Italian ancestor originally referred to the vulva of a pig

**to shake hands with one's best friend**, **with an old friend**, or **with one's wife's best friend** used of males urinating, from the fact that men commonly hold their penises while so doing. The expression is first recorded in 1952

**to spend a penny** perhaps the best-known of British urinary euphemisms: 'Venables hurried away up the tunnel . . . Given the club's debt of 18 million we knew he could not have gone to spend a penny,' *Guardian* 1991. It appears to date from around the World War II period, but those too young to remember when admission to a cubicle in a public lavatory cost one penny may be puzzled by the reference. Originally primarily a women's usage (there was no charge for using the urinals)

# DIARRHOEA

In the shrinking world of the early 21st century, the problem of diarrhoea impinges on speakers of English particularly in the context of foreign travel. Holidaymakers in hot countries regularly get laid low, and indeed in America this form of the malady is often termed **touristas** (a partial anglicization of Spanish *turista* 'tourist'). A popular way of referring to this delicate topic is by naming it from a city in the country visited, or from a person or group associated with it. American terminology tends to reflect the easy availability of Mexico as a holiday destination, while British usage (presumably reflecting the experiences of service personnel rather than tourists) often alludes to the Middle and Far East. The vogue for these terms probably arose around and just after the time of World War II, but there is a lack of early printed evidence for them (the first record, for instance, of many of the American expressions is in a 1962 issue of the journal *Western Folklore*).

**Adriatic tummy** diarrhoea suffered by visitors to resorts on the Adriatic coastline of Italy and the former Yugoslavia

**Aztec hop** or **twostep** suffered by visitors to Mexico – *Aztec* from the native Indian people of Mexico, *hop* (as in 'Saturday-night hop') and *twostep* from the rapid dance to the lavatory

**Basra belly** from the town in Iraq, but applied generally to visitors to the Persian Gulf, on which Basra is a port. Alliteration is common to many of these expressions

**Bechuana tummy** used formerly throughout British possessions in eastern and southern Africa, and taken from the name of Bechuanaland (now Botswana). The first syllable, incidentally, rhymes with *wretch*, not *wreck*

**Bombay crud** from the city in northwest India ('I got Bombay crud, I am suffering from looseness of the bowels,' Frank Shaw, Fritz Spiegel and Stan Kelly, *Lern yerself Scouse* 1966). *Crud* is a slang term, originally American, for any sort of illness (particularly fungal infections of the skin)

**Cairo crud** the sanitation system of Cairo has always had the reputation of being hazardous to foreign visitors. Cf. GIPPY TUMMY below (p 179)

**Delhi belly** from the capital of India, and one of a number of terms, presumably dating from the days of the Raj, connecting the names of Indian cities with the laxative effect of Indian food on some European digestions ('In Bombay, shortly after the First World War, our mess was periodically afflicted by a particularly virulent form of "Delhi belly",' *Daily Telegraph* 1980). The earliest printed record of it is in the US magazine *Newsweek* 1944

**Hong Kong dog** not a dog of the canine variety, but perhaps an abbreviation of the Australian slang *dog's disease*, a cover term for various maladies ranging from malaria to a hangover, and including 'gastroenteritis'

**Karachi cork** from the former capital of Pakistan: 'We had pet names for all our ailments – Lahore Looseness, Bangalore Bowels, Delhi Belly and Karachi Cork,' John Reid, 1962

**Malta dog** afflicting British seamen and other service personnel stationed on Malta

**Mexican two-step** or **fox-trot** from American tourists laid low in Mexico and dancing to the lavatory (cf. AZTEC HOP). From the same part of the world comes **Mexican toothache**, with a delicate substitution of a more mentionable complaint

**Montezuma's revenge** Montezuma II (1466–1520) was the ruler of the Aztecs at the time of the Spanish conquest of Mexico. His murder (probably but not certainly at the hands of the Spanish) is regularly avenged over four hundred years later by the dysentery and diarrhoea visited on American and European visitors to Mexico, and by extension other tropical countries. An alternative name sometimes encountered is the **curse of Montezuma**

**Rangoon runs** another alliterative formation, this time on the name of the capital of Burma

**Spanish tummy** a malady suffered annually by thousands of British tourists on the costas of Spain. The term is first recorded in print in a 1967 issue of the *Sunday Times*: 'They never seem to get Spanish tummy, and their children are never overtired brats'

**Tokyo trots** diarrhoea suffered by visitors to Tokyo, capital of Japan; first recorded in 1969

**Tunis stomach** a term in use amongst British service personnel in North Africa during World War II. *Stomach* euphemistically moves the site of the trouble higher up the digestive tract

Other strategies for avoiding the explicit naming of the affliction can be subdivided into:

## The Quasi-Medical

The condition **gastric flu** is not officially known to medical science, but the term is often used to disguise diarrhoea. **Gastroenteritis** can serve the same purpose. On a more colloquial level, so can **tummy bug**, **tummy trouble**, and **tummy upset**. Continuing the 'gastric' theme is the American **GIs**, short for *gastrointestinal* (*shits*). These circumlocutions also have in common the shifting of the affliction from the embarrassing intestines and rectum to the more inoffensive stomach. This is shared by ADRIATIC TUMMY, BECHUANA TUMMY, SPANISH TUMMY, and TUNIS STOMACH (see above), and also by the Briticism **gippy tummy** (first recorded in 1943), which associates the condition with Egypt (*gippy* is altered from *Egypt*; cf. also CAIRO CRUD above), or more generally with any hot foreign country.

## The Delicately Descriptive

The language pussyfoots around the increased liquidity involved in diarrhoea. The key word here is **loose**. This has been used since at least the 15th century to characterize active bowels. It is usefully vague in its range of application, from desirable laxity through excessive frequency to out-and-out diarrhoea. **Looseness** can be a synonym for diarrhoea: 'A violent looseness carried him off,' Thomas Gray, 1760. More explicit is **runny tummy**, a coinage of the second half of the 20th century (perhaps based on the model of *runny nose*).

Into the same category come **the squirts** and its originally dialectal variants **the squits** and **the squitters**: 'We went incessantly to those over-public latrines . . . My squitters were at their worst,' Lord Harewood 1981. The use of *squirt* to characterize the emission of over-liquid faeces (which nowadays strikes perhaps a too graphic note to count as truly euphemistic) dates back to the word's earliest history, in the 15th century.

## The Accelerated Sufferer

The earliest euphemism on record for diarrhoea was inspired by the speed and regularity with which the sufferer has to escape to the lavatory. It was **the trot**: 'My brother would be . . . asking me what was the matter with me that I was so *often hastily taken*; saying he was sure I was ill of the trot,' Ellen Weeton 1808. By the early 20th century this had been pluralized into the expression we are familiar with today, **the trots**. The same notion probably underlies **the runs** (first recorded in print in 1962), although there may well be some subconscious reference also to the runniness of the faeces. See also RANGOON RUNS, TOKYO TROTS above.

## Rhyming Slang

Colloquially, diarrhoea is *the shits*. Its frankness can be covered up in the mysterious obscurity of rhyming slang: **threepenny bits**, usually abbreviated to **threepennies**; and **tomtits**, most often encountered in the metaphorical sense 'attack of anxiety'.

# LAVATORIES

The problem with lavatories – both the apparatus and the room or building containing it – is that there is no neutral word for them. Virtually every term in common use began life as a way of avoiding a vividly embarrassing direct reference to their function – as in the ostracized *shit-house*. Even the classless, sanitized *WC* is the product of a euphemistic application of *closet* 'cupboard'. Of all the non-scatological expressions in current usage, possibly only the British *bog* does not represent some sort of an attempt at circumlocution – and it is still under a taboo. (The precise origins of *bog* are unclear. The *Oxford English Dictionary* traces it back to a verb *bog*, which it defines memorably as 'to exonerate the bowels', and describes as 'a low word, scarcely found in literature, however common in coarse colloquial language'; but it makes no suggestion as to the origins of this verb. Traces of the usage go back to the mid 16th century, and it is possible that its early application to non-flushing earth closets was prompted by a resemblance between the accumulated excrement and a swamp or morass.)

The battleground in 20th-century British English was mainly dominated by **lavatory** and **toilet**. Both are firmly euphemistic in origin, and both retain something of that genteel feeling of linguistic drapery covering something unmentionable. A *lavatory* was to begin with (in the 14th century) a vessel for washing. This reflects its etymology – it comes ultimately from Latin *lavare* 'wash'. It had extended its range by the 17th century to 'room with washing facilities', and by the middle of the 19th century it seems that this was widely taken to include a water closet too ('There are separate lavatories for the men and for the women and children,' *Morning Star* 1864). By the early 20th century the emphasis had shifted to 'room whose principal or only feature is a water closet', and *lavatory* was also being applied to the apparatus itself.

Likewise *toilet* originally denoted a piece of fabric used for wrapping clothes (it was borrowed in the 16th century from French *toilette*, a diminutive of *toile* 'cloth'). It progressed semantically via 'cloth cover for a dressing-table', 'dressing-table', and 'process of dressing' to 'dressing-room', and in America in the 19th century this became further restricted to 'dressing-room containing washing facilities, and also a water closet'. The modern range of applications (similar to those of *lavatory*) seems to have been in place by the 20th century.

The two words vied for precedence in Britain during the middle years of the century. *Toilet* laboured under the handicap of having been declared (by implication) 'non-U' by A S C Ross in his seminal 1954 article in *Neuphilogische Mitteilungen* (he did not specifically refer to *toilet*, but claimed that *toilet-paper* was non-U and *lavatory-paper* U). So the upper classes on the whole went to the *lavatory* and the lower orders visited the *toilet* and upwardly mobile parents in between actively encouraged their children to use *lavatory*, and proscribed the common *toilet*.

In the latter third of the century the battle faded, as the ground of both words began to be taken over by **loo**. It made its first serious inroads in *lavatory* territory, but now seems to be supplanting *toilet* too. It first appeared after World War I, but it does not appear to have made serious headway until the 1940s. No one is sure where it came from. The most commonly touted explanation is that it is shortened from *gardyloo*!, a warning cry shouted in the streets of 18th-century Edinburgh by someone about to empty the contents of a chamber pot out of a window. This in turn was based on *gare de l'eau*!, a pseudo-French phrase meaning 'watch out for the water!' But the gap between the apparent disappearance of this (there is little evidence for it after the early 19th century) and the emergence of *loo* makes the derivation dubious. Possibly there may be some connection with *Waterloo* (in the early 20th century *Waterloo* was a British trade name for iron cisterns). But the likeliest candidate is probably French *lieux d'aisances*, literally 'places of ease' (echoing English *ease oneself* for 'defecate' or 'urinate' – see p 165), hence 'lavatory'. This could well have been picked up and anglicized by British soldiers in France during World War I.

Several of the euphemisms in current usage pick up on the theme of washing, like *lavatory* before them. The reason, obviously enough, is that water closets have standardly been installed in rooms where washing facilities exist. The commonest is probably the American **bathroom**. In its transparent sense 'room containing a bath' it dates back at least to the late 18th century, but in American English, apparently in the first third of the 20th century, its euphemistic transference to 'lavatory' became institutionalized. Today, expressions such as 'go to the bathroom' (i.e. to urinate or defecate) are apt to cause transatlantic confusion. **Washroom**, also largely an Americanism, is used similarly. Military euphemism favours the 'washing' metaphor too, but in a more pompous guise. A defaulter told to clean the **ablutions** will know that the communal lavatory is meant, even though the main central sense of *ablution* is 'washing'. And **latrine**, another mainly army word, comes ultimately from a derivative of Latin *lavare* 'wash' (so it is a close relative of *lavatory*).

Another favourite diversionary tactic is to name the lavatory after some other function that could plausibly be performed by a room containing (or even adjacent to one containing) a WC. It is used particularly in the case of lavatories in hotels, shops, restaurants, and similar public buildings. **Rest room** is a good example, conjuring up the bizarre image of patrons taking a quick nap on the loo. It is hard to disentangle its origins from those of a genuine 'room for resting in', but it seems to be early to mid 20th century, and it started life, like many other euphemisms in this category, in the US. An even discreeter variant, now seldom encountered, is **retiring room**: 'the erection of public retiring rooms for both sexes in the street,' *Pall Mall Gazette* 1884 (Dr Johnson in his *English Dictionary* defined *privy* as 'place of retirement'). Similarly inspired are **powder room** (exclusively for the use of women, where they are supposed to go to 'powder their noses' (see p 164): 'During the days of Prohibition some learned speak-easy proprietor in New York hit upon the happy device of calling his retiring-room for female boozers a *powder-room*,' H L Mencken 1945); **cloak room** (or **cloaks** for short), a Briticism of around 1950 vintage, which is based on the notion that lavatories in public buildings are often situated next to the room in which outer garments are stored; and the clinical **personal hygiene station** for the in-flight use of astronauts. **Comfort station** appears at first sight to be first cousin to *rest room* but it could well be that the 'comfort' alluded to is not resting, but the relief of emptying the bladder or bowels (cf. RELIEVE ONESELF, p 165). It is an early 20th-century American coinage; the now defunct variant *comfort room* is first recorded in 1910, *comfort station* itself in 1923.

A similar and very widespread ploy is to refer to public lavatories by the sex to which they are assigned. Again, it is often not clear in early usage whether a lavatory is actually being alluded to (instances of **ladies' cloak room** and **ladies' room** recorded from the late 19th century may not be euphemistic), but by the second or third decade of the 20th century the circumlocution was firmly established. In the case of females, politeness at first dictated the use of *lady* rather than *woman*: **ladies(')**, now the commonest term in British English, dates from around World War I (American English retains the fuller form *ladies' room*), while **women's room**, an Americanism, is not actually recorded before 1961 (it has become better known outside the US since its use in 1977 as the title of a novel by Marilyn French; she employed it as a metaphor for the need to treat women as ordinary people rather than as little porcelain dolls on pedestals, about whom one must be conventionally polite). As far as available evidence can take us, such genteelism did not operate in the case of men's lavatories: both the polite **gentlemen('s)** and the more down-to-earth American **men's room** are first recorded in 1929. The familiar British **gents(')** emerged soon afterwards. In the more functional type of public building, such as offices, factories, and hospitals, a bare **men** and **women**, or even **male** and **female**, can indicate a lavatory, with no direct allusion to what a member of either sex may find behind the marked door (although they are increasingly being supplemented or replaced by non-language-specific stylized representations of men and women). At the other end of the scale come the jokiness of **guys** and **dolls** and the excruciating winsomeness of **(little) boys' room** and **little girls' room** (American coinages of the 1940s).

The location of the lavatory within a house often provides a peg for a euphemism. In the days when such facilities were commonly out of doors, they could hide under the term **outhouse**, particularly in American English, or even **woodshed**. Inside, they can be obliquely referred to as **along the passage** or as **upstairs** (as in 'Would you like to go upstairs before dinner?'). In America, lavatories in shops and other public places are often below ground level, so there **basement** serves the same purpose. But oddest of all is **the geography of the house**, or just **the geography** for short. This is first recorded in the mid 19th century in the general sense 'layout of the rooms in a house', but by the 1920s expressions such as 'Can you show me the geography of the house?' had become firmly established as coy ways of asking the location of the lavatory: 'The Business Man Jocular: "I say, where's the geography, old son?",' *Listener* 1967.

Vagueness is a time-honoured tactic when talking about the lavatory. It can hide behind such generalities as **the arrangements** or **the facilities** ('Would you like to use the facilities?'), or the more specific but still oblique **the plumbing**, as in 'show someone the plumbing'. But the extremes of circumlocution are represented by terms such as **whatchamacallit**, **whatsit**, and **you know what**, which are literally almost empty of meaning.

Vagueness also underlies the use of **article** for a portable receptacle for urine or faeces, first recorded in 1922 and stigmatized by Professor A S C Ross as non-U: 'A madman . . . crowned his amusement this morning by bringing an article which he . . . sat on,' *Spectator* (Calcutta) 1932. **Chamber pot** is now the neutral term for this object, but its origins (in the 16th century) were surely circumlocutory – a pot used in a chamber (i.e. a bedroom) could in theory serve several other functions (the *Oxford English Dictionary* notes (in 1889) that 'in the crockery trade, [*chamber pot* is] often euphemized as *chamber*'). Variants now disused include **chamber utensil** and **chamber vessel**. The simple **pot** has been used in the same sense since at least the late 17th century, but its diminutive **potty**, applied to chamber pots for children, is not recorded before the 1940s. Colloquially, but still euphemistically, the chamber pot was known from the mid 19th to the mid 20th century as a **jerry** – probably an abbreviation of *jeroboam* 'outsize wine bottle'. And going back as far as the 14th century, but now defunct, is **jordan**, which was originally the name of a sort of vessel used by doctors and alchemists. Even more in the true spirit of euphemism is **gazunder**, coined because the chamber pot usually 'goes under' the bed when not in use. **Bed-pan** has existed since the 17th century, but has only gradually evolved its present-day sense 'chamber pot specially adapted for a bed-ridden person, especially as used in hospitals'. It is based on a use of **pan** for 'lavatory (receptacle or seat)' which dates back at least to the early 17th century, but is now encountered mainly in the expression *down the pan* 'ruined, wasted'.

The classic British euphemism for a public lavatory, particularly one situated in the street, is *(public) convenience*. This appears to have its origins back in the 17th century as a general term for any useful appliance or utensil – for example, for spitting into ('A convenience to spit in appeared on one side of her chair,' Tobias Smollett 1748). The modern specific application seems to have become established in the first half of the 19th century. The main notion underlying the euphemism is no doubt that it is convenient to have somewhere close at hand if the need to urinate or defecate comes upon one in the street, but the *Merriam-Webster Collegiate Dictionary*'s definition of *convenience* – 'an appliance . . . conducive to comfort' – reminds us that there may also be connotations of the relief gained by satisfaction of an urgent need.

'Convenience' also lies behind **commode**. The word was acquired from French in the 18th century in the sense 'chest of drawers'. In its original language it was a noun use of the adjective *commode* 'convenient', and so etymologically it denotes a 'convenient' or 'suitable' piece of furniture. It was in the mid 19th century that *commode* began to be applied euphemistically to a piece of furniture containing a chamber pot (what had previously been called a **close-stool**), and thereafter to any lavatory. In the 20th century commodes faded away as plumbed-in lavatories proliferated, and their name went with them. But portable commodes, for use in camp and on campaign, survived longer, and acquired in the early 20th century the heroic name **thunder-box** – from the reverberations caused by the user? The most famous thunder-box in English literature is the one owned and cherished by Lieutenant Apthorpe in Evelyn Waugh's *Men at Arms* 1952, 'a mechanism of heavy cast-brass and patterned earthenware of solid Edwardian workmanship. On the inside of the lid was a plaque bearing the embossed title of *Connelly's Chemical Closet*.' In the end it blows up while Apthorpe is sitting on it. In Britain, the trade-name **Elsan** (registered in 1924) has often served as another euphemistic alternative. Mention of Apthorpe's chemical closet brings us to one of the most ancient lavatorial euphemisms: **closet**. This originally meant 'private room'. It was used in the 17th century in the expression **closet of ease** to denote a room containing a lavatory, and before long *closet* itself was doing the same job. It has now virtually died out as a solo item, but it remains very much in circulation in the term **water-closet**. This was originally applied in the mid 18th century to a room containing a lavatory flushed by water, but by no later than the early 19th century was being used for the lavatory itself. The abbreviation **WC**, which dates from about the same time, has since established itself alongside *lavatory*, *toilet*, and *loo* as one of the most socially acceptable ways of referring to the room and the apparatus it houses (albeit condemned as non-U by Professor A S C Ross). The abbreviation of the abbreviation, **W**, apparently dates from after World War II ('Talking to the lamp-post . . . Using language . . . Singing in the W,' Dylan Thomas 1953). *Closet* also lives on in **earth-closet**, denoting a lavatory in which the excrement is covered with soil.

The 'privacy' theme is carried on in the now obsolete **privy**. This dates from at least the late 14th century, and probably originated as a shortened form of *privy house* (not actually recorded until rather later) – that is, a private house, an apartment concealed from the general view. Along the same lines, **sanctum sanctorum** (in Latin literally 'holy of holies'), a general term for 'a place where one goes to be private', has in the past been used for 'lavatory'.

## Some other miscellaneous circumlocutions:

**blue room** a cabin-crew euphemism for the lavatory on a passenger aircraft

**can** an American English term, dating from around the turn of the 20th century. It is reminiscent of *pot* in its specific application of the general name of a vessel, but in this case it refers not to a chamber pot but to a water-closet, or more broadly the lavatory

**cottage** a public lavatory or urinal. A usage almost exclusively of male homosexuals, employed in the context of sexual assignation or chance encounters. It is first recorded in 1901

**dunny** an Australian colloquialism for 'lavatory,' or more specifically 'earth-closet'. It probably came from the obsolete British dialect *dunnekin* 'privy', but the origins of that are not clear. There may be some connection with *dung* and the obsolete slang *ken* 'house'

**heads** the nautical term for a lavatory. Dating from around the middle of the 18th century, it comes from the usual location of the latrines in the 'head' or bows of a ship. In American English, where the singular form is also encountered, it is additionally used for a lavatory on land

**house** enters into numerous lavatorial compounds, standing for the building or room containing the receptacle. Those in which it is the first element (such as **house of ease** and **house of office**) have died out. In some cases where it is the second element this is true too (e.g. **necessary house**), but it is still very much current in terms such as *bog-house, shit-house*, etc. In Tok Pisin, an English-based pidgin spoken in Papua New Guinea, a *smol haus* (i.e. small house) is a lavatory

**john** perhaps the most familiar of American euphemisms for 'lavatory', also used in Australian and New Zealand English. Written records of it go back no further than the 1930s, but there is an isolated instance from 1735 of *cuzjohn* (i.e. cousin John) in the same sense: 'No freshman shall minge [i.e. urinate] against the College wall or go into the fellows' cuzjohn,' *Harvard Laws*; so it would seem that the word is ultimately just a euphemistic application of the male personal name (if so, it could well have been modelled on the earlier and now obsolete **jakes** 'lavatory', which dates from the 16th century and may have been based on the personal name *Jaques* or *Jakes*). **Jane** has been used, particularly by feminists, as an alternative term for a females-only lavatory

**karzy** a Briticism of the mid 20th century. It is an alteration of Italian *casa* 'house', and may have found its way into English via British personnel serving in Italy during World War II

**lav** a distinctly down-market abbreviation of *lavatory*, which first appeared in the early years of the 20th century. It has spawned the inappropriately winsome **lavvy**: 'We stayed in a no-star hotel with a lavvy yard,' *Guardian* 1991

**parliament** a punning analogy between MPs sitting in parliament and someone sitting on a lavatory. In the same spirit are, or rather were, **house of commons** and **house of lords**

**shouse** the Australians thought up the most direct method of making *shit-house* more polite – running the two syllables together into *shouse* (rhyming with *mouse*). It is first recorded in 1941

**smallest room** in most houses the lavatory is indeed located in the smallest room (if you discount the cupboard under the stairs), even when it is en suite with the bath or shower. The euphemistic appellation is first recorded in 1930. (**Small room** is actually considerably earlier – Queen Victoria asked in a letter in 1858 'Has the railway carriage got a small room to it?' – but has not worn so well)

**throne** British speakers have been lèse-majestically comparing the monarch sitting on the throne with someone sitting on the lavatory since at least the 1920s.

# FARTS AND BELCHES

One of the world's most ancient euphemisms is the association of the gas produced in the alimentary tract as a by-product of digestion, with 'wind'. The early Indic peoples named the aubergine in Sanskrit *vatimgana*, which means literally 'wind go', and which, by a series of tortuous transformations, has given English the word *aubergine* (it is not entirely clear whether 'go' in this context meant 'be in progress' or 'depart', and hence whether the aubergine was regarded as promoting or discouraging intestinal gas). The English use of **wind** in this sense dates back to Anglo-Saxon times. It is applied to gas in both the stomach and the intestines, and indeed in former times it was also used for supposed gaseous eruptions in other parts of the body (Samuel Pepys, in his diary for 14 August 1661, mentioned 'his [Lord Hinchingbrooke's] pain (which was Wind got into the Muscles of his right side)').

The escape of this gas from the confines of the body has been genteelly described since at least the 16th century as **breaking wind**. This too has historically been applied to both ends of the alimentary canal, and in former times the two often needed to be lexically distinguished (Richard Huloet in his *Abcedarium Anglico Latinum* 1552 gave the synonyms 'belke [belch], or bolke, or breake wynde vpward', while Philemon Holland, in his translation of *Suetonius* 1606, wrote 'He would give folke leave to breake winde downward and let it goe even with a crack at the very bourd [jest]'). But in modern usage it tends to refer specifically to farting. The 'wind' of *put the wind up someone* 'to frighten someone' (an expression dating from the early 20th century) is based on the same idea.

Current verbal strategies for avoiding the word *fart* include **backfire** (from the backfiring of a car, and based on the rearward expulsion of gas), **blow off** (the metaphor of 'blowing' was used in Latin too, in the shape of *flatus* 'fart', formed from the past participle of *flare* 'to blow': this has given English the po-faced *flatulent*, and also the medical term *flatus* 'gas in the stomach or intestine'), **boff** (a British usage, apparently originally school slang), **let off** and **let fly**. Australians may use **breezer** for a fart, an obvious return to the imagery of wind.

In a curious subcategory of its own is **raspberry**. As a term for a derisive noise, it is short for *raspberry tart*, which was in turn a rhyming-slang circumlocution for *fart*. But there is little or no printed evidence for the use of either *raspberry tart* or *raspberry* to mean actually 'fart'. The earliest known records of it, from the 1890s, are fairly and squarely in the sense 'noise made (in imitation of a fart) by putting the tongue between the teeth or lips and blowing'. The American equivalent, *Bronx cheer*, has only ever meant 'derisive noise'.

*Fart* itself was once a perfectly respectable word (it probably dates back to the Old English period, and is first recorded in the well-known 13th-century ballad *Sumer is icumen in*). It was gradually driven out of polite circles (the *Oxford English Dictionary* in 1895 noted that it was 'not now in decent use'), but in common with other similarly frank terminology for bodily functions, it started to make a come-back to respectability towards the end of the 20th century. If it can be used unblinkingly in a guide to good manners and etiquette ('If a person suspects they are going to fart, their best move is to try to step away from the group,' Drusilla Beyfus, *Modern Manners: The Essential Guide to Living in the '90s* 1992), can complete rehabilitation be far away?

Allowing gas to escape from the stomach via the mouth has not been regarded as such a faux pas as farting, so it has not attracted as many euphemisms. Nevertheless, as we have seen, *break wind* has served both purposes, as does the modern *make a* **rude noise** (mainly used to and by children). And there is no doubt that many present-day English speakers shy away from the frankness of *belch* (the softer **burp**, which imitates the sound, is a comparative newcomer; it originated in post-World War I America). Food and drink likely to make one belch can be politely referred to as **windy** or (particularly in the case of beer and carbonated drinks) **gassy**.

# VOMIT

By far the commonest way of avoiding the rather direct verb *vomit*, especially in British English, is **be sick**. This originally meant simply 'be ill'. Then around the late 16th century *sick* began to be used in the sense '(possibly) about to vomit' (as in 'feel sick'), and by the early 19th century the modern usage was firmly established. In the latter part of the 20th century *sick* also began to be used fairly euphemistically as a noun, replacing *vomit*, but the overtones of the verb, *to sick up*, which dates from the 1920s, are far too harsh to qualify it as a circumlocution.

Other synonyms share the same frankness of imagery or harshness of tone, notably *throw up* (although this seems to have been fairly respectable when it first appeared in the late 18th century) and *puke*. But there are down-toning alternatives available. Australian and American English, in particular, have some colourful examples.

The Australian **chunder** may have originated around the middle of the 20th century, although its origins are not clear. It had a fairly restricted currency for thirty years or so, but was brought to a much wider audience in the mid-1960s by Barry Humphries, in his 'Barry McKenzie' cartoon strip in *Private Eye*, and now qualifies as a supposedly quintessential 'Aussie' word. No one is sure where it comes from. The most beguiling suggestion is that it was based on the name *Chunder Loo*, supposedly rhyming slang for *spew*. Chunder Loo of Akin Foo was a cartoon character who featured in advertisements for Cobra bootpolish in the Sydney *Bulletin* between 1909 and 1920. Other possibilities are that it is a worn-down version of *watch under*!, described by Barry Humphries as 'an ominous courtesy shouted from the upper decks for the protection of those below'; and that it is related in some way to *chunter* 'mutter', which was probably of imitative origin. The character Barry McKenzie's alcohol intake necessitated frequent reference to vomiting, and another imaginative Australian idiom popularized in the process during the mid-1960s was **technicolor yawn** – an allusion, presumably, to the varied hues of the regurgitated foodstuffs. Variants include **technicolor chunder**, **technicolor laugh**, and **technicolor yodel**. Also Australian is **call for Herb** – perhaps from a perceived resemblance between the name *Herb* and the sound of retching.

Many of America's rich arsenal of vomit euphemisms are based on the theme of losing possession of what one had swallowed. Into this category come **blow** or **lose one's doughnuts**, **blow one's groceries**, **lose one's lunch**, **shoot** or **toss one's cookies**, **shoot one's supper** and **toss one's tacos**. Also popular are references to the vomiter, perched over the lavatory bowl: **drive the porcelain bus** and **kiss the porcelain god**.

Other colloquialisms for *vomit*, many of them originating in college slang, include, in roughly chronological order: **upchuck**, **barf** (probably imitative of the sound of vomiting), **ralph** (perhaps from the personal name, but again with an imitative input), **boot** (perhaps from the notion of being sick into a boot), **flash** and **buick**.

British English has little or nothing to add, except for **honk** (another imitation of the sound of vomiting) and the now very dated verb **cat**. This probably came from the now obsolete expression **shoot** (or **jerk** or **whip**) **the cat**, meaning 'be sick, typically due to excessive alcohol consumption'.

Seasickness has its own particular euphemism: anyone vomiting over the side of a boat is said to be **feeding the fishes**.

# SPITTING

In present-day Western society, spitting in public seems generally to be frowned upon (although this taboo is apparently lifted in the case of professional footballers at play), but it is little euphemized. Few people would nowadays blanch at the thought of uttering the word *spit*, but for those who do there is an alternative verb in the long-winded **expectorate** (which etymologically denotes 'expel from the chest'). For the liquid when still in the mouth, the Latinate **saliva** is politer than the native *spittle*. In the days when public spitting was more widely practised, receptacles were provided. The standard term for these is *spittoon*, but if this seemed too vulgar there was also **cuspidor**, a euphemism with not just knobs but almost baroque curlicues on. First recorded in 1779, it was borrowed from Portuguese, and goes back ultimately to Latin *conspuere* 'spit on'.

# SWEAT

The subtle gradations of linguistic taboo are nowhere better illustrated than in the maxim 'Horses sweat, men perspire, and women glow' – implying an ascent from the basely animal to the virtually disembodied spiritual that was once merely coy but now strikes us as out-and-out sexist. But in fact it has never been a particularly faithful reflection of actual usage. There is very little evidence of the direct euphemistic substitution of **glow** for *sweat* when referring to females – and what there is is usually in conscious allusion to the maxim. It seems rather to have a more general application to raised body temperature, as caused by exertion, or even (metaphorically) by an abundance of animal spirits, and hence to the external manifestations of this, such as heightened colour and sweating (in 1884 W C Smith wrote of 'Girls, all glowing with the flush of life').

**Perspire** has since at least the late 18th century been used as a genteel alternative to *sweat* (a writer in the *Gentleman's Magazine* in 1791 noted that 'It is well known that for some time past, woman nor child . . . has been subject to that kind of exudation which was formerly known by the name of *sweat*: . . . now every mortal, except carters, coal-heavers and Irish Chair-men merely *perspires*'). However, the old maxim does illustrate how, as with many euphemisms, its power to disguise weakened over the years, so that it came to be regarded in some quarters as no longer a suitable word to apply to women. In the late 20th century the pendulum swung back in the other direction, and it is now widely scorned as mealy-mouthed. *Sweat* is coming back into its own.

It has not quite made it yet, though. Its full rehabilitation will not have been achieved until it appears in advertisements for sweat-control products. Here, ad-men's circumlocution still rules. In this world it is not so much the sweating that causes the problem – although **anti-perspirants** (an apparently post-World War II term) can be deployed against **underarm wetness**. It is the smell produced by stale armpit sweat that cannot be directly mentioned. Instead, it is termed **body odour**, or, for short, **BO**. This curious euphemism seems to have emerged in the late 1920s or early 1930s ('Do you ever ask yourself about Body-Odour?' Dorothy Sayers 1933; 'Those "B.O." ads. I laughed at – is the joke on *me*?' *Saturday Evening Post* 1933), but its finest hour came in the Lifebuoy Soap advertising campaign of the 1940s and 1950s, in which the offender's best friend whispered hoarsely in his or her ear 'BO!', causing them instantly to reach for the Lifebuoy. The average human body produces several different smells, of course, from various sites, but as if to disguise the feared and loathed armpit among the similarly offending but less unmentionable feet, breath, hair, etc, the potentially all-embracing *body odour* is narrowed down to just this one small area.

A disinclination to name the source of the smell also characterizes the use of **deodorant**, which, unless some other object is explicitly specified, can be taken to refer to the odour of the armpit (although actually, when they first appeared in the mid 19th century, *deodorant, deodorize*, etc. seem mainly to have been used with reference to sewage).

Other body-smells have got off surprisingly lightly. Offending feet, for instance, remain largely uneuphemized, except by advertisers of products designed to counteract **foot odour** or **perspiration odours**. But there is one triumphant exception: **bad breath**. As a term, *bad breath* lives in a strange and rather uncomfortable symbiosis with its synonym **halitosis**. This was coined, apparently in the 1860s or 1870s, as a piece of medical jargon (it is based on Latin *halitus* 'breath', and the suffix *–osis* means 'diseased condition'), and it is not until after World War I that we begin to see evidence of its wider use as a high-falutin, circumlocutious alternative to the rather savage *bad breath*. It has never succeeded in ousting *bad breath* altogether, though, even in advertising copy, perhaps because of a perception that it is a little too mealy-mouthed for its own good.

# TEARS

There are no very severe taboos in English-speaking societies against crying – not as far as women and children are concerned, anyway – so it is not an action that has called a great many circumlocutions into being. The now obsolescent **pipe one's eye** was originally nautical slang, dating from the late 18th century. **Break down** (an elliptical form of *break down in tears, break down and weep*, etc) is sometimes used when the speaker wishes to avoid the directness or frankness of *cry* or *weep*. And since as long ago as the 17th century, crying has been facetiously referred to as 'turning on the **waterworks**': 'Sneaking little brute . . . clapping on the water-works just in the hardest place,' Thomas Hughes 1857.

# SEMEN

There are occasions when the medical directness of *semen, seminal fluid*, etc and the earthiness of *spunk* will not do. The occasions are perhaps few and far between, semen not being a topic of everyday conversation, but one sort of text that often goes in for flowery circumlocution is pornography. This is where one is likely to come across the likes of **love juice** (first recorded in 1896) and **love liquor**: 'I could feel his lovejuice so hot, trickling down into the start of my stomach,' *Pussycat* 1972. (Both of these are also applied to vaginal secretions.)

Many euphemisms are based on a similarity, in appearance or consistency, with various foodstuffs – perhaps arising from a context of fellatio. Into this category come **cream**, **milk**, **butter**, **buttermilk**, **jam**, and **white honey**. On a more elevated plane, **essence** for *semen* implies the quiddity of a man's being.

But the commonest alternatives to *semen* are **jism** and **come**. The former emerged in the first half of the 19th century, no one knows where from, with the meaning 'energy, vigour'. It was towards the end of the century that it began to be used for 'semen'. It is an orthographically unstable word, with variants such as **chism**, **gism**, and **jissom**, and also **jizz**. *Come* (also spelled **cum**) is a nominalization of the verb *come* 'reach orgasm and ejaculate', and is first recorded in 1923. (A similar inspiration lies behind the American **jack**, which is based on the verb *jack off* 'masturbate' – itself probably a derivative of *ejaculate*.)

# MENSTRUATION

Given that it is the object of the strictest taboos in societies all around the world, it is not surprising that menstruation raises linguistic difficulties. For long the only words available for referring to it were technical terms or evasions and circumlocutions. Even today's relatively neutral *period* began life (probably in the late 18th century) as a euphemism (it was short for *period of menstruation*, and seems to have arisen out of a general medical use of *period* for 'duration of a disease').

The periodicity of menstruation is an ancient peg for naming it. Indeed the very word *menstruation* is based ultimately on it. It comes from Latin *menstruus* 'menstrual, monthly', a derivative of *mensis* 'month'. English has its vernacular equivalent in **monthlies** (Keith Allan and Kate Burridge (*Forbidden Words* 2006) report that 'when the Australian magazine *Woman's Weekly* came to be published monthly the name was specifically not changed to *Woman's Monthly* to avoid direct association with menstruation'). A similar notion lies behind the cryptic **that time of the month** (sometimes shortened even more allusively to **that time**) and the more up-front **wrong time of the month**. The use of **time** on its own for 'menstrual period' dates back as far as the 16th century: 'Certaine people maie not bleede, as women whiche haue their times aboundauntlie,' William Bullein 1564.

Another recurrent theme in euphemizing menstruation is ill health, as if it were a disease. All the main adjectives of illness have been used to characterize menstruating women: **ill**, **indisposed**, **poorly**, **sick**, **so-so**, **under the weather**, **unwell** ('When I was unwell for the first time it was she who explained to me, so that it seemed quite all right,' Jean Rhys 1934). More specific, but still intentionally vague, are **cramps** and **tummy ache**.

Blood, and particularly its colour, feature largely. *Bloody* itself is a little too direct to qualify as a euphemism, but a number of now rather dated expressions incorporate the colour red. The **reds** is described by the *Oxford English Dictionary* as 'obsolete', and the **red flag** or **rag**, **the Red Sea is in**, and *the visitor with the red hair has come* (see VISITOR below) all belong to a less outspoken age.

Another major strategy is the personification of the menstrual bleeding as a **visitor** or **caller**, someone temporarily (and perhaps inconveniently) present: 'It was shortly before my thirteenth birthday that I first had 'Visitors'. Mother . . . had told me about the menstrual cycle . . . My first 'visitor' was a light one,' *Quarto* 1980. This lies behind a range of more-or-less cryptic expressions, including **Charlie's come**, **my friend has come**, **having a little friend to stay** (these last two probably with the additional implication of relief at not being pregnant), **having grandmother to stay**, **having the painters in** (here there are also connotations of (red) colour – the association of paint and blood – and of the sanitary towels perhaps suggested by the painters' protective dust-sheets), **my relations have come**, and **the visitor with the red hair has come**.

A number of obscure references to the cloth or pad worn to soak up menstrual blood have served to euphemize menstruation: **the danger signal is up** (red for danger, from the blood-stained cloth), **the flag is up**, **flying the (red) flag**, **be on the rag**, **have the rag** or **rags on**, **riding the rag**. They all now have a very dated air.

The flow of blood itself lies behind the obsolescent **show** ('I was called to a young Lady, who had a Shew of the Menses at twelve Yeares old,' Richard Russell 1753) and the more modern **have a run on** and **wet weekend**. Some have claimed a similar influence in the dated **flowers**, but there is no evidence that the metaphor is anything other than botanical; any link with the verb *flow* is unlikely. Also from the garden comes **the roses**, a reference of course to the colour of blood.

Other themes include the temporary unavailability of the woman for sexual intercourse: **off duty**, **off games** (a punning association between school sports and sexual play), **out of circulation**, **unavailable**; the regularity of menstruation: **old faithful**; and its unwelcomeness: **bad week**, **problem day**, and – probably the most widely used menstrual euphemism, first recorded in 1930 – **the curse**, which brands menstruation as a sort of atavistic punishment visited on womankind by the fates.

The most curious and impenetrable metaphor for 'start one's period' is the American **fall off the roof**, often shortened to **fall off**. Its origins remain a mystery.

At the start of the 21st century the great majority of these menstruation euphemisms seem to belong to a vanished, more squeamish age, which regarded menstrual bleeding as somehow shameful. On the whole, people tend now to use the straightforward *period*, without embarrassment, and do not feel the need for the more outlandish circumlocutions of the recent past.

The non-appearance as well as the appearance of menstrual bleeding can give rise to circumlocution, particularly in the context of a possible unwanted pregnancy. Ways of alluding to this include **to be late**, **to be over one's time**, and **to miss**, first recorded in 1947 ('I think I have a baby on the way . . . I've missed twice,' Graham Greene 1961).

The naming of the cloths, pads, etc used for soaking up menstrual blood can cause embarrassment, as can the description of their disposal. In this area a sense of clinical detachment is invoked, particularly by those who package and market such items: *sanitary* and *hygiene* are the watchwords, as if the escaping menses were a public health hazard, to be quarantined at all costs. Use of the term **sanitary towel** dates back at least to the 1880s, and it was soon joined by **sanitary pad** and **sanitary napkin**. Getting rid of used ones in an approved receptacle is often subsumed under the usefully vague heading of **personal hygiene**, or just **hygiene** (but contrast 'LADIES!! Please do not put **unmentionables** in the Toilet but in the Receptacle Provided,' notice in a lodging-house lavatory, quoted by Auberon Waugh 1991). Manufacturers of deodorants to combat smells produced by menstrual bleeding, or more generally by the female genital and anal region, tend to hide behind the dainty generality of **personal freshness** or **feminine freshness**. *Feminine* is the keyword in this area: such deodorants are commonly described on packaging and in advertising copy as **feminine deodorants**.

The term *menopause* for the cessation of menstruation dates from the 1870s (it is an anglicization of *menopausis*, a modern Latin formation based on Greek *men* 'month' and *pausis* 'pause'). In present-day English it scarcely seems to call for a euphemism, particularly since the coining of *male menopause* (first recorded in 1949). But for those to whom it seems too much like forbidding medical jargon, the abbreviated **pause** has provided a softer alternative. Less often heard now than in the past, **climacteric**, or **grand climacteric**, is a specific application of a general term referring to a point or stage of particular importance in a person's life. Ancient theory reckoned that these points recurred at intervals of seven years or, according to some authorities, nine: 7 times 9 equals 63, an age of weighty significance, therefore termed the *grand climacteric*.

By far the commonest alternative to *menopause*, though, is **change of life**, with its gaunt message of transformation into a new mode of being, a rite of passage without the rite, simultaneously asserting a momentous event and yet somehow shying away from the plain truth. Records of it date back to the 1830s (at which time the variant *turn of life* also existed). Latterly it is often abbreviated to simply **the change**, pregnant with mysterious implications.

# ILLNESS AND INJURY

―――

## PHYSICAL ILLNESS

The impulse to avoid naming diseases directly increases in proportion to the fear or embarrassment they cause us. The fear factor is caused by lethality combined with a streak of insidiousness. In the 19th century the role of villain was filled by tuberculosis, which killed many people but whose causes were mysterious, giving it an extra dimension of fear. It was euphemized as **consumption** (a usage dating from the 17th century), in allusion to the way in which it 'consumed' its victims, giving them the pale and wasted appearance so fashionable amongst artists and poets of the time. Another circumlocution employed in the 18th and 19th centuries was **decline**, a specialization of the still current use of *decline* for 'progressive worsening of a person's health'. The dreaded word *tuberculosis* was not introduced into English until the middle of the 19th century (before that the doctors' word for the disease was the now disused *phthisis*), but *consumption* continued in lay use, and *tuberculosis* was also widely avoided with the abbreviation **TB** (first recorded in 1912). The supposedly romantic character of the disease was played up in the 19th century by what seem to us rather grisly euphemisms such as **raise colour** and **spill rubies** for 'cough up blood' (one of the symptoms of tuberculosis). The discovery of penicillin virtually wiped the disease out in Western society in the second half of the 20th century (though there are signs of its re-establishing itself in deprived inner-city areas), so now no one minds using the word *tuberculosis*.

Its taboo has been transferred to cancer, whose name many now dare not speak. The currently modish euphemism is **the big C**, first recorded in 1968 but probably given wider currency by John Wayne's use of it when he had the disease in the 1970s. In obituaries of cancer victims, death is usually identified discreetly as being 'after a **long**

**illness**', or occasionally 'a **prolonged illness**'. The rather drastic **incurable illness** is also sometimes used, which might seem a bit strong for a euphemism, but is evidently felt to be more acceptable than *cancer.* The cancerous tissue itself can be camouflaged with the vague terms **lump** or **growth**, and even **tumour** (with its chance of benignness) is deemed preferable to *cancer.* Doctors may choose to attack the problem from the other end, adopting as verbal disguises technical terms with which they imagine patients may be unfamiliar, such as **carcinoma** and **neoplasm**.

Heart disease is just as high-profile a killer as cancer, but it lacks the insidiousness that produces the fear factor necessary to taboo. We are not so afraid of talking about it. Nevertheless, like all areas of illness it is subject to the terminological obfuscation of medical jargon. **Cardiac arrest** and **cardiac incident** sound more dispassionate than the vernacular *heart attack*, and **myocardial infarction** is so obscure that with luck the victim or relatives may not know what you are talking about. The term **coronary** is widely bandied about when referring to heart disease ('A spot of coronary trouble, you know'), and it is also used as a noun (short for *coronary thrombosis*), meaning 'heart attack'. Strictly speaking this usage (first recorded in 1955) is inaccurate, since *coronary* actually refers in this context to the arteries that supply blood to the heart, but it appears to serve a euphemistic purpose. The alternative course is to make light of heart problems, for which **ticker** is available ('Liz has no bust, being about 92. She has, however, in her words a dicky ticker,' *Guardian* 1991). First recorded in 1930, it compares the beating of the heart to the ticking of a watch or clock. **Pump** (usually 'the old pump') serves the same purpose.

As we have seen, medicine offers ample opportunity for concealing unpleasant truths by the use of long words – a classic euphemistic ploy. It may be much less alarming to talk about **variola** than about *smallpox*, about **rubella** than about *German measles* (in the latter case there is now an additional reason for euphemism in the fear of a racist slur against the Germans). Embarrassment may likewise dictate the substitution of the official-sounding **haemorrhoids** for the smirk-producing *piles* (a coyer alternative is **unmentionables**; and someone who has had their piles surgically removed may for the same reason be discreetly described as having 'gone into hospital for a **minor operation**').

But the supreme example of the euphemistic substitution of a technical disease name is in cases where the lay term has come to seem offensive in some quarters. The classic instance is the officially endorsed replacement of *mongolism* with **Down's syndrome**. It came to be perceived in the 1950s and 1960s as demeaning to sufferers from the condition to identify them with a particular ethnic group because of their appearance (and possibly also as a racist slur on Mongols to identify them with mentally retarded people). So in a letter to the British medical journal *The Lancet* in April 1961 from G Allen and others it was proposed to introduce an alternative term. Amongst the suggestions were *Langdon-Down anomaly*, *Down's anomaly*, and *Down's syndome* (all commemorating the name of John Langdon-Down (1828–96), the English physician who classified the condition). The last gained the widest acceptance, and over the following three decades gradually established itself in the language at large. *Mongol* and *mongolism* are now comparatively rarely heard, particularly among younger speakers.

A similar case is that of leprosy. Strongly negative connotations attach to the terms *leper* and *leprosy* (uncleanness, rejection by society, etc), and it came to be felt that people suffering from the condition would get a better deal if they did not also have to suffer from its name. An alternative was available in **Hansen's disease** (first recorded in 1938), taking the name of G A Hansen (1841–1912), the Norwegian physician who discovered the bacillus that causes the disease. Pressure increased for its adoption in the 1970s and 1980s, but it has never really caught on among the general public to the extent that *Down's syndrome* has (for one thing there is not so much call in day-to-day Western society to name 'leprosy' as there is to name 'mongolism', so a new term has less chance to take root; and for another, there is no obvious derivative of *Hansen's disease* to denote 'leper').

Underlying distaste for the terms there must be some suspicion that there lurks fear for the conditions they name, and if that is the case, those who advocate a change in terminology must face the possibility that, like much euphemism, the new terms will eventually lose their power to disguise, and become in their turn taboo.

A popular strategy in pulling the verbal screens round an illness is to use a very vague term when referring to it. Amongst the favourites are **condition** (someone with a 'heart condition' has something wrong with their heart; see also CONDITION p 88), **complaint** (its use for 'ailment', and the parallel use of **complain of** for 'have or say that one has (a particular illness)', date from the 18th century; **feminine complaint** is a coy way of referring to a gynaecological illness), and

**episode**, denoting a brief attack of an illness (someone might, for example, be described as having 'a history of coronary episodes'). **Trouble** and **problem** could be far more serious than they purport to sound (someone with a 'heart problem' might be at death's door; **woman trouble** in the US is roughly equivalent in meaning to *feminine complaint*). A surgical operation may be described as a **procedure**; **discomfort** could well denote 'excruciating pain' (specifically, **motion discomfort** is airline-speak for 'travel sickness'). **Complications** are additional or previously undiagnosed symptoms that may well be more serious than the original condition (more euphemistically still, they can specifically be inflamed testicles brought on by a bout of mumps).

Understatement is a common element in the colloquial euphemisms for 'ill'. **Dicky** (as in 'a dicky heart'; there is a theory that it comes from the old saying 'as queer as Dick's hatband'), **funny** ('I feel a bit funny; I think I'd better sit down' might be the last words of a heart-attack victim), **queer**, **uncle Dick** (rhyming slang for 'sick'), **off colour** and **under the weather** all play down the seriousness of the conditions they refer to. It takes a very British stiff upper lip to say 'I'm afraid I'm not feeling very **well**' when you feel as though you are on the point of death. And in more formal contexts **unwell** makes a much less strong claim to sickness than *ill*. The language of hospital spokes-people describing how ill a patient is deploys the same sort of under-statement: someone who is **comfortable** is not actually in acute agony, while someone who is **poorly** (a curious adjective, mainly colloquial except in the context of hospital bulletins) may well be dying. If we are told that someone is (doing) **as well as can be expected**, we decode the comment as 'not at all well'. Someone who is **not long for this world** is on the point of death.

Colloquial terms for illnesses help to trivialize them and thereby chase away their terrors. **Lurgy** takes away the power of a disease (generally an infectious one) by making fun of it. The word was popu-larized in the early 1950s by the British radio *Goon Show*, and is usually used in the ironic 'the dreaded lurgy'. **Turn** has the additional advantage of vagueness: 'I had a funny turn,' 'She's had one of her turns' could refer to any of a range of symptoms, although there is often a suggestion of faintness or giddiness. The now rather superannu-ated usage dates from the 18th century; it is probably related to the sense 'sudden shock' (as in 'You did give me a turn!'), but there may be some link too with *the turn*, an obsolete term for a brain disease in sheep which causes giddiness, which was presumably based on the gyrations of affected animals.

Pneumonia was often euphemized in the past (in an unnecessarily sexist way) as the **old man's friend**, because it brought a quick and relatively pain-free death to old people who otherwise might be subjected to the lengthy suffering of other diseases. Glandular fever is sometimes given a friendlier face as the **kissing disease**, a reference to the supposed ease with which it is passed on by kissing. Someone who is seasick (originally but not necessarily depositing the vomit over the side of the ship) is said to be **feeding the fishes**. And the most celebrated euphemism for a 'wound suffered in battle' is the British slang **blighty** or **blighty one**, coined during World War I and denoting a wound so serious as to require a return to 'Blighty', as Britain was called by the troops (the term comes ultimately from Hindi *bila-yati-* 'foreign, English').

Perhaps the most embarrassing of surgical procedures, and therefore ripest for circumlocution, are castration and ovariectomy. Euphemisms in this area tend to be the product of veterinary practice, but there is some drift in usage from domestic animals to people, particularly in the context of vasectomy:

**alter** dating from the early 19th century, and mainly American and Australian in distribution. A usage of exquisite vagueness: anyone having their cat altered might reasonably be supposed to return home with a dog. There is some evidence of the use of **change** in the same sense, but it has never caught on to the same extent as the more up-market *alter*

**doctor** a usage first recorded by the *Oxford English Dictionary* at the beginning of the 20th century, in a book called *Cats* (1902) by F Simpson: 'It is necessary . . . to have your male cat doctored when he arrives at years of discretion.' The majority of its use is in relation to pets and farm animals, but in recent years it has also been applied to human vasectomies. Again, it operates on the vagueness principle, picking out only one amongst hundreds of medical procedures which a doctor could carry out

**fix** mainly American, but first recorded in 1930 in D H Lawrence ('Is he a gentleman or a lady? – Neither, my dear! I had him fixed'). It is based on the use of *fix* for 'mend', with the underlying assumption that there is something wrong with a sexually intact animal that needs putting right

**nick** originally used of the castration of animals (with reference to the cutting of the vas deferens), but in recent years also applied to human vasectomy

**nip** a rather graphic evocation of the action of the tool used in castrating farm animals. The imagery brings tears to the eye, so it is not surprising that it has not been reapplied to human beings

**snip** a noun, denoting a 'vasectomy', which involves cutting or 'snipping' the vas deferens

Cutting up a patient with a scalpel may sound a little less alarming when termed 'surgical **intervention**' (but there again it might not: coiners of euphemistic gobbledegook often have a tin ear). Drastic operations involving the removal of much tissue are euphemized by their exponents as **heroic surgery**.

Although the word *hospital* is itself a euphemism in origin – it is closely related to *host*, *hostel*, and *hotel*, and used to mean 'place where guests are received' – the tendency to euphemize hospitals is noticeably less marked than the urge to avoid direct reference to institutions for the mentally ill or for the very old (see pp 220, 232). Nevertheless, two or three slightly coy usages stand out. The bare *home* usually connotes senility or madness, but with **nursing home** we are in the area of general physical illness. First recorded in 1896, it is used to denote a relatively small establishment catering mainly for private patients, often those convalescing after an illness or operation (although in this context the more up-front **convalescent home** – first recorded in 1883 – may be preferred). Its force is in the avoidance of the bad vibrations of *hospital* and in the comforting connotations of *home*. **Sanatorium** (or **sanitarium**, as American English often has it) was introduced in the 1830s as a general term for a 'hospital', but before the end of the 19th century it was being used as a verbal fig-leaf for a 'hospital for people with tuberculosis', often with the subtext 'place where people with tuberculosis go to die' (a typical site for such institutions was in Switzerland or elsewhere with healthy mountain air). The use of **hospice** for a 'hospital for terminally ill people' dates from the early 20th century. Earlier it was applied to hostels providing shelter for pilgrims, destitute people, etc. These were usually run by religious orders, and as it was generally these orders who set up the first hospitals for incurables, they took the term *hostel* with them. It was the hospice movement, spearheaded in Britain by Dame Cicely Saunders, that brought it to wider public notice in the 1970s and 1980s.

Inside hospital or at home, patients are liable to find themselves patronized by the 'medical *we*' – as in 'How are we this morning?' Doctors like to use such expressions, in preference to 'How are you?', to euphemize the role of the patient: the responsibility for being a sick person is partially lifted from the patient's shoulders by the fiction that the doctor shares it. This usage of **we** probably dates from the early 19th century (it is first recorded in the works of Charles Dickens in the 1830s).

# VENEREAL DISEASE

The very name *venereal disease* epitomizes the art of euphemism: a world of pain, fear, embarrassment, ostracism, deceit, and in many cases death hides behind the fluttering eyelashes of Venus. The term *venereal* (etymologically 'of Venus') had been used in English since the 15th century to mean 'of sexual desire or sexual intercourse', but it was not until the mid 17th century that it was commandeered to denote diseases transmitted by sexual contact. (A home-grown alternative that exploits much the same idea is **disease of love**.) Since then, as is the way with euphemisms, it has lost its protective power (even in its abbreviated form *VD*, first recorded in 1920), but English-speakers' linguistic ingenuity has found a host of other disguises for syphilis, gonorrhoea, and the rest.

The 'disgrace' factor attaching to VD – the notion that you have brought it on yourself by doing something you should not have done, and that, particularly in the case of women, infection equates with moral degradation – has given rise to a high incidence of extraordinarily vague *VD* synonyms. For generations, the slightest hint of what one is actually referring to has been taboo, and those without a key to the code (such as inquisitive children) have been left mystified by a succession of impenetrable generalities. Who, for example, could make much of **a certain disease**, a favourite of the 19th and early 20th centuries?

Some use a shield of technicality or legalese: the obsolescent American **blood disease**, for instance, sounds quite plausibly medical if not examined too closely; **communicable disease** gives the impression of having the official approval of the public health department (although in the latter part of the 20th century the term in its true medico-legal application – to infectious diseases in general – became more widely known among lay people, and so its more specific connotations of disease communicated by sexual intercourse or by the dreaded public lavatory seat have faded away); and the fearsome **contagious and disgraceful disease** is an actual English legal term, applied to slanderous accusations of venereal disease. In US services jargon of the World War II period, **preventable disease** laid the blame fairly and squarely on the patient.

Technically, **general paralysis of the insane** is a disease resulting from the tertiary stage of syphilis, but those wary of the term *syphilis* have in the past often made use of it (or its abbreviation **GPI**) as a respectable-sounding alternative – nowadays the *insane* part rather damages its euphemistic credentials. (*General paralysis of the insane* is a translation of French *paralysie général des aliénés*, and came into English in the first half of the 19th century.)

But many of this class of 'vague' *VD* euphemisms have unmistakable undertones of disapproval. Terms such as **secret disease** (a 19th-century Americanism) and **unmentionable disease** proclaim the stigma in the very act of disguising the name. The devastatingly sexist **women's disease** neatly encapsulates the role of scapegoat with which women have been burdened for the spread of venereal disease (in this case, specifically syphilis), while at the same time maintaining impeccable 'vague' credentials – it could more logically, for instance, refer to cystitis or cervical cancer. But the most widespread VD fig-leaf is certainly **social disease** or **social infection**, which seems to have emerged in the US around the turn of the 20th century: '"I'd rather have a social disease," said one disk jockey, "than have a Pepsi in my refrigerator",' *Guardian* 1991. The mincing metaphor that underlies the usage is presumably that 'social intercourse equals sexual intercourse', that human contact in daily life presupposes a measure of sexual activity.

Despite the greater freedom in discussing sexual matters that grew up in the 1960s, we seem still to feel the need to avoid the term *venereal disease* – indeed, Keith Allan and Kate Burridge in *Euphemism and Dysphemism* 1991 report a new circumlocution: **special disease** (= syphilis). It may in fact be not the imputation of unchastity that bothers us any longer, but the very baggage of old hypocrisies that *venereal disease* carries with it. The latest terminology, **sexually transmitted disease** (**STD** for short) is clinical, no-nonsense. It mentions 'sex' and 'disease' quite openly, but its role in relation to *venereal disease* is unmistakably euphemistic.

If the context of the discourse provides the element of 'promiscuous or random sexual intercourse' that is an essential connotation of *venereal disease*, one's terminology can be vaguer still. So, amongst professional prostitutes, **ill** functions as a euphemism for 'suffering from syphilis, gonorrhoea, etc'.

The other verbal defence against venereal disease is to be brash about it, to make fun of it. That, for example, is the motivation behind the retention of that fine old English term **pox**. In past centuries it was used for a range of pustular illnesses (a usage which survives in compounds such as *smallpox* and *chicken pox*). Among its applications were *great pox*, *French pox*, and *Spanish pox*, denoting 'syphilis', and these led to its specific solo use for any venereal disease. It also underlies the coinage of rhyming slang such as **bang and biff** (=*syph*, short for *syphilis*, and no doubt with an ironic backward glance at the moment of contagion) and the American **hat and cap** (=*clap*).

**Clap** itself as a term for 'gonorrhoea' dates back to the late 16th century. It came from Old French *clapoir* 'venereal sore'. Originally a socially acceptable word, it was described by the *Oxford English Dictionary* in 1889 as 'obsolete in polite use', but it has remained vigorously alive in the lower reaches of the language. A gonorrhoeic infection is colloquially a 'dose of (the) clap', and for those who prefer obliqueness to directness this can be abbreviated to a **dose** (first recorded in this sense in 1914). To have **caught a packet** or **copped a packet** in World War II service slang was to be similarly afflicted; and of the same vintage was **catch a cold**, a metaphor perhaps drawn from the earlier sense 'be put at a disadvantage' rather than a direct medical comparison. To be **caught**, however, which denotes infection with a venereal disease, suggests a failure of luck, the drawing of life's short straw.

Also in the tell-it-like-it-is school is the American **crabs**. Originally denoting an infestation of crab lice, a sort of body louse that lives in the pubic hair, it has become semantically diverted to 'syphilis'.

In the past, a popular tactic in the euphemizing of venereal disease was to blame it on foreigners, particularly those from countries with a reputation for Latin lasciviousness. So in former centuries expressions like **French ache**, **French disease**, **French fever**, **Neapolitan favour**, and **Spanish gout** added a chauvinistic element to the camouflage of syphilis, gonorrhoea, etc. (This sort of buck-passing was by no means restricted to English-speakers: the Italians, for example, referred to syphilis as *mal Francese* 'French disease', and to the Dutch it was *Spaensche pokken* 'Spanish pox'.)

A favourite theme in the metaphoricizing of venereal disease is the painfulness of the symptoms. In particular, the stinging or burning sensation when urinating that affects gonorrhoea sufferers has produced the obsolete **pick up a nail** (which compares the pain with that of a horse with a nail in its foot), **hot**, and **piss pins and needles**. Syphilis in the past has been called **bone ache** (possibly a double entendre – *bone* is also slang for 'erect penis').

In former times, hospitals for the treatment of venereal diseases (what would now be called *VD clinics*) were termed **lock hospitals** or **locks**. The origin of the name was the Lock lazar-house, a 15th-century quarantine hospital in Southwark. The name, but not the hospital, just survived into the 20th century. The euphemizing of condoms as **prophylactics**, which dates from the World War II period, arose from their role as protectors against venereal disease rather than as contraceptives (*prophylactic* means literally 'preventing disease'). In the services from World War I onwards, an inspection of the penis for venereal disease has been known as a **short-arm inspection**, or **short-arm** for short (*short arm* is slang for 'penis', but there is also a punning reference to *small-arms inspection*, the inspection of rifles, pistols, etc).

AIDS has never been characterized as a 'venereal disease'. But although it is passed on by infected hypodermic needles, infected factor 8 given to haemophiliacs, etc, as well as by sexual contact, it *is* quite commonly categorized as a 'sexually transmitted disease' – further evidence that the term *venereal disease* is now avoided not because of its sexual connotations but because of the negative associations (moral and other) that it has built up.

The euphemisms of AIDS itself have made significant progress in a relatively short time. It has been suggested that even the name AIDS has euphemistic undertones: on the surface it is an acronym for 'acquired immune deficiency syndrome', but there may well be a subliminal message of helpfulness and friendliness in the resemblance to *aid*. The name originally given to the disease in Africa, *Slim*, may have been intended euphemistically, but the crudity of the reference to AIDS's emaciating effect soon became apparent.

A person whose body's immune system is impaired by AIDS may be said to be **immuno-compromised** (first recorded in general euphemistic use in 1987, although it has a longer history as a specialized medical term). Someone who actually has the disease is camouflaged as a **PWA** (='person with AIDS'), which avoids negative terms like *patient* and *victim*. Another AIDS-abbreviation (abbreviations are always useful smoke-screens) is **ARC** (='AIDS-related condition' – e.g. weight loss, fever, herpes zoster). Someone who befriends a PWA and acts as his or her companion and helper is a **buddy** (first recorded in 1982). And it is not unknown for the cause of death of PWAs to be announced as **pneumonia**.

# PHYSICAL DISABILITIES

Diseases are uninvited visitors. But lack of or dysfunction of any of the bits of our body – blindness, say, or the absence of a limb – touch us much closer to home. They are something wrong *with* us, rather than something happening *to* us. Perhaps that is the reason why we are so acutely sensitive about the language used to describe such falling short of physical perfection.

The traditional language of disability is of ancient lineage – *blind*, *deaf*, *dumb*, *lame*, *cripple* all go back to Anglo-Saxon times – and can sound brutally frank to modern ears. There have always been more circumlocutious ways of expressing these concepts – *blind*, for instance, might be puffed up to **sightless**, **eyeless**, **visionless** or romanticized as **dark** ('Mr Bathom has been totally dark for seven years,' *Annual Register* 1768); and **mute** (a 14th-century introduction from French) has a long history as an alternative to *dumb* – but it seems not to have been until the 20th century that we really started to avoid these particular 'four-letter' words in a big way.

The forerunner of modern disability euphemisms was probably **hard of hearing**. This actually dates back to at least the 16th century, but it seems to have been only gradually that the euphemistic meaning 'deaf' emerged from the literal 'having imperfect hearing'. It is often impossible to say which is meant, and intentionally so; euphemisms thrive on such ambiguity. And what is more, 'deafness', unlike 'blindness', is not an absolute concept: you can say 'I'm a bit deaf', but not 'I'm a bit blind'. So disclaimers such as 'Not deaf, you know, just a little hard of hearing' are apt to be uncharitably interpreted as 'some residual hearing, not far off stone-deaf'.

Circumlocution came of age with the terms **disabled** and **disability**, which became institutionalized with reference to physical defects in the 19th century, and **handicap**, which emerged early in the 20th century. Both are very firmly still in current usage, but are under attack from some quarters for being negative or condescending: *disabled* suggests a 'lack' or 'absence' of ability, *handicap* a demeaning 'disadvantage'.

In the 1980s and 1990s a whole new vocabulary for euphemizing physical defects emerged, mainly from America. It attempts to put them in a more positive light. Its key words are **challenged** (first recorded in 1985), which views the defect as something with the potential to evoke a positive response in the person; **different** – i.e. not necessarily better than 'able-bodied' people, but certainly not worse; **impaired** (see HEARING-IMPAIRED p 211, MOBILITY IMPAIRED p 212); and **inconvenienced**, which puts the disability firmly in its place – merely a little local difficulty (Hugh Rawson in his *Dictionary of Euphemisms and Other Doubletalk* 1981 reports that the American organization for blind, crippled, etc sportspeople is named the 'National Inconvenienced Sportsmen's League').

A round-up of contemporary 'physical defect' euphemisms, many of which incorporate one of these key words:

# Blindness

**nonsighted** a less ambiguous alternative to UNSIGHTED

**partially sighted** a more positive formulation than *partially blind* – a product of the *half full/half empty* school of verbal prestidigitation. Its precise denotation is usually 'nearly blind'

**sight deprived** establishing that the disability is not the blind person's fault, but perhaps not positive enough fully to satisfy the criteria of 1990s political correctness. First recorded in 1965

**unsighted** modelled on UNWAGED (see p 272) and the like, but potentially distracting for those who are aware of the other, earlier meaning, 'not having a clear view'. Chiefly American

**visual deficit** a classic piece of depersonalization which draws an analogy between blindness (total and partial) and a budget shortfall

**visual handicap/visually handicapped** an early entrant in the late 20th-century euphemization of blindness, but one which lost favour in the 1980s and 1990s owing to the negative vibes of *handicap* (see p 210). The politically correct replacement is **visually inconvenienced**

# Deafness

**aurally challenged** or **aurally inconvenienced** both have impeccable politically correct credentials, but in spoken English there is a potential confusion with ORALLY CHALLENGED (see below)

**hearing-impaired** a more serious, technical-sounding alternative to HARD OF HEARING (see p 209), but 'impair' sounds a jarring note of negativity that sorts ill with the euphemistic demands of the 21st century. The same stricture applies to **auditory-impaired**

**mutt and jeff**, or **mutt** for short. Amid the predominantly sombre 'disability' euphemisms, a gleam of humour in this piece of rhyming slang (= 'deaf'). First recorded in 1960, it commemorates two characters, the tall Mutt and the vertically challenged Jeff, in an American cartoon series drawn by H C Fisher (1884–1954)

# Dumbness and Other Impairments of Speech

There is a particular taboo on the literal use of *dumb* because of its alternative meaning 'stupid' (in its extended sense 'temporarily speechless', as in 'struck dumb with terror', there are no objections to it). But since dumbness is a comparatively rare condition, few euphemisms have been evolved for it.

**impediment** short for *speech impediment* – that is, a stutter, lisp, etc. 'She has an impediment, you know' is enough to tell us what is meant. The use of *impediment* in this context is traceable back to the late Middle Ages: 'He had an impediment in his tongue,' Robert Fabyan 1494

**orally challenged** or alternatively **vocally challenged**. Not much call for these, but **aurally-orally challenged** might conceivably have more of a chance, as a euphemism for the politically dodgy *deaf and dumb* and *deaf-mute*

# Lameness, Paralysis, etc

The terminology with which we characterize those who lack one or more limbs, who have malformed limbs, are partially or generally paralysed, etc was in turmoil in the last quarter of the 20th century. Words such as *disabled* and *handicapped*, themselves originally coined to avoid the stigma of *lame*, *crippled*, *spastic*, etc, came to be seen as negative and demeaning, and suggestive of 'abnormality'. A new vocabulary has been evolved which seeks to accentuate the positive features of such peoples' abilities, and enable them to meet life on their own terms. Some people find it risible, and it remains to be seen if it will catch on firmly:

**differently abled** a conscious amendment of *disabled*, which seeks to make the point, not 'worse', just 'different'. The adjective *abled* has been used by the disabled since the early 1980s to denote the able-bodied, and it served as the basis of *differently abled* in the mid 1980s. Parallel formations are **otherly abled** and *uniquely abled*. See also PHYSICALLY DIFFERENT

**physically different** again, the emphasis on difference rather than disability. First recorded in 1988: 'The society we [thalidomide victims] were born into is not adapted to physically different people,' *David Frost on Sunday* 1988. Related euphemisms are **physically challenged** and **physically inconvenienced**

**uniquely abled** an even more up-beat message than *differently abled*: there is no one else in the world who has precisely the capabilities of this person

Somewhere between the two extremes is **mobility impaired** (R.W. Holder in the *Oxford Dictionary of Euphemisms* 2003 comments: 'circumlocution which implies that the weakening is effected by some external agency').

# Shortness

**vertically challenged** people who are shorter than average can retaliate against oppressive heightism with *vertically challenged*, or alternatively **vertically inconvenienced** or **vertically constrained**. And those afflicted with actual dwarfism have been described as 'persons of **restricted growth**' (first recorded in 1987). Another convenient circumlocution is **below medium height**. See also PETITE (p 152)

Thickened heels and soles worn to increase a short man's apparent height can be euphemized as **risers**.

# MENTAL ILLNESS

Afraid of madness, of going mad, we shun the word *mad*. We have created a huge battery of colloquialisms to poke fun at it, to show that we do not really care about it, and also a range of dispassionate technicalisms, the verbal equivalent of padded cells, to keep it under control.

Virtually all the core 'madness' words whose literal frankness we now avoid (while allowing ourselves metaphorical extensions: 'You must be insane to even think it'; 'Don't get mad at me!') had their origins in euphemism. Latin *insanus*, from which we get *insane*, meant literally 'unsound', although it was used from earliest times for 'unsound in mind'. *Demented* goes back to a Latin formation based on *mens* 'mind' and the prefix *de-* 'away from, without'. *Lunatic*, from late Latin *lunaticus*, means etymologically 'affected by the moon' (it was, and no doubt still is, believed that recurrent periods of madness depended on the phases of the moon). The source of *cretin* 'mentally retarded person' is Swiss French *crestin*, which means literally 'Christian' – a euphemistic admission of mad people to the human race ('ordinary Christian folk') from which in practice they were commonly excluded. *Imbecile* 'mad person' is descended from a Latin word which denoted literally 'without a stick' (Latin *bacillum* = 'small staff or rod'), the underlying notion being that the mind 'lacks support', is 'feeble'. *Mad* itself appears to go back ultimately to a prehistoric Germanic root meaning 'change, adulterate'.

Other languages show the same euphemizing tendency in their madness vocabulary. Italian *pazzo* 'mad' comes from Latin *patiens* 'suffering', via the concept of 'ill person' (as in English *patient*). German *verrückt* 'mad' is the past participle of *verrücken* 'displace', and metaphoricizes the brain as a piece of machinery that is out of order. Serbo-Croat *mahnit* 'mad' is related to *mahati* 'swing', and apparently comes from the notion of a mad person swinging his arms round wildly.

But when it comes to madness, the path from euphemism to taboo is usually swift and straight. *Mad*, *insane*, *lunatic*, *demented*, *deranged*, *imbecile*, *moron*, *cretin*, and the rest can now cause a considerable shudder if used with reference to a mentally ill person. The typical course followed by such words is as follows: they are adopted as specialized terms by the medical profession (in former times, doctors tended to take over words for 'mentally weak' that already existed, such as *imbecile*, whereas nowadays psychiatrists are more inclined to coin their own – *mentally handicapped*, etc); as their euphemistic force wanes, they are dropped by doctors, but in the meantime they will often have been taken up by the law, where they will typically survive much longer – lawyers being less sensitive souls than doctors, and disinclined to tamper with established terminology; and finally they descend into the melting pot of more-or-less off-colour colloquialisms. In the 18th and early 19th century *lunatic*, for instance, was a perfectly respectable medical term; in 1903 the *Oxford English Dictionary* noted it as 'current in popular and legal language, but not now employed technically by physicians' (Henry Stephen in his *Commentaries on the Laws of England* (1845) made a distinction between *lunatic* and *idiot*: 'Persons insane (in which class are . . . to be included idiots who have had no understanding since their birth, as well as lunatics who . . . have lost the use of their reason)'); and nowadays its only generally acceptable usage is in the weakened sense 'wildly foolish'.

The turnover rate in 'madness' terminology is therefore high. Yesterday's soothing vagueness is today's embarrassment. In 1992, for example, there were moves to change the name of the British charity Mencap, on the grounds that its suggestion of 'mental handicap' – originally a euphemistic notion – might be likely to give offence. The modern history of 'madness' terminology really begins with *mental*, towards the end of the 18th century. The word had been in use in

English since the 15th century in general reference to the mind, but it is from the 1790s onwards that we find it applied specifically to disorders of the mind. The first such term on record is *mental derangement* (1794), and it was followed in the 19th century by *mental disorder*, *mental deficiency*, *mental illness*, etc. Shifts in usage between them have generally been motivated by the familiar decline from euphemism to taboo: for instance, in the 1959 Mental Health Act, the previously official British terms *mental deficiency* and *mental defective* were dropped in favour of *mental disorder*, presumably because *deficiency* and *defective* had come to seem demeaning in their suggestion of inadequacy. By the 20th century *mental* had clearly absorbed into itself its association with illness of the mind, reflected in usages like *mental patient* and *mental hospital* (see p 219). And in the 1920s we begin to see the first signs of **mental** being used on its own colloquially to mean 'mad' ('I gather she was a little queer towards the end – a bit mental, I think you people [nurses] call it,' Dorothy Sayers 1927). In the 1960s, **mental handicap** and **mentally handicapped** became the widely acceptable terms denoting incomplete or defective development of the mind, but by the 1990s *handicap* was under a general cloud on account of its negative connotations (see p 210), and alternatives were being sought. In 1991 the British Department of Health officially adopted the term 'people with **learning disabilities**'. The politically correct use of *mental* is deemed to be **mentally challenged**.

Other elements in the 20th-century official language of madness include **disordered**, which has its roots in the 18th century, and which suggests merely a mild mis-arrangement of the mind; **distressed**, which equates being mad with being upset; and **unbalanced**, which was probably inspired by THE BALANCE OF ONE'S MIND IS DISTURBED (see p 216). Note that all of these are not positive words, but are couched in negative terms – a classic euphemistic strategy. The politically correct terminology of the 1980s and 1990s dispensed with this subterfuge: it makes the statement that madness is not worse, merely not the same – hence **emotionally different**; it even claims a positive status for the mad – they are **special** or **exceptional**. But this flip-flop in attitudes has yet to catch on in the language at large, in British English at any rate. The most popular contemporary 'madness' euphemism is firmly in the negative school: **disturbed**. This evolved in the early years of the 20th century. The first record of it is in a translation of a German psychiatric text, so it may have been suggested by German *verrückt* 'mad', which can mean literally 'displaced, disarranged'. It has gradually seeped out from the specialist jargon of psychiatrists, social workers, etc into the public domain: '"Are you disturbed?" went on the lunatic . . . "No, just, er, tension." "I been disturbed for . . . a long time. Ever since my mum died, but they say it's nothing to do with that",' Kingsley Amis 1978. An allied term is **maladjusted**, which is used to cover a range of conditions, from being a social misfit to insanity.

**Eccentric** has a special place in the euphemism of madness. It does not merely neutralize madness; it makes a positive virtue of it. It takes behaviour traits which we might well be willing to ascribe to some sort of mental illness ('Not really mad, you know, just a little eccentric'), and turns them into something whimsically amusing and cosy. Edith Sitwell's *English Eccentrics* (1933) was written in praise of its subjects; and to this day many English people take a wry pride in the nation's reputation for eccentricity. Another term for strange behaviour verging on madness which has made great strides in recent years is **bizarre**. It is a favourite of journalists; it has become almost a cliché to describe any aberrant action as 'bizarre', whether or not it is literally 'strikingly or grotesquely strange': 'Why is it that the rest of us are unaware of such bizarre behaviour [compulsive washing],' *Guardian* 1990. But it lacks the positive connotations of *eccentric*. For more colloquial 'madness' euphemisms exploiting the notion of 'strangeness' see FUNNY (p 222).

One of the classics of 'madness' terminology is **nervous breakdown**, used by lay people to denote any of a range of sudden-onset mental illnesses from post-natal depression to schizophrenia (psychiatrists on the whole reject it as imprecise). It came into use around the turn of the 20th century, along with the synonymous **mental breakdown**. Its great advantage as a euphemism, apart from its vagueness, is that it suggests that behavioural oddities have their origin in some sort of physical trauma, some nervous lesion, rather than in mental weakness, which is seen as more shaming. It is often shortened to **breakdown**: 'After a breakdown you do [fear it will happen again], and the worst thing is, because of the stigma of mental illness, everybody else thinks so too,' *Observer* 1992.

The medico-legal world has a vocabulary all of its own to deal with madness. The key terms here are **while the balance of one's mind is disturbed**, which probably dates from the middle of the 19th century and is usually used to describe (or euphemize) the mental state of successful suicides (cf. UNBALANCED p 215), and **of unsound**

**mind**, first recorded in 1818. But even the lawyers have cleaned up their linguistic act. Those deemed insufficiently sane to be responsible for their criminal actions are now liable to be characterized by the coy phrase **diminished responsibility**: this was carefully defined in a British Act of Parliament in 1957 to make it applicable to people who are not actually barking mad, but at least temporarily a brick short of a full load. The formal legal procedures for sending a mad person compulsorily to a psychiatric hospital are strong targets for euphemism. Indeed, **certified** and **certifiable**, which date from the late 19th and early 20th centuries respectively, have moved beyond their original legal sphere to denote colloquially 'mad' (the system under British law by which two doctors and a magistrate had to sign a certificate in order to get a mad person locked away was abolished at the end of the 1950s). Alternative circumlocutions are **commit**, short for a range of longer expressions, such as 'commit to an institution', 'commit to an asylum', etc, **institutionalize**, first recorded in 1949, and, more colloquially, **put away** (as in 'He's been behaving very strangely lately; I think we'll have to have him put away'). The **men in white coats** are the doctors or attendants from the mental hospital who will come to **take away** the mad person. The latest British euphemism in this area is **section** ('So what do you want me to do? Keep her locked up here? Get her sectioned off to the funny farm?' *The Bill* 1992), which comes from the notion of applying the relevant 'section' of the mental health legislation. It bears a coincidental similarity to the American **section eight**, denoting discharge from the services on the grounds of insanity, which refers to section eight of US Army Regulations 615–360: 'You stay in until you are hit badly or killed or go crazy and get section-eighted,' Ernest Hemingway 1950.

A particular category of euphemisms attaches itself to those whose mental powers are abnormally low. *Retarded* (first recorded in G E Shuttleworth's *Mentally-Deficient Children* 1895) was no doubt meant kindly to begin with – the underlying image is simply of being 'held back' – but today it is unusably frank. Its colloquial counterpart, *backward*, whose roots lie in the 18th century, is now under a similar taboo. *Educationally subnormal* (first recorded in 1953) scarcely softens the verdict, although its abbreviation **esn** has a marginally euphemistic role. But the political correctness of the 1980s and 1990s yielded a number of circumlocutions. Most of them exploit the notion of 'development' (a positive concept): **developmental difficulties**, **developmentally challenged**, **developmentally different**, **developmentally**

**inconvenienced**. They recall the earlier euphemisms **late developer** and **slow developer**, denoting a dull child who may, with luck, blossom out later on, and **slow learner**, denoting a child of meagre intellectual gifts which keep him or her behind the rest of the class. **Under-achiever** too tries to be positive in suggesting merely temporary failure to reach full potential. A classic euphemistic strategy is represented in a range of terms incorporating *less*, which allow a positive note to be struck, even if it is compromised by the qualification: **less able**, **less academic**, **less gifted**, **less talented**. Amongst educationists in the 1980s, **learning difficulties** was widely used (but even this, abbreviated to *LD*, has been turned into a playground insult – it is the fate of euphemisms to be subverted). Another ingenious alternative is **the slower-minded**. See also SLOW (p 226). Adults as well as children of low intelligence can be characterized as **limited**, and other colloquial formulae for tiptoeing round the subject include 'She's **no scholar**' and 'He's **not a great reader**'. Children whose low level of academic achievement stems from idleness may be described as having a **concentration problem**. Children with alarmingly violent behaviour patterns – compulsively hitting their heads against the wall, for instance, or screaming uncontrollably at strangers – are now officially designated as exhibiting **challenging behaviour**: 'As many as 4,000 children in Britain have "challenging behaviour" – they may hurt themselves or other people,' *Radio Times* 1993. Strategies developed to make good any learning difficulties may be euphemized as **remedial** (e.g. 'remedial classes').

Schools too were the source of the concept of '**special needs**' – a classic euphemism, implying exclusivity in a weasely way and suggesting the possibility of nothing more serious than a mild allergy, but in fact covering a huge spectrum of deficits from physical handicap through low intelligence to emotional disturbance. In Britain, children judged by a local education authority to have such a need are **statemented** – that is, officially declared (in the vaguest possible terms) to have it (the procedure and its terminology were introduced by the Education Act of 1981). Meanwhile the concept of 'special needs' has spread beyond the classroom to the wider world (e.g. 'special-needs transport' could be laid on for the physically disabled of any age), so educationists have expanded it to '**special educational needs**' (often further euphemized by abbreviation to **SEN**).

Terrified of the stigma attached to the word 'failure', some early 21st-century educationists floated the idea of replacing it with

**deferred success,** but this triumph of the euphemizer's art, with its empty promise of jam tomorrow, not surprisingly met with little but derision.

Paradoxically, we often find it almost as awkward to refer to unusually clever people (particularly children) as to talk about people of low intelligence. The fashionable euphemism in this area is **gifted**, which appears to use the stratagem of playing down the cleverness: 'Peter MacMahon refuses to call his son a genius. Educationists prefer to talk about "gifted" children, often making comparisons with pupils with learning difficulties,' *Observer* 1992. The common factor is that both very high intelligence and very low intelligence are abnormal, and therefore in a measure threatening (the link is strikingly lexicalized in **exceptional**, used by educationists not just for unusually intelligent children but also, somewhat surprisingly, for unusually dull ones). (**Precocious** used of very clever or able children hovers on the edge of disapproval, but it serves a euphemistic function when applied to children who are bad-mannered and spoilt.)

The naming of the buildings in which mad people are kept is a particularly tricky business. *Madhouse* was a completely neutral term in the 17th and 18th centuries (an Act of Parliament of George III's time was entitled 'An Act for regulating Madhouses'), but today it would score 101 out of 100 on the offensiveness scale if used literally. *Asylum* was introduced in the 19th century, presumably in order to get away from the harshness of *madhouse* – its original connotations are after all of refuge and safety – but in the 20th century it also gradually became tainted. We now tend to avoid *asylum* and its compound forms *lunatic asylum*, *mental asylum* and *insane asylum*.

Many of our modern terms exploit the idea of a 'hospital': **mental hospital** (first recorded in 1898; now slightly dodgy, but probably still just counting as a euphemism); **psychiatric hospital** (apparently dating from around the same time); and just plain **hospital** ('Mentally handicapped adults are being sexually abused in homes and hospitals,' *Observer* 1992). This may partially be a hangover from the days when people with actual physical diseases, such as syphilis, were incarcerated in such places, but mainly it seems to reflect a growing tendency to regard madness as an illness (rather than as, for example, some sort of demonic possession). This fundamental change in the classification of madness probably had its roots in the late 18th century, but its first linguistic manifestations are terms such as *mental health* and *mental hygiene*, which began to emerge in the 19th century (*mental disease* and *mental illness* do not actually appear in the record until the 20th century, but they are probably older than that).

Another vague- and dispassionate-sounding candidate is **institution**. This probably got off the ground in compound forms such as **mental institution** ('She drove her daughter Sally literally so [i.e. insane], to the extent that Sally has spent most of her life in mental institutions,' *Independent on Sunday* 1992) and **psychiatric institution**, but it is now available in a solo role (as in 'He's behaving really strangely; he should be in an institution'). It does, however, have a rather harsh, inhuman edge to it which makes it not an ideal euphemism for the 21st century. Cf. INSTITUTIONALIZE (p 217).

An alternative and increasingly popular line of approach is **home**. Again, compounds came first (**mental home** is first recorded in 1928), but *home* itself now has a strong role in euphemizing 'place where mad people are kept'. This exploits the same connotations of security, refuge, and love that make *home* such an attractive term for places where old people, invalids, etc are kept (see p 232). An interesting linguistic development which has probably been boosted by the British government policy in the 1980s and 1990s of reducing the population of mental hospitals (euphemized as *community care*) is the evolution of the term **residential home** ('a young mentally handicapped woman who was moving away from her Nottingham residential home into the community,' *Observer* 1992) – as if a 'home' could logically be anything other than 'residential'.

The other way to take the terrors out of homes for the mad is to laugh at them. And coincidentally, many of the terms we use for doing this are based on the idea of lunatics' maniacal laughter: **giggle house** (an Australianism dating from the World War I period) and **laughing academy** both come into this category, and so possibly does **funny farm** (first recorded in 1963), although this may be more closely related to the use of *funny* for 'slightly mad' (see p 222). Other institutionalized jokey names are **loony bin**, or just **bin** for short (first recorded in 1919), which probably came from the notion of putting someone away as if in a bin; **booby hatch**, an American coinage of the 1920s which was actually used previously for a 'gaol' or 'lock-up' (the more logical-sounding **booby hutch** is often used instead); **bughouse**, another Americanism, dating from around the turn of the 20th century, which is based on *bug* 'person obsessed with an idea'; and **nuthouse**, first recorded in 1929 (American variants of this are **nut college** and **nut factory**).

The shift of emphasis in the latter part of the 20th century from the incarceration of the mentally ill in specialized establishments to their treatment at home gave rise to what many regard as its own euphemism: **care in the community** (first recorded in 1977).

Our colloquial language of madness often seems to have a cruel streak, betraying a willingness to poke fun at those with less than average mental powers. But two factors tend to soften its impact: much of it is reserved most of the time to extreme stupidity or foolishness rather than clinical insanity; and when it *is* applied to actual madness, the motivation, subconscious if not conscious, is frequently to euphemize it by making light of it:

**all there** nearly always in negative contexts: *not all there* = 'not completely sane'. First recorded in 1864. 'Absence' as a metaphor for mental incapacity is also exploited in various *out* phrases (see OUT) and also in lengthier euphemistic expressions such as 'the lights are on but no one's at home'

**barking** a Briticism, probably dating from the 1960s. Short for **barking mad**, it equates insanity with the barking of a mad dog

**barmy** originally **balmy** (first recorded in 1851), which probably draws an analogy between the 'softness' of balm and the 'softness' of a weak mind. The variant *barmy* emerged in the 1890s (based on *barm* 'froth'), and has since taken over as the main form. Another application of *barm* to 'madness' is **barmpot** 'mad or stupid person', originally dialectal: 'Thus a harmless schizophrenic will be classified by the staff as a "barmpot" and by the prisoners as a "nutter",' T & P Morris 1963

**bananas** first recorded in 1957, and often used in the expression *go bananas*. The connection between bananas and madness is a mystery. There may be a link with the obsolescent *banana oil* 'nonsense', but as no one knows where *banana oil* came from, it does not get us much further. Perhaps NUTTY and FRUITCAKE suggested some connection with the dessert course that might have been picked up in *banana*, but that is a pretty desperate throw

**bats** from the euphemistic expression **(have) bats in the belfry** 'be mad', which dates from around the turn of the 20th century. Another derivative is **batty**, first recorded in 1903

**bonkers** a Briticism which emerged in the 1950s. Its origins are entirely obscure. Common collocations are 'stark staring bonkers' and 'stark raving bonkers' (popularized by Lord Hailsham in 'If the British public falls for [Labour party policies], I think it will be stark raving bonkers' (1964))

**case** an extension and specialization of the sense 'patient' (which has its roots in the mid 19th century) to 'mental patient'. Originally probably medical slang, it is now firmly in the public domain (as in 'He's a real case!'). See also HEAD CASE and NUTCASE

**cracked** like *crazy*, which is too general a term to have much euphemistic force, *cracked* exploits the metaphor of the 'broken' mind. It dates back to the 17th century. The British **crackers** is much more recent; it is first recorded in 1928

**cuckoo** as an adjective meaning 'mad, crazy', originally an American usage, dating from the early 20th century. It comes from the noun use of *cuckoo* for 'fool', which is several centuries older

**doolally** a now obsolescent British services' usage, which evolved in India in the early 20th century. It is short for **doolally tap**: *doolally* represents a pronunciation of Deolali, a town in Marashtra where there was a British army camp; and **tap** comes from the Persian word *tap* 'fever'. The symptoms of someone suffering from malaria in the heat of a camp hospital no doubt resembled craziness

**dotty** there is a single isolated example on record of *dotty* being used for 'feeble-minded' in the 15th century, but its modern usage did not emerge until the late 19th century. It is probably related to *dote* 'be foolish', but 19th-century uses of *dotty* for 'unsteady on one's feet' suggest a possible connection with the now dated expression *dot and carry one* 'limp, be lame'. This is said to come from the 'dot' or impression left on the ground by a wooden leg

**flaky** an American usage, given international fame in 1986 when US president Ronald Reagan applied it to Colonel Qaddafi of Libya. First recorded in 1959, it may be based on the notion of someone 'flaking' out, as when under the influence of drugs. The derivative **flake** 'crazy person' dates from 1959 too

**fruitcake** a 'mad person'. It is American in origin, and comes from the expression 'as nutty as a fruitcake' (see NUT). Its earliest recorded use in the context of madness, from 1942, is actually as an adjective, in the phrase 'go fruitcake'; but it is the noun use, which emerged in the early 1950s, that has flourished

**funny** it is the 'funny-peculiar' sense of the word rather than the 'funny-haha' that has led to its use for 'mentally weak'. Other 'madness' colloquialisms based on the 'unusualness' metaphor include *odd*, *peculiar*, *queer*, *strange*, and *weird*. See also BIZARRE (p 216) and ECCENTRIC (p 216)

**head-banger** originally applied in the late 1970s to dancers gyrating to heavy-metal music (this style of dancing involved shaking the head frenziedly), but from the 1980s used for a 'crazy person' too

**head case** a 'mad person' – often with underlying implications of 'violent madness'. Mainly a Briticism, dating from the early 1970s. The metaphorical connection of *head* with 'madness' is an obvious one (see also *off one's head* at OFF (p 224) and HEADSHRINKER (p 227)); *case* in this context implies 'patient' (see CASE (p 222))

**limited** the limitation in this case is on intellectual capacity. The implication of low intelligence applies across the board, but is often aimed specifically at schoolchildren. A classic euphemism, which uses a very vague and ambiguous term to make a very specific charge

**loco** acquired by American English in the late 19th century from Spanish *loco* 'mad'. The origins of the Spanish word are not known

**loony** adapted from *lunatic*. Both the adjective, 'mad', and the noun, 'mad person', date from the last third of the 19th century

**loony tunes** like *loony*, both an adjective and a noun. It comes from the name of a series of Warner Bros animated cartoons, and was popularized by US president Ronald Reagan in 1985 in a reference to a hijacking of a US plane: 'We are . . . not going to tolerate these attacks from outlaw states run by the strangest collection of misfits, Looney Tunes and squalid criminals since the advent of the Third Reich'

**loopy** a coinage of the 1920s: 'glimpses . . . of the loopy world of the Telegraph letter-writer,' *Guardian* 1991. The underlying metaphor is presumably the twists and turns of a mad person's mental processes

**lose one's marbles** to lose one's mental faculties, typically as a result of old age. The idiom has a range of other manifestations, such as 'have all one's marbles' and 'have a few marbles missing'. It appeared in America in the 1920s, and may have arisen from an earlier use of *marbles* for 'personal effects or goods'. This in turn was an adaptation of French *meubles* 'furniture'

**natural** a now largely obsolete euphemism for a 'simpleton, fool', which dates from the 16th century: 'The man shuffled and bowed low, with the vacant grin of a natural,' Charles Gibbon 1878. It is short for the earlier *natural fool* or *natural idiot*, that is, someone who is by birth or nature mentally deficient

**nut** the wide range of 'madness' metaphors into which *nut* enters all depend on the slang use of *nut* for 'head', which dates from the first half of the 19th century. The adjectival **nuts** 'crazy' is of the same vintage; **nut** the noun, meaning 'mad person' or 'crank', is first recorded in 1903; and **nutcase** is a product of the 1950s (cf. CASE (p 222)). British **nutter** 'mad person, especially an aggressively violent one' is first recorded in 1958. The adjective **nutty** 'crazy' dates from the turn of the 20th century: a common expression in former years, but now rather passé, was 'as nutty as a fruitcake': '"He doesn't strike me as unbalanced." "On his special subject he's as nutty as a fruitcake",' P G Wodehouse 1967. See also NUTHOUSE (p 220) and *off one's nut* at OFF

**off** a range of colloquialisms define madness in terms of being 'off' something, implying removal or ejection from the normal state of affairs. One group uses the image of the 'head', suggesting a disengagement from the brain: **off one's head** (dating from the first half of the 19th century), **off one's chump** (also 19th century; the use of *chump* for 'head' is a metaphorical extension of an earlier sense 'lump of wood'), and **off one's nut** (first recorded in 1860). Another uses the metaphor of removal from some sort of support or conveyance: **off one's rocker** (*rocker* in this case is the curved piece of wood or metal on which something rocks) and **off one's trolley** (first recorded in 1896; *trolley* here is a small truck that runs on rails). The American **off the wall** is both more recent (it dates from the 1960s) and different in imagery. Its main sense is 'unconventional', but it is also used euphemistically for 'crazy'. It is not altogether clear what the metaphor is based on, but there may be some reference to a ball bouncing off a wall at a strange angle, as in the game of squash

**out** *out* rivals *off* for the number of madness metaphors it introduces. The image is of absence, particularly from the head, the site of the intelligence, if any: **out of one's head** (American in origin, and first recorded in 1825), **out of one's mind** (dating from at least the 15th century, and probably the original model for this group of phrases), **out of one's senses** (dating from the 17th century), and **out of one's skull** (first recorded in 1968). **Out of it** usually implies unconsciousness, but can also be applied to mental vacuity which mimics unconsciousness. **Out of one's tree** (coined in mid-1960s America) conjures up the image of a jungle animal infuriated to the point of madness by being driven out of its tree. **Out to lunch** (also American in origin, from the mid 1950s) equates someone absent from their desk with reason absent from the brain

**peculiar** see FUNNY

**postal** a curious American usage which arose out of a series of widely circulated news stories on the 1990s about deranged US postal workers who shot people at random and then killed themselves; hence, to 'go postal' is to have a fit of violent rage

**potty** began life in the mid 19th century as a general term of disapproval for anything trivial or feeble (possibly based on the expression *go to pot*), and was not used for 'crazy' until the early 20th century

**queer** see FUNNY

**right in the head** almost always negative: 'not quite right in the head'. The implication is not of utter insanity, but (most discreetly) of some mild mental weakness. In former times *not right* was used on its own in the same sense: 'We've got an old aunt of mine in the carriage who isn't exactly right,' J Hocking 1896

**round the bend** a 1920s coinage. If you are literally 'round the bend', you are out of sight, so the underlying image is presumably one of lack of contact with reality. The 'bend' in question is probably at least partly the S-bend in a lavatory

**sad** the patronizingly euphemistic shift in the use of *sad* in recent years has been interesting to observe. You feel 'sad' for (not angry about) someone who behaves in a way of which you disapprove – the implication being that they know no better. The epithet is transferred to the person – he or she is a 'sad' person to behave in that way. The behaviour trait may be ascribed to some moral or mental deficiency; and there is some evidence that *sad* is now being used to denote such a deficiency: in 1992 a 12-year-old girl wrote to the *Radio Times* complaining that a family which allowed the body of a dead relative to be shown on television 'must have been completely sad in the head'

**screwy** first recorded in America in the 1880s. It comes from the expression *have a screw loose*, which originally (in the early 19th century) denoted broadly 'be defective', but later came to be used euphemistically for 'be mad'

**sick** quite widely used in former centuries to denote mental weakness ('If they are not sick in their wits,' Simon Patrick 1692), but now replaced in this role by *ill*. In modern euphemistic usage, *sick* denotes a mental aberration characterized by taking pleasure in what others find repulsive

**simple** used as a euphemism for 'feeble-minded' since the 17th century; from the childlike lack of complex reasoning powers

**slate loose, have a** the imperfection in the roof of a building is transferred metaphorically to the human head

**slow** a very considerate way of referring to someone whose mind scarcely achieves walking pace. It is actually a very ancient use of the word, which dates back to the Anglo-Saxon period. Then, it was a straight, non-euphemistic usage; but over the centuries, as 'not moving quickly' has become the main literal sense of the word, it has moved into the realm of circumlocution. See also SLOW DEVELOPER, SLOW LEARNER, SLOWER-MINDED (p 218)

**soft** occasionally used independently to mean 'of low intellect', especially in the past ('One of the Grantlys was, – to say the least of it, – very soft, admitted as it was throughout the county of Barsetshire, that there was no family therein more widely awake to the affairs generally of this world . . ., than the family of which Archdeacon Grantly was the respected head,' Anthony Trollope 1867), but nowadays mainly in the expression *soft in the head*

**strange** see FUNNY

**touched** often said in a whisper, and accompanied by a knowing tap on the head. In origin, a shortening of 'touched [i.e. affected] by madness', which is how Isabella describes others' opinion of her in Shakespeare's *Measure for Measure*

**unhinged** a mechanical image – of a door or gate fallen off its hinges – to denote the disconnection of the mind. The usage goes back at least to the early 18th century

**wacky** or **whacky** often suggesting merely laughable, silly, or eccentric behaviour, but sometimes euphemizing genuine craziness. It first appeared in the 1930s, in the US. It may be an adjectival use of the earlier dialectal noun *whacky* 'fool', which itself came from *whack-head* 'person knocked senseless by a blow to the head'. The variant **wacko** or **whacko** came on the scene in the late 1970s, as both an adjective and a noun (='crazy person')

**wanting** that is, lacking normal intellectual powers (as in 'She's a bit wanting, poor dear'). The usage dates from the early 19th century

**weak in the head** having a subnormal intellect. The same idea is expressed by **weak-minded**

**weird** see FUNNY

**with it** originally used, from the 1930s onwards, to denote 'fashion-able, up-to-date', but since around 1960 also used for 'mentally alert, having all one's mental faculties'. Often in negative contexts (as in 'Poor old dear, she's not really with it these days')

As a coda to all these, a lexical pattern emerged in the late 20th century in which mental deficiency is described in terms of a single item lacking from a standard-sized group, as if to denote the absence of a measurable portion of the intellect. The number of ways in which this formula is realized is seemingly open-ended, but the highest-profile include **a brick short of a load**, **a few sandwiches short of a picnic**, **a card short of a deck**, **fifty cards in the pack** (a complete pack has fifty-two), and the Australian **not the full quid** (first recorded in 1944). One of the earliest models must have been **not sixteen annas to the rupee**, which dates from the days of the British raj in India.

Those whose job is to look after or cure the mad have a special euphemistic vocabulary applied to them. It is often found convenient to refer to psychiatrists discreetly as **doctors**, and to the attendants in mental hospitals (even the burliest of men) as **nurses**. **Alienist**, used in the past to denote a doctor who treated mental illness, and still current in America as a medico-legal term, gets its meaning from a euphemistic Latin use of *alienatus* (literally 'estranged, withdrawn') for 'insane'. A more colloquial approach is to call a psychiatrist a **head-shrinker**. The word originated in the 1920s as a term for a 'head-hunter who shrinks the heads of his victims', but around 1950 in the US the rather grisly metaphor was transferred to psychiatrists. The abbreviated **shrinker** and **shrink** date from the mid 1960s. See also MEN IN WHITE COATS (p 217).

# FADING OUT: OLD AGE & DEATH

———

## AGE

Despite all the anti-aging creams, monkey glands and assorted elixirs of life, the best defence we can mount against getting old probably remains – concealment under carefully applied verbal make-up.

The very word *age* is a living symbol of our need to ward off senescence. The Latin word from which it ultimately derives, *aetas*, meant simply 'period of existence, time of life'. But by the time it reached English via French in the 14th century, *age* was also being used for the 'latter part of life': old age commandeers the terminology of an entire lifetime, to try and roll back the years. The use of *aged* for 'old' dates back to the 15th century. *Aging* for 'growing old' (as in 'an aging population') is more recent, first recorded in the 19th century. It is new enough for us still to question its credentials: even a baby is 'aging', in the sense of 'growing older', though we accept that the word's message is always 'old', not 'older'.

It is hardly surprising, therefore, that perhaps the most notorious euphemism in the English language – the term with which many people would no doubt respond to *euphemism* in a word-association test – is a disguise for 'old person': **senior citizen**. This emerged in America in the 1930s, and has since proliferated around the English-speaking world (sometimes in the abbreviated form **senior**). Its natural habitat is officialese and the language of those who deal professionally with old people on a large scale, but it falls naturally from the lips of anyone who thinks it is more dignified to be described as 'senior' (implications of the top of a hierarchy) and as a 'citizen' (still a member of the polis, all marbles intact) than as simply an 'old person'. A relatively recent elaboration on this theme is **senior moment**, denoting an incident held to be indicative of senile decline (e.g. forgetting why one has come into a particular room).

As is almost inevitable with euphemisms that gain wide currency, *senior citizen* is beginning to lose its gloss. People have seen through it. But there is no shortage of alternatives.

A measure of subtlety is recommended for long-term success. Note the difference in resonance and connotation between 'an old person' and 'an **older** person'. The positive grade of the adjective makes a forthright statement that leaves no room for ambiguity, but the comparative succeeds in muddying the waters, even though the person so described may be in an advanced stage of senility. An institutionalized application of this, particularly in the advertising industry, is **the older woman**, who is decidedly in receipt of a bus pass. (In the context of sexual encounters, however, *older man* and *older woman* mean simply what they say.) A recent variation on the theme is the awkward and inelegant **elder abuse** for 'maltreatment of old people'.

Another subtle gradation that avoids the frankness and directness of *old* is **elderly**, first recorded in 1611. It began as a hedging adjective, meaning 'somewhat old', but in present-day English it has become a softer synonym for the *o*-word.

Other strategies for removing age's sting can be divided into two main categories: the solemn and reverential, and the more or less condescending.

The first works by selecting those words that put a positive gloss on oldness. It is obviously a good thing to be **mature**. We all reach physical maturity in our teens and mental maturity, in most cases, not much later; but in the cosy world of euphemism, the 'mature woman' or 'mature man' is decidedly middle-aged, if not downright old (see also MATURE FIGURE p 150). **Distinguished** overtly denotes a marked excellence, but we would be surprised to find it applied to someone without at least some grey in their hair. **Grande dame** suggests a respected senior (and therefore old) female in a particular area of activity (as in 'Elizabeth David, the grande dame of British cookery writers'), but its aura of ponderousness vitiates its usefulness as a euphemism; *doyenne* (or for a man, *doyen*) is less likely to give offence because we have not learnt to decode it as 'old'. **Seasoned** implies not just the second half of life, but also the wealth of experience gained in the first half. And **elder statesman**, ostensibly an honorific term for a senior politician, now above the party fray, whose wise counsel is sought, often connotes any old retired pol who is a bit past it (the term actually came into English in the early 20th century as a specific name for the members of the Genro, a body of retired statesmen consulted by the Japanese emperor in former times). American politically correct terminology of the late 20th and early 21st centuries (**chronologically gifted** and **experientially enhanced**) seeks to accentuate the positive.

Not all such circumlocutions are likely to be well received, however euphemistic their intentions. Nowadays, an old, and certainly a middle-aged woman would not take kindly to being called a **matron**, but previous generations used the term (literally 'married woman') to connote oldness and its dignity. Nor is **well preserved** liable to be seen as anything other than a back-handed compliment, however kindly meant.

*Years* figure largely in attempts to tiptoe around old age. Someone who is **of advanced years** is definitely old, but the expression is sufficiently blander than *old* to qualify as a euphemism. ('Advancement', incidentally, is the metaphor underlying **getting on** (as in 'He's getting on a bit. Can't do what he used to'), which is a cut-down version of the earlier **getting on in years** and **getting on in life**.) **Evening of one's days**, **sunset years** and **twilight years** are less direct, more sentimental, but still a bit gloomy (*sunset years* tries to capitalize on the glories of the setting sun, but cannot help reminding us of the darkness that follows). Much more upbeat is **golden years**, an American coinage which portrays old age as the best period of life, years of ripeness and fulfilment, suffused with a golden glow. Those who make it to this happy time are **golden-agers** (i.e. old people). (Older users of the Internet have been termed **silver surfers**.)

Another explicit reference to length of life is **the longer lived** or **the longer living** (note again the surreptitiously suggestive use of the comparative adverb), which began to oust *senior citizens* as the euphemism of choice for 'old people' in the US in the 1970s. **Ageful**, coined in the US in 1990, suggests an achieved maturity. Rather more subtle in its application is **a certain age**, probably a direct translation of French *un certain âge*, which first appeared in English in the mid 18th century. This certainly does not mean out-and-out 'old', but more an indeterminate age hovering between forty and sixty, and the underlying implication is that the person so described (typically a woman) is doing her best to conceal the facts, in both word and deed. **Middle age** can be just as slippery a term. On a purely actuarial calculation this ought to denote about 'thirty-five', but few 35-year-olds would admit to being middle-aged. The most strict interpretation would not start middle age until about forty, and in practice the euphemizing tendency usually pulls it up through the late forties into the fifties and even beyond. It's all relative, anyway: as the American financier Bernard Baruch said, 'To me old age is always fifteen years older than I am' (1955). The latest addition to this age-grouping terminology is **third age**. As a euphemism for 'old age' it is presumably based on the notion of youth and middle age as the first two 'ages', but there may well be a subliminal reference too to *Third World* as a euphemism for the poorest and least-regarded nations of the world. Someone who did not expect to have a long life might in the past have said that they would not **make old bones** (while no doubt secretly hoping to be **spared** – i.e. to remain alive).

The condescending school of euphemism winsomely perverts the terminology of youth in a vain attempt to turn back the clock. Here, old men are **boys**, and old women are jollied along (or indeed jolly themselves along) as **girls** ('Eyes down, girls,' says the bingo-caller to an audience, the majority of whom have left girlhood far behind). To call an old person **active** merely draws attention to their age by insisting that they have not actually reached a state of advanced decrepitude. The ingratiatingly saccharine 'so many **years young**' used to be a favourite method by which television game-show hosts patronized their more aged contestants ('Here's Ethel. She's seventy years young!').

Switching from positive to negative can always be relied on to soften the impact of a message: so 'he's **not as young as he was**' is readily interpreted as 'he's getting quite old', and 'she's **not in her first youth**' or '**not in the first flush of youth**' could easily mean that she is at death's door. More colloquially brutal but still euphemistic is **no spring chicken**. Flipping back from the negative to the positive, an old person could be congratulated on still being **above ground**.

Since the 18th century, old married couples have been known as **Darby and Joan** (the name appears to have originated in a popular ballad of the time). The first **Darby and Joan club** (the rather patronizing British term for an 'old people's club') is on record as opening in 1942.

Accommodation which specializes in housing and looking after old people (with or without medical care) has a mealy-mouthed vocabulary all of its own. Many of the terms exploit the 'end of the day' imagery we have encountered before: **eventide home**, **sunset home**, **twilight home** (and the whole business of looking after the old is somewhat cynically known as the **sunset industry**). **Convalescent home** and

**nursing home** put the emphasis on medical treatment, but we assume that the majority of the inmates are fairly old and may be there for the duration. **Rest home** comes cleaner about its geriatric clientele. All these euphemisms contain the cosy *home*, and indeed **home** itself is used in the same way: 'She's getting too old to look after herself; she'll have to go into a home'. Twee-est of all is **God's waiting room**.

A newish euphemism for machines, vehicles, etc that are obsolete is **life-expired**, first recorded in 1986.

# DEATH

It is a commonplace that death is the great taboo of present-day Western society. The Middle Ages feared it but faced it out, exorcizing its terror by boldly confronting the image of Death in religious and popular iconography. The Victorians, half in love with it, sentimental-ized it, and were not averse to referring to it openly. But today – while paradoxically glorifying it and trivializing it in the thanatopornography of war comics, TV crime programmes, and snuff movies, where death is a cheap thrill – we take considerable pains to avoid mentioning it directly. It embarrasses us.

Why should this be? Partly, no doubt, it reflects the circumstances of modern urban life. In the past, death was a more integrated part of life. People tended to die at home, and it was usual and accepted to see the bodies of those who had died. But present-day city-dwellers can pass their entire existence without ever encountering a real live corpse. (Television images of corpses are more readily available, of course, but even here there is a distinction. Actors playing dead cause us no discomfort (although before the 9pm watershed they must keep their eyes shut), but the showing of an actual corpse on a BBC television programme about undertakers in 1992 provoked a 12-year-old girl to write to the *Radio Times* complaining that the family of the dead person must be 'sad in the head' to permit it.)

But there must be more to our reticence than this. Keith Allan and Kate Burridge in their *Euphemism and Dysphemism* 1991 suggest that as a result of the modern abnormalizing of death, we in a sense almost expect not to die – so to mention death openly would be to shatter our collective self-delusion. Another factor they point to is that in the days before sophisticated medical technology we either dropped down dead on the spot or our bodies gave us some advance warning, but nowadays it is quite common for a doctor to diagnose a fatal condition out of the blue when the patient had not been feeling ill – hence a greater shock factor, breeding more fear, and more circumlocution.

Whatever the motivation, we now deploy a vast battery of terminology to avoid the words *die* and *death*. The most audacious of the death-denying strategies is to pretend that death is life. If you can convince yourself that the dead person has not really died, you are amply consoled. So those of a religious turn of mind will say that so-and-so is **alive with Jesus, lives in the bosom of the Lord**, etc. Such expressions strongly suggest a seamless continuation of earthly existence. A less startling claim, but one that appeals to the same euphemizing sentiments, is to suggest persistence of life in some altered mode: the **afterlife, eternal life**, a **higher life**. And on a more mundane level, the use of the term **life insurance** (first recorded in 1809) to denote insurance against death falls into much the same category.

But understandably this black-is-white approach is not widely taken. Subtler strategies have more chance of achieving their object. Of these, five in particular stand out as major sources of euphemism: death as rest or as some other form of non-consciousness; death as a journey or a leaving; death as a summons; death as a loss for those who knew the dead person; and death as an end.

The notion of being **at rest**, of being **laid to rest**, or of **reposing** has connotations of calmness and serenity, of relief from the struggles of life, that may ease the pain for the bereaved. It is an ancient euphemism, traceable back to our Anglo-Saxon ancestors. It finds expression too in the Latin *requiescat in pace* (*RIP*, 'may he/she rest in peace') inscribed on gravestones, and English has long used its own verb **rest** in the same way: 'I shall shortly be with them that rest,' John Milton 1671. English picks up on the *peace* metaphor too: **at peace** stands for 'dead', and **peace at last** can be found on tombs.

A closely allied idea is that of 'sleep' – a condition that mimics some aspects of death sufficiently closely to have been termed 'the little death'. Like *rest*, **sleep** has persisted down the centuries as a euphemism for 'be dead' – as in the familiar lines from Thomas Gray's 'Elegy written in a country churchyard' (1750): 'Beneath those rugged elms, that yew-tree's shade,/Where heaves the turf in many a mouldering heap,/Each in his narrow cell for ever laid,/The rude forefathers of the hamlet sleep.' The noun *sleep* is generally qualified in some way in this context: **last sleep, sleep of death**, etc. Sir Walter Scott's 'Sleep the sleep that knows not breaking' (1810) is typical of the more flowery circumlocutions. **Asleep** performs the same function: euphemisms such as **asleep in Jesus** and **asleep in the Lord** are recorded from as long ago as the 13th century, and **fall asleep** is a favourite way of saying 'die' on gravestones and in obituary notices ('In loving memory of my darling husband Percival William who fell asleep on May 21,' *Sun* (Melbourne) 1988, quoted in Keith Allan and Kate Burridge, *Euphemism and Dysphemism* 1991). **Close one's eyes**, with its Janus-like suggestion of both sleep and death, serves the same purpose.

Another off-shoot of the idea of 'rest' is the notion of being set free from the care, suffering, hardships, etc associated with earthly existence – as if life were a prison. **Release** is the key word here: 'Death's kindly touch . . . gave Soul and body both release from life's long nightmare in the grave,' Robert Browning 1878. In popular sentimentalese the usual phrases are **blessed release** and **happy release**. The same idea underlies **quietus**. This originally denoted a 'discharge given on payment of a debt', or a 'release from the responsibilities of an office'. But when Shakespeare put it into Hamlet's mouth ('When he himself might his quietus make with a bare bodkin') in the sense 'release from life', he opened the way for its modern use in expressions such as *make one's quietus* 'kill oneself' and *get one's quietus* 'die'.

Death as a journey from life to some specified or unspecified place or condition that is not life is an equally ancient and well-established theme. It is expressed at its pithiest in the simple verb **go** (as in 'I hope my husband goes first; he couldn't look after himself on his own'). Extensions include **go on**, which suggests translation to a different mode of existence, and **go over**. This is one of a small group of phrasal death verbs incorporating *over* (the others are **cross over** and **pass over**) which all imply the existence of some 'other side' to which the soul makes its way after death. **Pass** is a key word in the euphemism of death, both on its own and, more commonly, in **pass away** and **pass on**. The first is of considerable antiquity, dating back to the 14th century, the second apparently a comparative 19th-century newcomer, but both encapsulate perfectly the element of sentimental pretence that cannot even come straight out with *go*, but has to use the softer, more gradual *pass*. It puts in an appearance, too, in **passing** for 'death' (as in 'The whole nation mourned his passing'). Returning to *go*, **gone before** implies that the soul of the dead person has gone on ahead to wherever it is, where it will be joined at some later point by the souls of those as yet alive (it often crops up in the death-defying formula **not**

**dead** or **lost but gone before**); and the colloquial **goner** (dating from the mid 19th century) denotes a 'dead person'. **Depart** has a suitably sepulchral ring, introducing officialese into the obsequies: **depart this life** for 'die' dates back at least to the 16th century, and references to a dead person as **the departed**, or **the dear departed**, are first found in the 18th century. More colloquial 'journey' metaphors include **pop off** (first recorded as long ago as 1764) and the mainly American **check out**, which probably comes from the notion of leaving a hotel. **Take leave of life** preserves the gentilities in the face of extinction while at the same time subtly suggesting a measure of control or choice on the part of the leave-taker.

Many 'journeying' or 'leaving' metaphors are based on the supposed destination of the journey. This can range from the vagueness of the now obsolete *away* to something quite specific, such as the **happy hunting grounds** (to which the souls of dead American Indians reputedly go, although in fact there is no evidence that the term reflects any genuine Native American usage). Not surprisingly in the Judaeo-Christian tradition, the destination is often heaven, or the company of those who dwell there (equally unsurprisingly, the alternative option, hell, is not widely called on in euphemizing death). So the dead person will find himself described as **in heaven, in** or **with the Lord, in the arms of Jesus, in Abraham's bosom, with Jesus, with one's maker**, etc. Vaguer references include **aloft, in** or **to a better place, the other side**, and the more frivolous **upstairs**. Verbs associated with reaching the destination are *go* and *take* depending on whether the soul is viewed as taking an active or a passive role. So the dead person may be said to be **going home**, or to be being **taken home**, or to be moving in some other way towards **home** ('Heah [here] in de body pent,/Absent from Him I roam,/Yet nightly pitch my movin' tent/A day's march nearer home,' Ronald Firbank 1924, in imitation of a revivalist hymn); the metaphor of 'home', also expressed in the past as **long home** and **last home**, derives from the traditional Christian view of heaven as the soul's true home and the world as a place of temporary exile. Other Christian themes are represented in **go to one's reward** (an American coinage of the mid 19th century, and usually with the implication that the reward will be for good behaviour), **go to glory** (first recorded in 1814), **join the (great) majority** (which exploits the notion that the population of heaven is larger than that of the earth), and **meet one's maker** (God the creator of humankind, who resides in heaven). Harking back to a mythic, pre-Christian past is **go west**, which metaphoricizes the west as the land of the setting sun, the realm of darkness, winter, and death (although in fact, apart from one isolated 16th century example, the expression does not seem to have come into use until the World War I period). A bespoke twist to the theme is given by **gone to the big** (or **great**) … **in the sky**, where the gap is filled by the deceased's typical milieu or place of work ('Where are they now, those other renowned boozing hell raisers of yesteryear – Burton, Harris, Reed? All gone to the Great Pub in the Sky; only O'Toole is left', *Radio Times* 2007). And to counterpoint all these destinations, a point of departure: **land of the living**. It is generally used in negative or other non-assertive contexts (as in *if he is still in the land of the living* = 'if he is not now dead'). It is a direct translation of a Hebrew idiom, and entered the English language via the Bible ('Let us cut him off from the land of the living,' Jeremiah 11:19).

Another way in which people attempt to come to terms with death is to regard it as an imperative invitation from the authorities in the after-life. Linguistically this manifests itself in words such as **call**, **send for**, and **summons**: expressions such as 'final summons', 'the Lord sent for him', and 'called to a higher service' all imply the making of an offer that cannot be refused ('All the doctors in Christendom . . . can't save him. He's called,' *F Leslie's Popular Monthly* 1886). By way of response the dead person is said to have **answered the call**. At least it is all done with a semblance of a by-your-leave. A more peremptory attitude on the part of God and his agents is expressed by **taken** and **gathered** ('It was God's will that he should be taken,' Eugene O'Neill 1920). Both are widely used with a variety of euphemistic preposi-tional phrases, as in 'God took him to himself', 'she was taken from us *or* from the world', 'he was gathered to his fathers *or* ancestors' (the source of the last is the Bible, where it appears in several places – for instance, 'And also all that generation were gathered unto their fathers,' Judges 2:10). Casting God rather in the role of a commanding officer than a host or a farmer is the Salvation Army usage **promoted to Glory**, which views elevation to heavenly status as a step up the mili-tary hierarchy.

The notion of death as a deprivation of the living is a widely used source of euphemism, but much of the imagery coincides with the notion of 'mislaying', with potentially bathetic effect: 'We lost father last year' can sound disconcertingly like a confession of absent-mind-edness. This use of **lose** for 'be deprived of by death' dates back to the early Middle English period. **Lost** in the sense 'dead, killed' (as in *lost* *at sea* = 'killed by drowning') is somewhat more recent, as is the use of **loss** for 'bereavement' (as in 'We all commiserate with you on your sad/tragic loss') and 'death' ('Newton had to mourn the loss of his earliest and best friend,' David Brewster 1855). (A closely related use of *loss* is in **loss of life**, which covers up death or killing particularly in the context of large-scale slaughter in battle or decimation by natural disaster – as in 'Several ships were sunk; there was some loss of life'.) The concept of the dead person's absence is expressed by **no longer with us** (the positive **still with us** denotes 'still alive'); the reaction of their friends, relations, etc to their absence is that they are **missed**, or more usually **sadly missed** ('Jim. Nature's gentleman, sadly missed,' *Sun* (Melbourne) 1989, quoted in Keith Allan and Kate Burridge, *Euphemism and Dysphemism* 1991).

But although the dead are 'lost' to those who survive them, they do have the consolation of renewing acquaintance with those who predeceased them. The word **join** is much deployed to reinforce this concept: the dead person may be said to have gone to 'join their husband/wife', to 'join their dead comrades', to 'join their ancestors', etc – as if heaven is one big reunion party. **United** and **reunited** express the same idea.

Closely linked with the notion of death as loss is the comparison of death with taking leave of a living person. The verb **part** forms a metaphorical bridge, both from the point of view of the individual who dies ('[Falstaff] parted even just between twelve and one, even at the turning o' the tide,' Shakespeare, *Henry V* 1599) and reciprocally, denoting a mutual leave-taking ('Jim. We knew the time was coming and soon we'd have to part,' obituary notice, *Sun* (Melbourne) 1988, quoted in Allan and Burridge, *loc. cit.*). The person who is left alive following these adieus is euphemized as **left behind**.

Death as the end is expressed in a range of metaphors based on the word *last*. Someone's **last days** are the end of his life; when someone **breathes his last**, he dies; someone's **last words** are what he said just before he died. Death is also one's **latter end** (a usage that dates back at least to the 15th century), or, if it has been violent or in some other way unpleasant, a **sticky end**. **Late** is one of the most pervasive of all 'death' euphemisms, signifying 'recently dead' or 'now dead' (as in 'my late father'); the metaphor seems to be based on the notion of having been 'lately' (i.e. recently) alive, rather than on the concept of the 'late' period in life being next to death. And the logical consequence of reaching and passing the end is that you no longer exist, you are **no more**: 'But Cassius is no more,' Shakespeare, *Julius Caesar* 1601.

If none of the above five strategies seems appropriate to the circumstances in which one finds oneself, one can always in desperation try to pretend that the dead person is simply ill: 'Having decided that the man was dead, I tiptoed out of the room and went and told the nurse on duty, in the ghastly euphemistic language of our times, that I thought Mr Courtauld was not very well,' Auberon Waugh 1991.

The dignified, stiff-upper-lip approach is the external response of many people to death, and highly formal terminology helps to keep reality at a distance. **Demise** is a suitably high-flown alternative to *death* (although it did not begin to be used in that sense until the 18th century; it was originally a legal term denoting the transfer of an estate on the death of its owner). **Expire** similarly euphemizes *die* (etymologically it implies a last 'breathing out'). And **decease** is favourite officialese for *death* (the **deceased** as a verbal fig-leaf for 'the dead person' dates back at least to the early 17th century). Although it is distantly related to *cease*, the underlying metaphor is not of 'stopping', but of 'leaving': its ultimate ancestor is Latin *decessus* 'departure, death'.

Religious 'death' euphemisms tend to be solemn, too. The idea of the soul being allowed to leave the body is expressed in **resign one's spirit**, which also implies that God is going to hold on to it for keeps. Another way of saying the same thing is **give up the ghost**: originally (it dates back to Anglo-Saxon times) this was just as dignified as *resign one's spirit*, but in modern usage it has become diminished (as in 'This old car's just about given up the ghost'). **The Reaper** (more usually **the Grim Reaper**, occasionally **the Great** or **Old Reaper**) seems to suggest an older, pre-Christian religious stratum, but in fact it is not recorded until the middle part of the 19th century. It personifies death as a man with a scythe, gathering in lives as a farmer reaps corn. On a more frivolous level, a dead person may be said to be **playing his harp** (from the popular image of departed souls transformed into angels, sitting on heavenly clouds and playing harps). See also IN HEAVEN, WITH JESUS, etc (p 235).

The euphemism of death in battle swings between the two extremes of glorification and trivialization. The poetic vision of *pro patria mori* is summed up in the verb **fall**, which puts being killed by the enemy on a par in seriousness with tripping over a stone. The use of *fall* in this sense dates from at least the 16th century (it seems to have evolved from the earlier expression *fall dead*), and it has since become the respectable description of death in battle, to be pronounced in solemn tones and with downcast eyes, and omitting any direct reference to the actual (presumably unpleasant, messy, horrific, etc) circumstances of death. Similarly **the fallen** (first recorded in 1765) is used nominally for 'those killed in battle' (perhaps the best-known of the elegies for the dead of World War I is Laurence Binyon's 'For the Fallen': 'They shall grow not old, as we that are left grow old . . .').

The notion of giving up one's life for a greater cause, for one's country, etc provides specific euphemisms in such expressions as **the supreme sacrifice**, **the ultimate sacrifice**, and **the final sacrifice** (*supreme* is an important 'death' euphemism, also occurring in **the supreme penalty** 'punishment by death'). They seem to have emerged during the years of World War I (*supreme sacrifice* is first recorded in 1916), which might encourage the cynical to suppose that they were coined to bolster the morale of those offered up as cannon-fodder in that most pointless of wars. Similar in inspiration is **lay down one's life**, which was introduced into the English language by John 15:13 'Greater love hath no man than this, that a man lay down his life for his friends' (later adapted by Jeremy Thorpe, when characterizing Harold Macmillan's sacking of seven of his cabinet during a 1962 political crisis, to 'Greater love hath no man than this, that he lay down his friends for his life'). Potentially general in application, in practice it is most often used of people 'laying down their lives' for their country in war. Also not specifically military in origin, but now most commonly used in that context, is **cut off**. This generally connotes 'killed prematurely, without fulfilling average life-expectancy', and its most usual habitat is the expression *cut off in one's prime*.

Such dignified circumlocutions sanitize death in war mainly for the general public back home. Those actually in the midst of the fighting choose earthier metaphors to laugh off the reality of slaughter: a dead comrade is said to have **bought it** (a usage which apparently dates back to the early 19th century) or to have **copped it**, **copped out**, or **copped a packet**, or to have **got it** or **got his** (expressions of general misfortune – 'be killed' is only one among a range of senses, including 'be wounded', 'be severely punished', and 'be ruined'). American service personnel may say 'it's **taps**' when talking about death in action – an allusion to the earlier use of *taps* for the music played in a military establishment at sunset, or at a military funeral (it was originally a drum roll, but later came to be played on the bugle). In the US Air

Force, to **buy the farm** is to suffer a fatal air crash (the original rationale of the expression seems to have been that the farmer could pay off his mortgage with the money he got as compensation from the government for the damage done to his farm when the aircraft crashed into it). That, and variations such as **buy the ranch** and **buy the real estate**, have come to be used more widely, especially in the US military, for 'to be killed'.

Human beings are inexhaustably ingenious in verbally denying death. People connected with a particular sort of activity may well adapt an idiom expressing 'completion' or 'departure' in that activity to the notion of 'death'. **Slip one's rope** and **slip one's cable**, for instance, are of nautical origin, as may be the more generally applicable **slip off** and **slip away**. It must have been a cribbage player who first used **peg out** for 'die' (apparently around the middle of the 19th century; it originally denoted the completion of a game of cribbage by moving one's peg to the end of the board). **Cash in one's chips** is a metaphor derived from poker and other gambling games – from the exchange of counters for money when leaving the game – and **throw up the cards** comes from the same world. Australians in the past used an image from the game of marbles for 'dying': **throw in** (**toss in, pass in, chuck in**, and any number of variants) **one's alley** (an *alley* is a marble). **Strike out** comes from baseball, where it literally means 'be retired after failing to hit three pitches'.

## Other 'final act' images include:

**call it a day** it originated in the early 19th century as *call it half a day*. The literal meaning is 'consider that one has done a day's work and therefore stop', but it is widely used more generally for 'stop what one is doing' or 'give up on an activity', and occasionally for 'die'

**curtains** or sometimes **curtain** from the lowering of the curtain at the end of a play. It can just mean 'the end' in general, but often it is used specifically for 'death'

**hand** (or **pass** or **turn**) **in one's dinner-pail** originally American, and first recorded around the turn of the 20th century, but popularized by P G Wodehouse: 'My godfather . . . recently turned in his dinner pail and went to reside with the morning stars' (1964). The underlying image is presumably that when you are dead you need no more food

**hang up one's hat** if you are not going to need it any longer for going out . . . Other *hang up* = 'finish with' metaphors include **hang up the spoon** and, from the horse culture of the old American West, **hang up one's harness** and **hang up one's tackle**

**jack it in** British slang for 'stop what one is doing, abandon an enterprise' (first recorded in the 1940s), but also used occasionally for 'die'

**kick the bucket** a euphemism for 'die' first recorded in Francis Grose's *Dictionary of the Vulgar Tongue* 1785. Its origin remains notoriously in dispute. Very likely it comes from the notion of a slaughtered animal twitching while suspended from a beam by its legs (the now probably extinct dialectal *bucket* 'beam' may be a descendant of Old French *buquet* 'balance-beam'). But an alternative theory suggests the scenario of someone committing suicide by hanging, who stands on a bucket and then kicks it away from under him

**last roundup** a conceit based on the notion of a 'roundup' or gathering in of cattle in the Wild West. It seems unlikely that it was actually used by 19th-century cowboys; the earliest record of it is as the title of a song by G Brown (1932)

**pop one's clogs** from the idea of 'popping' (i.e. pawning) one's clogs when one no longer needs them for going out; first recorded in the 1970s, but probably around for much longer than that

**settle one's accounts** from the twin ideas of payment being the concluding phase of a transaction, and of leaving no debts outstanding on one's 'departure'. Of similar inspiration is **pay one's last debt**. And both call to mind **put one's affairs in order**, a euphemism commonly used in the context of someone preparing for death

**written out of the script** originally, in the 1960s, applied literally to a character eliminated from the story-line of a radio or television soap opera (as most famously in Frank Marcus's 1965 play *The Killing of Sister George*), but subsequently used metaphorically for 'dead'


Some other assorted metaphors for 'dying', 'dead', and 'death':

**bite the dust** or occasionally, in the past, **bite the ground** from the notion of falling down face first. First recorded in 1697 ('So many Valiant Heroes bite the Ground,' John Dryden), and subsequently widely used not just for literal 'dying' but also metaphorically for 'failing, being brought to an end'

**brown bread** rhyming slang for 'dead' – sometimes abbreviated to *brown*

**cold** 'dead' – from the rapid cooling of the body after death. The full-blown metaphor, which dates back at least to the 14th century, is mainly restricted to poetry, but the allied **before he/she was cold**, meaning 'shortly after death', is much more widespread

**conk out** or sometimes just **conk** a colloquialism which appeared during World War I, no one knows where from, and from the beginning meant both 'fail, break down' and more specifically 'die' (The British actor John Le Mesurier arranged for the following announcement to be placed in *The Times* after his death: 'John Le Mesurier wishes it to be known that he conked out on November 15th [1983]. He sadly misses family and friends'.)

**croak** a slang synonym for *die* that dates from the early 19th century. The source of the metaphor is generally assumed to be the gurgling sound in the throat of a dying person

**done for** commonly put by writers into the mouth of people mortally wounded or injured, but also used with reference to those actually (but recently) dead. It dates from the 18th century

**drop** historically used freely for 'die' ('I shall have the old place some day, when the old governor drops,' F Anstey 1889), but nowadays mainly restricted to a range of more or less fixed expressions such as 'drop like flies', 'until one drops', 'drop in one's tracks', and 'drop off one's perch'

**fade away** only very limited currency as a euphemism for 'die', and that as a result of the words of J Foley, 'Old soldiers never die, they simply fade away' (published in a song in 1920)

**feet first** in expressions like 'leave feet first', 'be carried out feet first', in allusion to the usual way of transporting corpses

**foul play** a piece of officialese, used particularly by the British police, which denotes 'actions causing death from other than natural causes' – i.e. murder. Reports on an unexpected death may conclude 'Foul play is not suspected' or 'has been ruled out' – which itself may well be a euphemism for 'probable suicide'

**go for a Burton** a Briticism that emerged from World War II. It was originally applied to pilots killed in action, but subsequently broadened out via 'be killed' in general to 'be destroyed or ruined'. No one knows for certain the source of the metaphor, but there may be some allusion to 'leaving in order to get a drink' (*Burton* is or was a type of beer made in Burton-on-Trent)

**go for one's tea** an abstemious euphemism employed by members of the IRA in the latter part of the 20th century, meaning 'to be murdered'

**grave** when talking literally about burial we seek to euphemize it (see p 253), but paradoxically (*the*) *grave* can serve as a euphemism for 'death' (as in 'from the cradle to the grave')

**had it** a piece of British World War II slang, which originally had, and retains, the more general sense of having lost one's chance of obtaining something alongside the more specific 'be killed'

**happen to** a particularly curious euphemism, which exploits to the full the value of vagueness. It generally occurs in such contexts as 'If anything should happen to me . . .', the subtext of which is to be interpreted as 'If I die'. The absolutely literal interpretation is so unlikely (it would be curious indeed if *nothing* happened to the person during the period in question) that we gloss 'anything' as 'death'

**hop off** a long-standing metaphor, which goes back to the 18th century. It is a shortening of **hop the twig** (an obvious reference to the departure of birds), which means generally 'leave' as well as more specifically 'die'

**inheritance tax** originally US, from the mid 19th century. A less stark alternative to the (not precisely synonymous) *death duties*

**kick off** a euphemism for 'die' which originated in the US in the early 20th century. It contrasts curiously with *kick off* 'begin', a metaphor based on the starting of a football match. The 'death' element is mainly carried by *off*

**negative patient-care outcome** a weasely circumlocution for 'death while under the care of a doctor'. It emerged in the US around 1980

**nonviable** originally used in biology of foetuses, cells, etc in the (somewhat euphemistic) sense 'incapable of sustaining life', but now, according to William Lutz, *Doublespeak* (1990), just plain 'dead' too

**push up the daisies** to be dead and buried. The tradition of regarding the daisy as the typical flower that grows above people's graves dates back at least to the mid 19th century. The first euphemism to exploit it was *turn one's toes up to the daisies* (see TURN ONE'S TOES UP below), followed shortly afterwards by **under the daisies** and, early in the 20th century, *push up the daisies*

**shuffle off this mortal coil** one of Shakespeare's contributions to the language of euphemism – *Hamlet* 3:1: 'For in that sleep of death what dreams may come when we have shuffled off this mortal coil, must give us pause.' *Coil* in this context has nothing to do with spirals; it means literally 'turmoil, bustle'.

**six feet under** dead and buried – from the standard coffin depth. Not recorded before 1942, but probably rather older than that

**terminally inconvenienced** 'dead' in the late 20th-century language of American political correctness

**time** the notion of 'one's time' is an important one in the euphemization of death: expressions such as 'His time has come', 'Her time is near', 'She went before her time' all disguise an underlying 'appointed time of death'

**turn up one's toes** to die – from the fact that in modern Western society dead bodies are placed on their back, with their toes pointing upwards. The expression dates from the mid 19th century, contemporaneously with the now obsolescent **toes up** 'dead': 'Ah, my Lord! – the poor thing! – toes up at last!' Lord Dufferin 1857

**underground** dead and buried

**way of all flesh** to 'go the way of all flesh' is to die. The image comes from the Bible, but only in an indirect way. It seems to be a blend of the Biblical 'go the way of all the earth', which has the same meaning ('And, behold, this day I am going the way of all the earth,' Joshua 23:14) and the expression *all flesh*, meaning 'all humankind', which appears several times in the Bible ('And all flesh shall see the salvation of God,' Luke 3:6). The mixture of the two idioms dates from the early medieval period

Public services who regularly encounter corpses have their own grim euphemisms for them. A body found in the water, for example by the river police, is a **floater** (a term of American origin, first recorded in 1890). A body, typically of a suicide, that has been run over by an underground train is a **one-under**.

# KILLING

The taboos against the deliberate killing of another human being, or of oneself, are powerful, and we have evolved a rich vocabulary of metaphor for glossing over it, excusing it, making light of it, and pretending it never happened. It ranges from the chillingly clinical language of state-sanctioned killing to the colourful terminology of gangland.

Violent criminals have more occasion than most of us to talk about killing, and they like to cover it up with dramatic, hard-edged imagery. Much although not all of it originated amongst the street gangs of 20th-century American cities:

**blow away** to kill, typically by shooting (although the imagery is more suggestive of an explosion)

**bump off** to kill violently. It originated in the US (it is first recorded in 1910), but unlike most of these slang 'killing' verbs it has seeped into the language at large

**burn** to kill, originally used with reference to execution in the electric chair, but subsequently broadened out to apply to any violent killing

**chill** to kill, with reference to the rapid drop in temperature after death

**cook** to kill. Probably, like BURN, originally a reference to execution in the electric chair

**crease** to kill. Originally to stun, or to 'wing' with a bullet, but later used with more finality

**croak** originally to die (see p 242), but already by the 1820s it was being used to mean 'hang', and it was a short step from that to 'kill, murder'

**cut** to kill, but not necessarily with a knife, so perhaps the origin of the metaphor is in CUT OFF (see p 239) or in the notion of *cutting out* or excluding someone

**drill** to kill by shooting (from the notion of drilling a hole in the body with a bullet). First recorded at the beginning of the 19th century, but typical of 20th-century 'tough-guy' American literature

We are coming close to the world of chilling political doublespeak in which not just individuals but entire communities or even peoples are wiped out by state action, which is at once denied and condoned by serpentine linguistic contortions. This is euphemism at its most Orwellian, draining unimaginable crimes of their power to shock by an application of bland officialese. The most notorious remains **the Final Solution** (a translation of German *Endlösung*), the name given to the German policy of killing all European Jews. Hugh Rawson in his *Dictionary of Euphemisms and Other Doubletalk* traces the German term back to 1938, but interprets early instances as implying deportation rather than extermination. Its full murderous intent did not emerge until 1941, and its English translation is not recorded before 1947. But it is in the nature of such linguistic perversions to be unpindownable. Other Nazi extermination euphemisms suggested removal rather than death: *Aussiedlung* 'evacuation,' for instance, and *Umsiedlung* 'resettlement'. And the impeccably vague *Sonderbehandlung* 'special treatment' makes genocide sound like quite a privilege.

But before the Nazis had even been thought of, the new Communist regime in Russia was anaesthetizing the language of official murder. The verb *likvidirovat* 'liquidate', originally applied, like its English counterpart, to the winding up of a company, was pressed into service to describe the removal of opposition by killing; and by the early 1920s English **liquidate** was being used in the same way. It was joined in the 1930s by **purge**, which comes on like a cleansing or purifying process but in fact generally conceals the murder of one's political opponents or other 'undesirables'. The latest addition to the vocabulary of state killing is **disappear**, which came into English in the 1970s, directly translating Spanish *desaparecer*, as a macabre euphemism for the murder of members of opposition groups in Argentina, Chile, and other Latin American countries. Those who are missing, presumed dead, are known as 'the disappeared'. See also ETHNIC CLEANSING (p 300).

Inspired by a similar desire to disguise murder behind a mask of bureaucracy are **eliminate** and **terminate**, two high-sounding words that appeal equally to small-time gangland bosses and to the heads of national security services. To increase the gobbledegook factor, American English has '**terminate** (or **eliminate**, or – more euphemistic still – **dismiss**) **with extreme prejudice**', 1970s CIA-speak for 'murder'. In the same spirit, an authorized assassination by a CIA operative is termed an **executive action**. The KGB's contribution to this vocabulary, which began to find its way into English in the 1970s, is **wet**: a *wet job*, *wet affair*, or *wet operation* is a political assassination, and to *get wet* is to be killed.

Returning to punishment by death, the man in the street is no more inclined to name it square-on than is the state. Circumlocutions abound. *Hang* has over the centuries lost its euphemistic force (in the Old English period it was applied to crucifixion, but by the 13th century it was being used for suspension by the neck), but it retains the characteristic vagueness of the verbal evasion. The same could be said of the verb **gas**: it could in theory have been used of anaesthetists administering gas to their patients, but in practice it always denotes 'wound or kill (specifically, execute) with poisonous gas'.

Colloquially, the preferred strategy when talking around methods of execution is to metonymize: hanging becomes **the rope** (or, in former times, **the gallows**); electrocution is **the chair** (or, with keener gallows humour, the **hot seat** or **hot squat**, or the **hummingbird**); burning is **the stake**. Sophisticated modern methods have their euphemisms too: a lethal injection of cyanide is termed in America the **green needle** (a grisly metaphor based on the colour of the victim's skin).

Making light of such horrors shields us from their full impact. To speak of **topping** someone trivializes their fate and makes it more bearable for us (the use of *top* for 'hang' dates from the early 18th century; nowadays it is often used reflexively for 'commit suicide'). The now rather dated **turn someone off** 'hang someone' performs the same function (it goes back to the 17th century, and derives from the earlier *turn off the ladder*, meaning 'thrust off the gallows steps'), as does the more graphic **string up** (a product of the early 19th century). From the victim's point of view, the process is trivialized by such verbs as **swing** 'be hanged' (as in 'You'll swing for this') and **fry** or **sizzle** 'be electrocuted'. The 18th and 19th centuries abounded in jokey metaphors for execution, and especially hanging, then the favoured method in the English-speaking world, which have now long passed their sell-by date: among them *necktie party* (an American term for a public hanging, particularly a lynching), *dance on a rope*, *go up a tree*, and *kick the wind*. The same defiant laughter in the face of the executioner comes through in the wry **electric cure** for death by electrocution.

Suicide is a particularly difficult area, requiring a good deal of verbal tiptoeing. The euphemism of suicide is for the most part restrained, self-effacing. A number of synonyms directly follow the Latin model (*sui-* = 'self'): **self-destruction**, despite the violence of its imagery, is less direct than *suicide*; **self-deliverance**, first recorded in

the mid-1970s, refers specifically to suicide by a seriously or terminally ill person, in order to end suffering (**planned termination** is a
suitably vague alternative in this area, but it has unfortunate echoes of
abortion); **self-immolation** is applied to people who burn themselves
to death, often for the purpose of making a political or other protest;
**self-violence**, first recorded in 1671, in Milton's *Samson Agonistes*, is
evasive but stark.

**Make away with oneself** dates back to the 17th century ('It seems
she . . . hath endeavoured to make away with herself often,' Samuel
Pepys 1666), and comes from a more general use of *make away with*
for 'kill', now largely lost. The metaphor of 'putting to one side, out of
the way' has been taken up more colloquially by **do away with
oneself**, which has a corresponding non-reflexive use meaning simply
'kill'. **Take one's own life** sounds disarmingly direct, but its effect is
far less harsh and clinical than *commit suicide*. **End it**, or **end it all**
(first recorded in 1911), is suitably vague, and the American **solitaire**,
from the name of various card games for one person, distracts one from
the enormity and solemnity of the act. The notion of 'taking the **easy
way out**' emphasizes the attractions of death compared with the
unbearableness of life. Somehow in late 19th-century America the
Dutch gained a national reputation for self-destructive tendencies, for
**the Dutch act** and **do the** or **a Dutch** emerged then as euphemisms for
'(commit) suicide'. They were also used to convey the notion of
'absconding' or 'escaping', so probably the underlying metaphor is
based on 'departure' rather than 'death'. A frequent modern circumlocution is **take an overdose**; it could in theory be an overdose of indi-
gestion tablets, but in appropriate circumstances we readily interpret
the veiled message as 'an overdose of a lethal drug': 'Mr Hook had
previously tried to take an overdose, but doctors believed he did not
show any obvious signs of wanting to commit suicide,' *Guardian* 1991.
See also FOUL PLAY (p 242).

Equally delicate is the language needed to refer to the deliberate
killing of a suffering person or animal, in order to end their pain. The
use of **euthanasia** to name this process dates from the middle of the
19th century, but the word itself is much older. It is an anglicization of
a Greek word meaning literally 'good death', and when it was first
used in English, in the 17th century, it was in precisely that sense – a
death that is gentle, without trauma or distress. An ideal base for a
euphemism. But for those for whom *euthanasia* is now too neutral, for
whom it does not proselytize the virtues of the practice, a more positive

alternative is the tendentious **mercy killing**. This emerged in America in the mid 1930s (an earlier alternative, **mercy murder**, first recorded in 1930, was evidently too frank to survive). Those who find *killing* too strong to take have another option in **humane death** (but this has the drawback of reminding one of *humane killer*, a term used for a painless implement or method for killing animals) or **assisted suicide**. When it is a question not so much of administering a lethal dose of a drug as of cutting off the life-support system of someone who would otherwise die, **pulling the plug** is the favoured colloquialism (from the notion of disconnecting the electrical and other apparatus that sustains life) – rather off-handedly callous, perhaps, but less direct than 'allow to die'.

People who have been fatally wounded by some violent action but are having difficulty in dying can be **finished off**, either by their original assailant or by a friend. It is the notion of the *coup de grâce*, the merciful stroke that ends suffering. **Despatch** functions in much the same way, conjuring up the image of the swift bullet or sword stroke that puts an end to pain. It can also be used with reference to wounded animals, as can **put someone out of their misery**, a usage first recorded in Parson Woodforde's diaries in the 1790s.

The painless killing of animals, and particularly domestic animals, that are ill, injured, too old to have a viable existence, or simply unwanted needs careful verbal handling. In the case of a pet, **put to sleep** is the favourite euphemism. First recorded in 1942, it picks up on the 'sleep' metaphor commonly used for 'death' (see p 233). **Put away** (as in 'We had to have the poor old dog put away') classically obfuscates the issue, suggesting storage in a cupboard. Less cosy, but still skirting well clear of the point, is **put down**. This was widely used from the 16th to the 19th century with reference to people, but since then it has been restricted to animals – for example, dogs caught worrying sheep. **Destroy** is more brutal still, and certainly would not be used by a parent explaining the death of a favourite pet to a child: its typical context is that of a working animal that has been so badly injured that it would not be possible or economically sensible to keep it alive: 'The bay five-year-old . . . was destroyed soon afterwards [after breaking its leg],' *Sunday Times* 1992. **Cull** is particularly mealy-mouthed. Its underlying etymological meaning is 'select', and in Australia and New Zealand in the late 19th century it came to be used in the sense 'pick out from amongst a herd of livestock'; not until the mid 20th century, apparently, did it begin to shade over into its currently most common meaning, 'select certain animals to be killed'.

**Country pursuits** and **field sports** euphemize the activity for which *blood sports* is the dysphemism.

**account for** originally, in the early 19th century, a term of the hunting field, implying that all the birds or animals to be shot have been ticked off on a list when killed. Subsequently used with reference to the killing of people (as in 'He accounted for the sentry with a single shot')

**assassinate** to kill for political reasons. The usage of the word is curious: it is applied mainly to the killing of people of high rank in public life, such as presidents and royalty, and it seems to want to pick out such an act as something special, above and beyond the common-place murder suffered by the hoi polloi; but its effect is to euphemize the act, making it somehow more glamorous, less heinous than the stark *murder* would have done. (It is striking that even **kill**, which most of the euphemisms in this section have been coined to avoid, can itself be used as a gentler, less sensational alternative to *murder*)

**bag** originally a hunting metaphor, from the notion of putting killed game into a bag, but later broadened out to include other targets – enemy aircraft, for example

**carry off** used mainly for the fatal effect of an illness (as in 'She was carried off by the flu'); first recorded in the late 17th century

**cut down** applied mainly to soldiers killed in battle – originally by a sword or bayonet, but latterly by gunfire (and especially machine-gun fire) as well. It is now also used for other analogous causes of death (as in 'She was cut down in her prime by cancer')

**do in** to murder, or sometimes more broadly to ruin or destroy. A Briticism dating from the early 20th century: 'My aunt died of influenza: so they said . . . But it's my belief they done the old woman in,' Bernard Shaw 1914. **Do for** can be used in the same sense, usually in the passive, but it is a veteran of the early 18th century, and is now showing its years

**frag** to kill one of your own officers deliberately in battle. The word is a legacy of the Vietnam war, where it was originally used to describe the use of fragmentation grenades for this purpose – hence *frag*. The usual victims were officers with an excessively gung-ho attitude towards battle

**put to the sword** to kill, originally with a sword (the expression dates from at least the 16th century), but latterly, and metaphorically, using a range of other methods. Its blandness suits it well to a frequent use, denoting large-scale slaughter or massacre by troops (as in 'The entire garrison was put to the sword')

**send** used in a wide range of 'killing' euphemisms which have a 'dying' counterpart incorporating *go*. The destination is heaven, hell, or some circumlocutious substitute for one of these, such as *long home* or *happy hunting ground*

**slay** essentially an archaism, and therefore romanticizing death – the subtext is 'nobly, in battle' – but revived in 20th-century American journalese to describe gangland and other murders ('10 slain in mob shoot-out')

**snuff out** to kill, murder. The original metaphor was 'to snuff out life', as a candle flame is snuffed out, but the use of the verb with a human object dates from at least the 1930s

**take out** to kill, with the underlying implication of an individual specially selected for elimination by murder. Used with reference to gangland killings, but also to the accurate fire of military snipers

**wipe out** the gentle action of rubbing lightly with a cloth is reapplied to large-scale slaughter. The agency is usually some natural disaster or plague, rather than a human being (as in 'The floods wiped out whole communities'). But *wipe out* is used with reference to individual murder too (cf. RUB OUT p 246), and the *out* may even be dropped

# FUNERALS

The USA is the spiritual home and natural habitat of English funeralese. The national need to euphemize the disposal of dead bodies, satirized by Evelyn Waugh in *The Loved One* 1948 and dissected in Jessica Mitford's *The American Way of Death* 1963, has spawned a bewildering array of funereal circumlocutions, designed to gloss over or even deny the fact of death.

The antennae of those in the burying business are acutely sensitive to any hint of a direct reference to death and any of the paraphernalia of funerals. In order to spare the dead person's friends and relatives the additional grief that such references will supposedly cause, they have constructed a verbal cocoon around the subject, which muffles all linguistic reality. The underlying approach seems to be that the context (arranger of funeral communicating with those to whom he offers his services) supplies the meaning, and so the language used can afford to be as vague, as semantically empty as possible. Both sides know they are talking about burying or burning a dead body – no need to say so.

So a grave becomes a **space** (if two people are buried side by side they are in **companion spaces**) and the plot where it is situated an **estate**. The embalming of the corpse is seen as an exercise in beautification (**restorative art**, done with **cosmetics**), or it is virtually handed over to the public health department (**hygienic treatment**, **sanitary treatment**). To avoid embarrassing references to improvidence in the face of death, the arrangements for those who neglected to pay in advance are termed **at-need** or **immediate need** (those with the necessary foresight are characterized as **pre-need** or **pre-arrangement**). The transaction of business itself, at which the scale of the funeral is discussed and payment agreed, is delicately termed the **arrangements conference**. A hearse is a **professional car**, a **service car**, or even, with grotesque inappropriateness, an **invalid coach** (and additional transport laid on for the living is usually in the lugubrious form of a **limousine**). A death certificate is, by some bizarre stroke of conscious or unconscious irony, a **vital statistics form**.

But if American English has gone furthest in verbally sanitizing the disposal of dead bodies, even to the point of suggesting that the bodies are not really dead ('Just resting', as unemployed actors euphemistically say in other circumstances), the same impulse is apparent in all varieties of the language. *Undertaker*, probably the most widely used lay term for an 'organizer of funerals', had extremely euphemistic origins, now lost sight of: it arose in the late 17th century as a specialized sense of *undertaker* 'one who undertakes or contracts to do work for another' (the association of ideas with '*taking* the body *under*' is purely fortuitous). Now it is so much the general term that it stands in need of euphemizing itself. **Funeral director** has since the late 19th century been a favourite of the profession, perhaps because it has a no-nonsense, businesslike, dispassionate air about it (it originated, not surprisingly, in America), but it does incorporate the slightly dodgy *funeral*. The search for a less direct alternative led to **mortician**, proposed in the February 1895 number of the American *Embalmer's Monthly*. By a subliminal appeal to *physician*, this seeks to establish clinical credentials, but it has never really caught on outside the USA – perhaps because the reminder of death in *mort-* is too overt. A more recent American alternative is **funeral service practitioner**, coined in 1959 (note again the implication of medical credentials in the reminder of *general practitioner* and *medical practitioner*). But the creepiest American alternatives are **bereavement counsellor** and **grief therapist**, which take the role of the body-burier out beyond that of the doctor to that of the psychotherapist and the social worker. A more down-to-earth euphemism for the undertaking business in general is **the dismal trade**.

The fiction that the dead are merely asleep or resting (see p 233) plays a major role in the mincing vocabulary of undertakers. **Slumber** is a key term in American funeralese: a **slumber room** (first recorded in 1936) is a room in which the undertaker lays out the corpse prior to the funeral; a **slumber box** is a coffin and a **slumber robe** is a shroud. The notion of resting underlies a range of other euphemisms alongside *slumber room*, including **chapel of rest** (one of the few funeral circumlocutions, oddly enough, to have specifically religious connotations), **home of rest** (the associations with REST HOME (see p 232), from which the deceased may just have come, are somewhat unfortunate), **reposing room**, and **restroom** (again, not a felicitous choice, given its other euphemistic use, for a 'lavatory' (see p 182)); and when buried, the dead person is said to have been **laid to rest**. The cosy connotations of *home* are also exploited in **funeral home**, which probably emerged in the US at the end of the 19th century, and in the now rather dated **funeral parlour**. Yet another circumlocution for 'mortuary', in the context of the relatives of the dead person coming in to look at the embalmed body, is **viewing room**; the process is delicately termed the **leave-taking**: 'Is there anything specially characteristic of your Loved One? Many like a musical instrument. One lady made her leave-taking holding a telephone,' Evelyn Waugh 1948; what the 'viewers' take away with them is, in a particularly cringe-making piece of morticians' jargon, a **beautiful memory picture**.

The other main theme is 'remembrance'. A **garden of remembrance** sounds suitably removed from death. The term appears to have originated as a name for a garden commemorating those killed in action, in the two world wars and elsewhere, typically with plaques recording their names (as opposed to actual graves), but it is now applied most commonly to the plot of ground next to a crematorium which mimics the commemorative function of a cemetery (another term for it is **garden of rest**, and for Americans it would be a **memory garden**). In America the equally horticultural **garden of honour** is a graveyard for dead service personnel. But the key American euphemism in this area is **memorial park**, a solemn disguise for a 'cemetery'. It heads a range of circumlocutions in which *memorial* is a fig-leaf for 'death': **memorial association** or **society** a club which people join to save up for their funerals; **memorial counsellor** a sales executive who sells plots in a cemetery; **memorial estate** such a plot; **memorial home** a building with commemorative plaques on the walls; etc.

References to the dead person follow the usual pattern – *the deceased*, *the dear departed*, etc (see pp 235–8) – but there are a few specific funeralisms. **The remains** (short for *mortal remains*) is now dying out, its euphemistic force long since swamped by an unfortunate suggestion of left-overs, but it did give rise to the bizarre **cremains**, coined in America to denote the 'ashes of a cremated person'. The award for unctuousness, though, goes to **loved one**, first recorded in 1926 and immortalized by Evelyn Waugh in the novel of the same name: "'What did your Loved One pass on from?' she asked. "He hanged himself'" (1948).

Every effort is made to avoid the dreaded word *coffin*. Lay people disguise it with a joke: **pine overcoat**, **wooden overcoat**, **wooden kimono**, the American **pine drape** (*drape* in this context meaning 'curtain'), and just plain **box** (first recorded in this sense in 1925). But the professionals, especially in America, prefer **casket**. It is sometimes claimed that Americans say *casket* where the British say *coffin* (much like *sidewalk/pavement*), but the truth is not so straightforward as that: *coffin* is very widespread in American English, and *casket* is mainly an undertaker's word, used particularly for the grander and more ornate (and more expensive) sort of receptacle. Trading on connotations of encrusted jewels and the suggestion that what is contained in the casket (the dead body) is precious, the usage emerged in the 1860s, and soon evoked the famous rebuke from the American writer Nathaniel Hawthorne, 'a vile modern phrase which compels a person of sense and good taste to shrink more disgustedly than ever before from the idea of being buried at all' (1863).

The place where bodies are buried has traditionally been called a *graveyard* or *burial ground*, but from the 17th century these have gradually been replaced by **cemetery**. In modern usage this generally denotes a large public burial ground, not attached to a church. It has the advantage of clothing the unpalatable in the obscurity of a dead language (its ultimate source, Greek *koimeterion*, was also deeply euphemistic, for it originally meant literally 'sleeping room'). But its gloss is wearing thin, and alternatives are being sought. America is to the fore again, with **memorial park** and **remembrance park**, and the whistling-in-the-dark approach of **marble orchard** and **marble town** (from the marble used for the headstones). A graveyard attached to a church is more discreetly termed a **churchyard**.

The process of burial can be solemnified as **interment**, or if something a little more light-hearted is required, you can speak of **planting** the dead person (a usage which originated in America in the mid 19th century): 'It was raining when we planted him, and I thought he'd get out of his coffin,' C Rougvie 1967. Once planted, you are *six feet under* (see p 244); those who have drowned or been buried at sea are said to have gone to **Davy Jones's locker** (the source of the name *Davy Jones* is not known, but *Jones* may be an alteration of *Jonas*, a variant of *Jonah*, the name of the Old Testament prophet who was swallowed by a whale). The whole funeral process is sometimes described as 'giving someone a **send-off**' ('Well at least we gave him a good send-off,' someone might say as the drink flowed, 'back at the house', 'afterwards') – an atavistic expression which recalls ancient rites of passage, and reminds us of the 'journey' on which the soul is embarked.

Cremation can be disguised by the high-falutin **calcification**, and the pseudo-Latin **crematorium** (based on Latin *cremare* 'to burn') was created in the late 19th century to give an air of gravity and solemnity to these newly introduced facilities (its anglicized version, **crematory**, now survives mainly in American English). In funeralese, the placing of the ashes of a burned body in an urn is **inurnment**.

# WORK

---

## EMPLOYMENT

The natural human urge to self-aggrandizement makes us name our jobs in the most imposing way we can get away with. If you are in some menial, low-paid occupation, at least you can make it sound good by borrowing a title from more exalted levels of the hierarchy, or by making it sound more difficult, technical, responsible etc than it really is. Whether the terminology that results from this can always be described as euphemistic is a moot point. Certainly such coinages tend to be pompous and jargon-ridden, but their hyperbole cannot be said to spill over into euphemism unless the terms they replace have some definite negative connotations – of menialness, servility, low status, unpleasantness, etc. It may boost a personnel officer's ego to be called a *human resources manager*, or make him or her think that the job is a different, more important, more challenging one (or there again it may not), but there is no particular stigma attached to being a personnel officer, so the reasons for avoiding the term *personnel officer* cannot be said to be euphemistic. It is more a matter of moving the lexical furniture about, spicing up the mundane with some high-sounding novelty.

Some general euphemistic trends can be discerned. As job titles in the latter half of the 20th century have lengthened from single words to multi-word compounds (often in response to the need for a non-sex-specific term to replace a word ending in *-man*), a range of key important-sounding elements has been evolved to raise lowly jobs in public esteem. In British English, **operative** has taken on this role. A **rodent operative**, for instance, sounds like a most respectable person, with no doubt a sheaf of professional qualifications, but behind him hides the *rat-catcher*, a low-status worker whose title comes much too clean about what he actually does, and reminds us of the dreaded rats that may infest our houses and give us the plague: 'When it comes to official jargon, can you beat turning our old friend the rat-catcher into a "Rodent Operative"?' *Sunday Times* 1944. Note the double vagueness, which disguises both the precise type of animal dealt with, and what the 'operative' does to it (even the *catcher* pulled its punches here, glossing over the 'killing' element). Logically, a 'rodent operative' could equally well be someone who does conjuring tricks with rabbits. Synonymous terms in the same vein are **rodent controller**, **rodent officer**, **rodent operator**, and **pest-control officer**. (In American English, *operative* is a partially euphemistic substitution for *detective* or *secret agent*.)

America favours the term **engineer**, which can enhance the status of a job which has nothing whatever to do with literal engineering. Still amongst the vermin, a rat-catcher in these terms is an **exterminating engineer**. And according to Judith Neaman and Carole Silver in *Kind Words* 1990, the person who cleans shoes in the US Senate is dignified by the title **footwear maintenance engineer**.

Exaggerated claims can also be made with **technician**, applied to jobs that require a remarkably low level of technical expertise, and **manager**, used for positions that involve nothing that would normally be considered managerial responsibilities (in America a dustman can be a **waste-reduction manager**, and in Britain, truancy officers have been transmogrified into **education welfare managers**).

The lowly calling of dustman has probably attracted more euphemisms than any other job. The association with waste matter, decomposing remains of food, and the attendant smells puts it at the bottom of the status ladder, so we try to disguise its nature by giving it fancy names. The word *dustman* goes back to the early 18th century, and is itself more than a little euphemistic in effect: dustbins contain many things less pleasant than dust. The American *garbageman* is much more honest. Of more genteel alternatives, the most widely used is **refuse collector**, which sounds disconcertingly like a hobby. British English also uses **cleansing operative** (the section of the local authority concerned with such matters is often known as the **cleansing department**), **refuse operative**, and the eco-fashionable **environmental cleaner**. American usage plays up the role of the dustman in safeguarding public health, with **sanitation engineer** and **sanitation worker**. And in addition to *waste-reduction manager*, it has **waste manager** and **waste management worker**. Then there is **garbologist**, an apparently serious coinage of the mid 1960s which imports the suffix *-ologist*, implying serious scientific study, into the world of waste disposal.

The similarly lowly public-lavatory attendant may have his or her status raised by the title **sanitary warden** or (for males) **sanitary man**, although this has had the knock-on effect of devaluing *sanitary inspector* (a coinage of the mid 19th century). To avoid any association with lavatories, these functionaries are now referred to as **public health inspectors**.

Another group near the bottom of the pecking order is servants, and there are decided taboos surrounding the use of the 'demeaning' word *servant* itself. **Staff** is conveniently broad and vague: 'Got someone to serve? . . . Oh God, get a couple of Philippinos in . . . You can be a socialist and have staff, you know,' *Absolutely Fabulous* 1992. The use of **domestic** (elliptically for *domestic servant*) dates back to the 17th century, and seems to be less taboo-ridden than *servant*, albeit now rather dated. The *domestic* theme is continued in **domestic help(er)**, **domestic operative**, and the American **domestic worker**. American English also favours **help** ('Help wanted' can be a specific advertisement for a domestic servant). In Britain the preference is for fuller forms such as **home help** and **daily help**. The latter (like the former) is almost always female, so **daily woman** is an alternative (inherently ambiguous) title, often colloquially shortened to **daily**. The use of *woman* in the name of a low-status job is somewhat anomalous: the grander sounding *lady* is generally preferred, as in **cleaning lady**, **dinner lady**, and **tea lady** (there is the story of the domestic servant hired through an agency who turns up at her new employer's door and says 'Are you the woman who asked for a lady to come and clean?'). The terms *waiter* and *waitress* are now under something of a cloud too, and not just because of their sexual discrimination. American officialese has spawned **dining-room attendant** and **catering service personnel**; the nonsexist lobby offers **waitron** and **waitperson**; and there is even some support for **server**, which might be supposed to crank up the meniality index.

Also suffering from an image problem, to judge by the range of names they go under, are people who travel around trying to sell things. *Travelling salesman* (a coinage of the late 19th century) has a definite touch of seediness to it – there are connotations of sexual opportunism. The vaguer **commercial traveller** and **traveller** (which are actually older) are a bit more respectable, if rather dated. The genteel British

**commercial gentleman** is now decidedly passé. Modern usage favours the bland **representative**, which may be qualified in various ways: **area representative** for someone who works a particular patch, **pharmaceutical representative** or **medical representative** for someone selling medicinal drugs, etc. Someone who sells things (such as cosmetics) part-time from door to door is known in American English as a **part-time merchandizer**.

The lowliness of the secretary is a problem not so much for (typically) her ego as for that of the person she works for. To enhance his prestige he will call her by the grander title **personal assistant** (usually **PA** for short), or in America **administrative assistant**, which suggests that his own status is high too. The subterfuge is perhaps colluded in by those who imagine that *personal assistant* is less sexually discriminatory than *secretary*.

The taboo on the British *navvy* is so strong that it has now virtually disappeared from general usage. An acceptably polite general replacement is **workman**, or perhaps if road construction work is being specifically referred to, **road mender**.

A particularly touchy area is the nomenclature of foreign people working in a country. *Migrant worker* may sound discriminatory or condescending; it is certainly on the politically-correct hit list. A suitably polite alternative is **guest worker**, probably a loan translation of German *Gastarbeiter*, which conjures up a whole scenario of graciously proffered invitations thankfully accepted (judging by the wages such people typically receive, there may also be some subliminal reference to the notion of the 'guest artist, guest star', etc who supposedly appears for no money). American English also uses the mealy-mouthed **seasonal employee** and **seasonal worker**.

On the use of TURF ACCOUNTANT for 'someone who takes bets on horses', see p 44.

Even the word *job* itself is too much (or too little) for some people. If a job is too humble for you to have, your alternatives are a **position**, a **post**, an **appointment**, a **berth** (jocularly), or a **situation** (now largely disused except in 'situations vacant'). It might be supposed that being given a job (as opposed to being sacked) was a matter for celebratory openness, not verbal camouflage, but even here euphemism puts out its insidious feelers: to be politically correct, any reference to the taking on of staff on any grounds other than individual merit (for example, their race or sex) must be in terms of **preferential hiring**, avoiding negative words like *discriminatory*; and in America, the following of this non-discriminatory hiring code is termed **affirmative action**.

Having a second job in addition to one's main employment is often frowned on if not actually disallowed, so it needs a verbal disguise: **moonlighting** (the subsidiary job is usually a night-time one).

People who pay for others' services are generally called 'customers'. But for some, it appears that the word *customer* will not do. It is just too ordinary. It does not have enough status. **Client** is much more upmarket – it was originally applied to lawyers' customers, but it is now used generally to add tone. Customers of would-be classy shops may be dignified by the title **patron**. British Rail, on the other hand, came to the conclusion in the early 1990s that it was rather demeaning to refer to the people who used its trains as 'passengers', so it decided to butter them up by calling them 'customers'. For the aliases used for prostitutes' customers, see p 100.

Money attracts euphemisms, and payment given for work done is a delicate linguistic area. *Wages* is déclassé. The high-status term is **salary**, which brings with it associations of regular payments made to professional people and senior non-manual workers. A more pompous effect can be achieved by **emolument** (etymologically a 'miller's fee for grinding grain') or **remuneration**.

# MARKETING

In no field of human endeavour is there more hyperbole and exaggeration than in advertising and selling. People with a product or service to exchange for money do not often resort to understatement. But little of the hyperbole is true euphemism, in the sense of concealing the unpalatable.

There are some areas, though, in which hyping the adequate shades into circumventing taboos. Even though small is supposed to be beautiful, for instance, it is quite hard to find a size of package described as 'small'. Marketers evidently feel that the notion of buying something of relatively low value in a small package does not appeal to people, so the smallest size will be labelled **regular** or **standard**. This has the knock-on effect of inflating the claims made for the larger sizes. A pack which no reasonable person would describe as anything other than 'average-sized' will be puffed up to **large**. And this leaves no terminology for the truly large apart from such hyperbolical flights as *jumbo*, *super* and *family*, and the euphemistic **economy** (which comes on as a mealy-mouthed alternative for 'cheap', but in practice connotes bigness). In America, where ownership of a 'small' car may for some seem like a confession of impotence, automobile sales staff describe the lower-sized end of their range as **compact** and **subcompact**.

This phenomenon of inflating a scale of epithets by taking the bottom one out and moving the rest down crops up in a variety of fields. In 1992, for instance, the English Football League renamed its four divisions. The former first division, little changed in composition, reappeared as the 'premier' division. The fourth division vanished, at least in name, although in fact it was still there, under the name 'third'. Likewise the third was now the 'second' and the second was the 'first'. A similar practice affects the naming of various categories of accommodation on aircraft, ships, trains, etc. The name of the lowest category undergoes an almost continual metamorphosis in order to salve the supposed vanity of those forced by economic necessity to use it. On British trains, for instance, the 'third class' has long since disappeared, and no one travels 'steerage' on ships any more. On aeroplanes, numerical class distinction is mitigated by calling the cheaper seats **tourist class** or **economy class**, while envy of 'first class' is dissipated by such exotic in-between formulae as **club class** and **executive class**. A similar devaluation affects the billing of leading performers in films: traditionally a film 'stars' its main actors, while subsidiary ones have to be content with 'with' or 'also starring'; but more recent practice has been to promote the stars to before the name of the film, with the result that the supporting players incongruously inherit the billing 'starring'.

The whole notion of cheapness is a difficult one for marketers to handle. Low price is clearly an asset as far as most purchasers are concerned, but to appeal to this too directly would risk making them seem tight-fisted or poor. So paradoxically, *cheap* is almost as much a taboo word as *expensive*. Circumlocutions need to be found for it (indeed *cheap* itself is somewhat euphemistic in origin; it began as a shortened form of *good cheap*, which at first meant 'good buy'). The key words here are **budget**, **economy**, **low-cost**, and, at a rather more genteel level, **inexpensive**. But a range of other formulae are available too ('amazing value', 'modestly priced,' etc), limited only by the marketers' ingenuity.

With cheapness, the problem is getting the message across in a not too obvious way – hence the euphemisms. But expensiveness generally needs to be swept under the carpet altogether, so it is not a much euphemized area. An exception is **exclusive**, which with a subliminal subtext of 'too expensive for someone like you' may incite the upwardly mobile to buy in retaliation.

A particular piece of marketeering subterfuge is the vocabulary used for suggesting that customers are getting something for nothing, when in fact the cost of it is hidden within the price they have paid. A *free* gift from a shop is really nothing of the sort. At least a part of the cost of a **complimentary** glass of wine turns up on your restaurant bill. A **courtesy** coach provided **for your convenience** is not paid for out of the pocket of the person running the company that sent it.

An area that demands careful handling is the selling of goods that are not new. The term *second-hand* has come to have decidedly negative connotations, and is unlikely to attract custom. **Used** was an early attempt at a fig-leaf, particularly applied to cars (it is first recorded in 1931), but its euphemistic credentials are now wearing rather thin. The main present-day alternatives are **nearly new**, **pre-owned**, which is a product of 1960s America, and **previously owned**. If something, such as a car, is not only second-hand but also old and expensive, it can be termed **classic**. And by a similar token, the promoters of a film, book, etc that is rather dated and restricted in appeal may try to boost its status by describing it as **cult**.

Second-hand items that are up-market enough can be classified as antiques. And antique dealers have their own vocabulary of circumlocution and obfuscation: a piece described as **commercial** is liable to be cheap and nasty; one that delights the untutored eye but is dismissed as unimportant by the experts is disguised as **pretty**, while one that sends the experts into transports of enthusiasm but is so ugly as to be unsaleable is **academically interesting**. A piece made up of disparate elements, such as a clock with a Georgian case and a Victorian movement, is a **marriage**; and the practice of taking the framework of old but clapped-out pieces of furniture, tarting them up with new veneer, and selling them as genuine antiques is termed the **carcass trade** (*carcass* is a cabinetmaker's term for the internal framework of a piece of furniture). No consideration of genuineness can pass by without mention of that most useful word in the world of art and antiques, **copy**, which sits firmly on the fence between bona fide imitation and fraudulent forgery.

But if there is one profession that is notorious for the euphemism of its marketing ploys, it is that of the estate agent. Indeed, the very term **estate agent** (a product of the last quarter of the 19th century) has euphemistic aspects. The subliminal suggestion of rolling acres of parkland dotted with trees and with a large country house at their centre strikes an incongruous note (particularly for Americans, who prefer *real estate agent*) when compared with the actual business of trying to sell poky flats, bleak bungalows, etc.

Estate agents have evolved a vocabulary of refined mendacity for putting the best possible gloss on their clients' property. Its cover is now so widely blown that it scarcely retains any true euphemistic power, but here for the record are the better established terms:

**bijou** tiny – scarcely room to keep, let alone swing a cat – but, so the implication goes, charming

**character** a house which 'has character' incorporates architectural aberrations of striking ugliness or vulgarity, or is old and in danger of falling down, or, paradoxically, is scarcely distinguishable in its banality from scores of similar ones all around it

**commodious** built like a barn and suitable only for a family of fourteen with servants

**convenient** so small that you can conveniently reach every cupboard in the kitchen without taking a step in any direction

**eat-in kitchen** no dining room, so you have to eat in the kitchen. An American real-estate agents' term, used to suggest smallness without actually saying 'small'

**Georgian** unspecifiedly old, certainly pre-World War II. As far as architectural historians are concerned, it refers specifically to the period covered by the first four Georges, who reigned in Britain from 1714 to 1830; but estate agents bear in mind that there were two further Georges in the 20th century

**gracious** old, probably quite large, and certainly expensive. Roughly the same ground is covered by **elegant**

**handyman's special** in dire need of renovation; if you're lucky has a roof. An American term

**historic** very old, a nightmare to keep up, and probably hedged about with regulations preventing you from modernizing it

**home** a house; used to cash in on all the positive associations (security, comfort, family, etc) of the word *home*

**ideal for modernization** in desperate need of modernization and/or repair

**immaculate** in a normal state of repair and upkeep; not in tatters and disgustingly dirty, but not redecorated throughout last week either

**landscaped** (of a new house) having a garden from which the builders have removed most of the rubble and laid a few turfs

**needs some work** in imminent danger of collapse if not seen to

**outstanding** in the top price bracket

**period** recognizably old, in both style and disrepair

**prestigious** prohibitively expensive – in theory because of some desirable attribute, such as situation, but in practice often no more than 'high in cost'

**quaint** claustrophobically small; an American equivalent of BIJOU

**secluded** miles from anywhere, cut off from public transport services, and suitable only for hermits

**select** with luck, marginally better than bog-standard

**snug** if two people are going to live in it they should be quite small and get on with each other well

**sought after** highly priced, but there is not necessarily a queue of prospective purchasers

**unique** unusual in some respect that may or may not be desirable

A notable feature of estate agents' descriptions is their geographical elasticity. The location of a property for sale will be represented as the most up-market and desirable that can be shoe-horned within the provisions of the Trade Descriptions Act. These are mostly local options that never achieve any wider status, but one that has become institutionalized in Britain is **South Chelsea** for Battersea – a name invented on the basis of the high fashionableness of Chelsea, which presumably helps to sell houses in Battersea.

# EXCUSES

Dissembling one's presence in the face of unwelcome callers is by no means restricted to the business world – probably the longest-established brush-off is 'X is not at home' when he or she most certainly is – but people who work in offices have evolved the most celebrated set of excuses with which secretaries ward off untimely telephone calls. It is probably euphemistic to call these excuses euphemisms – in truth they are generally just plain lies – but their users no doubt see them as mitigating the effect of the underlying message, 'He/She doesn't want to talk to you', which is bad for business and therefore taboo.

The two classics are **in a meeting** and **in conference**, which in the code of office behaviour establish uninterruptibility. Less specific but still effective is **tied up**. But **unavailable** is rather feeble, suggesting insufficient time or wit to think up anything better. Any number of extempore evasions will do as well, according to circumstances – 'She's on another line', 'He's not back from lunch yet', 'She's not at her desk just now', and so on – but it is important to make them plausible. The person who, wearying of an interminable telephone conversation, said 'I must go now, the phone's ringing' forgot this vital rule.

When it comes to excusing our own shortcomings, and particularly our failure to act, **pressure of work** is the cliché most commonly trotted out.

# DISMISSAL

Losing your job is a traumatic experience, so when we talk about it, we like to use a little verbal cotton wool, to soften its impact. In particular, those who have to inflict this unpleasantness on others are endlessly ingenious at inventing ways of pretending that they are doing something else.

The turnover rate of euphemisms in this area is high. No matter how thick the verbal disguise, people are well aware of what is being talked about, and the circumlocution soon becomes as painfully frank as the terminology it replaced. *The sack*, for instance, was no doubt intended to soften the blow (it emerged in the early 19th century, and has near equivalents in other languages, but the basis of the metaphor is not clear: possibly the original allusion was to an apprentice being given back his bag of tools when dismissed); but in present-day English one could scarcely say anything more blunt than 'I'm giving you the sack!'

The classically evasive approach is to try to give the impression that there is no question of enforced dismissal (with its unspoken undercurrents of incompetence or wrongdoing), but that employer and employed are parting company with mutual satisfaction. **Early retire-**

**ment** provides an excellent excuse, almost regardless of the age of the 'retirer'. Putting someone **out to grass** also suggests an age motive, albeit more brutally. Alternatively, you can suggest that the person's job no longer exists, rather than that they are incompetent to fill it: to be made **redundant** may be marginally less psychologically damaging than to be dismissed, even though the practical effect is the same. *Redundant* in this sense is a Briticism only, which emerged in the 1920s, and it baffles Americans; in the US, a similar notion is expressed by the verbs **excess** and **surplus**, denoting the dismissal of one or more employees because there are too many for the work available. To **lay off** an employee is to suspend his or her employment during a slack period. More circumlocutious still are **leave of absence** and **gardening leave**, the subtext of which is often 'kept out of the office while charges of malfeasance are being investigated'.

The right note of genteel evasiveness is struck by **release** and **let go** ('I'm afraid we're going to have to let you go, Ms Johnson'), which contrive to suggest that the employer is reluctantly acceding to the employee's request (an American variant of *let go* is **let out**). A colloquial way of putting it is **shelved**; and in American English an employee can be **retrenched** if the workforce in his or her company is being reduced due to economic stringency. More stiffly formal are **relieve someone of their duties**, **post**, etc, and also **dispense with someone's services** and **someone's services are no longer required** – note the euphemistic use of the archaic *services* to denote 'work'. The last implies, like *redundant*, that if the job were still there, you would be welcome to fill it. **Stand down** and **step down** insist that leaving is your own idea (even if in fact your superior suggested it or even ordered it). There is a kind (or self-exculpatory) impulse behind **not renewing someone's contract** – implying an act of omission, rather than a positive decision to dismiss. And someone thus got rid of may be said in hushed tones to be **no longer with us**.

A military officer who resigns early may be said (in Britain) to **send in his papers** (referring to the documents containing the sovereign's commission, and implying a certain involuntariness). Similarly a jobleaver who is **clearing his desk** may be suspected to have had the decision taken for him. **Spending more time with one's family** as an excuse (popular especially among politicians) for resigning had its profile raised in the early 1980s by the Conservative minister Norman Fowler, who quoted it in his resignation letter to Margaret Thatcher.

A frequent euphemistic strategy is to refer in some way to the mechanics of dismissal, thus shifting the focus from the dismissal itself. **Notice** is the key term here (first recorded in this specialized sense in the mid 18th century): to give someone *notice* or advance warning of dismissal is tantamount to dismissing them, even though the effect is more or less delayed. (**Warning** itself was used in the same way in the 19th century – as in 'to give a servant warning.') More colloquial alternatives are **cards**, first recorded in 1929 (one 'gets or is given one's cards,' originally literally a card recording employers' national insurance contributions, with which one was presented on leaving employment) and the American **pink slip** (also used as a verb: 'His wife had . . . left him the day after he was pink-slipped,' Thomas Pynchon 1966). **Marching orders** was originally, in the 18th century, an order for troops to set off at a march, but it has since been widely used (like its American equivalent **walking papers**) as a metaphor for 'dismissal', both generally and in the specific context of 'dismissal from a job'. Also with strong military associations is the American **separate**, used since the 19th century to denote 'discharge from the armed forces', but also applied in business and commerce: 'She [a spokeswoman] termed those losing their jobs as "separations" from the company,' *Boston Globe* 1992. To 'separate employees selectively' is to pick out individuals for the chop, to 'separate them involuntarily' is simply to give them the good old sack.

But it was during the last third of the 20th century, and particularly during the unemployment-ridden 1980s, that the vocabulary of dismissal was refined to hitherto undreamed-of extremes of mealy-mouthedness. The massive job losses associated with successive recessions have created a whole industry devoted to advising on how to dismiss staff, counselling those dismissed, and finding jobs for the unemployed. Devotees of this calling have evolved a new terminology that combines a chilling detachment (typified by the application of very vague inoffensive words like *reduction* and *adjustment* to an area charged with strong feeling) with an unconscious mincing coyness.

An early harbinger in British English was **rationalize**, which has been evolving since the 1920s as a general euphemism for 'reduce in scope' (the implied excuse being 'modernization through more rational methods'), and has come to be used specifically for 'reduce the size of a workforce (by dismissals)'. American English around the end of the 1960s contributed the chilling pair **outplace**, which originated in the 1920s as a general term for 'displace' ('Practitioners have even coined a euphemistic description for the process [of dismissing people]: "outplacing" executives who have been "dehired",' *Time* 1970) and **terminate**, which in many contexts sounds like a form of execution ('The current terminations . . . are expected to exceed 3,500 people by the end of this month,' *Boston Globe* 1992). They have been followed by a welter of pseudo-scientific circumlocutions masquerading as technical terminology. Typical examples are **executive culling** (when higher-grade staff are sacked), **head-count reduction**, **internal reorganization**, **personnel surplus reduction**, **vocational relocation**, **workforce adjustment**, and **workforce imbalance correction**. This is the world where dismissal is sanitized as **negotiated departure**, where a company that is subjected to massive job losses is described as **restructured**, where, in American government gobbledegook, sacking becomes **reduction in force**. Companies thus **slimmed down** are **lean**, or often even **leaner and fitter**.

Coiners of these linguistic evasions seem to have a particular liking for verbs beginning with the prefix *de-*. It is as if they are trying to pull the wool over people's eyes by using the positive term, suggesting expansion of the workforce, and hoping that the negative prefix will slip through unnoticed. Into this category come **degrow**, **dehire**, **deselect** (also used in the British Labour Party of a sitting MP who is not renominated for a seat by his or her local party), **destaff**, and the bizarre **decruitment**. (Of similar inspiration is **de-accession**, coined in the mid 1980s in the world of library and museum administration to disguise the selling off of books and other articles from public collections; it has also been redeployed to denote the dismissal of employees.)

But probably the keynote words of the late 20th-century science of dismissal are **downsize**, and its more mealy-mouthed successor **rightsize**. *Downsize* at least comes clean that it is all about 'reduction'. Introduced in America in the mid 1970s to denote the production of smaller cars, within the decade it was being applied to the reduction of workforces: 'Many of them will start the new year in fear of their well-paid jobs, as what is typically called "downsizing" sweeps through the securities industry,' *Economist* 1987. But that *down-* soon became too frank, and in the 1990s *rightsizing* came on the scene: 'Our reluctance to face facts these days is nearly as strong as our fear of fat, which has resulted in the notion of "rightsizing" a company or an arm of government,' *Boston Globe* 1992. In theory, of course, the 'right size' for a company could be bigger, but in practice the term always presages dismissals, not recruitment. The image conjured up is of a company structure as a Procrustean bed, which requires that extraneous employees be chopped off in order that the company may fit on to it.

From the employee's point of view, the best verbal defence against dismissal is mordant humour. To say that one has been **bounced** (possibly from the notion of hitting the pavement after being thrown out), been 'given the **bump** (or the **bullet**)', been 'shown the **gate**', or, in America, received a **kiss-off** is less stark than to admit that one has been sacked. If you have to go **down the road**, you are leaving your place of work for the last time. A British army officer who is demobilized is, or was, said to be **bowler-hatted** (a usage dating from the early 1950s), because for the sort of jobs such people went into, a bowler hat was until the 1970s part of the uniform. In the US Army, a **bobtail** is a dishonourable discharge – the reference to 'honorable and faithful service' being cut, or 'bobbed', off the bottom of the certificate of discharge. Someone dismissed from the navy is said to be **sent ashore**. Large-scale sacking of staff may be euphemized in American English as **house-cleaning**, especially when it follows from investigations into corruption or malpractice. But the wryest humour of all is perhaps in the chiefly American **DCM**, a pun on the initial letters of 'Distinguished Conduct Medal' which actually stands for 'Don't Come Monday'.

A particular class of rather colourful metaphor attaches itself to various forms of lump-sum payment given on dismissal, suggesting that this is an area which people do not like to refer to directly. The first in the field was **golden handshake** 'large payment made to someone retiring or being made redundant', which is first recorded in 1960. It has been followed by **platinum handshake** and **tin handshake**, respectively more and less generous than the golden variety ('Sir Robert Crichton-Brown, chairman of Rothmans, is understandably rather keen to be awarded the £750,000 platinum handshake which the board will propose,' *Daily Telegraph* 1988), and also by **golden parachute** and **tin parachute**, denoting contractual arrangements which guarantee a payment (large or small, according to the preciousness of the metal) in case of dismissal.

The final refuge for a dismissed employee (of executive grade) is a **consultancy** – a euphemism in both word and deed. If you can appoint the sacked one as a **consultant** instead of throwing him or her out into the cold hard world, you can continue to give them some remuneration without having to put up with their constant presence, and you don't necessarily ever have to consult them about anything.

When it is not people that are dismissed but documents – unwanted bumf and circulars, footling memos, etc – there is a jocular euphemism for *waste-paper basket* available: **circular file**.

Dismissal of another sort – from the field of play in sport, and specifically rugby league – is jocularly euphemized as an **early bath**, from the notion of a player sent off by the referee before the end of the game and able to enjoy a bath before his colleagues. The term was popularized in the 1960s and 1970s by the BBC rugby league commentator Eddie Waring. (Another notable sporting euphemism is **professional foul**, which seeks to disguise a cynically deliberate foul, committed to prevent a certain score by the other side.)

# UNEMPLOYMENT

The waves of unemployment that hit Britain in the 1980s and 1990s, following decades of relatively full employment, called forth a new vocabulary to cope with this traumatic condition. Indeed, the British government in the mid 1980s officially promulgated **job search**, institutionalizing what in less straitened times would have been known simply as 'job hunting'. And the place to which people go to look for a job, formerly known as a *labour exchange* (first recorded in 1869) or the more pompous *employment exchange* (first recorded in 1909), has been euphemized with the more user-friendly **job centre**.

For the socially conscious, the words for avoiding the over-frank *unemployed* in the late 20th century were **unwaged** (which actually emerged in the 1970s meaning 'working for no payment', but in the 1980s began to be used for 'without a job') and **nonwaged**. Larger mouthfuls produced by the American politically correct tendency in the 1980s include **indefinitely idled**, **involuntarily leisured**, and **temporarily outplaced**. In Britain in the 1980s, **UB40** became a euphemism for an 'unemployed person' – as in 'OAPs and UB40s half-price' (it comes from the number of the form filled in by claimants of unemployment benefit). And **claimant** itself is used in British English as a rather vague term for those in receipt of government welfare payments.

But unemployment is nothing new, and people have always been adept at finding words to cover up its embarrassment or shame. (In 1993, Chancellor of the Exchequer Kenneth Clarke decided to call the unemployed **jobseekers**.) A classic of the genre is **between jobs**, which confidently asserts that the unemployment is purely temporary. Also accentuating the positive is **at liberty**. An actor who is out of work is **between shows** or, more famously, **resting** (a term extended to cover sportsmen too). A sailor who has not found a job on board ship is **on the beach**.

'Promotion' to a grand-sounding new job which carries no higher pay than your previous one attracts racist metaphors, based on racial groups stereotypically regarded as stupid or substandard: in America it is a **Mexican promotion** or **Mexican raise**; in Britain, an **Irish promotion** or **Irish rise**.

# BANKRUPTCY

When a company is teetering towards bankruptcy, but still has hopes of surviving, it naturally favours discretion in public utterances about its position. 'Losing money hand over fist' would not encourage nervous investors. The most favoured low-key terms are **cash flow** and **liquidity**, which may be admitted into the same sentence as *problem* and even *crisis*, although preferably qualified by *temporary*: a 'temporary cash-flow problem' does not sound too bad at all.

If the worst happens, there is little that words can say to palliate it. The **receiver** can be 'called in' (a term designating someone appointed by a court to administer the property of a bankrupt), or the company can 'go into receivership', which has a more respectable ring than 'go bankrupt'. An **administrator** may be appointed. Insolvency may be wrapped up in the technical jargon of **over-geared**, which denotes that a company's borrowings exceed its assets.

But the main synonyms for *bankrupt* are colloquial and fairly unsympathetic. A company may be said to **fold** or **go under**. A bank which goes out of business has **closed its doors**. In British English, if a broker is **hammered**, he is declared to have defaulted (the origin of the metaphor is the three strokes of the hammer used in the Stock Exchange to secure silence for the announcement). If someone **takes a bath**, they make a large financial loss, typically following an injudicious investment. To land up in **Carey Street** (a now distinctly super-annuated expression, first recorded in 1922) is to be bankrupt – Carey Street, to the north of the Strand, London, was once the location of the Bankruptcy Department of the Supreme Court.

In American English, to **fall out of bed** is to suffer financial or commercial collapse. But if a company 'files' or 'goes' **Chapter 11**, it can continue trading while insolvent, under the provisions of chapter 11 of the Bankruptcy Reform Act 1978.

The nocturnal departure of those seeking to escape creditors is euphemized in a range of expressions based on the notion of 'moonlight'. The typical one is **moonlight flit**, which dates back at least to the early 18th century, but other collocations are recorded, with *march*, *walk*, *wander*, etc. The usual scenario is of a tenant in arrears with the rent decamping to avoid the landlord's wrath, but the terms can be used more widely to denote any departing debtor.

See also POVERTY p 284.

# TRADE UNIONS

Strikes seldom get a good press, and the word *strike* itself (first recorded – as a verb – in the industrial sense in the 1760s) has decidedly negative overtones. A rich circumlocutory vocabulary has been evolved by the trade union movement to name work stoppages without using the *s*-word.

The most notorious of these alternative terms is **action**, which is the butt of heavy-handed jokes from those who find it incongruous to describe something that involves stopping work as 'action'. Its commonest context is **industrial action**, first recorded in 1971, which in fact covers other forms of workers' protest than just strikes, and is therefore quite a useful cover term. A **day of action**, however, certainly involves not working for a day, with many of those involved taking part in protest marches. The American equivalent of *industrial action* is **job action**.

A variation on *industrial action* is **industrial dispute**, which actually dates back to the beginning of the 20th century (it is first recorded in Section 51 (xxv) of the Constitution of Australia, dating from 1900). It is often abbreviated to **dispute**, which transforms the strike into a restrained and gentlemanly falling-out.

Other roundabout terminology includes the vague **stoppage**, first recorded in 1902 ('1926 . . . The year of the General Stoppage,' *Publishers' Circular* 1926), the equally ambiguous **walk out**, which emerged in America in the late 19th century ('Twenty-two teachers at a Cardiff comprehensive school walked out on indefinite strike yesterday,' *Guardian* 1991), and the rather pompous **withdraw one's labour**. In American English, a strike by people who are forbidden by law from going on strike can be euphemized as a **sick-out** (first recorded in 1970) or a **sick-in** (also a 1970s coinage) – the pretext being 'absent ill'.

*Go-slow*, a coinage of the late 1920s, and its American equivalent *slowdown* are scarcely euphemistic, for they are quite up-front about the nature of the action taken. **Work-to-rule**, first recorded as a noun in 1950, purports to be so too, but it is slightly disingenuous, inasmuch as it attributes normality and legality to what is in practice a disruptive reduction in work-rate. Amongst the professions, the alternative **work-to-contract** has been used. In the late 19th and early 20th century another name for this sort of industrial action was **ca'canny**. This was originally a British dialect word for 'caution', made up of *ca'*, short for *call*, and *canny* 'cautiously'.

Work methods, conditions of employment, etc that are hopelessly out of date and inefficient but whose reform is opposed by trade unions are euphemized with the poker-faced **custom and practice**. When they are not merely inefficient but also irregular (for example, overmanning imposed on employers by unions, or excessive working of overtime) they are termed ironically **Spanish practices**, a reworking of the earlier **old Spanish customs**, and presumably some sort of reference to the supposed indolence of the Spanish.

To **organize** is to band together in a trade union, usually in the context of one particular company or place of work. The term **organized labour**, standing for 'unionized workforce', goes back to late 19th-century America.

The vagueness of **industrial relations**, first recorded in 1904, gives it plausible credentials as a euphemism: it could in theory stand for any of an almost open-ended range of relationships, between manufacturers, employees, customers, shareholders, etc, but in practice it refers to disagreements between employers and employees, their resolution and avoidance.

# MONEY

Money is traditionally an area hedged with taboos. People supposedly do not like talking about it, at least when it belongs to them. But the euphemistic fallout of this reluctance has been relatively low in conventional terms. We may prefer to talk about our **resources** or our **funds** or our **finances** than about our money. If we cannot afford something we may say that we haven't the **wherewithal** or the **needful**. But on the whole, the synonyms we use for *money* come into the category of robust colloquialism and outspoken slang: *ackers*, *brass*, *bread*, *dough*, *lolly*, *loot*, *Lsd*, *readies*, *shekels*, *spondulicks*, *wedge*, and the like. The number of these synonyms is remarkably large, and it is being constantly renewed. Speculation as to whether they too cover up a deep-seated aversion to mentioning 'money' directly, and are therefore basically euphemistic, is perhaps best left to amateur psychologists.

*Cheap* often collocates with *nasty,* and carries undeniable connotations of low quality, so the need for an alternative is often felt: **bargain** will do the job nicely (as in 'a bargain buy'), and **affordable** dismisses any possible hint of tat.

Those who handle money professionally have their own vocabulary of metaphors to draw a veil over some of their murkier dealings. The most notorious is **creative**, which essentially connotes 'verging on dishonest'. The general use of *creative* to suggest the embroidering of the truth is traceable back to the early 1950s, but its familiar modern use in such contexts as **creative accounting** and **creative bookkeeping**, denoting the most favourable presentation of accounts this side of illegality, seems to date from around 1970. Accountants and other money men who are blessed with this creativity may alternatively be said to **massage** the figures. An even more weasely word in this context is **adjust**. It comes on as if butter wouldn't melt in its mouth, but it can cover up all sorts of dubious manipulations. An **exchange-rate adjustment** or **currency adjustment** sounds much better than a *devaluation* (an alternative euphemism much heard during the enforced British devaluation of 1992 was **realignment**, which grew out of the pegging of currencies within the exchange-rate mechanism of the European Monetary System). When finance ministers are prepared to admit to a **downward adjustment** in the economy, we may be sure something serious is wrong. A **price adjustment** is most unlikely to be downwards (as is a **price revision**). Economic statistics that are **seasonally adjusted** somehow always turn out to be more favourable to the governing party. **Technical adjustment**, and **technical correction**, are used to try to suggest that a fall in stock-market prices has been caused by **technical factors** – mere formalities of stock-market operation – rather than by some event in the real world that will depress prices still further. (**Correction** may be used on its own for a large-scale collapse of stock-exchange prices.)

**Negative** is a useful word for verbal conjuring tricks in the financial world. It enables people in a backdoor way to describe something undesirable in terms of its more positive opposite. Economic contraction, for instance, may not seem so serious if you call it **negative growth**. **Negative savers** are people who spend more than they own. If a product makes a **negative profit contribution**, it sells at a loss. If your house has **negative equity**, it is worth less than the mortgage you have taken out on it.

It is vital to the interests of politicians, especially when elections loom, to play down the seriousness of an economic crisis. At all costs, doom-laden vocabulary must be avoided. For as long as is plausible, claim that the crisis is brief and will soon be over. This was the motivation behind Chancellor of the Exchequer Nigel Lawson's use of the word **blip** in 1989 to characterize a rise in the rate of inflation. If economic contraction continues, it may be conceded that it is a **downturn** (first widely used in economic contexts in the 1940s) or a **downtrend**. But as we move beyond that point, with a sustained fall in output and sales and growing unemployment, words must be chosen more carefully still. The economic state of Britain in the early 1990s made an instructive terminological case-study. The concession was gradually wrung from government ministers that it was a **recession**, a word first recorded in this economic sense in 1929. But as it continued to get worse, the question began to be asked, when does a recession become a depression or a slump? But neither of these latter words was ever countenanced by the government, and neither in fact was ever taken up to any extent even by those antagonistic to the government. *Depression* as an economic term appears to date from the early 19th century, and originally it was probably quite euphemistic in force, but its major connotation is of the ravaged Western economy of the 1930s, and no one wants to suggest the return of years that left lasting scars on the psyche of nations that suffered them. The use of *slump* in economic contexts dates from the early 1920s, but it has highly negative connotations of collapse that cause it to be shunned by government spokesmen. So the true answer to the question is that, although the economic situation of the early 1990s bore a resemblance in certain particulars to situations in the past that *had* been characterized as *depression* or *slump*, there was no chance that either of these dysphemistic terms would be sanctioned now. *Recession* does not *sound* so bad, so that is the euphemism of choice.

*Cartel* is a word businessmen like to avoid. More discreet ways of referring to this sort of illegal price-fixing between supposed competitors are **price-linking**, **orderly marketing**, **parallel pricing**, and, in America, **structured competition**.

## Some other miscellaneous financial euphemisms:

**black economy** that part of the economy consisting of money that has been earned but on which, illegally, no tax has been paid. This particular use of **black** to denote the contravening of financial or economic regulations dates back to the early 1930s. Its best-known manifestation, *black market*, is no longer euphemistic

**churning** the practice of a stock-broker continually buying and selling a client's shares simply in order to earn a commission on the deals, with no advantage to the client. A metaphor, mainly American, based on the notion of churning milk to cream off the best, and dating from the early 1950s

**easy terms** hire purchase, but not necessarily easy if your income does not keep pace with the repayments. The term dates back at least to the 17th century

**facility** a bank loan, or permission to overdraw one's account. A coy circumlocution for those who find talk of borrowing and lending embarrassing

**financial services** used generally for a range of services sold to the public by banks, building societies, and other financial institutions, but also more specifically and euphemistically for money-lending

**service** to 'service a debt, loan, etc' is to meet the interest payments on it. A quaint usage, arising in early 1940s America, which somehow recalls the other euphemistic use of *service*, for 'copulate with a female animal'

**unbundling** selling off individually some or all of the component parts of a business one has bought – in other (dysphemistic) words, 'asset-stripping'. In the late 1980s, the British financier Sir James Goldsmith was known as 'the Great Unbundler'.

# BRIBERY

The key euphemistic image of bribery is of removing friction, so that the wheels of a transaction may turn without hindrance. There is no hint of venality; it is merely a facilitating process. This is the world of *lubrication*, of *oil*, and of *grease*. The expression **grease someone's palm**, meaning to bribe them, is not recorded before the 19th century, but it has an ancestor in *grease someone's hand* going back to the early 16th century. **Grease** was used on its own in former times to mean 'to bribe', and it still survives as a noun in the sense 'bribery' (sometimes in the phrase **palm grease**). Other verbs that go with *palm* are *anoint* and *oil*, but **oil** in the context of bribery and corruption is most commonly encountered in the expression **oil the wheels** 'expedite matters by illicit or unofficial payment'. As an independent verb it is now rather dated. Also well past its sell-by date is the British slang **oil the knocker** 'bribe a porter or doorman'. The use of **lubricate** for 'bribe' – effectively as a euphemism for the more up-front *grease* and *oil* – is first recorded in 1928.

These terms are rather too crude and obvious, though, for use in the world of legitimate business. Here, more discretion is required. It is necessary to pretend that the money which changes hands serves some other, more admissable purpose. It may be disguised as **commission**, particularly when it involves payment to a foreign customer to persuade him to buy your product rather than a competitor's. Or you may choose to make a discreet **distribution** to those whom you wish to influence. A company which gives large sums of money to a political party in the hope of commercial favours may be said innocently to be making a **contribution**, as may an individual who does the same in search of a knighthood. A useful fig-leaf for bribes is to say that they are a **consultancy fee**, or an **introducer's fee** (for someone who brings two parties together), or that they are for the purposes of **entertainment** (as when a politician is 'entertained' on board the yacht of a wealthy businessman). A bribe concealed within an artificially raised selling price may be disingenuously described as **over-invoicing**. If you know someone within an organization who is open to bribery, you may say darkly that you have **connections** there.

The most elegant circumlocution for 'bribe' is **douceur**, borrowed in the 18th century from French (illegal or immoral activities generally sound less bad when referred to in a foreign language). It means in French literally 'sweetness', so it ties in with a vein of English 'sweet' bribery metaphor. You can **sweeten** a deal or a client with money or gifts, and a **sweetener** (first recorded in 1847) is a bribe. **Sugar** is used in the same sense.

Also at the genteel end of the spectrum is **inducement**: if someone 'offers you an inducement' to do something, you may interpret it as a prospect of secret payment for something rather underhand. Similarly if someone says they will make something '**worth your while**', a bribe is probably being suggested. A discreet inquiry 'Have you been **approached**?' is intended to ascertain whether you have been offered money **under the table**. In America, an **adjustment** is a payment made in order to have awkward matters settled according to one's wishes.

Colloquial alternatives tend to be more direct, but less crudely so than *bribe*. A surreptitious payment for services rendered may be a **backhander** (first recorded in 1960), a metaphor based on the notion of passing money clandestinely with the hand reversed behind the back. **Hush money** is a bribe paid to make someone keep silent about something you would rather not have revealed. **Bung** has become associated particularly with the nexus of bribes surrounding the transfer of a professional footballer from one club to another. A **kickback** (an American coinage of the 1930s) is a percentage paid to someone who allows the illegal appropriation of funds. **Payola**, of similar age and provenance, is a bribe paid to induce someone to abuse the trust of their position, and in particular to induce disc jockeys to plug a particular record. In American English a **hand-out** too can be a bribe, as can a **fix**. But the main slang term for 'bribery' in general is **graft**. This emerged in America in the middle of the 19th century in a range of senses denoting illegal or shady dealings for one's own profit, of which 'bribery' is only one. Its origins are not clear; it may be an adaptation of *graft* 'added part' to 'additional activity'.

The verbal euphemisms of bribery stress the theme of solicitousness, of concern for the well-being of the person bribed. If you **look after** someone, you may well be giving them money to do something they should not do, as you may if you **take care of** them. American English has the vague and enigmatic **see**: 'This, that or the other "professional" is "seen" . . . and lo and behold! the second game between the rival clubs is marked by a signal defeat,' *Ball Players' Chronicle* 1867. More bluntly, you can **pay** them **off**, or **fix** them.

The tipping of waiters and other servants can cause embarrassment, verbally as well as practically. The old euphemism for 'tip', **gratuity**, is no longer much encountered. But a curious scenario has emerged in American English in which payment is euphemized as a verbal act of thanks. So 'Have you **thanked** the waiter?' could mean 'Have you given him a tip?' It links back bizarrely to the world of bribery and corruption, where **gratitude** can be payment for doing something illegal.

# A COMMERCIAL AND INDUSTRIAL MISCELLANY

**bump** to refuse to allow a booked passenger to join a particular flight because it is overbooked. A piece of airline jargon, apparently originating in the late 1970s, which may have evolved from the American *bump* 'displace', a pre-World War II coinage

**Chinese copy** a product which is an exact copy of one made by another manufacturer, but for which no licence fee, royalty, etc has been paid. Cf. REVERSE ENGINEERING

**club** a selling organization which people pay to belong to. The main products sold in this way are books. The word *club*, with its associations of conviviality and companionship, disguises the purely commercial purpose of the undertaking

**competitor analysis** finding out about the financial and other affairs of competitor companies. When, as is often the case, such information is confidential, the term (a coinage of the 1980s) becomes a euphemism for *industrial espionage*

**dark** (of a theatre) not currently housing a production, closed – and therefore not illuminated. First recorded (in the American theatrical journal *Variety*) in 1916

**direct mail** junk mail – unsolicited advertising material sent through the post. 'Direct' because it comes straight from the sender, with no involvement from middlemen such as wholesalers and retailers. First recorded in 1930

**effluent** a moderately euphonious and harmless-sounding word used to cover up such unpleasantnesses as sewage, liquid waste from industrial plants, and radioactive waste from a nuclear power station. Etymologically it simply means 'flowing out'

**guest star** a perhaps over-polite way of referring to a performer who appears on a one-off basis rather than as a regular member of a company, and is after all paid for his or her trouble. Often the term seems to be used as a sop to the vanity of a moderately well-known performer appearing in a minor role. This particular theatrical use of *guest* dates from the late 19th century

**home equity loan** money borrowed using one's house as security. It sounds safer and less alarming than 'second mortgage'

**income protection** a discreet way of saying 'tax avoidance', which always sounds reprehensible even though, unlike 'tax evasion', it is not illegal

**message** an advertisement, particularly on television or radio. The notion of trying to sell something to the viewer or listener is artfully suppressed

**near** artificial, imitation. Used by manufacturers and their marketers to suggest a (spurious) affinity with the real thing. The first recorded example of the usage (*near cider*) is from 1822, but it was not taken up in a big way by the commercial world until the early years of the 20th century. Its commonest collocations are *near silk* and the rhyming *near beer*

**non-dairy** a piece of commercial weaselry denoting substances that mimic milk but contain no milk products – as in 'non-dairy coffee lightener'. It subliminally suggests 'milkiness' while overtly disavowing it

**operational** a word with a very high vagueness quotient, used in apologies for lateness or other shortcomings by the operators of train, air, and other transport services. Frustrated passengers informed that their plans have been disrupted because of 'operational difficulties' or for 'operational reasons' are unlikely to be mollified. The impression created is of either culpable ignorance or obsessive secrecy

**paper a house** a now rather dated theatrical euphemism denoting the filling of an auditorium (the 'house') by the management giving away free tickets – the intention being to give the impression of a popular and successful production. First recorded in 1859

**product placement** promotion of a product by having it appear on screen in a film or television programme or be referred to in the script

**public relations** an expression that began life innocently enough meaning 'relationship between an organization and the general public' (it is first recorded at the beginning of the 19th century in the writings of Thomas Jefferson) and gradually evolved in the hands of marketing men into 'presenting oneself or one's product in the best possible light'

**redlining** the automatic refusal of credit (e.g. for a mortgage) to any person living within a particular area. From the drawing of a red line on a map to designate the area, which contains low-income families, low-value houses, etc

**refer to drawer** a discreet formula used by banks to convey the message that they are not going to honour a cheque – presumably because the person who wrote it (the 'drawer') has not enough money in their account to cover it. Abbreviated in banking jargon to **RD**

**remainder** to dispose of unsold stock of a book at a reduced price

**reverse engineering** copying design features of a competitor's product. The metaphor is based on the notion of 'unbuilding' the product: taking it apart to find out how it is made. Cf. CHINESE COPY

**rubber cheque** a cheque that bounces, i.e. is not honoured by a bank because there are insufficient funds in the drawer's account to cover it

**unscheduled** unforeseen, caused by untoward events beyond the operator's control. Used mainly when a train, aircraft, etc is forced to stop (e.g. because of engine malfunction) at a place where it was not supposed to. The suggestion that it is merely not part of the timetable seeks to gloss over the fact that something has gone wrong

**vanity publishing** publication of someone's work that is paid for by the author him- or herself, because no publisher thinks it good enough to finance. A term which originated in America in the 1920s

# POVERTY

The shame of poverty makes it a natural target for euphemism. Neither individuals nor nations like to admit that they haven't enough money and cannot provide for themselves, and a range of alternative strategies has been evolved to avoid the dreaded word *poor*.

It was a particular growth area of the latter part of the 20th century – perhaps because the proliferation of 'politically correct' jargon coincided with an increase in poverty in the lower reaches of English-speaking Western societies. Typical circumlocutions of the 1980s and 1990s include **economically exploited**, **economically marginalized**, **culturally deprived**, **culturally disadvantaged** (nothing a few trips to an art gallery couldn't remedy, one would have thought), and the desperately up-beat **differently advantaged**, all meaning 'poor'. The tightrope of credibility is waveringly trodden by **negatively privileged** 'poor' and by **negative saver** (people whose expenditure exceeds their income).

Of longer standing is **disadvantaged**, which can imply not just lack of money but also a whole range of concomitant social disabilities; sociologists seem to have appropriated it in the 1940s. The point is made more explicitly (but still euphemistically) by **economically disadvantaged**. Similarly **deprived** and its noun **deprivation** suggest a whole range of lacks (they are commonly used with reference to children who have not enjoyed a normal family environment, education, etc), but the subtext underlying it is often 'lack of money'. And **under-privileged** (first recorded in 1896) when it comes down to it really means 'poor (with all the lack of opportunities and advantages that that implies)'.

Probably the most widely used, though, of all the social-workerese terms for 'poor' in the last quarter of the 20th century was **low-income**: 'Up to 60,000 children in low-income families have lost their right to free school meals,' *Guardian* 1971. First recorded in 1952, it probably began to establish itself in official gobbledegook in the late 1960s (Hugh Rawson, in his *Dictionary of Euphemisms and Other Double-talk* 1981, quotes from the *New Republic* 1971: 'The [US] Census Bureau has . . . decided to say "low-income" in its official releases'). It promotes the fiction that all poor people have at least some income, and suggests subliminally that they all have jobs. It is applied not just to people but also to the areas where they live, their houses, etc (a euphemistic role which it shares with **low-rent**). For those who are in work, but are poor, an alternative term is **low-paid**.

But such lexical pussyfooting is by no means entirely a recent development. The use of **distressed** for 'poor', and in particular for 'latterly impoverished' (as in 'a home for distressed gentlefolk'), dates back at least to the 1840s. As applied to people it is decidedly obsolescent, but it is still used in expressions such as 'distressed area', denoting a part of town where poor people live.

Such dainty circumlocutions are the province of the expert, but the man and woman in the street have their own 'poverty' euphemisms too. At the up-market end of the spectrum one can choose from **indigent** (which goes back to a Latin original meaning simply 'lacking'), **needy** and **penurious** or, if a noun is required, **want**, **need** (as in 'children in need'), **straitened circumstances**, and the opaquely discreet **reduced circumstances**, first recorded in 1886, which may go back to a now obsolete use of *reduced* for an army officer discharged from active service and put on half pay.

For circumstances where these would be too pompous, there are plenty of colloquial alternatives. The most widely used is probably **hard up**. First recorded in 1821, this may be a metaphorical extension of an earlier nautical expression *hard up* meaning 'with the tiller put as far as possible to windward' – done when a ship is in trouble in bad weather and has to turn away from the wind. Also available are **badly off** (with a number of possible adverbial variations – *miserably*, *worse*, etc); **embarrassed**, which dates from the late 19th century; **short**, as in 'I'm a bit short this week,' an elliptical usage for 'short of money' which goes back to the 18th century (**the shorts** is slang shorthand for '(temporary) poverty'); the American **whistling**, used particularly of addicts too poor to buy drugs, which is said to invoke the idea of wind whistling through an empty house; **on one's beam ends**, a nautical metaphor, based on the notion of a ship heeled over so far that its beams are touching the water, and it is in danger of capsizing; and **on**

**one's uppers**, or **down on one's uppers**, which emerged in the late 19th century, and comes from the idea of someone so poor that they have no soles on their shoes. The main rhyming slang contributions to the field are **boracic** (short for *boracic lint*, rhyming with *skint*), first recorded in 1959, and the now decidedly dated **hearts** (short for *heart of oak*, rhyming with *broke*), which was probably in part a pun on the name of a British friendly society.

It is not just individuals whose poverty must be euphemized. Areas and whole countries attract similar fig-leaves. Indeed, the unfolding list of 'poor'-euphemisms applied to the poor countries of the world in the post-colonial era provides a classic case study of the inherent fragility of such verbal evasion. The first in the field was probably *backward*, but to speak of 'backward countries' would now be so deeply taboo that its benign (in intention) origins have been completely obscured. Its patronizing connotations of mental dullness and lack of civilization had already begin to show through in the late 1940s, which is when we begin to note the appearance of its first euphemistic replacement, **underdeveloped**. First recorded in 1949 (in a speech of President Truman to the US Congress), it proliferated widely during the early 1950s, and quickly became the accepted term. But then it began to be perceived that *under-* had a certain negative tone to it which implied inferiority, so a new alternative was sought. **Less developed** and **lesser developed** had a vogue, but *less* is not much better than *under-*. A more positive note was struck by **developing**, first recorded in this sense in 1964, which has stood the course with rather greater success than its predecessors. (The strategy of hiding a deficiency under the notion of 'development', implying that although things are bad, they are getting better, is also apparent in **development area**, a term officially introduced in Britain in an Act of Parliament in 1945 to denote a poor part of the country. And of course it is not limited to a deficiency of wealth – see DEVELOPMENTALLY CHALLENGED and LATE DEVELOPER p 217.) It joined **emergent**, first recorded in 1954 in the sense 'newly independent' but soon picking up connotations of 'and therefore poor', and **emerging**; and also the rather twee **fledgling nation**, coined according to legend by Eleanor Roosevelt in the 1950s.

Increasingly in the 1970s and 1980s such terms came to be seen as preserving too much of a link with the notion of colonialism, and a new vocabulary was sought. A candidate presented itself in a term coined by the French economist and demographer Alfred Sauvy in the mid 1950s: *tiers monde*. Literally **third world**, this denoted those countries that were 'in the middle', between the two blocs of the US-dominated West and the Soviet-controlled East. In practice *third world* came to be applied to most of the countries of Africa, Asia and South America, but with important exceptions such as Japan and South Africa which confirm that criteria for membership include not just political non-alignment but also relative lack of wealth. It came into widespread use in English in the early 1960s, and its currency has held up, despite the fact that its credentials as a euphemistic cover-up for 'poor' are wearing thin (utterances such as 'Britain is in danger of becoming a third-world country,' in obvious reference to economic performance, reveal its subtext clearly enough). A more recent alternative is **the South**, which geopolitically denotes the poor countries of (mainly) the southern hemisphere, as contrasted with the rich industrialized nations of the northern hemisphere. First recorded in 1975, it came to greater prominence in 1980 with the publication of *North-South, a programme for survival: report of the Independent Commission on International Development* (known as the *Brandt Report*). A lesser known member of the set is **HIPC**, an initialism that hides the verbose but somewhat dysphemistic *highly indebted poor country.*

If being poor is hard to talk about, being given money to relieve one's poverty is also a delicate and for many people shaming topic to refer to. *Charity* can be a dirty word ('I don't want charity'), and a key concept in its euphemization is 'help'. On a personal level this is mainly lexicalized as **assistance**. If you are receiving **financial assistance** it may be assumed that someone, probably the state, is giving you money to live on because you do not have enough or you do not have any. In Britain between 1948 and 1965, money given by the government to the poor was known as **national assistance**. Administered by the National Assistance Board, this combined the previous categories of **public assistance** (a term still used in the US) and **unemployment assistance**. Someone who was **on assistance** was understood to be receiving such money: 'Ten quid's not going to put us on Assistance,' Angus Wilson 1956.

In a similar vein is **support**, a term much beloved of social workers and the like. In Britain, government payments to the poor are known as **income support** (a term which replaced *supplementary benefit* in 1986). In America the parallel term is **income maintenance**.

Internationally, financial 'help' comes in the form of **aid**. This use of *aid* for 'money or the equivalent given by a rich country to a poor one' is first recorded in 1940, and much of its early usage is in fact in the context of American payments to Britain.

The history of euphemizing such payments is a long one. The use of **relief** for 'help given to the poor' dates from the 14th century, and in later centuries it was applied specifically to money or other material help given to the poor under the terms of the Poor Law. Those receiving the payments would be known by a variety of phrases in the form *on the x*, 'x' representing the source of the money: **on the box** denoted money channelled via the church poor box; **on the club** meant that you were being helped out financially by a workers' club; **on the panel** meant that you were poor enough to be among those receiving free medical treatment; and **on the parish** (first recorded in 1632 but commonest under 19th-century poor law) signified that you were getting money and other benefits from the local parish (the Scottish equivalent was **on the board**) (see also ON ASSISTANCE above). The use of *dole* for a 'charitable hand-out', which became institutionalized in Britain after World War I, in the form *the dole*, for 'money paid by the government to the unemployed', probably began with the best euphemistic intentions, but latterly it has become synonymous with, and no less harsh than, *unemployed*.


Some other officialese designed to skirt round the concept of 'payment to the poor':

**benefit** originally, around the beginning of the 19th century, the money received from a benefit society, a club whose members' dues financed such payments to members who were poor because of sickness, old age, etc (such clubs were later called in Britain *friendly societies*, but the term *benefit society* lives on in America). Latterly, towards the end of the 19th century, *benefit* came to be used officially in Britain in various acts of parliament for government welfare payments. In modern British usage it generally implies poverty (as in *supplementary benefit*, the successor to NATIONAL ASSISTANCE (see p 287) and precursor of INCOME SUPPORT (see p 287)), but not always (*child benefit* is historically not means-tested)

**claimant** a poor person – that is to say, someone applying for or in receipt of money from the government. In Britain the term has become sufficiently institutionalized to appear in the *Claimants' Union*, the name of an organization which fights for the rights of those entitled to receive welfare payments

**concession** subsidy for those poor enough to be receiving government welfare payments – applied for example to cinema tickets (as in 'Concessions £1.50') and bus fares (as in 'concessional fares for UB40s')

**entitlement** euphemistic shorthand for the 'right to receive welfare payment of some sort from the state'

**needy and dependent person** an American euphemism for a 'person receiving government welfare payments'

**negative taxation** a term for state welfare payments apparently coined by the American economist Milton Friedman

**social security** the government provision of money and other help to those in need of it. An isolated record of the term survives from a letter written by Winston Churchill in 1908 (in which he writes of underpinning 'the whole existing social security apparatus with a foundation of comparatively low-grade state safeguards'), but it was not until the 1930s that it came into general use

**welfare** state provision for those citizens who are too poor to provide for themselves, or otherwise unable to do so. There are traces of the use of *welfare* in this sense dating back to the second decade of the 20th century, but it does not seem to have become firmly established until the term *welfare state* came on the scene. This is said to have been coined by Sir Alfred Zimmern in the 1930s, but the earliest instance of it on record is in the writings of William Temple (later Archbishop of Canterbury) in 1941

In the days of the Poor Law, the indignity of the workhouse or poorhouse was disguised with euphemisms such as **big house** and **union** (short for *union house*, a name given to workhouses in the 1840s, from their being administered by a 'union' of several parishes: 'I wonder sometimes if I am doomed to die in the Union,' Thomas Hardy 1874). For those who were not permanent residents but just dropped in from time to time (i.e. were only intermittently destitute) there was the **casual** (an abbreviation of *casual ward*).

In modern, more enlightened times, the **underclass** (a term for the poor, dispossessed and unemployed which entered English in the early 1960s, probably as a translation of Swedish *underklass* in the writings of the economist Gunnar Myrdal) is left to its own devices to cope with life in the **inner city** (an American coinage of the mid 1960s which holds a nosegay to what might previously have been termed *the slums*; contrast *city centre* – similar area, but no suggestion of poverty). Its accommodation is likely to be **social housing** – houses, flats, etc provided by a local authority for those unable to finance their own (if the incapacity is not poverty but infirmity, mental deficiency, etc, the euphemism is **sheltered housing**, denoting accommodation that has a supervisor to look after the people living there).

If the poor no longer have workhouses to go to, they can at least still use the services of the thriving pawnbroker, or **uncle**, as he continues to be euphemistically known (the usage dates from the mid 18th century, when those temporarily embarrassed would explain with great discretion that their pocket watch was 'at present at their uncle's').

# GOVERNMENT & POLITICS

———

Even in societies which proclaim themselves loudly to be 'open', it is in the nature of governments to be secretive. Ministers and civil servants cannot see a fact without wishing to conceal it from the outside world. And the language whose country of origin's ministry of defence makes a state secret of how many teaspoons it uses easily slips into subterfuge at the bidding of politicians and their spokespeople.

Such concealment and manipulation has an evasive vocabulary all of its own – for of course if dissembling, exaggeration and propaganda are openly avowed, their effectiveness is compromised. The key term amongst late 20th- and early 21st-century propagandists, who imagine that they have got the whole thing taped, is **news management**. Its underlying theme is that those in possession of information control the news, and that they will pass it on to the media, if at all, only at a time and in a form that is convenient to them. No direct imputation of falsehood is made, although the cynical might suspect it.

At a rather more colloquial level is **spin**, which denotes a favourable slant or gloss given to a piece of information – particularly for the purposes of what is known, not very euphemistically, as **damage limitation**. For example, if a political candidate gave what was obviously a not very impressive performance in a televised debate, his or her spokespeople might bombard the press with stories of how well in fact the candidate's particular style or policy went down with certain sections of the electorate. This is spin – trying to make things seem not so bad as they look. The term originated in America in the early 1980s. It comes from the notion of imparting spin to a ball – for instance, with the cue in pool – in order to make it behave in the way you want. Those whose job it is to reinvent the truth in this way are termed **spin doctors**, **spin meisters**, or simply **spinners**. Their job overlaps at several points with that of the **flak catcher** (an American coinage of the early 1970s – latterly often shortened to **flak**), who must deal with and deflect any comment, information, etc damaging to his or her employer or client.

The role of such functionaries is at once obfuscatory and Panglossic: that which is, or by any remote stretch of the imagination could be conceived as being, harmful, dangerous, controversial, etc is to be concealed; that which is bad is to be good, or at least not too bad. Even the language of secrecy cannot be straightforward. Something has to be pretty big to be termed 'secret' (or, with a touch of overtheatricality, 'top secret' or 'most secret'). Anything lower down the scale would be described as 'confidential', 'restricted' or, with curious euphemism, **classified** – a usage which emerged around 1940 in America, presumably as a shortening of 'classified as secret'. Government sources referring more generally to secret matters would nowadays be more likely to use the discreet **sensitive**: 'It has sown confidence and anxiety among researchers by giving birth to the ambiguous concept of sensitive but unclassified research,' *Guardian* 1991.

If something damaging or discreditable does come out, the next best thing is to minimize its awfulness. A leak of radioactivity from a nuclear reactor, for example, may be played down as an **energy release**, which sounds as though it could be both deliberate and benign and carefully avoids any mention of radioactivity. Someone whose political beliefs are changed by brain-washing may be described as **re-educated** (a term applied particularly to the Chinese Communists' treatment of their opponents). A virtually open-ended suspension of activity sounds less draconian as a **pause** (used in the 1960s in Britain to characterize bans on wage rises, but abandoned when people caught on to what it really meant; it was succeeded by **restraint**, notionally of the sort exercised rather than imposed). An economy, industry, etc ravaged by recession may be described as **lean**, a good positive term suggesting vigour and eagerness for action. Civil disturbances, even virtual civil war, can be verbally dismissed as **troubles** (a term applied particularly to the unrest and fighting in Ireland from 1919 to 1923, and in Ulster from 1970). And a crisis of considerable proportions can be airily brushed aside as a **little local difficulty** (a phrase made notorious by British prime minister Harold Macmillan in 1958 when talking about the simultaneous resignation of a large proportion of his cabinet).

Such language is not a million miles from the chilling doublespeak of totalitarian regimes, which contorts the truth with words. Unimaginable horrors are hidden surreally behind the blandest of language.

This is the world where mass exterminations of political opponents are **purges** (a term which emerged in the early 1930s), and where races are **purified** by killing citizens who do not belong to them (see also ETHNIC CLEANSING p 300). Where people sent to extermination camps are **relocated** or **resettled** (euphemisms originally dreamed up by Nazi propagandists for their treatment of the Jews; the term **resettlement** has also been used in South Africa for the forcible removal of blacks to their 'homelands'). Where opponents of the regime are **nonpersons** (a term first recorded in 1959). Where the philosophy of the leaders and the actions carried out in their name are deemed **progressive** no matter how stultifying or repressive they are in practice (a term annexed mainly by Communist regimes: 'The "progressive" view – the Communist view – was the only one allowed,' *Treatment of British P.O.W.s in Korea* 1955). Where the dictatorship of a ruling elite is disguised as the will of the people: a '**people's** republic' is likely to be a Communist totalitarian state. And where territory arbitrarily attacked, conquered and occupied can be euphemized as **lebensraum** (a term not coined but hijacked by the Nazis to give respectability to their plans for taking over large parts of eastern Europe – it means literally 'life-space', and denoted elbow-room for the German race to expand into. The main English version is **living space**).

Social class is an area prone to euphemism. Since at least the late 19th century the term *middle class* has had negative connotations, and **upper middle class** (first recorded in 1872) and even **middle middle class** (a coinage of the early 20th century) are in part attempts to circumvent these. But it is the bottom of the heap that presents the greatest problems. The term *lower class* (first recorded in 1772) is decidedly frank, and in the 20th century came to be regarded virtually as taboo. The alternative **working class** appeared in the early 19th century, but it too is under a cloud. Part of its problem is its perpetuation of the concept of 'class', a sensitive area. **Working people** (first recorded in 1871) gets round that. But the latter part of the 20th century preferred to incline to the view that in Western society (pace a legal decision to the contrary in a British court by Mr Justice Harman in 1990, arising out of a dispute over flats in Pimlico designated for 'working-class' tenants) the working class no longer exists, and euphemistic usage backs this up: the term **blue collar** designating manual or industrial workers, for instance (first recorded in 1950), makes no reference to social class, merely to occupation. A similar taboo has overtaken the Indian caste system: the negative term *untouchable*, once applied to the lowest caste, is itself deemed untouchable. An early replacement was **depressed class**, itself somewhat downbeat, and this was officially replaced in 1935 by the inscrutable **scheduled caste**.

The language of official communiqués has a secret code all of its own. In particular, a delicate veil of euphemism is interposed between what the atmosphere was really like at meetings between heads of government, diplomats, etc, and what is reported to the outside world. An **exchange of views** or **exchange of ideas** is likely to have been fairly chilly, and a discussion that is officially described as **cordial** has probably not gone well at all. The term **businesslike and friendly** implies little or no progress on the matters under discussion, while **full and frank** (a favourite of Harold Wilson when he was prime minister of Britain) and **serious and candid** suggest hotness under the collar if not actual blows struck. (The equivalent at the level of personal conversation is 'I **hear** you', the subtext of which is 'I disagree with you'.)

A miscellany of other circumlocutions from the world of government and politics:

**activist** often a cover term for someone prepared to break the law in pursuit of their political aims. Their activities are liable to be euphemized as **direct action**

**adviser** often, someone whose advice consists of practical demonstrations of how to fire guns. During the Cold War, the superpowers were addicted to sending in such 'advisers' to sensitive areas to bolster up a friendly regime – the Soviet Union, for instance, had many thousands in Cuba, and the US sent 200 to South Vietnam in 1954 who over the succeeding decade turned into a fighting army. The usage is first recorded in 1915 in the context of German military help given to Turkey

**alternative** not just alternative (to the established political, economic, social, etc set-up), is the implication, but better, because the established set-up is reactionary and harmful (for instance, an 'alternative lifestyle' will involve challenging current social mores by, say, taking drugs and flouting dress conventions). The usage is first recorded in 1970. As its cover has become blown, it too has been euphemized: 'alternative' medicine, for instance, is now often characterized as **complementary** medicine by those who fear that 'alternative' gives an impression of crankiness

**big brother** totalitarian rule that invades all privacy. When coined by George Orwell in 1949 for the name of the head of state in his novel *1984* it was intended to convey an overt but euphemizing benevolence, but its true nature has long since worn through the disguise

**community charge** the official designation given by the British government to the local tax, designed to replace domestic rates, that was introduced in England and Wales in 1990. *Community* is a comfortable, caring sort of word, popular with euphemizers in the latter part of the 20th century (see also p 221), and the government evidently hoped that the placatory name would make the tax less unpopular. Official spokespersons used it assiduously, but it failed to make much headway in the language at large in the face of its dysphemistic synonym *poll tax*. In 1993 its place was taken by a new system, with the more neutral name *council tax*

**correct** adhering without deviation to the party line, particularly in the context of parties of the extreme left and right. In the 1990s, **politically correct** denotes language (and opinions, behaviour, etc) regarded as acceptable by those with left-of-centre views: the nuttier politically correct coinages, such as *consensual non-monogamist* for 'wife-swapper' and *person with difficult-to-meet needs* for 'serial killer', are fair game for satirists (many of the most bizarre ones in fact have been dreamed up by right-wing critics to discredit those of a more liberal persuasion)

**cross the floor** to abandon your political party and join its opponents. A Briticism derived from the seating arrangements of the House of Commons, where government and opposition face each other across 'the floor of the house'

**deselect** to decide not to renominate a sitting member of parliament as a candidate in a forthcoming election. The weasely term entered British politics at the end of the 1970s, when the Labour party revised its reselection rules to make the practice possible

**disinvestment** withdrawal of financial investment as a political gesture. The term first appeared in the late 1930s with no political overtones, although even in its straight economic sense it has an element of mealy-mouthedness about it, as if seeking to minimize the seriousness of undesirable developments. In its modern usage it has been applied mainly to withdrawal of funds from South Africa in order to make that country abandon its racist policies. A rather more pompous synonym is **divestiture**

**fellow traveller** someone who sympathizes with but is not a member of a political organization, specifically the Communist party. When it was newly minted in the 1930s (probably modelled on its Russian equivalent *poputchik*) it had a positive ring, but over the years it was hijacked by the enemies of Communism and came to inhabit uneasy ground between insult and euphemism

**free world** in the era of the Cold War, the non-Communist countries of the world. As such the term (used of course by anti-Communists) includes several countries whose regimes offer their citizens the very reverse of freedom

**friendly** in the cynical parlance of international relations, friendly nations are countries that are under your thumb and from which you therefore have nothing to fear

**full employment** employment for most of the people who want to work – because it is an impossibility to have everyone in a society in work simultaneously, however worthy the aim. A euphemism that is at the same time a political slogan

**internal affairs** the usual implication of this bland-sounding term is 'investigation and rooting out of wrong-doers within the system'. The former Soviet Ministry of Internal Affairs (a translation of Russian *Ministyerstvo Vnutryennikh Dyel*, or *MVD* for short) oversaw the affairs of the secret police. And amongst Western civil police forces, *internal affairs* can be a discreet way of referring to the investigation of police corruption

**libertarian** a once honourable term, denoting a belief in political freedom. In recent years, however, the notion of 'freedom' has been hijacked by extreme right-wing thinkers, who use it to contrast a supposedly desirable open-ended self-determination for the individual with the 'regimentation' of left-wing societies. The word *libertarian* has been a victim of the take-over: 'In April a Sean Gabb . . . will give a talk to the right-of-sensible Libertarian Alliance,' *Guardian* 1991

**National Front** the name of an extreme right-wing British party, coined in 1967 to suggest that its fascist views were representative of the whole nation (an implication renewed by the later *British National Party*). *Front* is a term often adopted by political organizations which want to implant the idea of wide and unified support (as in the *Popular Front*, the name of various anti-fascist alliances of the 1930s)

**protectorate** in effect, a colony. From the mid 19th century the term has been used of a country or territory to a greater or less extent controlled by a superior power. The notion of protecting it from others is not usually uppermost in the mind of that power

**radical** politically extreme to the right or left; advocating far-reaching social change. A term used in the main by those sympathetic to such a position (although, particularly in American English, it has come to be a derogatory word for 'left-wing'). It dates from the 1830s

**social ownership** an alternative to *nationalization* for those who find the latter term too provocative. It was embraced by the British Labour party in the mid 1980s

**special** an all-purpose euphemism used by governments to disguise their more nefarious activities. 'Special treatment' in Nazi Germany, for instance, was mass murder of Jews and others; 'special education' in totalitarian countries is political indoctrination; and a 'special squad' may be a group of thugs put together by a government to harass and kill its political opponents

**sphere of influence** an area of the world effectively under the political and/or economic control of a superior power. The term came into use in the 1880s to designate territory, particularly in Africa and Asia, over which the then colonial powers claimed to exercise some sort of authority, in the context of the rivalry between Britain, Germany, etc at that time.

# WARFARE

––––

Since war is the most horrific self-inflicted collective experience human beings can undergo, it is not surprising that we should try to palliate its terrors and miseries with the words we use to talk about it. But it was the 20th century that made a macabre art form of the euphemism of war. Most of the standard words for 'war' in modern European languages – including English *war* and the related French *guerre*, German *Krieg*, Welsh *rhyfel*, and Serbo-Croat *rat* – are based etymologically on fairly straight forward concepts such as 'strife' or 'fighting', or 'tumult, confusion'; they do not represent an attempt by our linguistic ancestors to wrap up the idea of 'war' in verbal cotton wool. It may be that a combination of technological advances, which make it possible to kill many more of the enemy much more quickly and economically than in the past, and the greater impingement of war on civilian life, both via the television screen and by direct enemy action, has provided a much greater psychological impetus than in former centuries to cover up our shaming deeds with mild words.

So *war* itself is now a slightly dodgy word. It is not totally taboo, of course (we are quite happy to use it in the context of wars fought and won, even when they are of a brevity or one-sidedness – the *Falklands War*, the *Gulf War* – that would in former times not have qualified them for the term), but there are certainly times when we prefer to avoid its belligerent sound. Just as in the latter part of the 20th century countries rarely bothered to 'declare war' in accordance with the gentlemanly rules – as if wishing not to make things seem too bad – so the word *war* may be banished in favour of something less explicit.

The most daring approach is to refer to warfare as **defence**, or, more audacious still, as **peace**. A country with a high *defence capability* has large armed forces which can just as well be used for attacking another country as for defending its own. *Defence expenditure* goes on buying weapons, whatever purpose they may be used for. In Britain in 1964 the *War Office* (a regrettably aggressive-sounding ministry) vanished, subsumed under the more conciliatorily named *Ministry of Defence*. This backdoor use of *defence* dates from the 1930s (see also SELF-DEFENCE p 300). Rather more recent is the concept of *peace studies* as an academic discipline, which, while its avowed aim may be the elimination of war, necessarily spends much of its time studying war. It recalls the paradoxical nickname **peacemaker** given to the Colt .45 revolver in the old American West. **Peace-keeping** is often just verbal camouflage for 'military occupation' (while **pacifying** a population involves actively shooting at or otherwise attacking it). And the word *peace* has been sadly abused over decades of propagandizing by totalitarian governments of the right and left, with their cynical promotion of *peace offensives* ('China . . . publicly supported the various manifestations of the Soviet "peace offensive",' *Annual Register* 1952), *peace movements* and the like.

If calling black white seems too extreme, one can always play down the seriousness of the situation. A favourite circumlocution is **conflict**. This dates back to at least the 15th century as a word for a 'fight' or 'battle', but it was not really until the post-World War II period that it came to be taken up as a euphemism for 'war' – a development confirmed in the 1960s by its use in terms like *conflict research* and *conflict studies* for the academic study of war. (Another term for the discipline is **strategic studies**.) Franker, but still euphemistic, is **armed conflict**.

Along the same lines is **confrontation**, which does not have to be expanded to **armed confrontation** to be interpretable as 'fighting': 'Indonesia's "confrontation campaign" against Malaysia – an ingenious new expression for an unprovoked act of aggression – is one of the most futile minor wars of history,' *New Statesman* 1965. But probably the most notorious of mealy-mouthed circumlocutions for 'war' is **the late unpleasantness**, originally used in the late 1860s of the recently ended American Civil War, but subsequently employed as a more general distancing device of quite monumental incongruity.

The most difficult part of a war to explain away may be its start, particularly for an unprovoked aggressor. A variety of euphemisms is available. A popular strategy is to claim that you attacked to stop your victim attacking you. Into this category come **pre-emptive strike** (first recorded in 1959), **preventive strike**, **protective reaction** (an Americanism), and **anticipatory attack**. In the same vein, but even more outrageous, is the claim of **self-defence** used by an aggressor nation. Another excellent wheeze is to make out that the situation within the country you attacked was so bad that you had to invade it for its own good. Such an action may be described as an **incursion** (used by the Americans to characterize their invasion of Grenada in 1983), as an **intervention**, or, where the country invaded is held to be in breach of international law, as a **police action**, a term first recorded in the 1930s (the vague *action* is a popular component of 'war' euphemisms: a **limited action** is typically a swift war to defeat a weaker opponent, without any attempt at territorial conquest or at widening it to include other nations; and **enemy action** is a neat collective euphemism for bombardment, shelling, etc, as in 'This building was damaged by enemy action'). If the invaded population is up in arms it needs to be **stabilized** or *pacified* (see p 298), and if it is groaning under the yoke of an oppressive government it must be **liberated** (for all these read 'conquered'). If the aim is to bring about **regime change** (over-throwing a country's government), a **decapitation strategy** may well need to be pursued (i.e. killing its leader or leaders) If the country is occupied by invading forces it must be **cleansed** – a term put to even more chilling use in the former Yugoslavia in the early 1990s, when the forcible removal of Muslims from their territory by the Serbs was euphemized as **ethnic cleansing** (a translation of Serbo-Croat *etničko čišćenje* – the related *čistka* means 'purge'). If only a few stragglers remain to be killed or captured, they can be **mopped up** (a usage dating from the early 20th century). If those against whom military force is used have shown signs of rebelliousness, it may be termed **counter-insurgency**. And if the invasion is carried out mainly by para-troops, it may be camouflaged by the delicious piece of military gobbledegook **vertical insertion**. A war in which the ruling power, typically a colonial one, is trying to contain rebellion from within or without may be played down as an **emergency** (paradoxically, such 'emergencies' often seem to drag on for a long time: the war between British and Communist forces in Malaya, for instance, which was so euphemized, lasted from 1948 to 1960). A brief war in which the belligerents are 'minor' or third-world nations is a **brushfire war** (a term first recorded in 1955). An isolated armed encounter on a smaller scale than a war may be discreetly termed an **incident** – perhaps the best-known example of the genre is the Fashoda Incident of 1898, when British and French forces clashed in the Sudan over a territorial dispute, nearly precipitating a full-scale war. A war against members of another religion is dignified as a **holy war**.

The vocabulary of strategy and tactics, too, must be carefully weighed, to avoid any unnecessarily negative overtones. It is notable, for instance, how the word *strike* came to the fore in the latter part of the 20th century, taking over some of the semantic territory of *attack* (the first record of the usage dates from the early 1940s). It may be that it has connotations of impersonal detachment that are found preferable to the up-front aggressiveness of *attack*. So military tacticians may speak of *pre-emptive strikes* (see p 299), or of **surgical strikes** (a term first recorded in 1965, which avowedly denotes an attack, usually from the air, made with speed, precision, and minimal loss of life, but which in practice covers up more spilling of blood than on a surgeon's table), or of **air strikes** (bombing attacks). A *strike* may be no ordinary attack, but a launching of nuclear missiles: a **first strike** is an unprovoked nuclear attack, a **second strike** is a retaliatory nuclear assault by a country subjected to a first strike (both terms date from around 1960).

Dropping bombs from aircraft on to people on the ground sounds much less destructive if it is called **air support**, a term first recorded in 1941 (the implication being that the pilots are helping their colleagues on the ground by killing their enemies, but taken literally they could just be flying past waving their encouragement). The term's cover was comprehensively blown by a remark of Colonel David Opfer, US air attaché in Cambodia in 1973, quoted by Hugh Rawson in his *Dictionary of Euphemisms and Other Doubletalk*. Complaining about press coverage of American tactics, he said 'You always write it's bombing, bombing, bombing. It's not bombing. It's air support'.

Aerial bombardment, involving the killing of civilians, really got under way in World War II (following some practice rounds in the Spanish Civil War), and two early attempts to euphemize it were **area bombing** (which basically denoted the bombing of cities, as carried out by the Royal Air Force over Germany) and **precision bombing** (the term applied to American daylight bombing from 1943 onwards in an effort to suggest that the bombs would hit only targets of military importance). The disruption of enemy supply operations by bombing came to be dignified during World War II by the term **interdiction**, which more generally denotes 'prohibition' or 'restraint'. If for any reason you failed to find your designated target, you could attack instead a **target of opportunity** – i.e. drop your bombs on the first plausible-looking object in sight. During the Vietnam War, bombing became **armed reconnaissance**, terminology paralleled on the ground by **reconnaissance in force**. This designated a military operation in which troops advanced through a particular area and killed any (presumed) enemies found there. It was originally termed *search and destroy*, but this was deemed too explicit, particularly after the My Lai massacre of 1968, so euphemisms had to be deployed. Other alternatives included **search and clear**, **search and sweep**, and **sweeping operation**. Back in the air, a fight between two or more armed aircraft became in 1980s military gobbledegook an **air-to-air encounter**. It is in the nature of warfare that things do not always go as planned. In former times such things could be brushed under the carpet, but in the full glare of the 21st-century media some verbal camouflage may be necessary: hence a (deleterious) deviation from an original strategy becomes **mission creep**.

One of the most awkward features of warfare for military spokespersons to deal with is that people (or **soft-skinned targets**) tend to get killed and badly wounded. This stark fact needs to be considerately wrapped up. The key euphemism in this area is **casualty**. It came into use in the 15th century in the sense 'chance occurrence' (it is descended from Latin *casus* 'fall, chance'), and gradually evolved in meaning through 'mishap' and 'loss to a military unit caused by death or injury' until by the end of the 19th century it was being used for an 'individual killed or wounded in war'. Another comfortable word is **missing**, which leaves open the possibility that the person who disappeared following a battle may not actually be dead. The usage seems to have come out of World War I. Its fuller form, **missing in action**, is given a further euphemistic twist in the decent obscurity of the abbreviation **MIA**, first recorded in 1946.

Sanitizing the death of soldiers killed by the enemy is difficult enough, but there are worse scenarios. If by mistake you kill civilians (or obliterate non-military buildings) it is covered up as **collateral damage**, a term dating from the mid 1960s, or **civilian impacting**, a product of the Gulf War. And if by some oversight you succeed in killing someone on your own side, the death is attributed to **friendly fire**. This gruesomely inappropriate euphemism emerged from the Vietnam War, based on the somewhat earlier use of *friendly* for 'of one's own side' (as in 'friendly aircraft'). It gained a certain notoriety afterwards when it was used as the title of a 1976 book by C D B Bryan about an American soldier killed in this way in Vietnam, but its finest hour was perhaps in the Gulf War of 1991, when more Coalition personnel were killed in this way than by enemy action. Another coinage in similar vein is **friendly bombing**; bombs thus accidentally dropped on one's own side may be bizarrely euphemized as **incontinent ordnance**. In British military jargon, an unintentional attack on one's own troops is characterized as **blue on blue** (from the use of blue on maps to designate one's own side in a battle or exercise).

Getting killed is all part of the wear and tear of war, but retreat is a different matter. It touches the honour of the regiment. It virtually amounts to defeat. More ingenuity has been applied to wrapping it up in misleading verbiage than to any other aspect of warfare. Having **disengaged** (i.e. unilaterally stopped fighting, or given up), one may **retire to prepared positions** or **withdraw to prepared positions**. This makes it clear that one was thinking of going in that direction anyway, regardless of what the enemy did. A similar suggestion of pre-planning underlies **planned withdrawal** and **phased withdrawal**, and **strategic withdrawal** carries an implication of *reculer pour mieux sauter*. Alternatively one could try an **adjustment of the front** (*adjust* is a favourite word of euphemizers), a **retrograde manoeuvre**, a **strategic movement to the rear**, or a plain **disengagement**. One can **redeploy one's forces** (using the time-honoured euphemizer's tactic of vagueness), or **regroup,** or take the **route of egress**. A soldier who deserts or goes absent without leave may be said to take **French leave** – not a slur on the courage of the French, but a memory of a time when it was the done thing for guests at French receptions to leave without taking leave of their host. **Obstacle detachment** is a term used for units deployed behind German and Russian lines in World War II to capture and deal with soldiers attempting to retreat or desert.

We became shy in the latter part of the 20th century of talking about weapons of individual and mass destruction. Perhaps it is simply the sheer scale of killing of which we are now capable that has shamed us into circumlocution. A favourite cover term is **capability**: a country with 'nuclear capability' has at least one nuclear weapon, and if it has a 'first-strike capability' it probably has several hundred and can successfully use them in a sneak attack (see p 301). Similarly vague is **device**: it could be almost anything, but the collocation 'nuclear device' betrays its true nature. Popular amongst the military is **ordnance**, a venerable term for 'military weapons, ammunition, etc' which received a new lease of life during the Vietnam War. Its respectability made it a useful fig-leaf for the most sophisticated weaponry used by the Americans, and it was even perverted (in the expressions

**soft ordnance** and **selective ordnance**) to refer to napalm and related substances. **Hardware** is quite a jolly way of referring to implements of killing, as if they were the type of thing one could pick up at the local DIY centre. The usage actually dates back to the mid 19th century, but to begin with it was generally applied to small arms; the dismissive reference to large-scale military equipment is a fairly recent development: 'Tom retorts that Gulf War was nothing to do with religion, more a chance for macho man to test his new hardware,' *Guardian* 1991. The disjunction from reality is almost complete in **asset**, a term adopted by the American defence establishment in the late 1980s for any of the weapons in the Strategic Defense Initiative (Star Wars) system. Such weapons are for preference not 'fired' or 'shot' but **delivered**, as if they were parcels; and the missiles or other devices by which they are 'delivered' are **delivery systems** or **delivery vehicles**.

A weapon whose principal component is poison may be camouflaged as an **agent**: a **nerve agent** is a poisonous gas used for killing or disabling enemies, and a **chemical agent**, or **chemical warfare agent** (**CW agent** for greater disguise), will kill chemically. The American **incap** is short for 'incapacitating chemical agent', a cover term for such nasties.

Nuclear weapons give particular presentational problems. In the latter part of the 20th century, **strategic** took on an increasing role as a less fear-inspiring synonym. A 'strategic exchange' is readily interpretable as two sides firing nuclear missiles at each other, and 'strategic arms' are taken broadly to be nuclear weapons. Strictly speaking this is an oversimplification. The term was introduced in the late 1950s to designate nuclear weapons designed to destroy the enemy's productive capacity, in contrast to **tactical**, which denotes nuclear weapons used in battle to kill the enemy. But even in this official sense, the two terms have virtually become euphemisms for 'big' nuclear weapons and 'small' nuclear weapons respectively. In the navy nuclear weapons, and especially nuclear depth charges, are known as **special stores**. Nuclear bombs designed to kill people but leave buildings largely intact are disguised as **enhanced radiation weapons**, which while obnoxiously self-congratulatory in effect is at least preferable to the chilling *neutron bomb* (such bombs are also described as **clean**, a weasel word that serves additionally for a nuclear weapon with relatively low radioactive fallout). A side effect of all this coyness over nuclear is the coining of a term for non-nuclear weapons: **conventional** (first recorded in the early 1950s). A cosy, banal word for devices capable of slaughter on a massive scale.

On a more intimate note, bombs, mines, etc intended to kill individual human beings are designated **anti-personnel**, a coinage of the late 1930s which suggests animosity more than lethality.

The art of using human beings as weapons was deployed notoriously, but ultimately unsuccessfully, by Saddam Hussein of Iraq in the period running up to the Gulf War in 1990–91. Captured Westerners were kept at strategic places around the country, such as military installations, and their presence well publicized, so that the Coalition members knew that if they bombed the places, they might kill their own citizens. These unfortunate hostages were known as **human shields**, a term which emerged in the late 1970s but had to wait until the Gulf War for wider publicity. It is not uncommon for their captors to euphemize such hostages as **guests**. Indeed, the Iraqis used that term of their prisoners, who subverted it by coining the bland *guestage*.

'Soldiers' who are not part of an officially constituted army present a long-standing terminological conundrum. The classic formula is that *terrorist* (apparently a coinage in this sense of the 1940s) is the dysphemism, **freedom fighter** (first recorded in 1942) the euphemism, with *guerrilla* (adopted from Spanish during the Peninsular War) occupying neutral territory somewhere in the middle. But also into the scales on the euphemistic side can be put **irregular**, which goes back to the mid 18th century and suggests a certain devil-may-care independence, **insurgent** (literally someone taking part in an *insurrection,* and applied particularly to the various groupings fighting back in the wake of the US-led invasion of Iraq in 2003), and **partisan**, a 17th-century introduction which connotes loyalty and patriotism in the face of occupying forces. In the same vein is **patriotic front**, which those not in sympathy with its aims might describe less charitably as a 'terrorist organization'. A conflict in which regular forces are fighting against guerillas has been characterized as **asymmetric warfare**, a piece of jargon which has had a particularly high profile since the attack on the USA on 11 September 2001: '"Asymmetric warfare" is the term employed by the US military for fighting people who don't line up properly to be shot at', Steven Poole, *Unspeak* 2006.

The naming of those who do not fight against occupiers but help them poses an even trickier linguistic problem. **Collaborate** was first used in this context around 1940. It remains less frank than, say, 'betray one's country', but inevitably a word for such a despised activity quickly loses much of its euphemistic power. The vaguer **co-operate** has been used as a substitute. Into a similar category comes **co-belligerent**, literally 'one who fights on the same side', but used in World War II to designate a defeated former enemy which switched sides (e.g. Italy).

Colloquial understatement is a mainstay of the stiff-upper-lip school of military euphemism, particularly in British English. A war may be trivialized as a **lot** ('I got medals too, in the first lot,' Ray Galton and Alan Simpson 1967), a war or battle as a **show** ('I should very much dislike being blown up . . . but I should still more dislike missing the next show,' John Galsworthy 1924) or as a **party**, a military alert as a **flap**. In World War I the horrendous experience of climbing out of trenches into a hail of bullets and shells was made light of as going **over the top** (first recorded in 1916). And in World War II, tank crews referred to one of their or the enemy's vehicles being destroyed by burning as a **brew-up,** invoking the homely vocabulary of tea-making.

Compulsory military service provokes verbal subterfuge. The term **national service** was first used in Britain in 1916; its vagueness (it could in theory refer to an almost open-ended range of services to the nation) marks it out as a classic euphemism. The roots of the equally imprecise American **draft** lie in the late 18th century. The mealy-mouthed American **selectee** for 'conscript' was inspired by **selective service**, the name of a system of selective military conscription used in the US from 1917 to 1973.

# ESPIONAGE

The world of **espionage**, or to put it more bluntly *spying*, is by definition one that likes to wrap itself in mystery and subterfuge. Nothing is as it seems. And a major tactic in the obfuscatory game is the deployment of bizarrely misleading terminology. Much of it is mere verbal window-dressing, designed to put opponents or outsiders off the scent. But there is a hard core of genuine euphemism, used to avoid unseemly frankness.

The word *spy* itself, for instance, is hedged about with taboos. The underlying feeling about the activities of such people is that they are discreditable and sneaky, so although a government would refer to an enemy's 'spies', it would seldom own up to having them itself. The key euphemism in this area is **agent**. It is a shortening of **secret agent**, which is franker but still euphemistic vis-a-vis *spy*. As a term *secret agent* dates back at least to the early 18th century, but it is not clear that it began to take on the full modern range of connotations of 'spying' before the end of the 19th century. *Agent* itself is not recorded in this sense before 1932. Another frequent collocation is **undercover agent**; but the element of duplicity in *double agent* rather damages its euphemistic credentials.

Other verbal disguises for the spy include **attaché**, officially the designation of someone assigned to the staff of a diplomatic mission for some purpose, but in practice particularly in the case of military, naval, and air attachés often no more than a discreet fig-leaf; **chauffeur**, a lowly position on the embassy hierarchy which could conceal an international master spy; **plumber**, a term used for the political spies and burglars employed by the White House during the Nixon era to find and disseminate material damaging to the president's opponents – their original task was to plug 'leaks' of politically embarrassing information, hence *plumber* (first recorded in 1971); **source**, a piece of intelligence-community jargon for 'spy' which is also, and more widely, used for 'informant'; and **liaison officer**, behind which may lurk the controller of a spy ring.

A spy who infiltrates and remains inactive within an organization for a long time before being activated by his or her controller may be termed a **sleeper** (first recorded in 1955), or alternatively a **mole**. The latter usage, inspired by the animal's secret burrowings, can actually be traced back to the 17th century, but its modern currency is due to its use by the British espionage writer John le Carré. A spy who defects from one side to another is said to have **come across**; if the defection has been engineered by the other side, he has been **turned**. If spies are unmasked and expelled from a country, the discreet reason given may be that they have been engaging in activities '**incompatible** with their diplomatic status'. The subtext of the courtly phrase **persona non grata** (literally 'unacceptable person', and first recorded in 1904) may well be 'kicked out because of spying activities'.

The activity of spying itself is in need of some verbal camouflage. *Espionage*, as we have seen, is less brutal, more respectable, but it makes no attempt to cover up what is going on. For that we need to turn to **intelligence**. This has been used since the 15th century for 'information', and since the 17th century for the 'finding out of information'. In the 18th century the specific sense 'information of military value' evolved, and since then the word has specialized still further to 'secret information about an enemy', the 'gathering of such information', and an 'organization or staff engaged in such gathering' – spying and spies, in other words. It is now routine for governments to refer to their spying organizations as the *intelligence service(s)*, for the members of such organizations describe themselves collectively and rather matily as the *intelligence community*. Of the official agencies to incorporate the term in their names, the British *MI* (*Military Intelligence*), as in *MI5* and *MI6*, dates from the World War I period, and the American *CIA* (*Central Intelligence Agency*) was formed in 1947. From the 16th to the 19th century an **intelligencer** was a spy.

If spying on foreigners sounds more respectable as *intelligence*, spying inside one's own country, on people held to be a threat to the state, can be dignified as **security**. This usage evolved in the 1940s and 1950s out of the notions of safeguarding the well-being of the state and keeping its secrets. By the early 1950s, the term *security service(s)* had established itself for those organizations concerned with countering espionage, terrorism, etc. A broader alternative term is **secret service**, which goes back to the 19th century.

The activities engaged in by spies go under a range of innocent-sounding names. Probably the broadest and vaguest is **covert action** or **covert operation**. In theory it could refer to practically anything secret, but in practice it denotes spying, either of the respectable international sort, or of the more seedy internal variety (e.g. bugging one's political opponents). **Surveillance** ostensibly denotes nothing more than keeping watch, but in espionage contexts it can pass as cover for 'spying'. And if the spying is done by means of bugs and other electronic gadgets it will be termed **electronic surveillance** or **technical surveillance**, or **electronic counter-measures**. The bugs used in such operations can be verbally disguised as **highly confidential sources**. A building surreptitiously entered for the purpose of bugging or other 'covert' actions is said to have been **penetrated**. Such break-ins are termed in America **black bag jobs**, or simply **bag jobs** – possibly an allusion to the small bag in which the agents carry their burglar's tools.

Spying on your enemies from high-flying aircraft is innocently termed **overflying**. The mysterious **psyop**, short for *psychological operation* and first recorded in 1974, denotes an activity undertaken to destroy the morale of the enemy, as a part of psychological warfare (itself earlier euphemized as **psywar**). Plotting to overthrow an enemy government sounds politer when referred to as **destabilization**.

Organizations of spies are given deliberately bathetic nicknames, to ward off any unwanted drama or conspicuousness. The British intelligence service has long called itself **the firm**, suggesting a stolid and humdrum commercial undertaking. This was probably the main inspiration for **the company**, the colloquial name of the CIA, but it may also have been reinforced by the fact that *cia* is the abbreviation of Spanish *compañía* 'company'.

Suspects arrested by the CIA are deemed circumlocutiously to be **ill**, and when they have been jailed they are **in the hospital**. The practice of the CIA (particularly in the wake of the attack on the USA on 11 September 2001) of seizing terror suspects in one foreign country and transporting them to another one (typically one where a blind eye is turned to torture) is obfuscated by the gobbledegook term **extraordinary rendition**. On euphemisms for officially sanctioned killing by intelligence agents see p 248.

# RACE

A characteristic feature of present-day Western white society is the collective guilt it feels for subjugating, enslaving, marginalizing and in some cases exterminating other peoples throughout its history. One of the most obvious ways in which this manifests itself is the walking-on-eggshells nature of much of its vocabulary of race.

Even the word *race* is a bit dodgy. Perhaps its association with concepts such as 'master race', 'racial superiority', and 'racism' has amassed the cloud under which it finds itself. In certain fixed expressions it is still OK – *race relations* and *human race*, for instance – but in the context particularly of non-white populations it tends to be avoided. (Ironically, in the 1920s in America **race** was used virtually as a euphemism, to avoid the word *black*, mainly when talking about black musicians and their work.) Even more is *tribe* taboo, with its connotations of benighted people at a lower level of civilization than their white European discoverers. Along with it into the lexical sin-bin have gone *primitive* and the nouns *savage* and *native* (see NATIVE AMERICAN p 317). Acceptable late 20th- and early 21st-century terminology are **people** (as a countable noun, as in 'the English-speaking peoples'), **nation** (as in 'the Sioux nation'), and INDIGE-NOUS PEOPLES (see p 317). The notion of 'primitiveness' can be got across more discreetly with the term **preliterate**.

*Foreigner* is another sensitive term, with its excluding function and its subliminal suggestion of inferiority. In diplomatic (in both senses of the word) language, someone from abroad, and particularly one trying to enter your own country, is a **foreign national** or a **non-national**. In America, someone who enters the country without going through the legal formalities is not an *illegal immigrant* or *illegal alien* (very negative terms) but an **undocumented person** or **undocumented resident**. The early 21st century explored the euphemistic possibilities of

**asylum seeker** (taking over much of the semantic territory previously occupied by *refugee*), especially as contrasted with **economic migrant** (i.e. someone whose emigration is motivated by a desire for a higher standard of living rather than the need to escape political persecution).

Naturally, though, race euphemisms are mainly the product of the stresses in a society that are caused by the presence in it of unassimilated and politically weak racial groups. Such groups tend be regarded with at best suspicion, often hatred, which manifests itself linguistically in a range of insulting epithets and other dysphemistic language. Revulsion at such attitudes in turn produces euphemisms with which the sensitive topic can be discussed.

Key general words in this area are **community**, **ethnic**, and **minority**. The subtext of *community* can often be 'two racial groups in (hostile) contact': *community relations*, for instance, seek to enable the groups to get on well together; *community affairs* concern themselves with the interaction between the two; *community unrest* implies racial conflict. *Ethnic* became in the latter part of the 20th century the adjective of choice for 'not of the dominant racial grouping in a society'. In American English, it tends to be used specifically to refer to white minority groups, such as Italians or Poles, as opposed to blacks or Hispanics. In Britain, though, where it is a more recent introduction, it is a more general term: any racial group that is outnumbered by the white Anglo-Saxon majority can be characterized as an *ethnic minority*; and fighting between different racial groupings, as in Yugoslavia, may be *ethnic violence* or *ethnic conflict*. *Ethnic* has also come to be used as a noun, meaning 'a member of a minority racial group'. *Minority* is an open-ended word, encompassing anyone who is not part of the main crowd (and is therefore by implication at some sort of disadvantage) – adherents of a religion, the non-able-bodied, enthusiasts for a sport – but a major specific application is to racial groups. In American English, it traditionally denotes either blacks or Hispanics, although in practice there is a tendency for its application to leak out to other races, such as American Indians; and in Britain, no distinction on grounds of skin colour is implied.

On the whole *minority* is not applied to women as a disadvantaged sector of society – it would not be statistically accurate for one thing – but two key terms denoting a 'level playing-field' approach cover the sexes as well as racial groups. Both have a taint of euphemism. **Equal opportunity** suggests 'equal treatment for everyone in society', which is not *quite* the same thing as its underlying message, 'equally good treatment for disadvantaged groups as for white males'. An *equal-opportunity* employer undertakes not to discriminate against women, blacks, disabled people, etc in recruiting and promoting staff. The *Equal Opportunities Commission*, however, a UK body set up in 1975, is mainly concerned with sexual discrimination. **Affirmative action**, first recorded in America as long ago as 1935 but not widely used until the 1970s and 1980s, suggests merely a generally unexceptionable positiveness, but in fact designates preferential treatment given to women and racial minorities (in order to redress the built-in balance against them); another, less euphemistic way of putting it is *positive discrimination* (first recorded in 1967). The latest American alternative characterization of a member of a minority group is **emergent**, which tries to be encouragingly up-beat.

*Culture* can stand in for *race* in the euphemism game: **multicultural** often connotes a plurality of racial groups.

The dominant racial group within a society will commonly seek to distance itself from the other groups that share its territory, denying them access to their rights and institutions, forcing them to live in separate areas, etc. A probably subconscious awareness of the immorality of such practices taps a rich vein of hypocritical euphemisms. The most notorious example is **apartheid**, coined in Afrikaans in the 1920s but not recorded in English until 1947. It denotes the South African policy, set in train in the 1940s, of legal, social, educational, etc separation of the black population, with a view to promoting and maintaining the ascendancy of the whites. And yet it is such a simple and innocent-sounding word to carry such a weight of implication: translated literally into English, it means just 'separateness'.

The non-judgmental *separate* turns out to be a favourite of those who seek to euphemize such discriminatory policies. In South Africa, for instance, the term **separate development** (first recorded in 1955) came to be actively promoted once it became clear that the euphemistic power of *apartheid* was wearing thin. And in America the phrase **separate but equal**, apparently a coinage of Thomas Jefferson in 1776, was used from the late 19th century to the mid 20th century as a sop to keep the black population in its place, with its worthless assurance of theoretical equality in the face of unequal treatment.

A further layer of euphemism in South Africa was provided by the exploitation of the word **plural**. This had a dual circumlocutory role. It is used fairly benignly in World English, in terms such as **plural society**, to denote societies made up of more than one racial group. But in South African English this usage was perverted, in **plural society**, **plural democracy** and **plural relations**, to refer to the apartheid system.

The origins of the racial use of **segregate** (first recorded at the beginning of the 20th century) are no doubt euphemistic – before that it had simply meant 'separate' or 'isolate' – but the word and the concept have become so closely associated that the word's ability to disguise the concept has virtually disappeared.

American English uses the classic euphemism **harmonious** to denote 'segregated'. Thus a 'harmonious neighbourhood' would be inhabited only by whites. First recorded in the early 1970s, it implies that any racial mixture will jar. If the neighbourhood becomes black, it is said to **turn**. In British as well as American English, any area described as **middle-class** is liable to be lived in only by whites. In South Africa, the regions designated for the use of the black population went by the reassuring name **homelands**.

Amongst the weaselliest of racial euphemisms is the American **states' rights**. Ostensibly this denotes the right of individual states to control their own affairs in certain areas, but in practice it has been used in the South as a code for the right to continue official discrimination against blacks.

The most immediately obvious racial characteristic is, of course, skin colour, and a large number of racial euphemisms pick up on this. The broadest and vaguest distinction made in English is between white-skinned people and others, of which the obvious expression is **non-white**. First recorded in 1921, it exploits the understating effect of the negative. In the tortuous racial terminology of South Africa, it denotes specifically someone who is not of European descent or is not officially classified as 'white'.

**Coloured**, too, has complications in South Africa. In World English it denotes anyone with a dark skin, typically a black person but also, especially in British English, someone from the Indian subcontinent. In South Africa, however, it is used as a noun to designate anyone of mixed racial ancestry who does not come into any of the categories 'Asian', 'black', or 'white'. The specific use of **colour** for 'skin colour' dates back to around 1400, and its often euphemistic application to 'non-white skin colour' emerged in America in the late 18th century. Around this time was born the term **person of colour**, enthusiastically adopted by late 20th-century euphemists of the politically correct persuasion: 'The Bermudian pilots are men of colour,' *Naval Chronicle*

1803. (The even more right-on **skin-colour genetically different** for 'non-white' is, however, a much more recent coinage, as is **person of non-colour** for 'white person'.) *Colour* is also used euphemistically in compounds such as **colour prejudice** 'prejudice against non-white people' (first recorded in 1905), **colour bar** and the American **colour line** 'discrimination against non-whites' (coinages of the early 20th and late 19th centuries respectively), and **colour-blind** 'not discriminating against non-whites' (first recorded as long ago as the 1860s).

More explicit but still in the realms of euphemism is **dark**, as applied to skin, and by extension **dark-skinned**, used of people. Both are employed mainly in relation to those of African or subcontinental Indian birth or extraction. (The derivative *darky*, by contrast, is decidedly taboo.)

Non-white skin can be delicately referred to in such terms as **pigmentation** (a non-white person suffering discrimination may be said to have a 'pigmentation problem'; but the image is reversed in *pigmentocracy*, used in the 1950s for the whites-only rule in South Africa); **sepia**, a now dated Americanism (in 1944 H L Mencken noted 'some of them also use such terms as . . . *sepia* to get away from the . . . inaccurate *black*, and in 1944 there was a *Sepia* Miss America contest'); **tincture**; and **tinted** (as in 'tinted folk'), a facetious/satirical genteelism popularized by the Australian comedian Barry Humphries in his persona as Edna Everage. The modern politically correct alternative is **skin-melaninated**. All of these in practice refer mainly to people of African or subcontinental Indian descent, and they are certainly the referent in the case of **the tarbrush**. First recorded in 1796, this is used in expressions like 'a touch of the tarbrush' and 'a lick of the tarbrush' to suggest that a person is of partial black, Indian, etc ancestry. Its status is anomalous. To begin with its role was no doubt at least partially euphemistic; but since at the beginning of the 21st century black, etc ancestry is not a topic about which it is socially acceptable to be euphemistic, the term has flip-flopped into taboo territory, and is no longer much heard.

A particular British way of referring euphemistically to non-white people is **New Commonwealth**. This term, coined around 1960, literally denotes those member states of the British Commonwealth that became independent after World War II. In practice, that means countries in Africa, Asia and the West Indies, with largely non-white populations (as opposed to the white-dominated Old Commonwealth of Australia, Canada, South Africa and New Zealand). Many of the inhabitants of such countries came to live in Britain from the early 1950s onwards, leading to the euphemistic British use of **immigrant** for 'non-white person'.

The use of **Caucasian** for a 'white person' in non-anthropological contexts – particularly in American officialese – has more than a touch of the euphemistic about it. It appears to stem from a perceived taboo against classifying people by skin colour, which for a long time applied to *black* and still does to *yellow* and *red*: *white* can logically fall under the same ban. It is often made to encompass fair-skinned racial groups to whom in strict anthropological terms it does not apply: 'At first it was said that the candidates must be "Caucasian" but this evidently was aimed at Negroes, for Jews were later admitted,' C W Ferguson 1937. In American Black English **the man** for 'white people' (first recorded in 1963) is probably at least partly euphemistic in force.

The tortuous and sometimes self-contradictory history of the terminology applied to people of sub-Saharan African birth or ancestry in the 20th century is a microcosm of the fate of euphemisms: in areas covered by taboos, words created to circumvent the ban sooner or later get sucked in, and new euphemisms have to be introduced to replace them – and so on ad infinitum, or for as long as the taboo persists. Throughout the 19th century and well into the 20th century it was perfectly acceptable (at any rate in white society) to refer to such people as *black*, and even *nigger*, though often used contemptuously, was under no proscription. The reason for this was not of course that such words were not thought to be offensive to black people, but that few people in white society were much exercised about what might or might not be offensive to blacks. There was no taboo. But as the 20th century wore on, the social climate changed. Black people strove for and attained equality and independence. One result of this was that the terminology hitherto applied to them came to seem condescending if not downright insulting, and it was dropped. People, out of liberal sentiment or just common politeness, no longer used the term *black*, and *nigger* was firmly outlawed (although it remains available in Black English as a term of solidarity). The alternative to which white society turned was **Negro**, whose whiff of anthropological detachment made it ideally suited to its euphemistic task. It had been used since the mid 16th century to denote an African people with black skin and tightly curled hair, but it was in the 19th century that it began to be applied more widely to people of African descent living in North America, the

Caribbean and elsewhere. This gave it the impetus it needed to be taken up widely as an alternative to *black* in the 20th century.

But it was not long before taboo began to claw it back. In the 1960s, partly no doubt because of its similarity to the unacceptable *nigger*, *Negro* (and even more the female form *Negress*) came to be regarded as racist, and gradually passed out of acceptable usage. Its main replacement, ironically enough, was **black**, which in the interval since its banishment had come to be regarded as a term of pride rather than derogation by black people themselves. Its acceptance came slowly and step by step, for to begin with it seemed almost shockingly frank. Its bridgehead was as an adjective (as in 'black people'). This was followed up by its noun use, denoting 'black person', initially mainly in the capitalized form *Black*, but increasingly as the lower-case *black*. By the end of the century it was a generally accepted neutral term in World English (although in Britain it can cause offence to Indians, Pakistanis and Bangladeshis included under its umbrella).

An alternative used for American blacks is **African-American** (preferred now to the somewhat earlier **Afro-American**), and the political correctness lobby has come up with **member of the African Diaspora**. A further alternative is **African-descended** (which, like the other two, glosses over the fact that many African peoples are not negroid). British English uses **African-Caribbean** and **Afro-Caribbean**.

An equally touchy area has been the terminology applied to Jews. Astonishingly (to early 21st-century sensibilities), in the late 19th century **Arab** was used as a euphemism for 'Jew', and **Hebrew** and **Israelite** continue in occasional use as pompous circumlocutions. This particular vein of pedantic polysyllabic terminology used to avoid the stark monosyllable *Jew* finds its most high-profile expression in **anti-Semitic** (first recorded in 1881), which has been found more acceptable than the frank *anti-Jewish*. *Jew* is if anything increasingly under a cloud, and the female form *Jewess* can give positive offence; the tendency is to use the watered down **Jewish person**. In Nazi Germany *arisch* – and hence English **Aryan** – was used as a euphemism for 'non-Jewish', although its earlier coiners had intended the term to denote any of the peoples who speak Indo-European languages.

The latter part of the 20th century saw an increasing sensitivity to condescending nomenclature applied to minority racial groups, and a tendency, particularly in North America, to replace traditional English racial terminology with the names that peoples use for themselves.

Hence **Inuit** (first recorded in English in 1765) is now more politically correct in English than *Eskimo* (it means literally 'people'). It is applied to the 'Eskimos' of Canada; those living in Alaska have adopted the name **native Alaskan** (but see NATIVE AMERICAN below). The terms *Red Indian* and *redskin* have long since been banished as racist; their replacement, *(North) American Indian*, is under a cloud because of its gratuitous reference to Indians, which was the product of a 15th-century geographical error; and even the politically approved **native American** (or **native Canadian** for Canada) has attracted adverse comment both for its use of *native*, a tricky word in racial contexts (see p 310), and because the reference to *America* defines such peoples in terms of Amerigo Vespucci and his fellow Europeans, who 'discovered' America only after its aboriginal peoples had been there for many millennia. A general cover term for those who inhabited a part of the world before the arrival of Europeans is **indigenous peoples**. Roughly equivalent in application, but differing in connotation, is **sun people**, which encompasses the native peoples of Africa, Asia, America, Australia – everyone, in fact, except Europeans and their descendants, who are classified as *ice people*. **First Nations** and **first people** likewise assert indigenousness.

The designation of people from Asia also presents problems. *Oriental*, with its freight of stereotypes, is now firmly taboo, and in the 20th century *Asiatic* lost favour. The currently approved term for Americans of Asian descent is **Asian-American**.

Gypsies are a frequent target of racial prejudice, and therefore attract euphemisms: **traveller**, **travelling people** and the more pompous **itinerant** reflect their lifestyle (although all three are also applied to non-gypsies who follow the same way of life), and the now obsolescent **tinker** alludes to a once common trade of male gypsies.

# INDEX

# INDEX

# INDEX

# INDEX